PENGUIN BOOKS

Selling Hitler

'A masterly account.'
Literary Review

'Brilliantly chronicled.'
New Statesman

'Probably the best book about contemporary journalism in
more than a decade and certainly the most entertaining.'
Columbia Journalism Review

About the Author

Robert Harris is the author of fifteen bestselling novels:
the Cicero Trilogy – *Imperium*, *Lustrum* and
Dictator – *Fatherland*, *Enigma*, *Archangel*,
Pompeii, *The Ghost*, *The Fear Index*, *An Officer and a
Spy*, which won four prizes including the Walter Scott
Prize for Historical Fiction, *Conclave*, *Munich*,
The Second Sleep, *V2* and *Act of Oblivion*. His work
has been translated into forty languages and he is a
Fellow of the Royal Society of Literature. He lives in
West Berkshire with his wife, Gill Hornby.

ROBERT HARRIS

Selling Hitler

The Story of the Hitler Diaries

PENGUIN BOOKS

PENGUIN BOOKS

UK | USA | Canada | Ireland | Australia
India | New Zealand | South Africa

Penguin Books is part of the Penguin Random House group of companies
whose addresses can be found at global.penguinrandomhouse.com

First published in the UK by Faber & Faber Ltd in 1986
First published by Arrow Books in 1996
Published in Penguin Books 2023
020

Typeset in 9.25/12.5 pt Sabon LT Std by Jouve (UK), Milton Keynes
Printed and bound in Great Britain by Clays Ltd, Elcograf S.p.A.

The authorised representative in the EEA is Penguin Random House Ireland,
Morrison Chambers, 32 Nassau Street, Dublin D02 YH68

A CIP catalogue record for this book is available from the British Library

ISBN: 978-0-099-79151-5

www.greenpenguin.co.uk

Contents

Acknowledgements

This account is based upon interviews with the main participants in the Hitler diaries affair; upon the many hundreds of pages of prosecution evidence generated by the subsequent trial; and upon the so-called *Stern Report* – the findings of the internal commission set up by *Stern* to examine how the fiasco occurred. Almost all of this information came to me on the understanding that its various sources would not be identified publicly. It would be invidious to try to single out the few who did speak freely; I hope I shall be forgiven if I thank them here collectively rather than individually.

My editor at the BBC, David Dickinson, was once again extremely understanding. My colleague Jane Ellison collaborated on the research, from the first interview to the last document: without her help, this book could not have been written.

ROBERT HARRIS

September 1985

Note

Most of the financial transactions concerning the Hitler diaries were conducted in Deutschmarks. In April 1983, when the diaries were published, the rates of exchange were:

£1 = 3.76 marks

$1 = 2.44 marks

List of illustrations

Dramatis Personae

Wilhelm Arndt: Adolf Hitler's personal servant, entrusted with escorting the Führer's 'testament to posterity' out of Berlin in April 1945

The Marquess of Bath: Owner of the world's largest collection of Hitler's paintings

Hans Baur: Hitler's personal pilot

Randolph Braumann: 'Congo Randy', a close friend of Gerd Heidemann

William Broyles: Editor-in-chief of *Newsweek*

Gerda Christian: One of Hitler's secretaries

Barbara Dickmann: Television journalist hired by *Stern* to help launch the Hitler diaries

Charles Douglas-Home: Editor of *The Times*

Manfred Fischer: Managing director of Gruner and Jahr, owners of *Stern*

Dr Max Frei-Sulzer: Swiss 'handwriting expert'

François Genoud: Swiss lawyer representing the families of Hitler, Goebbels and Bormann

Frank Giles: Editor of the *Sunday Times*

Rolf Gillhausen: *Stern* editor

Otto Guensche: SS adjutant who burned Hitler's body

Major Friedrich Gundlfinger: Luftwaffe pilot who flew Wilhelm Arndt out of Berlin in April 1945

Gerd Heidemann: *Stern* journalist responsible for obtaining the Hitler diaries

Gina Heidemann: Wife of Gerd Heidemann

Dr Josef Henke: Senior official of the West German Federal Archives

Dr Jan Hensmann: Deputy managing director of Gruner and Jahr

Peter Hess: Publishing director of Gruner and Jahr

Wolf Hess: Son of Rudolf Hess

Ordway Hilton: American 'handwriting expert'

David Irving: British historian

Eberhard Jaeckel: Professor of History, University of Stuttgart

Medard Klapper: Arms dealer and confidence trickster who alleged he was in touch with Martin Bormann

Peter Koch: *Stern* editor

Peter Kuehsel: Financial director of Gruner and Jahr

Konrad Kujau: Forger of the Hitler diaries

Edith Lieblang: Konrad Kujau's common-law wife

Heinz Linge: Hitler's valet

Brian MacArthur: Deputy editor, the *Sunday Times*

Werner Maser: West German historian

Rochus Misch: Führerbunker switchboard operator

Maria Modritsch: Konrad Kujau's girlfriend

Reinhard Mohn: Chief executive, Bertelsmann AG

SS General Wilhelm Mohnke: Commander of the Führerbunker

Rupert Murdoch: Chairman, News International; owner, *The Times, Sunday Times* and *New York Post*

Henri Nannen: Founder and publisher of *Stern*

Lynn Nesbit: Senior Vice-President, International Creative Management

James O'Donnell: Author, *The Berlin Bunker*

Dr Klaus Oldenhage: Official of the West German Federal Archives

Maynard Parker: Editor of *Newsweek*

Leo Pesch: Journalist employed in *Stern*'s history department

Billy F. Price: Collector of Hitler paintings from Houston, Texas; author, *Adolf Hitler: The Unknown Artist*

August Priesack: Self-styled 'professor' and expert on Hitler's art, consulted by Fritz Stiefel and Billy Price

Kenneth Rendell: American 'handwriting expert'

Arnold Rentz: West German forensic chemist

Felix Schmidt: *Stern* editor

Christa Schroeder: One of Hitler's secretaries

Gerd Schulte-Hillen: Manfred Fischer's successor as managing director of Gruner and Jahr

Richard Schulze-Kossens: One of Hitler's SS adjutants

Wilfried Sorge: Member of the management of Gruner and Jahr, responsible for selling the Hitler diaries to foreign news organizations

Franz Spoegler: Former SS officer, who offered Heidemann forged correspondence between Churchill and Mussolini

Fritz Stiefel: Stuttgart businessman, collector of Nazi memorabilia

Jakob Tiefenthaeler: Collector of Nazi memorabilia who acted as agent for Gerd Heidemann when he tried to sell Goering's yacht

Hugh Trevor-Roper (Lord Dacre of Glanton): Master of Peterhouse, Cambridge; Independent National Director, Times Newspapers

Thomas Walde: Head of *Stern*'s history department

Gerhard Weinberg: Professor of Modern History, University of North Carolina

Peter Wickman: *Stern* correspondent based in London

Louis Wolfe: President, Bantam Books

SS General Karl Wolff: Heinrich Himmler's Chief of Staff; Military Governor of northern Italy, 1943–45

Introduction to the New Edition

One evening, just before Christmas 1982, I had an unlikely festive drink with the far-right historian, David Irving.

I was twenty-five years old, a reporter on the BBC's *Newsnight* programme, specialising in films about historical subjects. Irving, 44, had long been notorious for his revisionist views about the Nazis. In particular, he had seized on the fact that there was no direct order from Hitler linking him to the Holocaust and had used it to advance the ludicrous argument that the murder of the Jews had somehow taken place behind the Führer's back. But journalists cannot always be too squeamish about their contacts. Still, he was not quite the pariah he later became – at least he didn't claim then, as he did later, that the Holocaust had never happened.

Anyway, our conversation that night – I holding a glass of wine, he (a teetotaller) sipping a soft drink – was to have far-reaching consequences for us both.

HARRIS: How are things?

IRVING: Annoying! I've been in Germany all week on the trail of Hitler's secret diaries, but it's turned out to be a waste of time – and money.

HARRIS: They don't exist?

IRVING (bitterly): Oh, they exist – I've seen some pages from them – but they're complete forgeries!

I thought little more of it until four months later, on Friday 22 April 1983, when the German magazine *Stern* announced that it was about to start publishing Hitler's diaries, and that serial rights had been sold to Times Newspapers. The moment I heard, I rang Irving at his flat in Mayfair. Were these the same diaries he had mentioned before Christmas? 'Exactly the same: I'm looking at my photocopies now,' he answered. Would he like to come on to *Newsnight* that evening and confront the editor of *The Times*, Charles Douglas-Home, who insisted they were genuine? He most certainly would . . .

Thus began my involvement in what remains probably the most famous and fantastical publishing fraud of all time. Over the next couple of years, as the great scoop unravelled and the prosecutions began, I made two films on the subject for *Newsnight*. I visited most of the main locations – the forger's shop in Stuttgart, the *Stern* offices in Hamburg, the Swiss city of Zurich where the diaries were kept in a bank vault. I met the forger (I was reading a biography of Göring at the time, and he signed it for me – *from Göring*). I obtained the confidential police interrogations of the key witnesses, and the internal report *Stern* commissioned into the disaster. I interviewed some of the central players, from Henri Nannen, founder and publisher of *Stern*, to the hapless Hugh Trevor-Roper, who authenticated the diaries for Rupert Murdoch. I attended the final day of the trial of the two fraudsters.

I can't remember the exact point at which I decided to turn all this into a book, but once I did, it preoccupied me to the exclusion of almost everything outside my BBC work, including summer holidays, to the understandable irritation of my then-girlfriend, now-wife. The Elvis Costello hit of the time, 'Every Day I Write the Book', became our signature tune.

Selling Hitler pulled together for the first time many of the themes that have preoccupied me throughout my writing life: the workings of the media, the endless fascination that Hitler and the Third Reich continues to exert (on me, I confess, as much as anyone), the allure of archives and of hidden documents, the way that history hangs over the present and continues to shape us, however much we may like to think we have escaped our collective past.

In deciding how to approach the story, I was greatly influenced by *Indecent Exposure* by David McClintick (1982) which told the story of corruption in Hollywood in the most elaborate detail. I decided to take a similar approach. Although I stuck closely to the facts, like McClintick, I found myself shaping the story and deploying the characters rather as a novelist might. (Indeed, my book was eventually turned into a six-part drama series on ITV, with a deliciously mischievous cast, including Barry Humphries as Rupert Murdoch and Alan Bennett as Hugh Trevor-Roper.)

And *Selling Hitler* has an important place in my heart for another reason. Reading Hitler's monologues about his post-war plans for Europe gave me the idea for my next book: an examination of how the world might have looked if Germany had won the war. My plan was to write it as a parody of a travel book – a kind of *Baedeker Guide* to Hell – illustrated by the maps, plans and architectural models drawn up by the Nazis in the early 1940s, detailing every aspect of the victorious Reich, from the autobahns of the colonised Eastern territories to Albert Speer's grand new capital of the Reich: Berlin, renamed Germania.

But that, in turn, brought me up against the limits of factual writing. These twenty million German settlers who were supposed to settle in Ukraine, for example – would they really have wanted to live there? And what would a victorious Germany have had to say about the disappearance of the Jews of Europe? I thought again of Irving's malevolent but still (as far as I am aware) unrefuted assertion that no order with his signature on it directly links Hitler to the destruction of European Jewry. Why *was* that, I wondered? Was he envisaging a post-war world in which he could deny such a crime had even occurred? The only way to answer these speculative questions was to use the tools of fiction. A novel began to take shape in my mind, which eventually became *Fatherland*, published in 1992. Fifteen novels later, I have never returned to non-fiction.

A few kind friends, when they want to wind me up, still maintain that *Selling Hitler* is my best book. And in a corner of my mind, in the watches of the night, it crosses my mind that they may be right. There are some true stories that are simply better than fiction – that say more about human gullibility, credulousness, greed and self-deception. No novelist would dare to dream up the outlandish characters and complicated plot twists that are described in the pages that follow; they defy all logic. I owe a lot, therefore, to Konrad Kujau, Gerd Heidemann, Hugh Trevor-Roper, the Marquess of Bath, Billy F. Price and the rest of the cast of *Selling Hitler*, almost all of whom are now dead, but who I hope are still capable of providing the reader with some cautionary entertainment in this fortieth anniversary year of the publication of Hitler's 'diaries'.

Robert Harris, 2023

Prologue

On April Fool's Day 1983 the distinguished British historian Hugh Redwald Trevor-Roper, first Baron Dacre of Glanton, was telephoned at his country home in Scotland by the Assistant Editor of *The Times*, Mr Colin Webb.

Among his many honours, Trevor-Roper had, in 1974, accepted an invitation to become an Independent National Director of Times Newspapers. For nine years his telephone had rung periodically with news of strikes, sackings and closures. But this call had nothing to do with routine *Times* business. It concerned a discovery of great historical significance. It was strictly confidential. The German magazine *Stern*, said Mr Webb, had discovered the private diaries of Adolf Hitler.

Trevor-Roper, a former Regius Professor of History at Oxford, was startled and immediately sceptical. 'I said to myself, there are so many forgeries circulating in the "grey market": forged documents about Bormann, forged diaries of Eva Braun, falsified accounts of interviews with Hitler ...' Besides, it was well known that Hitler disliked putting pen to paper and had virtually given up writing in his own hand altogether after 1933. As far as he was aware there was no evidence, either in the German archives or in the recollections of Hitler's subordinates, to suggest that the German dictator had kept a diary. If he had, and if it had now been discovered, it would certainly rank as one of the greatest historical finds of modern times: Hitler, as Trevor-Roper himself had written, was the twentieth century's Genghis Khan, the 'political genius' whose murderous influence upon mankind was still being felt four decades after his death. If this diabolical figure, contrary to all accepted beliefs, turned out to have kept a *diary*, it would provoke a sensation.

Webb explained that *Stern* was offering to sell the foreign serial rights in the diaries. Rupert Murdoch, the owner of Times Newspapers, was considering bidding not merely for the British and Commonwealth, but possibly for the American rights as well. The syndication negotiations were about to begin. In the meantime the diaries themselves were being kept in a bank vault in Switzerland. Webb said that Murdoch wanted an expert's opinion before making an offer for the diaries. Would Trevor-Roper, as an authority on the period and a director of the company, be willing to act as an adviser? Would he fly out to Zurich and examine the material?

Trevor-Roper said he would.

In that case, said Webb, *Stern* would expect him in Switzerland at the end of the following week.

By the time Adolf Hitler had passed his fifty-second birthday, there was no longer a human being left in history who could provide a precedent for his impact on the earth. In January 1942, whilst he picked at his customary vegetarian supper at his headquarters in East Prussia, his soldiers were guarding U-boat pens on the Atlantic coast, shivering in dugouts on the approach roads to Moscow, sweating in tanks in the Libyan desert. In less than twenty years, he had passed from brawling provincial politician to imperial conqueror. He was remaking the world. 'Mark my words, Bormann,' he announced one evening over dinner, 'I'm going to become very religious.'

'You've always been very religious,' replied Bormann.

But Hitler was not thinking of himself as a mere participant in some future act of worship: he was to be the object of it.

'I'm going to become a religious figure,' he insisted. 'Soon I'll be the great chief of the Tartars. Already Arabs and Moroccans are mingling my name with their prayers. Amongst the Tartars I shall become Khan . . .'

When the warm weather returned he would finish off the Red Army. Then he would 'put things in order for a thousand years'. Giant roads would be built into Russia and the first of twenty million Germans, 'soldier-peasants', would start making their homes in a colony whose frontier would extend 250 miles east of the Urals. The Russians, denied churches and schools, educated only to a point at which they could read road signs, would be confined to vast, disease-ridden cities, patrolled from the air by the Luftwaffe. The Crimea would be exclusively German. Moscow would be razed to the ground and turned into an artificial lake. The Channel Islands would be handed over to the Strength Through Joy organization 'for, with their wonderful climate, they constitute a marvellous health resort'. Every nation would have its part to play in Hitler's New Order. The Norwegians would supply Europe's electricity. The Swiss would be hotel keepers. 'I haven't studied the problem as regards Sweden,' joked Hitler. 'In Finland, unfortunately, there is nothing to be done.' Opponents would be confined behind barbed wire in the lengthening chain of concentration camps now opening up in the Eastern territories. At the first sign of trouble, all inmates would be 'liquidated'. As for the Jews, they would simply be 'got rid of'. The future was a vista of endless conflict. A man's first encounter with war, stated Hitler, was like a woman's first experience with a man: 'For the good of the German people, we must wish for a war every fifteen or twenty years.' And in Berlin, renamed Germania, at the centre of this ceaselessly warring empire, would sit the Führer himself, in a granite Chancellery of such proportions that 'one should have the feeling that one is visiting the master of the world'. The Berghof, his private home on the Obersalzberg, would, in due course, become a museum. Here, propped up in bed, while the rest of the household slept, Hitler had found the inspiration for his dreams, gazing out 'for hours' at 'the mountains lit up by the moon'. When his dreams were reality, it would become a place of pilgrimage for a grateful race. 'I can already see the guide from Berchtesgaden showing visitors over the rooms of my house: "This is where he had breakfast . . ." I can also imagine a Saxon giving his avaricious instructions: "Don't touch the articles, don't wear out the parquet, stay between the ropes . . ."'

Almost half a century has now passed since Adolf Hitler and his vision were buried in the rubble of Berlin. All that remains today of the Berghof are a few piles of stone, overgrown with moss and trees. But the repercussions of his career persist. '*Si monumentum requiris, circumspice*,' concludes Alan Bullock's study of Hitler: 'If you seek his monument, look around.' The division of Germany, the exhaustion of British power, the entrenchment and paranoia of Soviet Russia, the denials of freedom in the Eastern half of Europe, the entanglement of America in the Western half, the creation of the State of Israel and the consequent instability of the Middle East – all, in a sense, have been bequeathed to us by Adolf Hitler. His name has become a synonym for evil. Even the physical act of uttering the word 'Hitler' necessitates a grimace. In 1979, the British historian J. H. Plumb described him as a 'curse', the 'black blight' that overshadowed his youth:

> The trauma of Hitler stretched over fifteen years for my generation, breaking lives, destroying those one loved, wrecking my country. So it has been difficult, well-nigh impossible, to think calmly of that white, moustachioed face, eyes ablaze like a Charlie Chaplin turned into a nightmare. Even now when I recall that face and hear that terrifying, hysterical, screeching voice, they create a sense of approaching doom, disaster and death.
>
> Yet, hard though it may be, Hitler has to be understood...

In an attempt to come to terms with this phenomenon there were, by 1980, according to one estimate, over seventy biographies of Adolf Hitler in existence. There are twice as many biographies of Hitler as there are of Winston Churchill; three times as many as there are of Roosevelt and Stalin. Only Jesus Christ has had more words devoted to him than Hitler. The public appetite for these books is enormous. In 1974, Joachim Fest's biography sold over 250,000 hardback copies in Germany alone. Two years later, John Toland's *Adolf Hitler* sold 75,000 copies in the United States (at $15 each) and went into four printings within weeks of its publication. When David Irving began work on *his* study he wrote that 'it was possible to speculate that "books on Hitler" outnumbered page for page the total original documentation available. This proved a sad underestimate.' By 1979 the British Library and the Library of Congress listed over 55,000 items relating solely to Hitler and the Second World War. There are specialist books about Hitler's childhood, his years in Vienna and his service in the army; at least half a dozen works are devoted specifically to his last days and death. There have been investigations into his mind, his body, his personal security, his art. We have first-hand accounts from his valet, his secretary, his pilot, his photographer, his interpreter, his chauffeur and a host of adjutants, ministers and generals. From one doctor (Morell) we know all we ever want to know – and considerably more – about the movement of Hitler's bowels; from another (Giesing), the appearance of the Führer's genitalia. We know that he liked cream cakes, dumb blondes, fast cars, mountain scenery; that he disliked lipstick, modern art, opinionated women and the screech of an owl.

The detail is immense and yet, somehow, the portrait it adds up to remains oddly unconvincing. Despite the millions of words which have been poured into explaining the gulf between Hitler, the private individual, and Hitler, the political prodigy, the two remain unreconciled. 'We seem to be left with a phantom,' wrote J. P. Stern, 'a centre of Nothing.' This inner emptiness helped enable Hitler to use himself like a tool, changing his personality with shocking abruptness to suit the task in hand. The charm of an Austrian gentleman, the brutality of a gangster, the ranting of a demagogue, the assurance of a diplomat succeeded one another in a kaleidoscope of performances which left his innermost thoughts a mystery. In the 1930s, an astonished official watched him carefully work himself into an artificial rage for the sole purpose of frightening an English diplomat; the performance over, he returned to his advisers chuckling, 'Gentlemen, I need tea. He thinks I'm *furious*.' Hitler remained an enigma, even to his most intimate advisers. 'I got to know Adolf Hitler more closely in 1933,' wrote Joachim von Ribbentrop at the end of the war.

> But if I am asked today whether I knew him well – how he thought as a politician and statesman, what kind of man he was – then I'm bound to confess that I know only very little about him; in fact nothing at all. The fact is that although I went through so much together with him, in all the years of working with him I never came closer to him than on the first day we met, either personally or otherwise.

'When a decision has to be taken,' Hermann Goering told one diplomat before the war, 'none of us count more than the stones on which we are standing. It is the Führer alone who decides.' And General Jodl, at Hitler's side throughout six years of war, was equally baffled. 'To this very day,' he wrote in 1946, 'I do not know what he thought or knew or really wanted.' He was utterly self-contained, mysterious, unpredictable, secretive, awesome. He was, as Hugh Trevor-Roper put it, 'the Rousseau, the Mirabeau, the Robespierre and the Napoleon of his revolution; he was its Marx, its Lenin, its Trotsky and its Stalin.' What a sensation it would cause if it were now discovered that such a man had left behind a *diary*...

On Friday, 8 April 1983, exactly one week after his initial conversation with *The Times*, Hugh Trevor-Roper presented himself at Terminal 2 of London's Heathrow Airport. There he was met by *Stern*'s London representative, Peter Wickman, and at 11.15 a.m. they took off for Zurich.

Wickman, plump and garrulous, proved an amiable companion and the sixty-nine-year-old historian was soon launched into one of his favourite topics of conversation: the inordinate superiority of Oxford over Cambridge. (He once said that leaving an Oxford professorship for a Cambridge mastership was rather like becoming a colonial governor.) It was not until the stewardess had served lunch that the two men settled down to business.

Wickman gave Trevor-Roper a twenty-page, typewritten document, bound in a clear plastic cover and entitled *Plan 3*. Based on the so-called diaries, it told the story of how Hitler's deputy, Rudolf Hess, had undertaken his abortive peace mission to Britain in May 1941. The accepted view among historians was that Hess had made his dramatic flight on his own initiative. But according to the diary entries quoted in *Plan 3*, Hitler knew of Hess's intention in advance.

On 25 June 1939, Hitler was alleged to have written in his diary:

> Hess sends me a personal note about the England problem. Would not have thought that this Hess is so sharp-witted. This note is very, very interesting.

Other entries followed:

> *28 June*: Read the Hess note again. Simply fantastic and yet so simple.

> *6 July*: Hess should work over his thoughts which he has informed me about in his note and I anticipate seeing him for a one-to-one meeting.

13 July: Have also talked to Hess again. As soon as he has thought everything over properly, he will call me back. I would not have thought Hess capable of this. Not Hess.

22 July: Have Goering with me once more. I carefully inquire what range our best planes have. Hess said that one would have to build a special plane and that he was already working on the plans. What a man. He does not want any more said to Goering about his plan.

Finally, Hitler was supposed to have outlined three contingency plans:

1 Should the mission go well and Hess be successful, he acted in agreement with me.
2 If Hess is arrested in England as a spy, then he informed me some time ago of his plan, but I rejected it.
3 Should his mission fail completely, I declare Hess acted in a fit of delusion.

When it became clear that Hess's mission *had* failed, 'Plan 3' had duly been adopted. This, according to *Stern*, was the solution to one of the great mysteries of the Second World War, proof that six weeks before the invasion of Russia, Hitler had made a genuine attempt to negotiate peace with Britain.

Even as he took detailed notes from the document, suspicions began to accumulate in Trevor-Roper's mind. *Stern*'s version of the Hess story was in conflict with all the available evidence. Albert Speer, for example, had been outside Hitler's study door at the precise moment that the Führer had learned of Hess's flight to Britain. 'I suddenly heard,' Speer recalled, 'an inarticulate, almost animal outcry.' Trevor-Roper had been told the story by Speer in person. He had subsequently described in his own book, *The Last Days of Hitler*, how the Nazi leadership had been hastily summoned to the Berghof to discuss the damage Hess had done: hardly the behaviour one would have expected if Hitler had known of Hess's intention in advance. He told Wickman immediately that he thought the *Stern* story was rubbish and Wickman, who had long nursed his own private doubts, agreed.

By the time the plane landed in Zurich, Trevor-Roper was finding it difficult to keep an open mind about the diaries. He was almost certain it was a wasted journey, but having come so far he thought he might as well at least see them. The two men took a taxi into town, dropped off their luggage at the Hotel Baur au Lac, and while Trevor-Roper waited, Wickman telephoned ahead to the bank where the diaries were being kept. The *Stern* people were already waiting. Wickman told them that he and the historian were on their way over.

Shortly after 3 p.m., Trevor-Roper was ushered into a ground floor room of Zurich's Handelsbank. At the end of a long table, three men rose to meet him. One was Wilfried Sorge, the salesman who had flown round the world alerting newspapers in America, Japan, Italy, Spain and Britain to the existence of the diaries. Another was Dr Jan Hensmann, the financial director of *Stern*'s parent company, Gruner and Jahr. The third German was *Stern*'s bullet-headed editor-in-chief, Peter Koch.

When the introductions had been completed, Koch gestured towards a side table. On it were fifty-eight volumes of diaries, carefully piled up in a stack more than two feet high. Another set of documents was in a metal safety deposit box. There was a bound volume of original drawings and paintings. There was even a First World War helmet, allegedly Hitler's. This was no mere handful of notes. It was, as Trevor-Roper later described it, 'a whole coherent archive covering 35 years'. He was staggered by its scale.

He picked up a couple of the books. They were A4-sized, with stiff black covers. Some bore red wax seals in the form of a German eagle. Others were decorated with initials in gothic script. Most carried typewritten labels declaring them to be the property of the Führer and signed by Martin Bormann. The pages inside were lined, some densely filled with old Germanic script, some bearing only a couple of sentences, some completely blank. At the foot of each page was Hitler's signature – a jagged oscillation in black ink, like a seismographic record of some distant earthquake.

The *Stern* men met Trevor-Roper's queries point by point. They produced three separate reports from handwriting experts authenticating the documents. They described how the diaries had come into their hands. They confirmed that the magazine knew the identity of the supplier. It was enough.

> When I entered the back room in the Swiss bank [wrote Trevor-Roper in *The Times*], and turned the pages of those volumes, my doubts gradually dissolved. I am now satisfied that the documents are authentic; that the history of their wanderings since 1945 is true; and that the standard accounts of Hitler's writing habits, of his personality, and even, perhaps, some public events may, in consequence, have to be revised.

Twenty-four hours later Rupert Murdoch was sitting in the same bank vault leafing through the diaries with the former head of Reuters at his side translating their contents. By mid-afternoon on 9 April he had offered the delighted Germans $3 million for the world rights.

What happened next is described in detail later in this book: how Murdoch and the *Newsweek* company fell into an ill-tempered auction which at one stage pushed the price of the diaries up to $3.75 million, until *Stern*'s greed and *Newsweek*'s alleged unscrupulousness punctured the whole deal; how *Stern* nevertheless managed to sell subsidiary rights in the diaries to newspapers and magazines in America, Britain, Australia, France, Italy, Spain, Norway, Holland and Belgium – a contract carefully calculated to squeeze the last marketable drop out of Adolf Hitler, dividing the diaries into twenty-eight separate extracts whose publication would have spanned more than eighteen months; how news of the diaries' discovery was rushed into print despite growing evidence that some of the material was of post-war origin; and finally how this elaborate but increasingly shaky pyramid of subsidiary deals and serial rights was sent crashing two weeks later by a short laboratory report from the Federal police.

The diaries, announced the West German state archives on 6 May, were not merely fakes: they were '*eine plumpe Fälschung*', a crude forgery, the grotesquely superficial ('*grotesk oberflächlich*') concoction of a copyist endowed with a 'limited intellectual capacity'. The paper, the binding, the glue, the thread were all found to be of post-war manufacture. By the time this was disclosed, the management of *Stern*, in the course of more than two years, had handed over twenty-seven suitcases full of money to enable their star reporter, Gerd Heidemann, to obtain the diaries. $4 million had disappeared, making the Hitler diaries the most expensive and far-reaching fraud in publishing history, easily dwarfing the $650,000 handed over by McGraw-Hill for the faked autobiography of Howard Hughes. Scores of reputations apart from Trevor-Roper's were damaged by the diaries fiasco. At least four editors in three different countries lost their jobs as a result.

The affair was a reminder of Adolf Hitler's continuing hold on the world's imagination. News of the discovery of the diaries made headlines in every nation; it ran on the front page of the *New York Times* for five consecutive days. Shrewd businessmen showed themselves willing to pay enormous sums for material of which they had read only a fraction. It did not matter that the diaries' content was perfunctory and tedious: it was sufficient that it had been written by *him*. The diaries briefly put Hitler back in the arena of international diplomacy, a weapon in the Cold War which his career had done so much to create. Radio Moscow alleged that 'the affair of the Hitler diaries clearly reveals the CIA style'. America's Ambassador to the United Nations, Jeanne Kirkpatrick, suspected the communists of producing the diaries 'to sow distrust between the United States and its German friends'. In the middle of the furore, the East German leader, Erich Hoenecker, cancelled his planned trip to Bonn complaining of a hostile Western press campaign: repeated allegations that the diaries originated in an East German 'forgery factory' were bitterly resented in Berlin. When the real forger, Konrad Kujau, confessed to the police on 26 May, it was difficult to believe that so much international confusion could have resulted from the work of this jaunty and farcical figure.

How did it happen? How did a hard-headed German publishing company come to spend so much money on such palpable fakes, and persuade almost a dozen foreign partners to invest in the project? To answer that question, we have to go back more than forty years: back through the expanding market in Hitler memorabilia, back through the activities of the surviving members of the Führer's inner circle, right back to the figure of Hitler himself, malevolent to the last, but no longer confident of his destiny, preparing for death in his bunker in the spring of 1945.

PART ONE

'For mythopoeia is a far more common characteristic of the human race (and perhaps especially of the German race) than veracity. . .'

Hugh Trevor-Roper, *The Last Days of Hitler*

I

On 20 April 1945, Adolf Hitler celebrated his fifty-sixth and final birthday. Russian artillery shells were falling on the centre of Berlin and 6000 Soviet tanks were moving into the outskirts of the capital. Bremen and Hamburg in the north were about to fall to the British; Stuttgart, in the south, to the French. The Americans had captured Nuremberg and the Stars and Stripes was being unfurled over the podium from which Hitler had once addressed the annual Nazi Party rally. To escape the constant Allied air attacks, the Führer and his staff were now forced to live cooped-up in a bunker fifty-five feet beneath the Reich Chancellery. 'It was not,' observed Martin Bormann in his diary, 'exactly a birthday situation.'

At 2 p.m. Hitler shuffled out of his bedroom exhausted from lack of sleep. His doctors gave him three injections, including one of glucose. His valet administered eyedrops. He wrapped himself in a heavy grey overcoat, turned up the collar, and slowly climbed the spiral staircase out of the bunker and into the Chancellery garden to inspect a waiting contingent of Hitler Youth. Their leader, Arthur Axmann, was shocked by his appearance: 'He walked with a stoop. His hands trembled.' He passed along the short line of boys and patted a couple of them on the cheek. He uttered a few hoarse and scarcely audible words about his faith in an ultimate victory, turned, and retreated back underground to preside over the day's main war conference.

That same afternoon, while Hitler and his generals were surveying what remained of the German armed forces, Sergeant Rochus Misch, the bunker's switchboard operator, took the opportunity to slip upstairs into the fresh air for a cigarette. He was standing smoking amid the rubble of the Ehrenhof, the Chancellery's Court of Honour, when two men appeared. One was Sergeant Wilhelm Arndt, a wounded veteran of twenty, who acted as one of Hitler's personal servants. The other was a young soldier-valet named Fehrs. Between them they were dragging a large metal trunk. Misch offered to help.

There were approximately ten trunks which had to be loaded on to the back of an antiquated, three-wheeled delivery truck parked in the courtyard. It was heavy work. Misch reckoned that each of the metal containers weighed over one hundred pounds. To heave one on to the back of the truck took two men. Misch did not ask what was in them and Arndt did not tell him. 'It was only,' he recalled, 'when Arndt, now in full field uniform and armed with a machine pistol, clambered on top of the chests, that I realized it must be a mission with a one-man escort.' The truck drove out of the courtyard. Misch watched it disappear. 'Poor Arndt,' he reflected years afterwards. 'At the time we all thought he was the lucky one, escaping embattled Berlin and heading for the mountains.'

Arndt was taking part in a mission known as Operation Seraglio: the evacuation from the Berlin bunker of about eighty members of Hitler's entourage, together with a mass of official government papers, personal property and valuables. Their destination was the so-called 'Alpine Redoubt' in the south of Germany, near Berchtesgaden, where the Nazis had a half-formulated plan to establish a new centre of command in the event of the capture of Berlin. The evacuation was being conducted by air. General Hans Baur, Hitler's personal pilot, who was responsible for the provision of aircraft, had managed to muster ten planes for the operation, dispersed between four different Berlin airstrips. The lorry carrying Arndt and the metal trunks was directed towards a grass runway at Schoenwalde, about ten miles north of the city. Two planes were waiting there. One was to be piloted by a Luftwaffe flying officer named Schultze; the other by a veteran of the Russian front, Major Friedrich Gundlfinger.

Allied aircraft had been celebrating Adolf Hitler's birthday all day with an almost continuous stream of air raids on Berlin. At 10 p.m. they struck again. Arndt and the other passengers heading in convoy for Schoenwalde were obliged to stop and seek shelter. The raid lasted four hours. At the airfield, Schultze and Gundlfinger were growing increasingly anxious. Time was running short. They had to take off under cover of darkness to avoid the Allied fighters which now had command of Germany's skies during the day. The two pilots discussed tactics. Schultze favoured flying high to make use of every available scrap of cloud cover. Gundlfinger preferred hedge-hopping at low altitude.

The passengers finally began struggling on to the airfield shortly before dawn. Arndt attended to the stowing of the trunks in Gundlfinger's plane, then clambered in after them. He was one of sixteen passengers. Schultze took off first. Gundlfinger followed a few minutes later, at about 5 a.m. on the morning of 21 April. His destination lay 350 miles to the south: Ainring, near Salzburg, the airfield closest to Berchtesgaden.

In the event, Gundlfinger completed less than one-third of the journey. He had been in the air for little more than half an hour and had just passed what was left of the city of Dresden when something went wrong. Possibly the plane was shot up by a patrolling American fighter; possibly it was hit by fire from a German anti-aircraft battery which mistook it for an enemy plane. At any rate, it was next seen shortly before 6 a.m. skimming the treetops in flames before crashing into the Heidenholz forest close to the Czech border. Villagers from the nearby hamlet of Boernersdorf ran to the scene. The plane – a large Junkers 352 transport aircraft – had ploughed nose-first into the ground and was burning fiercely. Trapped in the wreckage, a figure writhed and screamed at the onlookers for help. But the intense heat and the ricochets of exploding ammunition made rescue impossible. The aircraft had to be left to burn itself out.

Schultze, meanwhile, had also run into trouble. Shortly after taking off he had discovered that one of his fuel pipes was fractured. He was forced to divert to Prague, then still in German hands, to refuel. It was 8.30 a.m. when he finally landed at Salzburg, expecting to find Gundlfinger waiting for him. All the other eight planes were there. But of the major and his aircraft there was no sign. This information was relayed to General Baur in Berlin and he, in turn, broke the news to Hitler that one of the planes involved in Operation Seraglio was missing. Hitler, he recalled, 'became very pale' and asked which one. Baur said it was the one with Arndt on board, at which Hitler appeared 'very upset'. According to Baur, he then uttered the words which were to cause so much mischief almost forty years later. 'In that plane,' he exclaimed, 'were all my private archives, that I had intended as a testament to posterity. It is a catastrophe!'

'After I'd seen how much that affected the Führer,' said Baur, 'I tried to calm him and explain that Gundlfinger was an old fox from the First World War, that the Americans wouldn't have got him that easily: probably he'd made an emergency landing somewhere. But we didn't know, and our investigations were without success.'

On 22 April, the day after Arndt's disappearance, with heavy fighting reported in the suburbs of Berlin and with no sign of the counter-attack he had ordered, Hitler at last admitted defeat. 'That's it,' he shouted, scattering a handful of coloured pencils across the map table. 'How am I supposed to direct the war in such circumstances? The war's lost.' He walked out of the military conference. At about 4 p.m. he summoned Julius Schaub, the crippled soldier who had been his secretary, bodyguard, companion, messenger boy and valet for more than twenty years. Together they opened the steel safe in Hitler's bedroom. Four feet high and three feet wide, it was brimming with his personal papers. The material was stuffed into suitcases, carried up into the Chancellery garden, tipped into a bomb crater and set on fire. Hitler stood for a while in the fading light, watching as this record of his private affairs went up in smoke. 'Richelieu once said, give me five lines one man has penned,' Hitler is reported to have lamented subsequently. 'What I have lost! My dearest memories! But what's the point – sooner or later you've got to get rid of that stuff.' To complete this task, he instructed Schaub to fly to Berchtesgaden and destroy all his remaining personal files.

Schaub is believed to have arrived at the Berghof on his errand of destruction on the night of 26 April. Berchtesgaden, which had been subjected to a 300-bomber raid the previous day, was in a chaotic state. The homes of Bormann and Goering had been badly damaged. One wing of the Berghof was wrecked. Schaub was in an equally dilapidated condition. Eva Braun's sister, Gretl, who met him in the Führer's apartments, was shocked to discover him drunk and on the arm of his mistress. He had flown down bearing Hitler's keys but whether he actually carried out his master's instruction and destroyed everything is unclear. According to a US intelligence report, Gretl confided to an American undercover agent a few months after the war that in her view 'Schaub probably selected the most interesting things with the help of his mistress and hid them away.' In the 1970s, the British historian David Irving, an indefatigable hunter of original documents, received information that Schaub had 'sold Hitler's papers to a former magistrate now living on Lake Starnberg in Bavaria'. The magistrate, however, 'proved unapproachable'.

Before lurching off into the Führer's private quarters with his girlfriend, Schaub handed Gretl a letter which had been entrusted to him in Berlin two days earlier by Eva Braun. 'My darling little sister,' it began

> How it hurts me to write such lines to you. But there is nothing else to do. Each day and each hour may be our last, and so I must use this last opportunity to tell you what must be done . . . Please keep your head high and do not doubt. There is still hope. It goes without saying, however, that we will not let ourselves be captured alive.

In what was effectively her last will and testament, she provided a list of friends who were to receive her effects.

> In addition I must request the following. Destroy all of my private correspondence, especially the business papers . . . Destroy also an envelope which is addressed to the Führer and is in the safe in the bunker. Please do not read it. The Führer's letters and my answering letters (blue leather book) I would like packed watertight and if possible buried. Please do not destroy them. . .

In a reference to Gundlfinger's plane and its cargo of Hitler's property, Eva asked her sister if Arndt had arrived 'with the letter and suitcase? We heard here only that the plane had been attacked.' The letter ended 'with heartiest greetings and a kiss'. A few days later, Eva Braun achieved her life's ambition and married Adolf Hitler. On 30 April, the couple killed themselves and their bodies were set alight.

The following morning, at almost exactly the same moment as the charred corpses of the newly-weds were being interred in a shell hole in Berlin, their personal effects were being burned in Berchtesgaden. The rooms of the Berghof were systematically emptied of clothes, furniture, linen and crockery. The contents were taken outside and destroyed to prevent them falling into the hands of the approaching Americans. Hitler's library of 2000 books, along with his collection of press cuttings, was hidden in a nearby salt mine. (These volumes, each with a garish swastika bookplate bearing the inscription '*Ex Libris Adolf Hitler*', were later found by American troops, transported to Washington, and in 1953 catalogued as a collection by the Library of Congress.)

On this same day, 1 May, Gretl decided the time had come to comply with her sister's last request. For assistance she turned to a young SS major named Johannes Goehler. According to a post-war investigation by US intelligence, 'Gretl said that she would like him to take charge of the safekeeping of a large chest of letters which had been entrusted to her. They were letters between her sister, Eva Braun, and Hitler. The chest, about the size of an officer's trunk, was in a cave near the Berghof.' Goehler promised to help. He rang one of his subordinates, SS Captain Erwin Haufler, and instructed him to send a truck to Berchtesgaden immediately. That night Eva Braun's chest, along with a clothes basket, was evacuated to the local SS headquarters in Fischhorn Castle in Austria.

For the next week they stood, objects of intense curiosity, in a corner of Haufler's office. The basket, which was open, was found to contain Eva Braun's photograph albums of life at the Berghof, 'a few small framed pictures' and some rolls of film. The trunk was locked. After several days of speculation, Haufler and his SS cronies eventually plucked up the courage to break it open. Inside was a treasure trove of Hitler memorabilia. There was an assortment of the Führer's architectural drawings: 'made in pencil', Haufler told the Americans after the war, 'depicting floor plans and the like. I saw one sketch which seemed to represent a church.' There was a box of Hitler's stationery. There was a book belonging to Mussolini and another, in Eva Braun's handwriting, in which she had made notes of her letters to Hitler. There was an album entitled 'Enemy Propaganda in Stamps'. 'Then there was a pair of black trousers,' recalled Haufler, 'badly ripped, or rather slit, and also a coat, which was field grey,' bearing the insignia of the German eagle. This, the SS men correctly assumed, was the uniform Hitler had been wearing at the time of the attempt on his life in July 1944: in an emotional moment, the Führer had sent it to Eva to keep as a souvenir. But what most captured the soldiers' interest were the letters. The trunk was three-quarters full of them: 'at least 250,' estimated Haufler, with another thirty or forty postcards. These were Hitler's letters to Eva Braun, a lovingly preserved record of their ten-year relationship. Haufler picked up one. 'My dear Pascherl,' it began, 'I send you my heartiest greetings.' It was signed 'your Adolf Hitler'.

Precisely what happened next is unclear. According to Haufler, he handed the trunk over to his administrative officer, Franz Konrad, with instructions to burn it to prevent its contents falling into Allied hands. But Konrad, a notoriously corrupt SS captain, whose activities during the German occupation of Warsaw had earned him the title 'King of the Ghetto', disobeyed him. In the final hours of the war he sent a truck loaded with looted treasure to his brother's house in the nearby Austrian town of Schladming. Hidden among the canned food, the liquor and the radios were two suitcases and a metal trunk with Eva Braun's name tag attached to it. 'Make sure you get through,' the driver alleged Konrad told him. 'If you get stopped on the way, take the two bags and the chest and make off. If everything else should go wrong, you must save those three things.'

Acting on this information, on 24 August 1945, agents from the US Counter-Intelligence Corps (CIC) raided the home of Konrad's brother and seized the Hitler uniform, Eva Braun's private photograph albums, her silverware, the notes she had made of her letters to Hitler, and the stamp collection. A second cache of material, which Konrad had given to his mother to hide, was recovered in October. This haul included twenty-eight reels of colour film – Eva Braun's home movies of her life with Hitler. All these objects were turned over to the American Army and shipped back to the United States. But of Hitler's letters, by far the most interesting items, there was no sign. Thirty years later, David Irving once more set out to track them down. His conclusion, after months of inquiry, was that they were discovered near

Berchtesgaden by one of the CIC officers who promptly stole them for himself. They have now disappeared into the archives of a private collector in the USA.

In addition to the property of Eva Braun, Konrad also appears to have stolen the correspondence between Hitler and the leader of the SS, Heinrich Himmler. The files had been transferred for safekeeping from Himmler's headquarters to the library at Fischhorn Castle where they were kept in a steel cabinet, guarded by Himmler's orderlies. After Hitler's suicide, Konrad was assigned to help destroy them, but admitted to the Americans after the war that he put a set of the most interesting documents to one side. Shortly afterwards he turned up at the home of his secretary, Martha von Boskowitz, and gave her a package 'about 18 inches long, 6 inches thick and 4 inches wide'. He told her that the tightly wrapped parcel contained his 'personal letters' and asked her to hold on to them, 'in case anything should happen to me'. About six weeks later another SS man called and took the package away. It, too, has disappeared.

In the course of their investigations, the CIC also began picking up rumours of the existence of Hitler's 'diaries'. According to Colonel Wilhelm Spacil of the Reich Main Security Office (RSHA) Franz Konrad boasted to him at the beginning of May 1945 that, in addition to all his other treasures, he was in possession of 'the diary of Hitler, written on very thin paper' which he had hidden in a specially made zinc box. The CIC asked Captain Haufler what he knew of such diaries. Haufler described how two weeks before the end of the war he had been at the Berghof when an air raid alarm sounded. He and Gretl Braun, along with the Berghof's housekeeper, Frau Mittelstrasser, took shelter in the underground bunker. The two women showed him around part of the labyrinth of tunnels which extended for nearly two miles beneath the mountain.

> I was only allowed to stand at the doorway to the Führer's room [recalled Haufler]. Frau Mittelstrasser pointed out several things in the room: for example, there were 5000 phonograph records stored there. Among other things, she pointed out the 'personal notes' of the Führer. These were contained in four or five large books which stood

near the desk. Of course, everyone knew that Hitler kept a diary. The books were firmly bound, and not quite as big as a *Leitz-Ordner* [a loose-leaf file]. I can't tell you anything more about them, for I only saw them from a distance, and didn't even have them in my hand. I never saw these books again.

In the absence of any other hard information, the CIC investigation petered out. Gretl Braun dismissed Haufler's story. 'Hitler didn't keep any diaries,' she told a CIC agent. 'The books which were standing in the air raid shelter in the Berghof were not diaries, but rather minutes of the day's activities, which were kept by whoever was the Führer's adjutant at the time.' And Franz Konrad, despite prolonged interrogation, insisted that he knew nothing of such books, that Spacil was mistaken, that he must be muddling the 'diaries' with Eva Braun's notebooks which he confessed to having stolen. At the height of the debate over the Hitler diaries' authenticity in 1983, the *Sunday Times* clutched at the straw offered by the CIC files. Quoting only the testimony of Spacil and Haufler, the paper used the information to try to refute claims that there had never been any suggestion that Hitler kept a diary. But given the paucity of evidence, and even allowing for the unreliability of the witnesses, the likelihood is that the references to 'diaries' which creep into a couple of CIC reports are actually the result of a misunderstanding.

The Third Reich had dissolved into chaos. In Berlin, in Munich, in Berchtesgaden, Allied soldiers as well as German picked through the detritus of Hitler's Germany and carried off whatever seemed of value. A gang of Russian women soldiers ransacked Eva Braun's apartment in the Berlin bunker and emerged, according to one witness, 'whooping like Indian squaws', waving Frau Hitler's underclothes above their heads, carrying off lamps, vases, bottles, carpets, crystal glass, Hitler's monogrammed silver, an accordian, a tablecloth, 'even a table telephone'. At the Berghof, French and American troops wrenched off light-fittings and doorknobs and pulled out the springs from the Führer's bed. Eventually, every inch of plaster was stripped from the walls; stairs and handrails were torn up; the members of one enterprising unit even took a sledgehammer to Hitler's marble fireplace and sold off the pieces as ashtrays. At the Führerbau, the monumental stone building on the Königsplatz in Munich where Hitler had met Chamberlain and Daladier, dozens of GIs plundered the storerooms, using a wooden crate as a stepping stone as they explored the waterlogged basement. When one anonymous soldier from the US 14th Division staved in the lid of the crate he found yet another hoard of Hitler's private property: two gold-plated pistols, a swastika ring, a miniature portrait of the dictator's mother painted on ivory, a framed photograph of Hitler's favourite dog, Blondi, a gold watch bearing the initials 'A.H.' and valuable monogrammed crystal glasses, carefully wrapped in newspaper. 'The next thing I picked up was a diary,' recalled the soldier, many years later. 'It was a red diary with gold lettering and Hitler's insignia on it, his initials on it. But I flashed right through it and it was all in German. I just threw it right aside and it dropped into the water on the floor.' He returned to retrieve it some time later but the 'diary', or whatever it was, had gone. There are many such stories. As recently as 1984, a family in British Columbia found a crateful of personal papers belonging to Heinrich Hoffmann, Hitler's court photographer, lying discarded in their attic: it had been brought back by their father at the end of the war and forgotten. Years later it is impossible to guess how much of historical value may have been carted away from the wreckage of Nazi Germany and may still come to light.

Reviewing such documentary evidence as exists, it is conceivable that of five sets of Hitler documents supposedly destroyed in the spring of 1945, four of them – the private files held at the Berghof, the letters to Eva Braun, the correspondence with Himmler and even possibly part of the cargo entrusted to Arndt – may actually have survived. Only the contents of the safe in Berlin, whose incineration was personally supervised by the Führer, can definitely be regarded as lost.

This tantalizing state of affairs was to provide the perfect scenario for forgery.

2

Outside the entrance to the Führerbunker in Berlin, a shell crater
was strewn with sheets of charred paper. Rummaging beneath the
blackened litter, a Russian soldier discovered a pair of scorched and
crumbling bones. He called his commanding officer over. 'Comrade
Lieutenant Colonel!' he shouted, 'there are legs here!'

Thus, on 2 May 1945, if the Soviet writer Lev Bezymenski is to be
believed, Private Ivan Churakov of the 1st Byelorussian Front stumbled on the most sought-after Hitler relic of them all. 'So!' exclaimed
Stalin when he first heard of the Führer's death, 'that's the end of the
bastard. Too bad that we did not manage to take him alive.'

Disinterred from the crater, the remains of Hitler and Eva Braun
were placed in a pair of rough wooden boxes and taken to the Soviet
Army headquarters in the northern Berlin suburb of Buch. Hitler's
corpse had been so badly damaged by fire that parts of it disintegrated
on the mortuary table. According to the official autopsy report, the left
foot was missing; so was the skin: 'only remnants of charred muscles
are preserved.' The mouldering cadaver was displayed in a clear-
ing in a wood outside Berlin at the end of May to one of the Führer's
bodyguards. By August it was in Moscow, where, quite probably, it
remains to this day. ('Hitler's body,' boasted one Russian official in
1949, 'is in better keeping with us than under the Brandenburg Gate
in Berlin.') Hitler's teeth – a bridge of nine dentures in yellow metal
and a singed lower jaw consisting of fifteen teeth – were handed over
to the Soviet counter-intelligence agency, SMERSH. These, together
with the dictator's Iron Cross, his party insignia and the teeth of Eva
Braun, were last seen in Berlin in May 1945 in a cigar box, being

offered around by a SMERSH officer to fashionable German dentists for identification.

But, abetted by the Russians, even in this reduced form, Hitler was still capable of making mischief. The autopsy report and the various proofs of Hitler's death were suppressed by the Soviet Union for more than twenty years: officially, to have them 'in reserve' in case an imposter appeared claiming to be 'the Führer saved by a miracle'; in reality, to embarrass the British and Americans. At least twice in the Kremlin and once at the Potsdam Conference, Stalin lied to the Allies, telling them that Hitler had escaped and was in hiding. As part of his campaign against fascist Spain, he even suggested that Hitler was being sheltered by General Franco. Senior Soviet officers in Berlin, who had at first admitted to the discovery of the body, hastily changed their stories and followed Stalin's line. The Soviet newspaper *Izvestia* went so far as to allege that Hitler and Eva Braun were living in a moated castle in Westphalia in the British Occupation Zone of Germany.

The post-war appetite for stories about Hitler and the Nazis, which was to culminate in the diaries fiasco, found its first sustenance in this confusion. Throughout the summer of 1945, newspapers trampled over one another to bring their readers the 'true story' of the Führer's fate. First Hitler was said to be working as a croupier in a casino in the French resort of Evian. A few days later he resurfaced as a head waiter in Grenoble. Then, in bewildering succession, he was reliably reported to be a shepherd in the Swiss Alps, a monk in St Gallen, and an Italian hermit living in a cave beside Lake Garda. Some newspapers maintained that Hitler was posing as a fisherman in the Baltic, others that he was working on a boat off the west of Ireland. He had escaped by airplane. He had escaped by submarine. He was in Albania. He was in Spain. He was in Argentina.

Hitler's progress across the world's front pages was followed with increasing embarrassment in Whitehall. When the Russians hinted that the British might be shielding him in Westphalia, the Government decided to act. In September 1945, Brigadier Dick White, a senior official in the British security service, later to be chief of both MI5 and MI6, was asked to prepare a report on what had happened to Hitler. He was given six weeks to complete the task. White delegated this urgent mission, code-named Operation Nursery, to a particularly bright young intelligence officer named Hugh Trevor-Roper.

At the outbreak of war Trevor-Roper had been at Oxford completing a biography of Archbishop Laud. Recruited into British signals intelligence, the twenty-six-year-old research student was obliged to switch his mind from the study of seventeenth-century clerical politics to the analysis of intercepted German radio traffic. He became one of the foremost experts on the German intelligence service, the *Abwehr*. He had a penetrating intellect, a sharp tongue, and a natural combativeness which caused one of his superiors in the Secret Intelligence Service to threaten him with court martial.

He arrived in Germany in the middle of September. His method of solving the mystery of Hitler's fate owed something to the novels of Agatha Christie. He was the amateur detective; the Führerbunker the country house where the crime had been committed; its survivors the witnesses who could provide the vital clues. He quickly demolished the stories of some of the more obvious fantasists: the doctor who claimed to have treated Hitler for a lung wound sustained during fighting around the Berlin Zoo; the female Gestapo agent who swore she could take him to the Bavarian estate where Hitler was living in a secluded foursome with Eva, Gretl, and Gretl's husband, Hermann. To uncover the truth he compiled a list of everyone who had attended Hitler in his final days and travelled the country tracking them down. He interrogated Keitel, Jodl, Doenitz and Speer. In their prison camps he questioned the Führer's SS guards. At Berchtesgaden he caught up with two of Hitler's secretaries, Johanna Wolf and Christa Schroeder; he almost captured a third, Gerda Christian, when he turned up at the home of her mother-in-law – he missed her by only a couple of days. By the time he came to write his report he had found seven witnesses who were with Hitler in the final week of his life, including the chauffeur, Erich Kempka, who provided the gasoline with which his master's body was burned, and a guard, Hermann Karnau, who witnessed the funeral pyre.

On the night of 1 November 1945, Trevor-Roper presented a summary of his findings to an audience of sceptical journalists in the Hotel-am-Zoo in Berlin. One of them, the *Newsweek* correspondent,

James P. O'Donnell, later recalled the confident impression he made: a 'dapper' figure in his wartime uniform, crisp and sarcastic, 'a master of tart understatement'.

That evening, Trevor-Roper told for the first time the story of Hitler's death which has since become familiar: the final appearance of the Führer, accompanied by Eva Braun, to say goodbye to his staff; their retirement to his sitting room; their deaths – his by a revolver bullet, hers by poison – and their subsequent cremation in the garden of the Chancellery. Trevor-Roper fixed the time of death as 'shortly after 2.30 p.m. on 30 April 1945' and he concluded with a magisterial rebuke to the press:

> There is no evidence whatever to support any of the theories that
> have been circulated and which presuppose that Hitler is still alive.
> All such stories which have been reported have been investigated and
> have been found to be quite baseless; most of them have dissolved at
> the first touch of fact and some of them have been admitted by their
> authors to have been pure fabrication.

'As of that evening,' wrote O'Donnell, 'most of the international press stationed in Berlin was finally convinced that Hitler was indeed dead.' His handling of the case earned Trevor-Roper the title 'The Sleuth of Oxford'.

The inquiry was an unprecedented opportunity for an ambitious young historian. With the permission of British intelligence Trevor-Roper turned the information he had collected into a book. *The Last Days of Hitler* appeared in 1947. It was hailed in Britain as 'a masterpiece'. In the United States, Arthur Schlesinger Jr declared it 'a brilliant professional performance'. The book has since been reprinted thirteen times in Great Britain alone. By 1983 its world-wide sales amounted to almost half a million copies. Trevor-Roper bought a Bentley on the proceeds and for a while was said to hold the record for driving from Oxford to London in under an hour.

Behind the Iron Curtain, the book was banned. 'The Polish edition was stifled in the publisher's office,' wrote Trevor-Roper, 'the Bulgarian edition destroyed by the police on its appearance.' The Russian position remained unchanged. 'It was never allowed that Hitler might be

dead. It was assumed, and sometimes openly stated, that he was alive.'
This doctrine officially remained in force until 1968 when the communist author Lev Bezymenski was allowed to publish the autopsy
report in his book *The Death of Adolf Hitler*. Even then the truth had
to be distorted for political effect. In his anxiety to avoid being captured alive, Hitler appears to have simultaneously pulled the trigger
of a revolver held to his head and bitten on a glass ampoule of cyan-
ide clenched between his teeth. But despite the unanimous evidence of
the witnesses in the bunker that they heard a shot, despite the fact that
the autopsy report itself stated that 'part of the cranium' was 'missing', Bezymenski insisted that Hitler had only taken poison and had
thus died 'like a dog': it was apparently still important to the Soviet
Union that Hitler should be depicted as too cowardly to take the soldier's way out. Twenty-three years after the concealment of its discovery, the corpse had not lost its propaganda value.

Researched at first hand in the interrogation cell and the secret service
registry, *The Last Days of Hitler* was unique: the insight of an historian combined with the scholarship of an intelligence officer on active
service. Trevor-Roper was given access to the diaries of Goering's chief
of staff, General Koller, as well as those of Schwerin von Krosigk, the
Minister of Finance. He was the first to make use of the diary kept
by Hitler's valet, Heinz Linge, discovered by a British officer amid the
ruins of the Chancellery in September 1945. In the middle of November, after the completion of his original report, he was summoned back
to Germany from leave in Oxford to authenticate Hitler's last will
and testament. Shortly afterwards, in pursuit of two missing copies of
that document, he led a group of CIC officers in a midnight raid on a
house near the Austrian border. After a long interrogation session he
finally broke the resistance of a German major who admitted possessing a copy of Hitler's will. The major led him into the garden of his
home and in the darkness broke open the frozen ground with an axe
to retrieve a bottle: 'breaking the bottle with the axe, he drew out and
handed to me the last missing document. . .'

Such colourful adventures set Trevor-Roper apart from more conventional academic historians. His experience taught him that Nazi

documents could surface unexpectedly in all manner of unlikely places. He also appreciated that it was sometimes necessary to deal with unorthodox and even unsavoury characters. One could not afford to be too squeamish. In 1952, he met François Genoud, a Swiss lawyer whom he described at the time in the *Sunday Express* as 'an unrepentant Nazi sympathizer'. Genoud, a former member of the SS, whose name was later to be linked with the Palestine Liberation Organization, had obtained over a thousand typewritten pages known as the *Bormann–Vermerke*: the 'Bormann Notes'. They were meticulously kept in Martin Bormann's personal custody and he had written upon them, 'Notes of fundamental interest for the future. To be preserved with the greatest care.' They proved to be the transcripts of more than three hundred of Hitler's mealtime monologues: the interminable, rambling soliloquies which had passed for conversation at the Führer's dinner table and which had been recorded on Bormann's orders as if they were Holy Writ. The material legally belonged to Genoud. After the war he had acquired the copyright in Hitler's literary estate from the dictator's sister, Paula. Similar contracts had been agreed with Bormann's widow and the heirs of Josef Goebbels ('these poor people,' Genoud later called them, 'whose rights and property have been plundered'). Trevor-Roper edited, introduced and helped arrange publication of Genoud's material, which appeared in 1953 as *Hitler's Table Talk*.

Fascinating, yet simultaneously tedious and repellent in its grinding prose and vertiginous imagery, the book captures the authentic voice of Hitler. Lunch might find him lecturing Dr Porsche on the superiority of the air-cooled engine; over dinner he would hold forth on the origins of the planet. He had an opinion about everything: the inability of the English to perform Shakespeare, the 'harmfulness of cooked foods', the legends of ancient Greece, the toad ('a degenerate frog'), Winston Churchill ('an utterly immoral, repulsive creature'), the 'negroid' appearance of Eleanor Roosevelt, prelunar civilization and the mental capacity of a dog. In his brilliant introductory essay, Trevor-Roper depicted Hitler's mind as 'a terrible phenomenon, imposing indeed in its granitic harshness and yet infinitely squalid in its miscellaneous cumber – like some huge barbarian monolith, the expression of giant strength and savage genius, surrounded by a festering heap of refuse – old tins and dead vermin, ashes and eggshells and ordure – the intellectual *detritus* of centuries'.

For Trevor-Roper, *Hitler's Table Talk* was the first of a series of such commissions. In 1954, he edited Martin Bormann's letters. In 1956 he wrote the introduction to the *Memoirs* of Dr Felix Kersten, the faith-healer and masseur who treated Himmler and other senior Nazis. When Genoud produced what purported to be the final entries of the *Bormann–Vermerke* in the late 1950s, covering the last few weeks of the war, Trevor-Roper provided the foreword. For more than thirty years, if a publisher had documents from the Third Reich whose presentation required the imprimatur of a well-known academic, he was the first person they turned to. In the 1970s, when the West German company of Hoffmann and Campe acquired, from mysterious sources behind the Iron Curtain, 16,000 pages of Josef Goebbels's diaries, Trevor-Roper was appointed to edit the section devoted to 1945. And all the time he continued to turn out articles and essays about the Nazis and their Führer, many of them written in a vituperative style typical of academic debate in general, and of Trevor-Roper's technique in particular. He denounced the so-called 'memoirs' of Hitler's sister-in-law Bridget as a fake. He ridiculed the inaccuracies of *A Man Called Intrepid*. He attacked A. J. P. Taylor's thesis about the origins of the Second World War as 'demonstrably false'. Errors were punished, positions defended.

'Trevor-Roper,' complained Taylor in 1983, 'thought he had taken out a patent in Hitler.'

3

Hitler's bunker in Berlin was blown up by the Russians in 1947, his house at Berchtesgaden by the Americans in 1952. The motive in each case was to deny any renascent Nazi movement a shrine. But interest in Hitler could not be destroyed. It continued to grow, like weeds amidst the rubble.

Although *The Last Days of Hitler* put a stop to much of the outlandish speculation about the Nazi dictator's fate, it did not end it entirely. A close personal following of cranks, misfits, fantasists and criminals continued to attend Adolf Hitler in death as in life. In December 1947 a German pilot calling himself Baumgart swore in an affidavit that he had flown Hitler and Eva Braun to Denmark a few days before the end of the war. 'Baumgart afterwards retired to a lunatic asylum in Poland,' noted Trevor-Roper. Six months later a film actor from the South Tyrol named Luis Trenker produced what he claimed were Eva Braun's diaries. *Wochenend*, a romantic magazine for women, based in Munich, undertook to publish them. For a short time, *Wochenend*'s breathless readers were treated to Eva's intimate reminiscences: how Hitler forced her to wear leather underwear, how naked dances at the Berghof turned into midnight orgies, how Hitler feared water but loved having his feet bathed. It was exotic drivel of a high order, but unfortunately a few weeks later it was officially declared a forgery. In 1950 the proprietor of *Tempo Der Watt*, a pro-Nazi magazine, claimed to have heard from Martin Bormann that Hitler was living in a Tibetan monastery. 'We shall not give up the fight as long as we live,' Bormann was quoted as saying. A French magazine reported sightings of Hitler, minus his moustache, in Caracas, Buenos Aires and Tokyo. In 1956

The Times reported rumours that recordings of Hitler's voice, allegedly made in the previous twelve months, were being produced and sold in West Germany.

Another German periodical, *Herzdame*, adopted a fresh approach in the autumn of 1949. Hitler, it revealed, had fathered an illegitimate son in Munich some time before the First World War. The son, Wilhelm Baur, had committed suicide shortly after his father, in May 1945, but his children – the Führer's grandchildren – were still alive, 'somewhere in Germany'. This baseless story nevertheless engendered a spate of imitations until, by the mid-1970s, there were enough Hitler children clamouring for attention to fill a sizeable nursery. Most were straight-forward confidence tricksters like Franz Weber-Richter who swindled 15 million pesos and 50,000 marks out of a group of ex-Nazis in Argentina: their suspicions apparently were not aroused even by his additional claim to have spent eighteen months on the planet Venus. In 1965 the daughter of Tilly Fleischer, a famous German sportswoman who had competed in the 1936 Berlin Olympics, was persuaded by her boyfriend to compile a book, *Adolf Hitler Was My Father*. Extracts appeared in a German picture magazine under the headline 'If Only Hitler Knew', before police put a stop to the hoax. Claimants were still coming forward twelve years later. In 1977 a Frenchman, Jean Loret, told an international press conference in a fine display of filial loyalty that he had decided to reveal the secret of his parentage in order 'to let the world know that Hitler was not impotent'. The stories have varied over the years but two characteristics have remained constant: their inherent implausibility and the willingness of someone, usually a journalist, to believe them.

Mercifully, despite the fears of the Allies, the post-war interest in Hitler generally centred on the man rather than his ideology. To this day there has been no popular resurgence in support for Hitler's ideas. In 1983, the West German government estimated the number of active neo-Nazis at less than 2000, a feeble legacy for a movement which once dominated every level of German society and conquered much of continental Europe. One of the most singular features of the Nazi phenomenon was the extent to which National Socialism ultimately proved to be totally dependent upon its creator. Hitler occasionally used to picture himself as a spider at the centre of an enormous web. Without him, in the spring of 1945, this complex system of interlocking institutions, which had once appeared so powerful, simply melted away. It was not merely Hitler's state which died with him: the beliefs which had underpinned it died too. As Professor J. P. Stern put it, people who had once followed him had 'real difficulty in recalling the message now that the voice was gone'. Afterwards this served to focus yet more attention on Hitler. How did he do it? What was he like?

To begin with, in Germany at least, the enormity of Hitler's career made it difficult even to ask such questions. The period from 1933 to 1945 was largely ignored in school curricula. Anyone displaying Nazi mementoes or even publishing photographs of the period was liable to prosecution. Hitler was a subject of acute sensitivity. As late as 1962 the West German embassy in London felt compelled to make an official protest over a British television play, *Night Conspirators*, which imagined that after seventeen years of exile in Iceland, Hitler had returned to Germany. *Mein Kampf* was banned. When Hutchinson's, owners of the British copyright, decided to republish it, the Bavarian State authorities declared their 'strong opposition'. 'The German authorities regret our decision,' acknowledged the publishers in a note at the front of the book, 'thinking that it may prove damaging to new understandings and friendships.' In 1967, when a publisher in Spain also proposed a new edition, the Bonn government intervened and bought the Spanish rights itself to stop him.

But in the decade which followed, this reticence about the past was gradually transformed. The curiosity of a generation born after the collapse of the Third Reich coincided in 1973 with the fortieth anniversary of the Nazis' rise to power. That year saw an unprecedented surge of interest in Adolf Hitler, a tide of books, articles and films which the Germans dubbed the *'Hitler-Welle'*: the Hitler Wave. Joachim C. Fest, a former editor-in-chief of NDR television, published his monumental biography, the first comprehensive account of Hitler's life in German to appear since 1945. Fest began his book with a question unthinkable a decade earlier: 'Ought we to call him "great"?' *Hitler* became a bestseller, serialized in *Stern* and described as 'the Book of the Year' at the

Frankfurt Book Fair. The Führer's domination of the display stands at Frankfurt was such that the German satirical magazine *Pardon* hired an actor to impersonate him. Their 'Hitler' visited the Fair to demand a share of the royalties. He was arrested.

The effects of the Hitler Wave were felt across the world. In America more than twenty new books about Hitler were published. Two film producers, Sandy Lieberson and David Puttnam, released a documentary, *Swastika*, which included the Eva Braun home movies seized by the CIC in 1945: the cans were discovered by a researcher in the archives of the US Marine and Signal Corps. In February, Frank Finlay starred in *The Death of Adolf Hitler*. Three months later, Sir Alec Guinness appeared in *Hitler: The Last Ten Days*. The film was banned by the Jewish management of the ABC–EMI cinema chain. The Israelis denied it a licence. 'The figure of the assassin,' complained the Israeli Censorship Board, 'is represented in a human light without giving expression to the terrible murders for which he is responsible.'

Guinness confessed that in playing the part he had found it 'difficult not to succumb to Hitler's charm. He had a sweet smile and a very sentimental Austrian charm.' The BBC, despite protests, showed Leni Riefenstahl's Nazi propaganda film, *Triumph of the Will*. To Hutchinson's commercial pleasure but editorial embarrassment, the reissued *Mein Kampf*, despite an artificially high price to discourage mass sales, had to be reprinted twice. A delegation from the British Board of Deputies tried to dissuade the company from bringing out a paperback edition. They failed, and Hutchinson's sold a further 10,000 copies. Foreign language editions appeared in Denmark, Sweden and Italy. The *Sunday Telegraph* wrote of 'the astonishing resurgence of the Hitler cult'. *Time* reported a 'worldwide revival' of interest in the Nazi leader: 'Adolf Hitler's presence never vanishes. His career is still the fundamental trauma of the century.'

The 1970s also witnessed a corresponding boom in sales of Hitler memorabilia. In the immediate aftermath of the war this activity, too, had been discouraged by the German authorities. In 1948 a ruling by a denazification court that 'Hitler was an active Nazi' enabled the State of Bavaria to seize his personal property – principally his private apartment in Munich, some money owed to him by a Nazi publishing company, and a few valuable paintings. (Eva Braun's home, bought for her by Hitler in 1935, was also confiscated and donated to a restitution fund for the victims of Nazism.) Three years later, the Bavarian government made use of its powers to prevent Hitler's former Munich housekeeper, Frau Anni Winter, from selling a trunkful of the Führer's private property. Under the terms of Hitler's will, she was entitled to 'personal mementoes' sufficient 'for the maintenance of a modest middle-class standard of living'. She inherited such relics as Hitler's gun licence, his Nazi Party membership card, some of his watercolours, a copy of *Mein Kampf* and the original letter from President Hindenburg inviting Hitler to become Chancellor in 1933. For these and other treasures, Frau Winter was offered $250,000 by an American collector. The authorities promptly intervened and impounded the bulk of the collection, leaving her, bitterly resentful, with what they imagined to be a handful of valueless scraps.

But following Frau Winter's death, in 1972, these supposedly worthless items were put on sale at an auction in Munich. Telephone bids were taken from all over the world for lots which included family photographs, an eleven-word note for a speech and a War Loans savings card. Prices were reported to have 'exceeded all expectations'. The average price simply for a signed Hitler photograph was £450.

In the succeeding years the Nazi memorabilia market took off spectacularly. Hitler's 1940 Mercedes touring car – five tons of armoured steel and glass, twenty feet long with a 230 horsepower engine and a 56-gallon fuel tank – was sold in Arizona in 1973 for $153,000. A rug from the Reich Chancellery fetched $100,000. A millionaire in Nevada paid $60,000 for the crateful of Hitler's personal property rescued from the basement of the Führerbau. The Marquess of Bath acquired Himmler's spectacles, removed from his body after his suicide. He also bought a tablecloth which had belonged to the Commandant of Belsen concentration camp. A military dealer in Maryland, Charles Snyder, sold locks of Eva Braun's hair for $3500, and – following a deal with the official American executioner – strands from the ropes which hanged the Nuremberg war criminals.

It was against this background, in 1973, with the Hitler Wave at its height, that Mr Billy F. Price of Houston, Texas, heard of a new prize about to come on the market. Mr Price – owner of Hitler's napkins and cutlery and on his way to possessing one of the world's largest collections of Hitler paintings – discovered through contacts in Germany that Hermann Goering's old yacht was for sale. Price expressed an interest. But before he had time to put in a bid, the boat was sold. The purchaser, he learned later, was a figure hitherto unknown in the close-knit memorabilia market: a German journalist named Gerd Heidemann.

PART TWO

'For in his male he hadde a pilwe-beer,
Which that he seyde was Oure Lady veyl:
He seyde he hadde a gobet of the seyl
That Seint Peter hadde, whan that he wente
Upon the see, til Jhesu Crist hym hente.
He hadde a croys of latoun ful of stones,
And in a glas he hadde pigges bones.
But with thise relikes, whan that he fond
A povre person dwellynge upon lond,
Upon a day he gat hym moore moneye
Than that the person gat in monthes tweye;
And thus, with feyned flaterye and japes,
He made the person and the peple his apes.'

Geoffrey Chaucer: 'The Pardoner',
General Prologue to *The Canterbury Tales*

4

The boat was lying low against the harbour jetty when he first saw her, ageing and dilapidated, with the freezing waters of the River Rhine seeping into her hold. She had been built in 1937 and presented as a gift by the German motor industry to Hermann Goering, architect of Hitler's rearmament programme and commander-in-chief of the Luftwaffe. The sumptuously finished motor yacht took its place amongst the other trappings of the Reichsmarschall's grandiose lifestyle: his luxurious private train, his 100,000 acre hunting estate, his enormous hoard of looted art treasures. In honour of his first wife, who had died prematurely in 1931, Goering named her *Carin II*. The yacht survived the wartime air raids guarded by three soldiers in a private anchorage in Berlin. She also survived the death of her owner in Nuremberg in 1946. During the Allied occupation she was impounded by Field Marshal Montgomery and presented to the British Royal Family who rechristened her the *Royal Albert*. Following the birth of the Prince of Wales, she was renamed the *Prince Charles*. In 1960, after more than a decade in the service of the British Rhine Flotilla, the Queen returned the yacht to Goering's widow, his second wife, Emmy.

It was on a bleak day in January 1973, thirteen years later, that Gerd Heidemann found her moored on the waterfront in the West German capital, Bonn. She now belonged to the owner of a local printing works. More than eighty feet long, expensive to maintain and in need of extensive repairs, the yacht had become a financial liability. The owner told Heidemann he wanted to sell her.

Heidemann subsequently maintained that at that time he had no particular interest in the Nazis. He was a photographer and reporter on *Stern* and had simply been commissioned to take pictures of the boat for a feature article. He was forty-one years old, his third marriage had recently collapsed, and he was looking for an opportunity to make some money. He concluded that the yacht, once renovated, could be sold for a large profit. A few weeks later, in March, he bought her for 160,000 marks. It was a huge sum of money for an ordinary journalist to find. He had to mortgage his house, a bungalow in the Hamburg suburb of Flottbeck, to raise it.

Heidemann knew little about sailing. For help he turned to an acquaintance, a twenty-five-year-old seaman named Axel Thomsen who was studying for his captain's qualifications at the naval school in Hamburg. 'I went down to Bonn and saw the ship,' recalled Thomsen. 'It was in a miserable condition. Of the three engines, only one diesel was working. She was also taking in water and had constantly to be emptied.' She was too badly damaged to withstand the open sea, and late that summer the two men sailed her back to Hamburg along the inland waterways of northern Germany. She had to be put in dry dock for a year to be made watertight.

Heidemann soon had cause to regret his impulsive investment. He had hopelessly underestimated the amount of work which *Carin II* 's restoration would involve. By 1974 he was in a financial trap: he could hope to sell the boat only if he completed the repairs; he could pay for the repairs only by selling the boat. Meanwhile, interest rates on the money he had already borrowed and the cost of keeping the yacht in dock bit deep into his salary. 'He permanently seemed short of money,' said Thomsen ten years later. 'He was always trying to pump loans out of other people. He was worried that things were going to be taken off him because he hadn't paid his debts.' In desperation, Heidemann even asked Thomsen to lend him 15,000 marks. Word went round the Hamburg shipyards that the naive and over-confident new owner of 'Fat Hermann's boat' was financially shaky. Neither for the first time in his life nor the last, Heidemann was in danger of making a fool of himself.

Gerd Heidemann was born on 4 December 1931 in the Altona district of Hamburg, the illegitimate son of Martha Eiternick. When his

mother married a former sailor turned policeman called Rolf Heidemann, Gerd took his stepfather's surname. His parents were apolitical. Gerd, like most boys his age, was a member of the Hitler Youth.
When, at the end of the war, the Allies produced evidence of the scale
of the Nazis' atrocities, he went through the same sequence of emotions as millions of his fellow countrymen: disbelief, anger, guilt and
a desire to reject the past.

A quiet and unassuming adolescent, Heidemann left school at the
age of seventeen to become an apprentice electrician. The passion of
his life was photography and eventually he found work as an assistant in a photographic laboratory. He went on to become a freelance
photographer for the German newsagency DPA, for Keystone and for
various Hamburg newspapers. In 1951 he won his first commission
from *Stern*. On 1 September 1955 he became a permanent member of
the magazine's staff.

Twenty-eight years later, when his bewildered and humiliated
employers were pressed into holding an internal inquiry into his activities at *Stern*, they found there was almost nothing to say about his
early days on the magazine. 'His colleagues do not have any particular
memories of him, except that he used to enjoy playing chess,' reported
the inquiry. His shyness effaced him to the point of anonymity.

Stern had been founded in 1948 by a charismatic journalist and
businessman named Henri Nannen. The magazine prospered on a diet
of scandal, consumerism, crime and human interest, skilfully designed
to appeal to a war-weary population. The picture stories Heidemann
worked on give an idea of the quality of the magazine at that time.
One was 'Germany's Starlets'; another, 'Hospitals of Germany'. He
investigated organized crime in Sardinia and smuggling on the border
between Holland and West Germany. On one occasion he was dispatched to Goettingen to locate the son whom Chou En Lai was
rumoured to have fathered during the 1920s when he was studying
in Germany. Heidemann found a woman who had once had an affair
with a Chinese student called Chou; their son was killed in the war.
Unfortunately, as Heidemann reported to Nannen, her lover turned
out to be Chou Ling Gui – a different Chou entirely. Nannen's reply,
according to Heidemann, was 'Chou is Chou' and the story appeared

beneath the dramatic headline, 'Chou En Lai's Son Fell For Germany'. Looking back on his work during this period, Heidemann described it as 'mediocre'.

In the mid-1950s Nannen was astute enough to recognize that the shock and humiliation of the immediate post-war era was gradually being replaced by a growing public interest in the Nazis. Heidemann became involved in features about the Third Reich: Auschwitz, fugitive war criminals and the reminiscences of the widow of Reinhard Heydrich. 'Heidemann's routine activities were generally speaking outside my daily concern,' Nannen told police in 1983. 'I had the impression that he was a competent researcher. I didn't know of any mistakes in his work.' There was something about this intensely serious young man, with his pale complexion and earnest expression, which reminded Nannen of a priest fresh from a seminary.

From 1961 Heidemann worked abroad as a war photographer. He saw action in the Congo, in Biafra, Guinea Bissau, Mozambique, Iraq, Jordan, Israel, Uganda, Beirut and Oman. In 1965 he won an international press award at the Hague for the year's best photo-report: a feature about white mercenaries in the Congo. He frequently worked in a partnership with Randolph Braumann, a *Stern* reporter of the macho school, known to his colleagues in Hamburg as 'Congo Randy'. 'We both enjoyed war reporting and enjoying life and experiencing danger away from Europe,' recalled Braumann. In 1970 they covered the Black September civil war in Jordan and were almost killed trying to run from a Jordanian tank to a German embassy car Heidemann had parked nearby. Even Braumann was impressed by his photographer's exuberance under fire:

We jumped out of the tank and were immediately shot at from a house a few hundred metres away. I threw myself to the ground but Heidemann marched up to the bullet-ridden car and shouted to me: 'Randy! Come on! It's just like *Kismet*!'

Braumann was awed by his composure. 'The man had absolutely no fear.'

Back in Hamburg, Heidemann attempted to recapture the excitement of his foreign adventures. According to Braumann:

He used to collect war games and toy soldiers. In the cellar of his house was a great panoramic battlefield with enemy infantry and tanks, columns of pioneers, rocket silos, fighter aircraft – I really don't know where he got the time to build up such a huge installation. He used to buy the toys from all over the world. He had catalogues from New York, London, Paris and Hong Kong.

Visitors to the Heidemann household would be taken down to the cellar by their host to be shown the toy battlefield. Later, upstairs, if they were particularly unlucky, Heidemann would bring out mementoes from his trips abroad.

In the sixties [recalled Braumann] he'd collected everything he could about the Congo rebels. He had recordings, notebooks, photographs. As I knew quite a lot about them, I found it quite interesting when he played all his recordings for me. You could hear a lot of shooting on them. He called them 'Conversations Under Fire'. Other guests – among them his wife at the time, Barbara – found the whole thing idiotic. I was the only one amongst his friends who knew what it was like to drive round with these rebel convoys.

Basically, we were both always longing to escape from Europe.

Heidemann's obsessional nature inevitably had its effect upon his personal relationships. He had first married in 1954, at the age of twenty-three, and had a son. A year later he and his wife were divorced. In 1960 they remarried and had a daughter. But in 1965 the marriage finally foundered. Divorced once more, in 1966 Heidemann married his second wife, Barbara. This relationship lasted for five years, until Barbara too tired of his collections, his stories and his frequent absences abroad. The couple separated in 1971.

As a journalist, Heidemann was a curious amalgam of strengths and weaknesses. In research he was indefatigable, hunting down documents and interviewees with a dogged persistence which earned him the title 'der Spürhund' – the Bloodhound. His approach was uncritical and indirect. He flattered and insinuated and was often rewarded with the sort of confidences that a more aggressive approach would have failed to solicit. But this tendency to submerge himself in the opinions of others was Heidemann's principal failing. He was such a compulsive collector of information that he never knew when to stop, and although he strove to be more than a photographer and researcher, he failed to become one of *Stern*'s major writers. He lacked any sense of perspective. Invariably the editor would end up asking him to hand over his boxes of files and transcripts. Someone else would have to boil down the mountain of information into a story. According to *Stern*'s 1983 inquiry: 'He never actually wrote any of his reports himself.'

In 1967 Heidemann became involved in an exhaustive investigation to try to uncover the real identity of the German thriller writer, B. Traven. Long after the essentials of the story had been published in *Stern*, Heidemann continued his researches, to the exasperation of the magazine's editors who wanted him to work on other projects. He went to Chicago, San Francisco, Mexico and Norway. He toured German antique shops collecting Traven memorabilia. 'I acquired everything I could,' said Heidemann. Even the patience of Congo Randy became strained. 'Heidemann would talk about nothing else but Traven,' he later complained. In 1972, Heidemann asked Braumann to help him turn his information into a book.

> He showed me everything that he'd collected about Traven. There must have been at least twenty ring-folders full of material. I said: 'My dear friend, I'd have to read for half a year before I could even start.'

Undeterred, Heidemann spent almost a decade immersed in the Traven story. By the time he had finished he had seventy files of information. He became convinced that the writer was the illegitimate son of Kaiser Wilhelm II. As proof, he showed Braumann two photographs: one of a man he believed to be Traven, and another of the Kaiser's eldest son. 'Don't they look similar?' he asked. Braumann was not impressed. 'I thought the story was far too improbable. It was typical of Gerd Heidemann that he should believe in something so crazy and unlikely.'

Braumann thought it was equally 'crazy' that Heidemann, short of money and ignorant of ships, should have plunged himself into debt to buy Hermann Goering's yacht. But knowing this restless, diffident, obsessive man as well as he did he was not in the least surprised by what happened next. 'I knew that after the mercenary phase and the

Traven phase there would be a new phase for Heidemann: the Nazi phase.'

By 1974, *Carin II* had at least been rendered watertight. She was taken out of dry dock and moored in a Hamburg marina. 'Only the most urgent repairs had been done,' recalled Axel Thomsen, 'because Herr Heidemann was deterred by the high cost involved. He said that further work was too expensive.'

With the yacht's renovation temporarily halted for lack of money, Heidemann set about researching her history. In Munich he made contact with Goering's daughter, Edda. She was in her mid-thirties, attractive, unmarried and devoted to the memory of her father. According to his colleagues, Heidemann had always been remarkably successful with women. Apparently Edda too saw something in this tall, slightly pudgy, quietly spoken journalist who listened so attentively to her stories of her father. Shortly after their first meeting, when Heidemann visited her to show her photographs of *Carin II*, the couple began having an affair.

Slowly, imperceptibly, through his ownership of the yacht and his relationship with Edda, Heidemann began to be drawn into a circle of former Nazis. A *Stern* reporter, Jochen von Lang, introduced him to former SS General Wilhelm Mohnke, the last commander of the German garrison defending the Reich Chancellery. The sixty-three-year-old General had lived quietly since his release from Soviet captivity in 1955. He even declined to attend the reunions of the SS *Leibstandarte Adolf Hitler*, the Führer's bodyguard, of which he was a founder member. One reason for Mohnke's low profile was that the British still had an outstanding war crimes charge against him, alleging he had been responsible for shooting prisoners at Dunkirk. Mohnke, silver-haired and craggy-featured, still lithe and powerful, looked as if he had stepped out of a Hollywood war film. 'Herr von Lang took me to the yacht,' stated Mohnke, 'where, among others, I met Edda Goering.' He and Heidemann established what he called 'a very friendly rapport' and were soon addressing each other with the familiar '*du*'.

Another SS general introduced by Jochen von Lang became friendly with Heidemann around this time: Karl Wolff, one of the most senior of the surviving Nazis. Wolff had been Himmler's liaison officer with

Hitler. He was sufficiently close to the SS Reichsführer for Himmler to call him by a pet name, 'Wolffchen', an endearment which Heidemann later adopted. In Minsk in 1941, on the one occasion Himmler steeled himself to stand at the edge of a mass grave and watch his SS troops massacre a hundred naked men and women, it was Wolff who caught hold of him when he seemed to faint and forced him to carry on watching. Wolff was heavily implicated in the Final Solution. As the Nazis' military governor in Italy, he was alleged to have sent at least 300,000 Jews to the Treblinka death camp. He was also accused of arranging the liquidation of partisans and Jews in the Soviet Union. Wolff saved his neck by secretly negotiating with Allen Dulles the surrender of the German forces in Italy to the Americans. In 1946 he was sentenced to four years' hard labour but spent only a week in prison. In the 1950s Wolff became a successful advertising agent in Cologne. But in 1962 he was rearrested. Fresh evidence was produced, including a letter written in 1941 in which he professed to be 'particularly gratified with the news that each day for the last fortnight a trainload of 5000 members of the "Chosen People" has been sent to Treblinka'. He was found guilty of complicity in mass murder and sent to prison, but in 1971, in view of his 'otherwise blameless life', he was released. He was seventy-four when Heidemann met him: charming, energetic and unrepentant.

Heidemann began to hold regular Third Reich *soirées* on *Carin II*. About a dozen friends and former Nazis would be invited, with Wolff and Mohnke as the guests of honour. 'We started to have long drinking evenings on board,' recalled Heidemann, 'with different people of quite different opinions talking to each other. I had always been a passionate reader of thrillers. Suddenly I was living a thriller.' He started to devour books on the Third Reich. 'I wanted to be part of the conversation, not just to sit and drink whisky.'

Heidemann's only problem was the continuing cost of the yacht. Merely servicing the debts he had incurred in buying it was proving 'a bottomless pit'. In the hope of a solution, he decided, in 1976, to seek help from Henri Nannen.

The *Stern* of 1976 was very different from the *Stern* which Heidemann had joined in the 1950s. With the advent of the sexual revolution in the 1960s, it had begun sprinkling its pages with glossy pictures of nudes. Following the growth of protest politics, its editorial line had swung to the left, with strident articles on student unrest, the Vietnam war, and the perfidy of the NATO alliance. The magazine's financial strength was a reflection of the power of the West German economy. It sucked in enormous advertising revenue and regularly produced issues running to 300 pages. Always abreast of the latest fashion, with a circulation of over 1.5 million, it easily outsold its major competitors. Its publisher, Henri Nannen, shaped the magazine in his own image: prosperous, bulging, glossy and bumptious.

In 1976 this 'hybrid of money and journalism', as one of his left-wing writers called him, was sixty-three. He had never been a member of the Nazi Party, but he had a past which sat uneasily with his present position as purveyor of radical *chic*. He had appeared as a sports announcer in Leni Riefenstahl's film of the 1936 Berlin Olympics. He had written articles praising Hitler in *Kunst dem Volk* (*Art for the People*), a Nazi magazine. During the war he had worked for a military propaganda unit. *Stern*, under his guidance, gave extensive coverage to the Third Reich and there were some who detected an ambivalence in his fascination with the period. 'It was subconscious,' claimed Manfred Bissinger, Nannen's left-wing deputy at the time. 'For Nannen, the less bad the Nazi past turned out to have been, the less bad his role in it was.' He had a powerful personality and Heidemann revered him: according to Braumann, 'he obeyed his great master Nannen's every word'.

Heidemann had been pestering Nannen to visit *Carin II* for months. In the summer of 1976, Nannen finally agreed. He was, in his own words, 'surprised and fascinated' by what he saw. Heidemann had turned the yacht into a kind of shrine to its first owner. Goering's dinner service was on prominent display, as were Goering's tea cups and Goering's drinking goblets. On the table was Goering's ashtray, in the cupboard, his uniform. The cushion covers were made out of Goering's bathrobe. Working from old photographs, Heidemann had even tried to fill the bookshelves with the same books Goering had kept there. Most of these mementoes had been given to Heidemann by Edda Goering; the rest had been acquired from dealers in Nazi memorabilia.

Heidemann showed Nannen an album filled with photographs and newspaper cuttings about the yacht which included a picture of Princess Margaret on a trip to Basle. 'Simply everything was there,' said Nannen later. 'The photographs didn't just come from one source. They couldn't have been forged. He'd actually collected the whole lot. I found it an incredible journalistic performance.'

Having put his employer in this receptive mood, Heidemann outlined his plan. Nannen recalled:

> Heidemann told me he needed a loan of 60,000 marks, otherwise he would be in difficulties. He was having to pay the interest on a loan of 300,000 marks he'd taken out to pay for the renovation of the Goering yacht. He needed money to put a new engine into his boat.

Heidemann proposed that he should write a book for *Stern* based upon the conversations he was holding with Mohnke, Wolff and other old Nazis. He told Nannen that he had already begun tape recording some of these reminiscences and had some interesting material on the Odessa network, the supposed Nazi escape route to South America. 'Because Heidemann had already reported on this subject for *Stern*,' said Nannen, 'I agreed.'

On 12 October 1976 Heidemann concluded an agreement with *Stern*'s parent company, the large Hamburg publishing house of Gruner and Jahr. He undertook to write a book provisionally entitled *Bord Gespräche* (*Deck Conversations*) with the subtitle 'Personalities from History Meet on Goering's Former Yacht *Carin II* '. The contract was unusually generous towards Heidemann. He was paid an immediate advance of 60,000 marks, but no date was stipulated for the delivery of the manuscript and he was not required to return the money should he fail to write the book. All he had to do was undertake to maintain *Carin II* in a satisfactory condition. The contract was signed, on behalf of Gruner and Jahr, by Henri Nannen and by the company's managing director, Manfred Fischer.

With the official blessing and financial support of his employers, Heidemann's descent into the world of the old Nazis now began in earnest.

5

While Heidemann poured whisky and adjusted his tape recorder aboard *Carin II*, another journalist was also busy tracking down survivors of the Third Reich. One hundred and fifty miles south-east of Hamburg, in his office in West Berlin, James P. O'Donnell, bureau chief of *Newsweek* magazine, was compiling a card index of more than 250 people who had been with Hitler during his last days in the bunker. His researches were to have important consequences for Heidemann.

O'Donnell's first assignment in Berlin for *Newsweek*, in July 1945, had been to visit the Führerbunker. The memory of those forty-five minutes beneath the ground – the stench of blocked latrines whose effluent flooded the narrow corridor, the blackened walls, the tiny rooms littered with broken glass and bloodied bandages – had stayed with O'Donnell ever since. 'Adolf Hitler,' he wrote, 'exercises over my mind, and that of many others, I suspect, a curious kind of fascination.' He decided to write a book, an expanded version of *The Last Days of Hitler*, describing what had happened in the bunker. Between 1972 and 1976, operating out of Berlin, he visited scores of eyewitnesses, 'cruising Hitler's old autobahns, clocking more than 60,000 miles'.

Like Heidemann, he found himself increasingly fascinated by the network of characters he uncovered. Thirty years after the end of the war many of the people close to Hitler still kept in regular contact. Gossiping amongst themselves, divided into cliques, their relationships still traced ancient patterns of loyalty and animosity forged in the heyday of the Third Reich. Once, while he was interviewing Albert Speer at his home in Heidelberg, the postman arrived and handed Speer a package which turned out to contain an autographed copy of his book, *Inside the Third Reich*. Speer had sent it to Christa Schroeder, his favourite among Hitler's secretaries, whom he had not seen since his arrest and imprisonment in 1945. She had sent it back with a brief covering note saying that she was sorry, but she was returning the book because she had been 'ordered to do so'. 'Who has the power to issue such orders?' asked O'Donnell. 'The Keepers of the Flame,' replied Speer: the adjutants, orderlies, chauffeurs and secretaries who had formed Hitler's inner circle and who habitually referred to themselves as *die von dem Berg'*, 'the Mountain People', in memory of their pre-war days at Berchtesgaden. Speer, once Hitler's favourite, was generally detested for his 'betrayal' of the Führer at Nuremberg. For his part, Speer contemptuously dismissed them as the *Chauffeureska*.

It was this group that O'Donnell, and later Heidemann, succeeded in penetrating: the adjutants, Otto Guensche and Richard Schulze-Kossens; the pilot, Hans Baur; the valet, Heinz Linge; the chauffeur, Erich Kempka; and, above all, the secretaries, who maintained a fierce loyalty to their dead employer. To them he was still *der Chef*: the Boss. The oldest, Johanna Wolf, had been recruited to work for Hitler by Rudolf Hess in 1924 and had remained his principal private secretary for more than twenty years. *Stern* was reputed to have offered her $500,000 for her memoirs. She turned them down. 'I was taught long ago,' she explained to O'Donnell, 'that the very first and last duty of a confidential secretary is to remain confidential.' None of Hitler's four main secretaries had married after the war; none had much money. When O'Donnell finally persuaded Gerda Christian to meet him at the home of an intermediary in 1975 she was working as a secretary in a bank in Dortmund. Of all the Keepers of the Flame, she was the most fanatical. 'Do nothing to let the Führer down,' was Frau Christian's repeated exhortation to her colleagues. She had divorced her husband, a Luftwaffe general, in 1946, and like the other secretaries, she chose to remain single. O'Donnell once asked her why. 'How could any of us have remarried,' she replied, 'after having known a man like Adolf Hitler?'

It was in the autumn of 1972 that O'Donnell first heard the story of Sergeant Arndt's ill-fated mission to fly the ten metal trunks out of Berlin. From Heinz Linge he had obtained the address of Rochus Misch, the bunker's switchboard operator. Misch, by then in his fifties, turned out to be the proprietor of a paint and varnish shop less than a mile from O'Donnell's Berlin office. Misch was happy to talk about his wartime experiences. The interview began in his shop and continued during a walk through the city. From a vantage point in Potsdamer Platz the two men stood for a while, looking out across the Eastern sector, to the grassy mound in the shadow of the Berlin Wall which is all that now remains of Hitler's bunker. It was not until the early evening, when they were sitting in O'Donnell's office, that Misch mentioned the loading of the chests on to the lorry and described Arndt's departure from Berlin.

> In my office [recalled O'Donnell] I had for years been using my own US Army officer's standard-issue footlocker to store back-copies of the overseas editions of *Time* and *Newsweek*. Misch spotted this, and in order to describe the German chests pointed to the footlocker: 'Something like that, only cheaper, and with wooden ribs.' To get the heft and thus a guess at the weight, Misch and I together were just able to lift it three feet into the air to simulate the 1945 loading operation.

Using this as a rough guide, O'Donnell estimated that Arndt had been escorting almost half a ton of documents. He decided to pursue the story further and a few months later drove down to the Bavarian village of Herrsching, on the shores of Lake Ammersee, to see Hans Baur.

Baur had tried to break out from the Führerbunker two days after Hitler's death but had been cut down by Russian machine-gun fire. He was hit in the leg and the wound had turned septic. 'There was no surgeon available,' Baur wrote later, 'so the German surgeon amputated with a pocket knife.' O'Donnell found a tough and irascible old man of seventy-seven, who used his wooden leg as if it were an elaborate stage prop, noisily tapping it with his signet ring or occasionally hobbling round the room on it to enact some dramatic scene. In November 1945 he had been taken by cattle truck to Moscow's Lubianka prison where, night after night for weeks on end, he had been interrogated about Hitler's final hours. He was made to put his account down on paper, only to have the pages snatched off him and torn up before his eyes.

Sometimes he was grilled on his own; sometimes the Russians dragged in other bunker survivors: the commander of Hitler's SS bodyguard, Hans Rattenhuber, his naval attaché, Admiral Voss, Otto Guensche and Heinz Linge. The questioning went on for three and a half years. In 1950 he was asked if he had ever flown Hitler to meet Mussolini. Baur answered that he had, four times. He was promptly accused of 'having taken part in war preparations, because during those discussions Hitler and Mussolini had hatched their criminal plot to attack the Soviet Union'. Despite Baur's horrified protests that he 'bore no more responsibility than a train driver', he was sentenced to twenty-five years in a labour camp. In the end, he spent ten years in Soviet captivity. He was released in 1955 and shortly afterwards he decided to write his memoirs. They were not designed to be a work of scholarship or history, but – as he told Trevor-Roper soon after his return to the West – a book to be read 'by the fire, in the evening, with pipe in mouth'. It was in this book, *Hitler's Pilot*, buried amid the anecdotes of his adventures with the Boss, that Baur had first described Hitler's reaction to the news that Arndt's plane was missing.

The original manuscript had contained ten pages on Operation Seraglio, but his publishers had cut them – as they cut more than two-thirds of his rambling reminiscences. Baur told O'Donnell that he had been anxious to set matters straight because of accusations from the relatives of some of those killed that the operation had been poorly planned. He had contacted the Luftwaffe's Graves Registration organization who told him – erroneously as it turned out – that the aircraft had crashed in a Bavarian forest (it had in fact crashed in what is now East Germany). That was all he knew. He had no idea what Hitler had meant by 'valuable documents' for 'posterity'.

O'Donnell considered what could possibly have been of such value to Hitler that its apparent loss could cause such distress.

From the autumn of 1942 onwards, a team of stenographers had taken down every word uttered during the military conferences at the Führer's headquarters. These verbatim transcripts were compiled at Hitler's insistence as a means of establishing his strategic genius and his generals' incompetence: 'I want to pin down responsibility for events once and for all,' he explained to one of the stenographers. If there was one set of records which Hitler intended as 'a testament to posterity' it was this. He stated at the time that his words were to be 'taken down for later historical research'.

One of Hitler's secretaries, Christa Schroeder, told O'Donnell that in her view it was these transcripts that were on board the crashed plane. Else Krueger, Martin Bormann's former secretary, agreed with her. She rejected O'Donnell's initial theory that the papers might have been the missing notes of Hitler's 'Table Talk' from 1943 to 1944: these were Bormann's responsibility and would have been among his files, not Hitler's.

At this point, in 1975, with the deadline for the completion of his book looming, O'Donnell decided he had taken the story as far as he could. He was content to have obtained a minor historical scoop: establishing for the first time a link between Baur's account of Hitler's reaction to the loss of Arndt's plane, and Misch's description of the evacuation of the ten heavy chests. To round off the story, and to cover all possible eventualities, he ended his account of the episode with what he hoped was an appropriately teasing last paragraph:

> As all police reporters know, documents have a way of surviving crashes in which humans are cremated. While even metal melts, a book or a notebook does not burn easily, above all when it is packed tightly into a container excluding oxygen. Paper in bulk tends, rather, to char at the edges . . . One is left with the nagging thought that some Bavarian hayloft, chicken coop, or even pigsty may well have been waterproofed and insulated with millions of words of the Führer's unpublished, ineffable utterances, simply hauled away at dawn as loot from a burning German transport plane.

O'Donnell's book was published in Germany under the title *Die Katacombe* in 1976. Not long afterwards, General Mohnke, one of the book's main characters, presented a copy to Gerd Heidemann.

6

O'Donnell was aware of *Stern*'s increasing interest in the survivors of Hitler's court. 'During the years when I was on the road talking to the "Mountain People", and above all from 1975 on, *Stern* approached at least a dozen of the old Hitler retainers and encouraged them, in the words of Heinz Linge, "to get something, anything on paper".' Linge, who lived in Hamburg, recalled one occasion when he joined Wolff, Mohnke, Hanna Reitsch (the famous Nazi test pilot) and 'several others' aboard *Carin II* for a day trip to the North Sea island of Sylt. Linge described the yacht as 'a kind of sentimental bait for all of us old Hitler people'. In the course of the two-hundred-mile voyage, Heidemann 'between bouts of champagne and caviar' tried to entice his guests to dictate their memories into his tape recorder. The results were disappointing: hardly surprising, observed Linge, 'with so much champagne flowing'.

The Sylt excursion was, unfortunately for Heidemann, fairly typical. The rambling and tipsy old Nazis enjoyed his hospitality but produced little of practical value. By 1978 it was becoming apparent that Henri Nannen's 60,000 mark investment in Heidemann and his 'deck conversations' was not paying off. Around this time, Erich Kuby, an experienced *Stern* writer, joined forces with Heidemann to investigate the Nazis' relations with Mussolini. *Carin II* was supposed to be the key which would unlock the participants' memories. SS Major Eugen Dollmann, formerly a senior officer in the German security service in Rome, was among those lured aboard. In the visitors' book aboard the yacht Kuby wrote that 'on this calm and quiet sea – if one can ever describe the Elbe as such – in the company of General Wolff, we allowed the Third Reich to come alive again'. But despite Kuby's melo-dramatic description, these sessions also proved to be largely worthless.

> Heidemann's research practice [according to Kuby] consisted of switching on his tape recorder and letting it run as long as possible so that he didn't break into the flow of the other person's conversation with pointed questions. . . During our work together, Heidemann delivered to me from time to time transcripts of all his tape recordings. I think that in total there were some 500 pages or so. But he wasn't filtering the information. He was simply writing it up word for word and a lot of it didn't even have any questions.

'Until this time,' said Kuby, 'I had no particular reason to think that Heidemann was pro-Nazi in any way. But as we worked on the project, my conviction about this began to waver.' His colleague, he realized, no longer had any 'critical perspective' in his dealings with the former Nazis: he was beginning to identify with them. Piecing together Heidemann's activities from now onwards is to witness a man slowly sinking into a mire of obsession and fantasy about the Third Reich.

Heidemann married his third wife at his fourth wedding ceremony in May 1979. His new bride was not Edda Goering, from whom he had parted a few years previously, but one of Edda's friends. Gina Heidemann had been introduced to her future husband in the early 1970s. She was a former *au pair* girl and airline stewardess, tall and elegant with long blonde hair. At the time her affair with Heidemann began she was still married to her first husband and had two children, daughters, aged nineteen and sixteen. She shared Heidemann's interest in the Nazis and had spent many happy hours on board *Carin II*. The two witnesses at the wedding were not Joseph and Heike Friedmann – Gina's closest friends and the couple who had first introduced her to Gerd – but SS Generals Wolff and Mohnke. 'We asked the Friedmanns whether they'd mind,' Gina explained to the *Sunday Times* in 1983. 'They are Jews you see. Joschi said that, no, he thought it would be interesting. And it was. They were all very interested in talking to each other.' Not all the Heidemanns' guests were as phlegmatic. 'My wife and I went to the wedding ceremony,' recalled Randolph Braumann, 'and I said to him, "Aren't you going a bit far? The SS as wedding witnesses?" "That's just a tactic," said Heidemann. "I need these people in order to get to the old Nazis in South America."'

Heidemann wasted no time in exploiting his contacts. On 24 June 1979, he and Gina set off on their honeymoon – accompanied by General Wolff. Their destination was South America, where the trio spent the next nine weeks looking for fugitives from the Third Reich. The lustre of Wolff's name ensured that the Heidemanns had access to some of the most notorious of the Nazi refugees. They visited Argentina, Chile, Paraguay, Bolivia and Brazil. They saw several high-ranking SS officers who had served in Italy. In Chile they met Walter Rauff, Wolff's former subordinate, who had been in charge of the mobile 'gassing vans', precursors of the gas chambers. He was wanted in West Germany for the murder of 97,000 Jews, mostly women and children. In La Paz in Bolivia, Wolff arranged a meeting with Klaus Barbie, the 'Butcher of Lyons', wanted by the French for torture, murder, and complicity in the Final Solution. Barbie gave Heidemann a long interview, and the reporter afterwards referred to his 'friendship' with the war criminal.

'The point of the trip was to find Mengele and Bormann,' Wolff told the police in 1983, 'or at least to find traces of them.' Josef Mengele, the notorious chief doctor at Auschwitz, had, it has since turned out, drowned in the sea at São Paulo only four months before Heidemann came looking for him: his trail, said Heidemann, was 'cold'. But the search for Martin Bormann was a different matter. From the summer of 1979 onwards, Heidemann was convinced that Bormann was alive.

Such a belief was not without precedent. By 1972, sixteen different 'Martin Bormanns' had been arrested in South America: there was Rohl Sonnenburg, for example, the forty-three-year-old priest picked up in 1966 by the Brazilian police in a monastery near Recife; there was Juan Falero, the itinerant Mexican carpenter who had never even heard of Bormann, who was arrested in Guatemala in 1967; five years later there was the case of the septuagenarian jute and banana planter, Johann Hartmann, who was plucked from his shack in a remote Indian village in Colombia, photographed and fingerprinted, and reported all over the world as being Hitler's former secretary. All of the alleged Bormanns were later found to be innocent and released, but the speculation that

Bormann had survived persisted. 'I believe that Martin Bormann is alive and well,' wrote Stewart Steven, Foreign Editor of the *Daily Express,* in March 1972. 'His story would be certainly the most fascinating of all.' Eight months later, Steven collaborated with the American writer Ladislas Farago on a five-part 'World Exclusive' serialized in the *Daily News* in New York and the *Express* in London. According to the two newspapers, Bormann was living as a prosperous businessman in Argentina. This 'great manhunt saga', as they called it, was accompanied by a 'snatched' photograph of an 'Argentine intelligence officer' face to face with his 'quarry' in the border town of Mendoza. Subsequent investigation established that the picture was actually taken outside a café in the heart of Buenos Aires and showed two friends talking. 'Bormann' proved to be a fifty-four-year-old Argentine high school teacher named Rudolfo Siri.

The journalist who did most to discredit the rumours that Bormann had survived was Jochen von Lang – the man who had first introduced Heidemann to Mohnke and Wolff. In 1965, von Lang had published an exhaustive investigation in *Stern* which concluded that Bormann had died during the break out from the Führerbunker on 2 May 1945. *Stern* was sufficiently confident of von Lang's conclusion to hire a bulldozer and a team of labourers to dig for his body in Berlin's Invalidenstrasse. They found nothing. But seven years later, on a snowy morning in December 1972, workmen excavating a site a few yards from the scene of the original *Stern* dig found two skeletons. Identified from dental records, one proved to be Hitler's last doctor, Ludwig Stumpfegger, and the other, Martin Bormann.

This evidence satisfied most people. The West German public prosecutors, who had been searching for Bormann since 1945, shut down their inquiry. Hugh Trevor-Roper, who had regarded the question of Bormann's survival as 'open' for twenty-five years, stated that it could now be 'closed'.

Ladislas Farago, naturally, disagreed. In 1974 he produced a book – *Aftermath* – supposedly containing new evidence that Bormann was still alive. The book's credibility was not enhanced by Farago's highly coloured prose style. ('Turning to Hugetti, he said, "I think this gentleman needs the picana." Dieter winced. He knew what the picana was – the dreaded torture instrument ... ') The climax of Farago's imaginative tale was his personal confrontation with 'Bormann' in a convent hospital run by nuns of the Redemptorist Order 'somewhere in southern Bolivia':

> I saw a little old man in a big bed between freshly laundered sheets, his head propped up by three big downy pillows, looking at me with vacant eyes, mumbling words to himself, raising his voice only once, and then only to order us out of the room rather rudely. 'Dammit,' he said, not only with some emphasis, but with a vigour that astounded me, 'don't you see I'm an old man? So why don't you let me die in peace?'

For this, Farago was reported to have been paid an advance by his American publishers, Simon and Schuster, of more than $100,000.

Heidemann, like Farago, believed Bormann had survived. He subsequently claimed to have been given information to this effect by Klaus Barbie. When he returned to Germany from his honeymoon on 30 August he told Braumann 'he was more convinced than ever that Bormann was alive: there was a whole series of indications'. He showed Erich Kuby a collection of twelve by ten inch photographs, which he had brought back from South America. 'They included a set of pictures supposedly of Bormann,' recalled Kuby. 'Heidemann said he had not taken them himself but had been given them.' As had been the case with the pictures of the Kaiser's son six years earlier, the photographs fascinated Heidemann. He spent hours poring over them, tracing the subject's profile and the shape of his ears. 'He was convinced,' said Kuby.

His employers on *Stern*, however, were less impressed. Before he left, Heidemann had persuaded them to help pay for the trip. His expenses – excluding air fares – amounted to 27,000 marks. But once again they found themselves with little to show for their money. 'After his return from South America,' noted the *Stern Report*, 'although he had masses of tape recordings and transcripts, none of it produced very much which was usable for the magazine.' This failure, combined with the high cost of the South American expedition, put Heidemann's position on the magazine 'in jeopardy' for the first time in almost twenty-five years. Heidemann retaliated by spreading rumours that he was considering offers for his services from *Stern*'s rivals, *Bunte* and *Quick*.

*

The extent of Heidemann's gullibility, of his almost pathetic eagerness to believe what he was told, was clearly demonstrated in 1979. There was the affair of the 'Bormann' photograph; there was also the affair of the Churchill–Mussolini correspondence.

While working with Kuby, Heidemann had become involved with a former SS officer named Franz Spoegler. Spoegler, who had been one of Mussolini's German adjutants, claimed to have access to thousands of pages of transcripts of Mussolini's telephone conversations with his mistress, Clara Petacci. He also said he could produce some sensational correspondence between the Duce and Winston Churchill. Heidemann was enormously excited. 'Over a period of about eighteen months,' recalled Kuby, 'he was always chasing Spoegler to get hold of these documents.'

On 17 February 1979, Heidemann approached David Irving, who was in Hamburg to take part in a television programme. Irving had edited the diaries of Goering's deputy, Field Marshal Milch, and Heidemann – with his mania for collecting anything to do with *Carin II* – asked Irving for a copy of an entry referring to a conference aboard the yacht. Then he told Irving about the Churchill–Mussolini correspondence. 'He knew that I was writing a Churchill biography,' said Irving. 'He wanted to use me to get to English newspapers with these Mussolini letters.' That night, in his diary, Irving made a note of his conversation with Heidemann:

> He has at his private address a few letters from WSC to Mussolini, in English, dated up to 1941 (!) in which latter letter for instance WSC complains about the pro-German attitude of the Pope. The purpose of the WSC letters (to which G.H. does not have Musso's replies) was to try to break Mussolini out of the Axis. The letters are both typescript originals and photocopies.

Irving was intrigued and immediately on his return to London he wrote Heidemann a letter 'in order to confirm in writing my interest in the Churchill letters to Mussolini which you mentioned'. Nine months later, at the end of November 1979, Heidemann rang the British historian and asked him to come to Hamburg as quickly as possible. On 2 December, Irving arrived at the Heidemanns' flat.

Heidemann [recalled Irving] took me into the office next to his living room. On the bookshelves were between 50 and 70 large loose-leaf folders. He opened two or three of them and showed me transcripts he had written up himself of conversations with Karl Wolff and other leading figures from the Third Reich. Some of the conversations had taken place in South America. . . He described Karl Wolff as someone who had opened doors. I think the name Mengele was mentioned.

From one of the folders, Heidemann produced photocopies of correspondence between Mussolini and Churchill covering almost six years. The first letter, dated 20 May 1939, was from Churchill, urging Mussolini not to sign the so-called 'Pact of Steel' with Hitler. The last letter, from Mussolini, written in April 1945, was a cryptic appeal to the British Prime Minister to remember their 'earlier agreements'. In addition to the correspondence already in his hands, Heidemann, according to a memorandum Irving wrote shortly afterwards, had:

> a two-page typed list from his source listing all the other correspondence on offer, giving dates and synopses of the letters concerned. They display a close knowledge of the politics of the era, for example in July 1940 (?) Churchill offering Mussolini a revision of the frontier between Uganda and Kenya to Italy's advantage if Italy would withdraw from the Axis; he also offers a separate peace to Italy, at France's expense. . .

For a moment, Irving was electrified. Here was evidence of secret dealing between the leaders of two warring nations. If it were true, it would create a sensation.

Unfortunately for Heidemann, as Irving pointed out after a careful examination, the letters were obvious fakes. In what purported to be a handwritten Churchill letter to Mussolini dated 7 May 1940 there were four clues to suggest it was a forgery: the Chartwell letterhead was centrally placed rather than printed on the right; in the text, Churchill referred to his impending appointment as prime minister – something which did not occur for another three days and which at that stage he was unlikely to have anticipated; the letter contained a misspelling of 'wich' for 'which' – 'a common spelling error made by foreigners', commented Irving; and finally the handwriting itself, in his view, was 'slightly too ragged'.

This was a bitter disappointment to Heidemann. Spoegler, according to Kuby, had demanded 65,000 marks for the correspondence, and Heidemann told Irving he had 'mortgaged one-quarter of *Carin II*' to pay for it. Having spent more than a year pursuing the documents he now saw their authenticity virtually demolished in the space of an afternoon. When Irving returned to London, he sent a copy of the letter dated 7 May 1940 to Churchill's official biographer, Martin Gilbert, for his opinion. On 17 December, Irving wrote to Heidemann telling him that Martin Gilbert 'clearly dismisses the possibility of authenticity... Under no circumstances should you part with more money unless you are absolutely convinced.' For Heidemann, the news that his investment had been wasted could not have come at a worse moment.

Despite the 60,000 marks he had been paid by Nannen in 1976, Heidemann's financial position had steadily worsened. To ease the problem temporarily, on 9 May 1977, under a scheme open to Gruner and Jahr employees, he had taken out a two-year company loan of 10,000 marks. Exactly a year later, on 9 May 1978, he had borrowed a further 30,000 marks. Adding together this new loan, the balance still outstanding on the old one, and the money he had been paid for *Bord Gespräche*, Heidemann at this point owed his employers 94,960 marks: considerably more than a year's salary.

In 1979, unable to extend his borrowing any further, Heidemann resorted to a new tactic to raise money. On 23 May, despite his failure to write the promised *Bord Gespräche*, he signed another agreement with Gruner and Jahr. In return for a further 30,000 marks he now undertook to deliver *three* books: a study of Mussolini, to be written in collaboration with Erich Kuby; a volume of autobiography, with the working title *Gerd Heidemann: My African Wars;* and a book about Nazi escape routes, *SS Export*.

The problem, as he confided to General Mohnke, was the cost of *Carin II*. He earned 9000 marks per month; the yacht alone took up 6000. In desperation, in June 1978, he finally decided he would have to sell her. He advertised her in the catalogue of the Munich auctioneers,

Hermann, specialists in the sale of military memorabilia. His asking price was 1.1 million marks. The boat remained unsold. The consequences of this failure were to lead Heidemann directly to the Hitler diaries.

Mohnke suggested Heidemann try getting in touch with an acquaintance of his who might be able to help sell the yacht: a former junior member of the SS living in the town of Augsburg near Munich. His name was Jakob Tiefenthaeler.

Tiefenthaeler was fifty-three years old. He worked at the local US airbase where he was in charge of audio-visual instruction. He had an extensive network of old Nazi contacts, Mohnke, Wolff and Hans Baur among them. He was also deeply involved in the secretive world of Nazi memorabilia collectors, specializing himself in the acquisition of photographs from the Third Reich. At the beginning of 1979 Heidemann rang him. 'He said he'd got my name and telephone number from General Mohnke,' remembered Tiefenthaeler.

> I'd known Mohnke for a long time. Heidemann said in the telephone conversation that Mohnke had told him that I might be able to find buyers for his yacht. I asked Heidemann to send me technical details and pictures of the ship and I said that I'd try to find somebody.

Heidemann complained sorrowfully to Tiefenthaeler that he couldn't bear the thought of being parted from the yacht, that he'd turned it into a 'perfect museum' full of Goering treasures, but that the cost of berthing and insurance were such that he could no longer afford the luxury of keeping it.

Tiefenthaeler advertised the yacht in the United States for a price of 1.2 million marks. When this proved unsuccessful, he made contact with a millionaire Australian who ran a war museum in Sydney. Despite the fact that Heidemann twice dropped the price – first to 800,000 marks, then to 750,000 – the Australian pulled out. An Arab oil sheik from Abu Dhabi expressed an interest, but Heidemann was not keen: he told Tiefenthaeler he was worried that the yacht would be damaged in the hot sun. The Ugandan dictator Idi Amin sent a German mercenary, Rolf Steiner, to inspect the ship, but again the deal fell through. Amin would have loved to have cruised around Lake Victoria in Hermann Goering's yacht, but the problems of transporting it to that landlocked country were felt to be insuperable.

While Tiefenthaeler was busy pursuing these potential foreign purchasers, he gave Heidemann the name of a wealthy South German collector of Nazi memorabilia who might be interested in buying some of the smaller Goering pieces. Accordingly, some time in 1979 – it is difficult to be sure of the precise date – Heidemann turned up in Stuttgart. Seven miles east of the city, in the quiet suburb of Waiblingen, he found a small engineering factory belonging to Fritz Stiefel; immediately next door to it was Stiefel's house. He rang the bell and a thickset, taciturn man appeared.

According to Stiefel, Heidemann handed him a visiting card and introduced himself as a reporter from *Stern*. 'He said that the reason for his visit was that he wanted to ask me if I was interested in buying the table silver from his yacht, the *Carin II*.' Stiefel invited him in. Like some medieval pardoner peddling holy relics, Heidemann then laid out his wares. 'There was a small silver sugar bowl, a silver water goblet and a gold coloured match-holder,' recalled Stiefel. 'The Goering family crest was engraved on all the objects.' This trinketry appealed to Stiefel and he promptly bought it. 'I can't say exactly how much I paid for these objects,' he claimed subsequently, with an unconvincing show of vagueness. 'It was certainly over 1000 marks.' Heidemann tried to tempt his customer into buying a couple of larger items. Stiefel was interested in the reporter's expensive set of Goering table silver, but decided against taking it after consulting his wife. Nor did he want Goering's ceremonial uniform which Heidemann also produced for his inspection.

Returning to Hamburg, impressed by Stiefel's interest and by his obvious wealth, Heidemann telephoned Tiefenthaeler and suggested a new scheme: in return for an investment of 250,000 marks they should offer to make Stiefel a partner in the yacht. Tiefenthaeler promised to speak to Stiefel and shortly afterwards, towards the end of 1979, he rang Heidemann back. He was in a state of some excitement, having just been shown round Stiefel's collection of Nazi mementoes; among them, he told the reporter, was a Hitler diary.

7

On 6 January 1980, a few days after David Irving had passed on Martin Gilbert's judgement that the Churchill–Mussolini correspondence was faked, Heidemann returned to Waiblingen to see Fritz Stiefel.

Heidemann opened the conversation by outlining his proposal that Stiefel should become part-owner of *Carin II*. In his quiet, urgent voice he conjured up a glowing vision of the future: the yacht, fully restored to her former splendour, would be permanently moored off the coast of 'an island in the Atlantic' (Heidemann's suggestion was Jersey); it would be 'a floating museum' full of Nazi memorabilia, dedicated to the memory of Hermann Goering. Stiefel was unimpressed. 'I turned him down flat,' he said.

Disappointed in one fantasy, Heidemann grasped at another. Was there, he asked Stiefel, any truth in the rumour that he had a Hitler diary? The businessman, according to Heidemann, was 'startled' but after some hesitation agreed to show it to him.

Stiefel led Heidemann to an armoured steel door upon which was a large sign: 'BEWARE. HIGH VOLTAGE. DANGER TO LIFE.' Stiefel unlocked it, swung it open, and the two men stepped over the threshold.

Heidemann was later to tell colleagues of his astonishment at what he saw. The room was large and windowless. On display, in beautifully lit cabinets, was a staggering assortment of souvenirs from the Third Reich. There were swastika flags, Nazi uniforms, photographs, paintings, drawings, books. In one corner was an exhibition of porcelain made by concentration camp inmates; in another, a collection of military decorations, including a *Pour le Mérite*. It had to rank as one of the largest private collections of its kind in Germany.

Stiefel handed Heidemann a slim, A4-sized book, with hard black covers and gothic initials in the bottom right-hand corner which Heidemann took to be 'AH'. Stiefel allowed him to hold it briefly. He flicked through it. It covered the period from January to June 1935. There were a hundred or more lined pages; some were half full, some blank; some written in pencil, others in ink. Many of the pages bore Hitler's signature. The writing itself was virtually indecipherable. After a few moments, Stiefel took it back and locked it up.

Heidemann began asking questions. Where did the book come from? Stiefel said it was salvaged by local peasants from a plane crash at the end of the war. Who gave it to him? A man in Stuttgart, replied Stiefel, who had relatives in senior positions in East Germany – no, he wouldn't reveal his name. Were there more diaries? Stiefel said he understood there might be another twenty-six, each of them, like the one in his possession, covering a six-month period. That was all he could say.

Heidemann returned to Hamburg in a state of great excitement. In the *Stern* offices he described how he had actually *held in his hands* Hitler's secret diary. He had managed to memorize a few sentences about Eva Braun and her two pet dogs which he recited endlessly.

Any journalist claiming to have stumbled upon such a scoop would have expected to face a certain amount of scepticism. Heidemann was greeted by an almost universal incredulity, bordering on derision. This was, after all, the man who had had two SS generals officiating at his wedding, who had spent his honeymoon looking for war criminals, who had claimed to have a recent photograph of Martin Bormann and who had thought he could prove the existence of secret dealing between Churchill and Mussolini. When Heidemann broke the news of the Hitler diary to Henri Nannen in the *Stern* canteen, the response was frankly insulting. According to Nannen: 'My word-for-word answer was: "Spare me all that Nazi shit. I don't want to hear about it and I don't want to read about it."' Heidemann fared no better with Peter Koch, the magazine's aggressive deputy editor, who treated him as if he were mentally deranged. 'Keep away from me,' he shouted, 'with your damned Nazi tic.' He warned Heidemann to stay off subjects connected with the Third Reich and added, ominously, that 'he'd better produce something soon'. 'The trouble with *Stern*,' complained Heidemann bitterly, 'is they don't want to hear about history any more.'

Only one man seemed to take Heidemann seriously. He was Thomas Walde, an earnest and sober character in his late thirties whose chief distinguishing feature was a large brown moustache. Walde had joined *Stern* in 1971 as an editorial assistant and had risen to become news editor. When, at the beginning of 1980, *Stern* had established a new department specifically to deal with historical stories, Walde had been put in charge of it. He had been in his office little more than a week when Heidemann turned up asking if he could come and work for him. Leo Pesch, Walde's young assistant, recalled how Heidemann told them 'he had seen a Hitler diary in the possession of a South German collector'. He would not stop talking about it. One evening in April, he threw a party for the history department on board *Carin II*. 'The idea,' said Walde, 'was to meet outside the context of the normal office routine. We wanted to get to know the boat. And we wanted to discuss future projects.' Among those 'future projects' was the Hitler diary.

Walde was interested in Heidemann's tale. The problem was that almost nobody else was. 'Heidemann and Koch didn't get on,' he recalled, 'and Koch opposed Heidemann's request to research Nazi topics.' Walde therefore decided to embark on what was to prove a disastrous strategy. Without telling Koch and the other editors he went behind their backs and commissioned Heidemann to search for the Hitler diaries. 'I didn't believe in their existence,' he claimed later. 'I just hoped Heidemann would do enough research to kill the subject once and for all.'

The most obvious course was to try to discover the identity of the man who had supplied the diary to Stiefel; once he had his name, Heidemann reasoned, he could approach him directly. Stiefel, however, flatly refused to cooperate. Therefore, in the summer of 1980, Heidemann once again turned to the man from whom he had first learned of the diary's existence, Jakob Tiefenthaeler. Tiefenthaeler, who had by now given up his attempts to sell *Carin II*, told Heidemann that he understood the supplier was an antique dealer in Stuttgart named Fischer. Armed with this information, Heidemann and Walde waited one night until everyone had gone home and then began combing through every Fischer in the Stuttgart telephone directory: a task – given the commonness of the name

Fischer in Germany – not unlike searching an English phone book for a particular Smith. When this yielded nothing, Walde asked *Stern*'s correspondent in Stuttgart to make discreet inquiries around the city about this mysterious dealer; again, there was no trace.

With this line of inquiry temporarily at an end, Heidemann adopted a fresh tactic. He knew from Stiefel that the diary supposedly came from a plane crash. From O'Donnell's book, *Die Katacombe*, and Baur's, *Hitler's Pilot*, he knew of the mysterious documents shipped out of the bunker whose loss had so distressed Hitler. He was convinced that this must be where Stiefel's diary originated. If he could substantiate the story of the plane crash by pinpointing its location it would be a strong argument in favour of the diary's authenticity. On Monday, 13 October 1980, he rang the Wehrmacht information bureau, the *Wehrmachtsauskunftstelle*, in Berlin to inquire if they had any information about the pilot of the missing plane, Major Friedrich Gundlfinger. He was not hopeful. Given the chaos in Germany in those closing days of the war it was asking a great deal to discover the fate of a single aircraft after an interval of thirty-five years. Heidemann was therefore surprised when, after a pause, a voice at the other end of the line replied that the bureau did indeed have records relating to Major Gundlfinger: he had died in a plane crash on 21 April, close to the little village of Boernersdorf near Dresden in East Germany on 21 April 1945; he was buried close to the crash site; his death certificate in the local register was 16/45.

From this moment, Heidemann and Walde were hooked and the tempo of their search quickened. Two days after Heidemann's discovery of the location of the crash site, on Wednesday 15 October, Walde travelled to East Berlin. Through a contact in the East German security service he arranged a visit to the Dresden area to be undertaken in one month's time. The cover story was that Heidemann was a relative of one of the victims of the plane crash. On Monday 27 October, Heidemann went to see Hans Baur in Herrsching, who once again confirmed the details of Gundlfinger's last flight.

Heidemann's unexpected success left Thomas Walde with a problem and in the last week of October, while Heidemann was talking with Hans Baur, he took the opportunity of a vacation to think things over.

For the past three years he and a close friend, Wilfried Sorge, had left their wives and families and gone on an annual walking holiday together. The two men, almost the same age (Sorge was three years younger than Walde), had known one another for the best part of twenty years. They had both attended the same school in the small town of Uelzen, not far from Hamburg. Now they both worked for the same company: Walde as a *Stern* journalist, Sorge as a junior executive with *Stern*'s owners, Gruner and Jahr. They kept few secrets from one another.

Accordingly, when they were safely alone in the middle of a Bavarian forest, Walde told Sorge of his involvement with the Hitler diaries and of the difficulties he was now in. The trouble, said Walde, was that Peter Koch, who was likely to take over from Henri Nannen in the New Year as editor-in-chief, had expressly ordered Heidemann 'not to pursue any further researches into the Nazis'; Walde had disobeyed him. Meanwhile, Heidemann's tale about Hitler's diaries, far from being 'killed' by further investigation, was beginning to look as if it might be true. To compound his problems, Walde was about to undertake what he described as a 'risky journey' to East Germany, unable to tell his superiors about it because he had been deceiving them for the past six months. 'Herr Sorge advised me to take the chance,' recalled Walde.

Agreeing to keep the conversation confidential, they continued their walk.

But the sudden spectre of Hitler had clearly infected the holiday mood. Nursing their secret, the two men crossed over the border into Austria. They inspected Hitler's birthplace in Braunau, and the town of Leonding, near Linz, where the Führer had spent part of his youth, before returning to Hamburg on 31 October.

On 15 November 1980, Heidemann and Walde drove through one of the checkpoints from West to East Berlin, picked up Walde's contact who had arranged the trip, and travelled 120 miles south to Dresden. Another hour's drive brought them to a tiny cluster of farmhouses and barns, nestling amid hilly fields and gentle woods three miles from the Czech border, in a region known as 'Saxon Switzerland'. With its tiny kindergarten and scattered population of 550, it was difficult to imagine a sleepier village than Boernersdorf.

The *Stern* men parked their car on the side of the main road outside Boernersdorf's small church. Behind it, in the cemetery overlooking the village, in the south-eastern corner, half hidden amongst the weeds and the long grass, they found eight weather-beaten wooden crosses. Attached to each one was a small white tile giving the name of the person buried there, the date of their birth and the day of their death: 21.4.45. They found Gundlfinger's grave and Wilhelm Arndt's; two graves were simply marked 'unknown man' and 'unknown woman'. This physical evidence of the plane crash thirty-five years earlier made a profound impression on the two men. 'The discovery of the graves,' said Walde, 'was like another stone in the mosaic.'

Anxious to avoid drawing attention to themselves, Heidemann and Walde did not stay for long. They made notes of the names on the crosses and took some photographs. Half an hour later they returned to their car and drove back to Berlin.

Heidemann and Walde now sensed they were close to a breakthrough. On their return from East Germany, Walde informed Wilfried Sorge of the success of their visit.

The story as they had pieced it together seemed simple and credible. Papers of great value to Hitler undoubtedly had been loaded on to a plane in Berlin; that plane undoubtedly had crashed in East Germany; part of its cargo, a diary, had surfaced in the West. The remaining task was to find the link between the wrecked aircraft and Fritz Stiefel – and to find him before anyone else did.

A few days after their arrival back in Hamburg, Heidemann and Walde renewed their contact with Jakob Tiefenthaeler. They asked him to pass on to the mysterious 'antiques dealer' an offer generous enough to tempt him out of his seclusion. They were prepared, they told Tiefenthaeler, to guarantee a payment of 2 million marks in return for the complete set of Hitler's diaries; this sum could be paid, according to his preference, in either cash or gold. If necessary, they would be prepared to accept photocopies of the diaries rather than the originals. The whole matter would be dealt with in the strictest confidence:

even if the West German government tried to force *Stern* to disclose the identity of the supplier, they would stand by the traditional prerogative of a newspaper to protect the anonymity of its informants. It was a remarkable offer, all the more so considering it was made without the knowledge of the magazine's editors. It showed the extent to which Heidemann and Walde had already convinced themselves that the diary held by Stiefel must be genuine.

While they waited for Tiefenthaeler to bring them the supplier's response, Heidemann, using the notes he had made from the graves in Boernersdorf, set about tracing the victims' relatives. On 1 December, in the Ruhr steel town of Sollingen, he found Frau Leni Fiebes, the widow of Max Fiebes, one of Hitler's bodyguards who had been among the passengers. She had been notified of her husband's death in 1948. She showed Heidemann the official report which had been forwarded to her, recording the discovery of:

> a male corpse with the remains of a grey-green uniform with two stars on the collar, a wallet containing a number of passport photographs, and the name Max Fiebes, Oberscharführer of the SS, born 27 March 1910 in Sollingen. No personal property could be found as it had been completely burnt.

This was of interest to Heidemann only in so far as it showed that oddments of paper could have survived the crash. But Frau Fiebes was at least able to give him the name of the plane's rear gunner, Franz Westermeier, and on 10 December, the indefatigable reporter tracked down his family in Haag in Upper Bavaria. Westermeier, he learned to his surprise, had actually survived the crash, thrown clear of the burning wreck on impact, together with an SS guard, Gerhard Becker. Becker had died of his injuries two days later, but Westermeier had lived on into old age, dying in April 1980 of a kidney tumour: Heidemann had arrived just eight months too late.

Another trail seemed to have gone cold, leaving them no further forward. All Heidemann and Walde could do now was hope that the offer being relayed by Tiefenthaeler would flush out their prey.

8

The New Year arrived, cold and bleak, with a symbolic reminder of Germany's Nazi past and the conflicting emotions it aroused.

On 6 January 1981, a crowd of about 5000 German naval veterans and right wingers gathered in the snow at Aumuehle near Hamburg for the funeral of Grand Admiral Karl Doenitz, Hitler's successor as leader of the Third Reich. Doenitz, who had died on Christmas Eve at the age of 89, had been a devoted Nazi and the West German government announced that it would be boycotting the ceremony. 'But in buses, cars and trains,' reported *The Times*, 'mourners came to his funeral, many of them old men with an upright military bearing, Iron Crosses glinting on their breasts and evident nostalgia for what Doenitz stood for.' Rudolf Hess sent a wreath from his cell in Spandau. Serving naval officers – some in uniform, despite an official ban – formed an honour guard around the grave. As the coffin, draped in the red, black and gold flag of the Federal Republic and bearing Doenitz's service dagger, was lowered into the frozen ground, the mourners broke into the militaristic first verse of *'Deutschland über Alles'*. At a rally afterwards, speakers from the extreme right were applauded as they denounced the craven behaviour of the republic's politicians. It was an ugly start to the year and the ensuing political row lasted several weeks.

SS General Wilhelm Mohnke, who lived close to Aumuehle, marked Doenitz's passing by arranging a small reception at his house on the day of the funeral. Otto Guensche and Richard Schulze-Kossens, two of Hitler's SS adjutants, attended; so too did Gerd Heidemann. They all met at the graveside and then went back to Mohnke's for his little party. 'It was on this occasion,' remembered Mohnke, 'that Herr Heidemann

71

told us for the first time that there were supposed to be Hitler diaries.'
Heidemann described the story of the plane crash and revealed that he
had discovered its location in Boernersdorf. When he insisted that a set
of Hitler's diaries had survived, the three old SS men were sceptical.
'That was thought by the people there to be impossible,' declared
Mohnke. Schulze-Kossens, who had helped found Hitler's SS honour
bodyguard in 1938 and who had often been in the Führer's company,
doubted if Hitler had had the time to write a diary. Heidemann was
undeterred. Nothing could now shake his conviction that somewhere
out there were Hitler's diaries.

Nine days later, his confidence appeared to be vindicated. On Thursday 15 January, after an interval of more than seven weeks, Jakob Tiefenthaeler at last rang back. Herr Fischer, he reported, *was* interested in
Heidemann and Walde's offer and had authorized him to pass on his
telephone number. It was 07152 41981. The reporter noted it down. He
could hardly contain his impatience. 'I remember that Herr Heidemann
was in a real hurry to end the conversation,' recalled Tiefenthaeler. 'He
thanked me and promised to keep in touch.'

Heidemann turned in triumph to Walde. 'I have the number.'

A man's voice, gruff and heavily accented, answered the number which
Heidemann dialled. 'I have been trying to reach you for more than a
year,' Heidemann told him. He talked about his ownership of *Carin
II*, his friendship with the old Nazis and his collection of Third Reich
memorabilia, before finally coming to the point. 'We are very interested in the diaries.'

Fischer said that he was a dealer in militaria. He was originally
from East Germany. His brother was still there – a general in the
East German army. The general had been in touch with peasants in
the area where Hitler's transport plane had crashed at the end of the
war. In return for money and consumer goods he had acquired from
them a hoard of material which had been salvaged from the burning aircraft and hidden locally for more than thirty years. It was not
simply a matter of diaries, said Fischer. There were other Hitler writings involved, including a handwritten third volume of *Mein Kampf*
and an opera.

An opera? Heidemann was taken aback.

Yes, said Fischer, an opera entitled *Wieland the Blacksmith* which Hitler had written in his youth in collaboration with his friend August Kubizek. There were also letters and papers belonging to Hitler and original Hitler paintings. Heidemann asked about the material's whereabouts. Some of it was in the West, said Fischer, but most of it was still in the East. He had already had offers for it from the United States.

Heidemann repeated the proposition he had made to Tiefenthaeler: 2 million marks for the diaries and a guarantee of absolute secrecy. Fischer sounded doubtful. His brother was prepared to deal only with discreet private collectors. He would never agree to the sale of the material to a publishing company: if his involvement ever became known, his career, possibly even his life, would be endangered. Again, Heidemann promised complete confidentiality. Fischer hesitated. He could, he supposed, keep *Stern*'s name out of it and pass Heidemann off to his brother as a wealthy Swiss collector. Certainly, he was adamant that if they were to do business, no one else could be brought into the arrangement. He would deal only with Heidemann. This suited the reporter perfectly and by the time the conversation ended, half an hour later, the foundations of a deal had been laid.

Heidemann and Walde now needed money and the following week was devoted to putting together a suitably tempting prospectus to obtain it. Heidemann assembled the information and photocopied the relevant extracts from *Die Katacombe* and *Hitler's Pilot* but as usual he passed his material on to someone else to write up – on this occasion, Walde. The two men gave the project the cover name 'The Green Vault', after '*Grünes Gewölbe*', the treasure chamber in Dresden Castle which housed a famous military museum. On Sunday, 24 January the document was completed. After outlining the story of the trunks full of documents, the plane crash and Hitler's reaction to it, the prospectus went on:

> Farmers found the crates containing the documents. One man from
> southern Germany, who was a visitor in East Germany, managed to
> rescue the treasure from the farmers and safeguard it. Many years

later, it was smuggled into the West. Part of the archive is still in East Germany. For around 2 million marks I could obtain 27 handwritten volumes of Hitler's diaries, the original manuscript of *Mein Kampf* – so far unpublished – and an opera by the young Hitler and his friend August Kubizek, entitled *Wieland der Schmied*. There are also many other unpublished papers.

The conditions are that the names of the people who brought the material out of East Germany should not be revealed and the money must be handed over to the supplier by me, personally, abroad. Part of the money has to be paid into East Germany.

I have actually visited the place in question [Boernersdorf]. Dr Thomas Walde came with me. We were there last year. There can be no doubt about the authenticity of the material. I know personally almost all those who survived from Hitler's bunker and I have checked the story with them. If our company thinks that the risk is too great, I suggest that I should seek out a publishing company in the United States which could put up the money and ensure that we get the German publication rights.

The document was signed by Gerd Heidemann. It was put into a folder together with the extracts from the books of O'Donnell and Baur, and the photographs which Heidemann had taken in Boernersdorf.

Under normal circumstances, the next step would have been for Walde and Heidemann to have taken their story to *Stern*'s editors. But the deception which the pair had been practising for more than six months had boxed them in. Not only would they have been accused of lying, they had no guarantee that their story would have been accepted. Koch's attitude towards Heidemann's Nazi fixation had not changed. Only a few days earlier, according to the reporter, Koch had called him in and instructed him to research a series about the arms race. Heidemann had tried to avoid the assignment and had broached the subject of the Hitler diaries but Koch had brushed him aside angrily: 'You! Always with your SS topics!' And Walde had another fear: *Stern* was short of sensational stories at the moment. The magazine's aggrieved editors, he claimed later, might have 'wasted the tale of the diaries as a quick scoop'. It is also likely, although naturally neither man has ever admitted it, that they realized the discovery of the diaries could make them a great deal of money. Why should they simply give it away to their ungrateful editors?

Walde had already initiated Wilfried Sorge into the secret. At about noon on Tuesday 27 January, the two journalists visited him in his office to show him their 'Green Vault' dossier. They told him that they needed 200,000 marks as a deposit to secure the first volumes. Sorge promised to see what he could do.

Four hours later Heidemann and Walde were summoned up to the offices of Gruner and Jahr on the ninth floor of the *Stern* building. Sorge had shown the folder to his immediate superior, Dr Jan Hensmann, the company's deputy managing director. Hensmann was enthusiastic and at once telephoned the firm's managing director, Manfred Fischer, to ask if he could spare a few minutes. 'Heidemann has found something,' said Hensmann. 'We need to talk about it.' Full of curiosity, Fischer made his way to Hensmann's office.

Five men took their places in the room for the first of what would eventually prove to be dozens of conferences on the diaries, extending over a period of more than two years. Heidemann and Walde were the journalists present; Hensmann was the financial expert; Sorge, the salesman; Manfred Fischer, the dynamic executive whose love of instant decision making was to start the whole calamity.

The dossier was handed to Fischer. He read it, fascinated, and began asking questions. 'Heidemann,' he recalled, 'explained that many of the documents were in the hands of a highly placed officer in the East German army. The books had to be smuggled into the West by secret and illegal means. No names could be revealed in order not to jeopardize the informants.' Fischer asked what Henri Nannen thought of it all. Heidemann described Nannen's derogatory remarks in the *Stern* canteen; he talked of his 'difficulties' with Peter Koch; neither of them knew anything about it, nor should they be told. Walde pitched in to support Heidemann. Fischer was impressed by his manner of calm assurance; Walde, he said later, added a 'seal of authority' to the story.

Things might have gone very differently for *Stern* if at this point Fischer had insisted that the magazine's editors be let in on the secret. But Fischer was a supremely self-assured character. He had reason to be. At forty-seven he was the favourite protégé of the mighty Reinhard

Mohn. Mohn controlled 88·9 per cent of Bertelsmann AG, the West German printing and publishing conglomerate with an annual turnover of almost $2 billion. Bertelsmann in its turn owned 74·9 per cent of Gruner and Jahr. Fischer was expected to take over the running of the entire Bertelsmann empire in the next few months. If Heidemann and Walde wanted to keep the discovery of the diaries secret from their editors for a while, he was not the kind of man to shirk responsibility for that decision. He was flattered that two such experienced journalists should turn to him. Personally, he did not blame them for being reluctant to trust Koch – Fischer did not like the *Stern* editor either: he was too abrasive and much too left wing for his liking. Fischer was excited at the prospect of obtaining Hitler's diaries. It would do him no harm to arrive at Bertelsmann with a reputation as the man who had engineered the biggest publishing coup of the decade. He postponed his next appointment and asked Walde and Heidemann how much they needed.

It was eventually agreed that Heidemann would offer, on Gruner and Jahr's behalf, 85,000 marks for each of the twenty-seven volumes. The company would also be willing to pay up to 200,000 marks for the third volume of *Mein Kampf* and 500,000 marks for the remainder of the archive, including the pictures. Heidemann said that he needed 200,000 marks as a deposit. Ideally, he would like to fly down to Stuttgart that night. Fine, replied Fischer, he should have the money at once. He summoned the company's financial secretary, Peter Kuehsel.

Kuehsel, an accountant in his forties, had been with the firm for only three weeks. He wandered into the office and was suddenly ordered by Fischer to produce 200,000 marks in cash – immediately. It was after 6.30 p.m. and Kuehsel had been on the point of going home. He protested that all the banks were closed. 'Get the money,' said Fischer, and with a parting injunction to Heidemann to keep him fully informed, he departed for a reception being held by one of Gruner and Jahr's consumer magazines.

'I didn't know what the money was for,' Kuehsel said afterwards. 'It wasn't necessary for me to know. According to the company's internal rules, Dr Fischer could authorize payment.' The only bank he could think of which might still be open was the Deutsche Bank at Hamburg airport; he rang and checked; they were. Heidemann, Sorge, Kuehsel and a representative of the company's legal department piled into a car and drove off into the night.

At the bank, a bemused cashier handed over 200,000 marks in 100-, 500- and 1000-mark notes. 'Herr Heidemann gave me a receipt,' said Kuehsel, 'and put the money into his briefcase.' Heidemann had booked himself on to the final flight out of Hamburg for Stuttgart. According to Kuehsel: 'We took Herr Heidemann to the departure hall. I told him he was carrying a lot of money and he had to be careful.' In addition to the cash, Heidemann had also taken the precaution of packing what he hoped would be his trump card in persuading Fischer to hand over the diaries – the pride of his collection, the full dress uniform of Hermann Goering.

Heidemann was now playing the part he relished most. Settled into his seat on flight LH949, a suitcase containing 200,000 marks at his side, he took off for Stuttgart on a secret mission to buy Adolf Hitler's diaries.

At Stuttgart airport, Heidemann hired a car and drove into the city to the International Hotel. He rang Gina to let her know he would not be coming home that evening and went to bed.

The following morning, using the address given to him by Tiefenthaeler, Heidemann drove to Fischer's shop at number 20 Aspergstrasse. The building was four storeys high, a solid, red brick affair, part of a terrace on a steep hill. Fischer's shop had a pair of windows at the front, heavily shuttered. Heidemann rang the bell. There was no reply; the place was deserted. He tried to peer through the windows at the back, but they too had heavy metal bars and lace curtains.

Heidemann waited in his car in the bitter January cold all morning with only the money and Goering's uniform for company. In the afternoon he decided to try to find Fischer's home. From the area code prefixing Fischer's telephone number, he worked out that his house must be in the Leonberg area, about ten miles west of the centre of Stuttgart. Heidemann drove through the darkening countryside, through neat fields and brightly lit villages, until, at about 7 p.m., he reached the tiny hamlet of Ditzingen. He drove past a row of small houses, parked by a phone box and rang Fischer's number. 'It's Heidemann,' he said, when Fischer answered, 'from *Stern*.' Fischer asked him what the weather was like in Hamburg. 'I'm not in Hamburg,' replied Heidemann. 'I'm five minutes away from your house.' Fischer gave him his address – it was literally only across the street – and moments later, Heidemann was ringing the doorbell of one of the small houses he had just passed.

The door opened to reveal a short, round-faced man with a bald head and drooping moustache.

9

In Konrad Paul Kujau, alias Konrad Fischer, alias Peter Fischer, alias Heinz Fischer, alias Doctor Fischer, alias Doctor Kujau, alias 'The Professor', alias 'The General', known to his many friends as Conny, Gerd Heidemann had at last met his match: someone whose talent for inventing stories was equal to his own capacity for believing them.

Konrad Kujau, who began by forging luncheon vouchers and who ended up responsible for the biggest fraud in publishing history, was born on 27 June 1938 in the Saxon town of Loebau in what is now East Germany. He had three sisters and a brother; of the five children, he was the third eldest. His father, Richard Kujau, was a shoemaker. Unlike Heidemann, whose background was relatively apolitical, Conny was reared in a typically working-class, pro-Nazi household. Richard Kujau was an active supporter of the Nazis from 1933 onwards and his beliefs rubbed off on his son: seven years after the end of the war, at the age of fourteen, Conny was to be found painting an enormous swastika on his grandmother's kitchen wall.

Kujau's childhood was overshadowed by the poverty which descended on his family after his father was killed in 1944. His mother was unable to support the family and they had to be sent away to various children's homes. Conny, the brightest in the family, did well at school but was too poor to stay on beyond his sixteenth birthday. In September 1954 he became an apprentice locksmith, a position he held for less than a year. Then came a succession of temporary jobs, none of them lasting more than a few weeks, as a textile worker, a building-site labourer, a painter, and finally as a waiter in the Loebau Youth Club. In 1957 a warrant was issued for his arrest in connection with the disappearance of the Youth Club's microphone. Shortly before dawn on 7 June 1957, Kujau fled to the West.

He made his way first to the home of his uncle, Paul Bellmann, in West Berlin. But Bellmann had no room for his troublesome, nineteen-year-old nephew, and Kujau found himself in the first of a series of refugee camps. Rootless, alone, with no family to fall back on, the young Kujau was eventually resettled in Vaihingen, on the outskirts of Stuttgart. He lived in a succession of homes for single men and drifted into a world of casual labour and petty crime. His biography is written in his police record. In November 1959 he was arrested for stealing tobacco from a local cooperative and fined eighty marks. In 1960, together with an accomplice, he broke into a storeroom and stole four cases of cognac. He made so much noise he woke up two nightwatchmen who pursued and caught him. The police found he was carrying an air pistol, a small revolver and a knuckleduster. A court in Stuttgart found him guilty of serious theft and he went to prison for nine months. In August 1961, he was in trouble again, this time for stealing four crates of pears and a crate of apples whilst employed as a labourer for a fruit merchant; again, he spent a short period in prison. Six months later, working as a cook in a Stuttgart bar, he was arrested after a fight with his employer.

It was at this time that Kujau met and fell in love with a waitress at the same establishment, a homely girl named Edith Lieblang. Edith, like Conny, was plump, in her twenties, and a refugee from East Germany: she had worked as a salesgirl and was training to be a nurse when she decided to cross into the West in April 1961, a few months before the erection of the Berlin Wall. She came to seek her fortune and found Conny Kujau, upon whom, for a time, she seems to have been a steadying influence. In the summer of 1962 he rented premises in Plochingen, fifteen miles outside Stuttgart, and opened the Pelican Dance Bar. 'For the first time,' he claimed later, 'I began to make money.' He also began to rewrite his personal history.

To call Kujau a compulsive liar would be to underrate him. It would not do justice to the sheer exuberant scale of his deceptions. In 1962 he told people his surname was 'Fischer' and asked them to call him 'Peter'. He made himself two years older, by changing his date of birth to March 1936. He altered his place of birth from Loebau to Goerlitz. He painted a touching but sadly fictitious picture of his childhood: separated from his parents during the bombing of Dresden, he had, he said, been brought up in an orphanage until his mother found him with the help of the Red Cross in 1951. He had not been a waiter in the Loebau Youth Club but an 'organization manager'. He had attended the Dresden Academy of Art. He had been persecuted by the communists because his family was not working class. He had fled to the West to avoid conscription into the East German army. He had worked as a commercial artist in an advertising agency. There was no particular reason for most of these lies: Kujau simply liked telling stories.

By 1963 Kujau was once again in financial trouble. He gave up his dance bar and returned to Stuttgart to work as a waiter in a beer cellar. He soon resumed his old ways and for the first time his police record shows a conviction for forgery. He counterfeited twenty-seven marks' worth of luncheon vouchers and was sentenced to five days in prison. According to the court records, Kujau – who was tried under the name Fischer – had added some new stories to his repertoire: he now claimed to have been born in June 1935, so adding yet another year to his age; he also pretended he was married.

In the year that saw his first conviction for forgery, Kujau persuaded the long-suffering Edith Lieblang to put up the money for his latest money-making scheme: window cleaning. He now had the distinction of having two criminal records, one under the name of Fischer, the other as Kujau. As Kujau he was actually supposed to be in jail, serving time under an old suspended sentence. The company therefore had to be registered in Edith's name as the Lieblang Cleaning Company, with the slogan, 'Guaranteed Clean as a Housewife'. Although the firm eventually picked up contracts from a large Stuttgart department store, a chain of fast-food restaurants and South German Television, Kujau and Lieblang initially did not make much money from the business. For seven years they could not afford to buy a flat together and continued to live apart, Edith working part time as a textile worker and as a waitress in a coffee shop.

In March 1968 the police carried out a routine check at the Pension Eisele, Kujau's lodgings in Alfdorferstrasse. Kujau was registered as a cook and waiter named Peter Fischer from Goerlitz. He told the police that he was a resident of Berlin and gave them his uncle's address. Unfortunately he was carrying papers which gave a different name (Konrad Fischer), a different address (Stuttgart) and a different date of birth. He was arrested. At the police station he gave a third version of events. His name, he said, was Peter Konrad Fischer, of no fixed address. He had given a false name because he was in fact a deserter from the East German army: he had escaped to the West in 1963 after training as a lieutenant in chemical warfare at the Rosa Luxemburg officer academy. A few hours later, he changed his story again: now he had come to West Germany immediately after leaving school in order to evade military service. He confused his interrogators in Stuttgart as he was subsequently to confuse journalists and the Hamburg police in 1983, by appearing to give precise details which only hours of investigation would later establish to be false – in this case that he had entered West Germany using a friend's passport made out in the name of Harald Fuchs. Finally, his fingerprints proved that he was none of the people he said he was: he was the same old Konrad Kujau, conman and petty thief, who was wanted for evading a suspended jail sentence. Still protesting his innocence, he was taken away to Stuttgart's Stanheim Prison.

In the late 1960s, following Kujau's release from Stanheim Prison, the Lieblang Cleaning Company began to flourish. By 1971 it had half a dozen employees and was making an annual profit of 124,000 marks. Kujau and Edith bought a flat together in Schmieden, near Stuttgart, and Edith became Conny's common-law wife. In 1970, the couple returned to East Germany for a visit to Loebau. Kujau now had a new idea for making money, one which was far more in tune with his private interests than cleaning people's windows. Since childhood he had been obsessed with militaria – guns, medals, uniforms – especially from the Nazi era. There was a flourishing demand for such objects in the West, and in the East, in the attics and junk shops of communist Germany, there was a ready supply. They were also cheap: on the black market, the western deutschmark was worth five of its eastern counterpart. Through his relatives in Loebau, Kujau let it be known that he was interested in buying military memorabilia for hard cash. Carefully worded advertisements were placed by his family on his behalf in East German newspapers: 'Wanted, for purposes of research – old toys, helmets, jugs, pipes, dolls, etc.' Kujau claimed to have been 'swamped' with relics as a result. It was an illegal trade. The East German government had introduced legislation to protect the state's 'cultural heritage', forbidding the unlicensed export of objects made before 1945. Kujau and Lieblang had to smuggle their merchandise over the frontier. Normally, the border guards did not bother to search them. It was not until 1979 that Kujau was stopped trying to carry out a sabre; Lieblang was also caught on one run and had her consignment confiscated.

Kujau at this time cut a curious figure, simultaneously comic and sinister. He was only in his thirties but his thinning hair, bulging waistline and old-fashioned clothes made him look much older. He loved weapons of all kinds. Guns and swords brought back from East Germany decorated the walls of his house. According to his employees, he frequently wore a pistol which, after an evening's consumption of his favourite drink of vodka and orange, he would fire into the air at random. Mostly he would shoot off a few rounds in a field by the Schmieden railway station, but he had been known to take potshots at bottles in his favourite bar. On 13 February 1973 he lay in wait outside the Balzac night club in Stuttgart for a man who had allegedly been slashing the tyres of vans belonging to the cleaning company. At 4 a.m., roaring drunk, he leapt out brandishing a loaded machine-gun. The man ran off. In the darkness and confusion, Kujau blundered into a doorway where he came face to face with a prostitute. The woman screamed. The owner of the night club and a waiter heard the commotion, overpowered Kujau and summoned the police. He told them his name was Lieblang. When the police raided his flat they found a machine-gun, a double-barrelled shotgun, three air pistols, three rifles and two revolvers. He confessed to having given a false name, apologized for being drunk and was let off with a fine.

By 1974, Kujau's militaria was taking up most of the couple's home and Edith's attitude became threatening. According to Kujau she told him: 'Either that goes out of the window or we separate.' Kujau then began renting the shop in Aspergstrasse, filling its fifty square metres of floor space with his collection. It became the venue for long drinking sessions at which Kujau would entertain some of his friends: collectors with strong heads and simple minds like the local policeman, Ulli Blaschke, who is occasionally supposed to have acted as Kujau's bodyguard; the post office official, Siegmund Schaich, a collector of military drinking jugs; and Alfons Drittenthaler, a blacksmith from the nearby town of Burlafingen. 'The President of Police came several times,' boasted Kujau. 'Sometimes a prostitute would sit next to the State Prosecutor. It would go on until late at night.' Another regular visitor was Wolfgang Schulze, a resident of Miami, who was Kujau's agent in the United States, dealing on his behalf with the extensive network of American collectors.

Business was conducted both by barter and by cash. Drittenthaler, for example, gave Kujau a nineteenth-century grenadier's helmet in exchange for 3000 marks and a reservist's beer mug; on another occasion, in a straight swap, he obtained a set of mugs from Kujau in return for three uniforms. Drittenthaler described Kujau's collection as 'very large and valuable'. It included an almost complete set of Third Reich decorations, 150 helmets, 50 uniforms, 30 flags and, according to Kujau, the largest collection of military jugs in West Germany. 'He told me that the majority of his things came from East Germany,' said Drittenthaler. 'He said that he had a brother there who was a general.' Using this flourishing business as a cover, Kujau was now able to exploit to the full what he had discovered to be his greatest and most lucrative skill: forgery.

By his own account, Kujau first discovered his latent artistic talent at the age of five when his next door neighbour in Loebau, a 'Professor Linder', taught him how to draw. From childhood, painting was his main hobby. In Stuttgart, in the early 1960s, he began to sell a few canvases. He discovered that there was an especially large market for pictures depicting battle scenes; he claims to have painted his first in 1962: 'They were simply torn out of my hands.' He developed a technique of putting his customers into the centre of famous scenes – one client was painted sitting in a staff car next to Field Marshal Rommel – and these paintings, according to him, could fetch as much as 2000 marks, 'a lot of money in those days'. It was in 1963 that Kujau applied his talent to copying out luncheon vouchers, his first known act of forgery. How he graduated from this to larger frauds is unclear. At his trial in 1984 he told a typically colourful story of how his talent was first spotted by the legendary Nazi intelligence officer and head of the West German secret service, Reinhard Gehlen. Kujau claimed that Gehlen gave him forty pages of handwriting and signatures to copy out in 1970 and thereafter hired him to do a number of freelance jobs. Gehlen is dead and the story impossible to check – which no doubt explains why Kujau told it.

What *is* clear is that in the 1970s Kujau began introducing forgeries into the genuine material he was smuggling out of East Germany. The Hamburg police later filled two rooms at their headquarters with examples of his handiwork. To an authentic First World War helmet he attached a faked note, supposedly signed by Rudolf Hess, stating that it had been worn by Hitler in 1917. To an ancient jacket, waistcoat and top hat he added an 'authentication' stating that it was the dress suit Hitler wore to the opening of the Reichstag in 1933. 'When I had completed a piece,' bragged Kujau after his arrest in 1983, 'I framed it and hung it on the wall. People went crazy about them.' He passed off a Knight's Cross, one of Nazi Germany's highest decorations, as having once belonged to Field Marshal Keitel. He could execute a passable imitation of the handwriting of Bormann, Hess, Alfred Rosenberg, Keitel, Goering, Goebbels and Himmler. The forgeries themselves were invariably crude. Kujau used modern paper. He created headed stationery simply by using Letraset. He aged documents by pouring tea over them. But he guessed, rightly, that his customers would never take them to experts to check. Public display of Nazi memorabilia was illegal and collections were generally kept, a guilty secret, behind locked doors.

At some stage, Kujau even executed an outstandingly clumsy forgery of the agreement signed by Hitler and Chamberlain at Munich. Spelling and grammar were not Kujau's strong suits, even in German; when, as in this case, he tried to forge something in English, the results were farcical:

> We regard the areement signet last night and the Anglo-German Naval Agreement as symbolic of the desire of our two peoples never to go to war with one another againe.

We are resolved that method of consultation shall be the method adopted to deal with any other questions that may concern our two countries, and we are determined to continue our efforts to remove possible sources of difference and thus to contribute to assure the peace of Europe.

When it came to Hitler, Kujau had even more opportunities for forgery: not only could he copy Hitler's handwriting, he could also forge his paintings.

In 1960, the Marquess of Bath had paid £600 for two Hitler watercolours auctioned at Sotheby's: *The Parliament and Ringstrasse, Vienna* and *A View of the Karlskirche, Vienna*. It was the first step on the way to accumulating what eventually would be the world's largest private collection of Hitler's art. By 1971 he had forty-eight paintings in his 'Hitler Room' at Longleat; by 1983 he had sixty. Lord Bath acquired the pictures for posterity and confessed to a certain 'admiration' for the Nazi leader: 'Hitler did a hell of a lot for his country,' he explained. Other collectors followed Bath's example. Billy F. Price, owner of Price Compressors of Houston, Texas, built up a private exhibition of twenty-four paintings, housed behind bullet-proof glass in his company's boardroom. The cost of the paintings escalated as the demand grew. By the mid-1970s they were fetching over £5000 (15,000 marks) apiece.

The paintings' sole attraction was that they were by Hitler; their intrinsic merit was negligible. Hitler took a layman's view of modern art: Impressionists, Expressionists, Cubists and Dadaists were 'scribblers, canvas scrawlers, mental defectives or cultural Neanderthals'; once in power, he banned their work. (When someone demonstrated to him that one of the outlawed painters, Franz Marc, was capable of producing 'traditional' pictures, Hitler was genuinely puzzled. 'He could even draw properly,' he commented, 'so why didn't he do it?') Hitler himself was a painter of such meagre talent that he rarely attempted to depict human beings; he confined himself to stilted pictures of buildings and landscapes. Even to Kujau, a painter of limited ability, their technical poverty made them easy to copy. The other advantage, for a potential forger, was the scale of the Führer's output. Whatever Hitler

lacked in artistic merit he made up for in industry. He is estimated to
have produced between 2000 and 3000 drawings, sketches, watercolours and oils.

Kujau was not far behind, turning out fakes literally by the hundred.
He added to their plausibility using his favourite trick of attaching a
forged letter or certificate confirming their authenticity. On the back
of a large painting of German infantrymen in Flanders in 1918 Kujau
wrote, in Hitler's handwriting: 'I painted this picture in memory of the
comrades who fell in the field.' Next to this he pasted a note supposedly signed by a Nazi official: 'This work was created by the Führer
and Reichschancellor Adolf Hitler in the year 1934.' Close inspection of the painting reveals Lance-Corporal Adolf Hitler standing in
the midst of the battle clutching a hand grenade. Another of Kujau's
efforts, *Nude on Green Background*, was passed off as a painting by
Hitler of his niece, Geli Raubel. 'Picture remains in flat. Adolf Hitler,'
reads a scrawled note. 'Geli sat as a model for this for over twenty
days.' Kujau earned tens of thousands of marks for such forgeries. He
did not even have to go looking for customers: furtive, wealthy, and
eager to believe, they came looking for him.

IO

Fritz Stiefel, forty-seven years old, owner of a flourishing engineering works, first noticed Kujau's shop in Aspergstrasse in 1975 as he was driving past it. The windows were full of military memorabilia. Stiefel was a collector himself. He pulled up outside and rang the bell. The shop was deserted. He came twice more but on each occasion there was nobody there. Then one day he happened to be passing when a small, fat man appeared outside cleaning the windows. 'I spoke to him,' recalled Stiefel. 'He introduced himself to me as Fischer.' He was taken inside and shown around the Aspergstrasse collection. He bought a Nazi decoration for 650 marks. Before long, seduced by Kujau's patter, he had become the shop's best customer.

Stiefel collected militaria of all types, but his specialist interest was in documents and autographed photographs. He was amazed by Herr Fischer's ability to produce these. 'I assumed that he must have really good connections. He certainly gave me that impression. He told me often of his journeys to East Germany. He said he had relatives there.' Stiefel's gullibility was matched only by his willingness to spend money. Kujau could scarcely believe his luck. 'He always got excited when he saw something new,' he said later. 'If I'd told him I'd got Hitler's underpants he'd have got equally worked up.' In six years, according to the Hamburg state prosecutor, Stiefel spent approximately 250,000 marks in Kujau's shop. He bought 160 drawings, oil paintings and water-colours supposedly by Hitler, along with eighty handwritten poems, speech notes, letters and manuscripts. Stiefel's obsession led him into fraud. He transferred 180,000 marks from his company's accounts to the Lieblang Cleaning Company, allegedly to meet 'cleaning costs' but actually to pay for Hitler memorabilia. As a result, he was eventually forced to repay over 120,000 marks to the German tax authorities.

In return for this outlay, Stiefel acquired one of the largest collections of fakes in West Germany. His 'Hitler' pictures ranged from a design for Hitler's parents' tomb, dated 1907, to a portrait of Eva Braun at the age of twenty-four. Some of the paintings were drawn from Kujau's fervid imagination (for example, a series of cartoons purportedly drawn by Hitler for his regimental newspaper in 1916); others were copies of existing works. One female nude executed in chalk signed 'Adolf Hitler' and dated 1933 was a copy of a drawing by Erhard Amadeus Dier. Another, entitled *Female Nude, Chubby, Fraulein E. Braun* was a poor imitation of Julius Engelhard's *Bathing in the Bergsee*: when Kujau persuaded Stiefel to buy it, he actually showed him a copy of the Engelhard painting and, with characteristic cheek, accused Hitler of plagiarism. Kujau also sold Stiefel a leather box, lined with silk, which he had bought at Stuttgart railway station, containing 233 handwritten pages of the 'original manuscript' of *Mein Kampf*. Kujau had simply copied it, verbatim, from the published book. On the title page he wrote, also in Hitler's hand: '*The Struggle of the Times*, or *The Struggle* or *My Struggle*. Which title impresses more? Adolf Hitler.'

Kujau subsequently claimed that he copied out the *Mein Kampf* manuscript as a means of practising Hitler's handwriting and there can be no question but that he became extraordinarily proficient at it. He slipped in and out of other people's handwriting as he did his various pseudonyms and biographies, with complete ease. It is difficult to say with precision when he first hit on the idea of writing a Hitler diary. Kujau's American agent, Wolfgang Schulze, told Gitta Sereny of the *Sunday Times* that he handled 'unbound' sheets of Hitler writing supplied by his client as early as 1976. According to Kujau it was in 1978 that he sat down and began typing out a chronology of Hitler's daily life, using an official Nazi Party yearbook for 1935. Having done that he decided to see how it would look in Hitler's handwriting.

In the cellar of his and Edith's new home in Ditzingen were some school notebooks, bought for a few marks in a shop in East Berlin. Kujau had originally intended using them to keep a catalogue of his collection. Now he took one out, dipped his pen in a pot of black ink, and started to write. When the ink ran out, he switched to a pencil. 'It was easy,' he said later. As a finishing touch, he stuck some imitation metal initials in gothic script on the cover. The initials were bought by Kujau in a department store, were made of plastic in Hong Kong, and were in fact 'FH', not 'AH' as Kujau had thought. It was, like all his forgeries, slipshod and homemade. It would not have withstood an hour's expert examination.

Two weeks later, during one of Fritz Stiefel's regular visits to Aspergstrasse, Kujau brought out the book and laid it on the table in front of him. '*That*,' he told him, 'is a Hitler diary.'

Stiefel examined it carefully. 'He was not so much fascinated by the contents,' said Kujau, 'as by the initials I'd stuck on the front of it.' He asked if he could borrow it and Kujau agreed. 'I took it home with me and read through it,' recalled Stiefel. He then locked the book away in his safe with the rest of his faked Hitler manuscripts.

At around the same time that he received the diary from Kujau, Stiefel decided that the time had come when he should seek an expert's opinion on his remarkable Hitler archive. He asked Kleenau, a firm of Munich auctioneers who handled important manuscripts, if they could recommend an authority on Hitler's art and writing. Kleenau gave him the name of August Priesack.

'Professor' Priesack, as he styled himself, had been employed by the Nazi Party between 1935 and 1939 to track down Hitler's paintings. His task was to buy up as many as possible and sort out the genuine Hitlers from the fakes which, even then, were polluting the market. For Priesack, as for so many of the 'Keepers of the Flame', those years in the sun before the war, when he was young and enjoying the patronage of the Führer, represented the best time of his life. He had piles of yellowing press cuttings and photographs from the Third Reich, his private archive, stored in his cluttered Munich apartment. He was seventy-six years old, a former secondary school teacher, listed in the Munich police records as a well-known sympathizer with the ideals of the Hitler era. He was working on a book of previously unpublished pictures of the Nazi Party rallies. He had also been hired by the

American millionaire Billy Price who was compiling a complete catalogue of Hitler's art. Stiefel invited Priesack to visit him in Stuttgart and evaluate his own collection.

For Kujau, this was a decisive moment. Hitherto he had had to fool only amateur enthusiasts. Now his work was to be judged by a supposed expert. In May 1978 he had signed an agreement with Stiefel guaranteeing that everything he had sold him to date and might sell him in the future was 'original' and 'contemporary'. Under the terms of the contract, if anything turned out to be fake, Kujau had to give Stiefel a complete refund. A great deal therefore depended upon Priesack's verdict. He need not have worried. The old man took one look at Stiefel's collection and declared it to be of 'great historical significance'. He pointed to a watercolour. 'I last held that in my hands in 1936,' he told Stiefel and Kujau. 'It was then,' said Kujau later, 'that I knew what kind of an expert *he* was. I had only finished that painting ten days before.'

Priesack was sufficiently impressed to contact one of Germany's leading authorities on Hitler: Eberhard Jaeckel, Professor of Modern History at the University of Stuttgart. Jaeckel, the author of *Hitler's Weltanschauung, A Blueprint for Power*, had been engaged for some years in the compilation of a complete collection of Hitler's writings from 1905 to 1924. Priesack had passed on to him some material from his own archive in 1974 (subsequently dismissed by Jaeckel as 'a few pieces of paper, copies, without any value'). Now he urged the historian to meet with Stiefel and his astonishingly well-connected supplier, Herr Fischer. Jaeckel, aware that important Hitler documents were in the hands of a number of private collectors, agreed. An appointment was arranged for Friday, 21 September 1979.

Priesack arrived at Stiefel's house before Kujau and Jaeckel. For the first time the industrialist opened his safe and showed him the Hitler diary. Priesack spent an hour reading through it. He was hugely impressed by the existence of such a book, although he had to confess to a certain disappointment in its contents. (Kujau had filled it almost entirely with lists of appointments and proclamations lifted out of the Nazi yearbook.) He made a few notes. 'I can only remember one page which I copied,' recalled Priesack. 'The others were really for the most part just headlines from the *Völkischer Beobachter* [the Nazi Party newspaper].' The fullest entry, the one written down by Priesack, was for 30 June 1935:

> The explosion catastrophe in Reinsdorf is all I needed. One ray of hope today was the dedication ceremony of the House of German Art in Munich.
>
> But at any rate I can relax a bit with the architects. E. [Eva Braun] now has two little puppies so time does not lie too heavily on her hands.
>
> Must have a word with E. about Goering, too. His attitude towards her just isn't correct.
>
> All quiet on the health front.

Despite the triviality of the content, Priesack had no doubts that the book was genuine. When Kujau arrived he paid him an emotional tribute. 'You are our salvation,' he told the former waiter and window cleaner. 'You must find more documents. History will thank you.'

Jaeckel was also impressed by Stiefel's collection as the industrialist laid it out before him. 'There were drawings, paintings and documents signed by Hitler,' he remembered. He was handed the diary and 'leafed through it quickly'.

> I remember a place where Eva Braun and a dog were mentioned. As far as I recall, only the right-hand pages were written in ink and signed by Hitler. . . I was told it came from East Germany and had been kept there since 1945. The question of how it was brought to the West was not answered – I was told it could be dangerous to the people who'd brought it out. It was also suggested to me that there was a senior official involved in East Germany called Fischer.

Kujau watched Jaeckel going through the book. There was a discussion about how many more diaries there might be. Kujau said that he understood from his sources in East Germany that the diaries spanned thirteen years, from 1932 to 1945. Priesack cut in: assuming that each of the missing books also covered six months, there would be twenty-seven books in total. Jaeckel urged Stiefel to try to obtain them. Kujau claimed later to have sat and listened to all this 'in amazement'.

Jaeckel's particular interest was in material up to the year 1924. Stiefel had plenty to show him, including some previously undiscovered poems by Hitler written during the First World War. These included 'It was in a thicket of the Artois Forest', an illustrated ballad, and 'An Idyll in the War', a work in four verses in which 'Hitler' described how a German soldier delivered a Frenchwoman's baby:

> As the medical orderly Gottlieb Krause heard as he came through Arras,
> The sudden dull cry of a woman from the closest house:
> I must help! was his thought, even a German in the field remains helpful,
> And a newborn baby Frenchman arrived in the world with Gottlieb
>   Krause's help.
>
> And with his typical great care he looked after the child,
> Washed it, cared for it, to show we're not barbarians
> And held the babe with pleasure in front of his comrades;
> This little worm knows nothing of Iswolski and Delcassé's intrigues!
>
> Milk was rare and needed in a hurry; in the meadow grazed a cow,
> And two soldiers from the next troop commandeered her at once,
> And milked her! It ran in spurts and in rich amounts,
> Shrapnel fell close by but didn't stop the work.
>
> Right afterwards, he gave the bottle to the child he had delivered,
> And pulled two zwieback out of his pocket for the mother
> An idyll proving once again the German's noble creed,
> If the Limeys haven't destroyed it, the house is still there.

Each verse had an accompanying illustration: the soldier tending the mother and her baby; the soldier showing the baby to a comrade; the soldier milking a cow; the soldier saying goodbye to the Frenchwoman with the child in her arms. Jaeckel saw no reason to believe it was not genuine. Attached to it and to most of the other pieces in Stiefel's collection was an 'authentication' on official Nazi Party stationery. The following year, Jaeckel reprinted 'An Idyll in the War' in his book of Hitler's early writings, along with *seventy-five* other forgeries produced by Kujau.

At the end of this productive meeting, Jaeckel gave Kujau a lift back into Stuttgart. The 'antiques dealer' had scarcely opened his mouth all afternoon. He struck the historian as 'reserved' and 'uneducated'. Jaeckel told him that if he could discover any more volumes of Hitler's diaries, he would very much like to edit them.

Kujau was by now leading a life of bewildering complexity. He was running the shop in Aspergstrasse. He was organizing the illegal export of memorabilia from East Germany. He was forging documents and paintings. He was still nominally in charge of the Lieblang Cleaning Company. He was answering to at least two different names. And as if this was not enough, he had now begun deceiving Edith by taking a full-time mistress.

Kujau's corpulent figure had long been familiar to the working girls of Stuttgart's red-light district where he was universally known as 'The General'. His favourite haunts were the Pigalle night club and the Sissy Bar. Using the money he was making from Nazi memorabilia, he entertained lavishly. The girl he was with was always well paid; the others were regularly bought bottles of champagne. In March 1975 he met Maria Modritsch, a twenty-five-year-old Austrian girl who was serving drinks in the Sissy Bar. She had left school at fifteen to work in a factory, come looking for work in West Germany and ended up as a bar girl. She was thin, quiet and of homely appearance. Kujau took a liking to her and they began what Maria primly called an 'intimate relationship'. She gave up work in the Sissy Bar and in May 1978, he set her up in an apartment in Rotenbergstrasse where she lived alone with her pet rabbit, Caesar. Kujau had a key, kept some clothes in the flat, and provided Maria with a monthly allowance of between 1000 and 2000 marks. 'Conny gave me a loan for the furniture,' said Maria. 'He had more money than I did and he spoiled me. He visited me almost every day. We would go out together. Then he would go back to his own flat. From time to time he'd stay overnight. As far as I'm aware, Edith didn't know about my existence.' Kujau told Maria he was married to Edith. 'It was not until later,' said Maria, 'that I learned he only lived with her.' She helped out in the shop occasionally and was under the impression that her lover was some sort of painter.

Three weeks after the meeting with Jaeckel and Priesack, on 15 October, Kujau and Maria went out for a drink. After some schnapps in the

Korne Inn they moved on to the Melodie Bar. Shortly before midnight, a group of immigrant workers, Yugoslavs, burst into the bar brandishing guns. While most of the clientele threw themselves to the floor, Kujau, in a fit of drunken bravado, leapt to his feet and attacked them. In the ensuing struggle he was struck on the head and had to be taken to hospital with blood streaming from a three-inch gash in his forehead. He was interviewed by the police and once again could not resist spinning them a story. He was 'Dr Heinz Fischer', Maria was his secretary, he worked for the Baden-Wuerttemberg authorities. When this was checked and found to be false, he lied again. He was 'Dr Konrad Kujau', until last year a colonel in the West German army, and soon to become a professor. The police searched a briefcase he had with him and found artists' materials, an air pistol and a photograph of himself posing in the full dress uniform of a general. Kujau said that he had bought the pistol at an auction. He confided to the policeman interviewing him that it had once belonged to Field Marshal Rommel. The policeman told his colleagues that Kujau was either mentally unstable or a military fanatic.

This curious episode was not over yet. Less than a week later, Kujau was invited to return to the police station to explain why he was going around falsely claiming to have a doctorate. Charges were laid against him for misrepresentation. Even the most blatant confidence trickster would by now have given up, but Kujau swore that he was the author of eleven books on Nazi Germany, including *Adolf Hitler the Painter, Adolf Hitler the Frontline Soldier, Adolf Hitler the Officer*, and a five-volume study, *Adolf Hitler the Politician* – all published by the Ullstein company in Munich. He declared that as a result of his work he had been invited all over the world to lecture on the Nazis; he possessed not merely one but three doctorates, awarded to him by the universities of Tokyo, Pretoria and Miami. The incredulous police asked him for proof of these honours.

The documents [stated Kujau] are at home, but my office is currently being renovated and everything is packed in cartons. These documents are also in the cartons and therefore I cannot show them to you at the moment. I shall have them photocopied and sent to you as soon as the renovation work is finished. I should mention that although I received my award from the University of Tokyo in 1977, the date on the document is 1952. This is because in Tokyo the year 1952 corresponds to our 1977.

The police waited but the documents never materialized. The following July, Kujau was fined 800 marks for the misuse of titles. He described his occupation in court for the first time as 'painter'.

On 20 October 1979, five days after the fight in the Melodie Bar, ignorant of his supplier's difficulties with the police, Fritz Stiefel invited Kujau and Edith to his house for a party. The celebration was supposed to be in honour of the birthday of Frau Senta Baur, wife of Hans Baur, but at the last moment Frau Baur was unable to attend. As a result there were only six guests: the Stiefels, Kujau and Edith, and the former SS man Jakob Tiefenthaeler and his wife.

It was a convivial evening. Stiefel had known Tiefenthaeler as a fellow collector for several years; Kujau had been introduced to Tiefenthaeler as 'Herr Fischer' by Stiefel over dinner the previous March, although on that occasion, said Tiefenthaeler, Kujau 'had kept very much in the background'. This evening was different: the drink flowed, and as the number of empty bottles steadily mounted, so did Kujau's loquacity. 'He said that he was a businessman,' recalled Tiefenthaeler.

> Then later he explained that he had an antiques shop in Stuttgart. He told me that he didn't have any employees there, that he was often away travelling, that for much of the time the place was shut. He also boasted that evening of his good contacts in East Germany. In this connection he told us that his brother was a general in the East German border service: he had a great deal of authority but that wouldn't exempt him from punishment if he was found to be involved in something illegal.

After a few more glasses, Kujau began talking about the Hitler diaries. According to Tiefenthaeler he boasted that 'he could bring to the West diaries which had been on board one of the Führer's planes' which had crashed in East Germany at the end of the war.

These diaries had been hidden in a safe place by local peasants. He said there were 27 volumes, but he could only bring them out to the West one at a time. They had to come out at intervals of between one and two months: more journeys than that would be suspicious.

Tiefenthaeler, whose own Third Reich collection was largely built around autographs and pictures, was fascinated.

This is the first occasion on which Kujau is reported to have used the plane crash to explain the provenance of the diaries. When he had given the first diary to Stiefel sixteen months earlier he had merely said that he had 'got it from East Germany' along with his other militaria. At the meeting with Jaeckel only four weeks earlier he had been equally vague. This suggests that at some point in the period 21 September to 20 October, Kujau discovered the story of the crash.

According to Stiefel, he and Kujau had visited Hans Baur at his home in Herrsching some time around September 1979. Priesack had also been there. 'It was in the evening,' said Baur, 'and my wife and I went with them to have dinner in a neighbouring village.' Baur subsequently claimed to have no recollection of discussing the loss of Gundlfinger's plane, but the coincidence of this meeting with Kujau's adoption of the story suggests otherwise. Stiefel admitted to the police that he had certainly heard an account of the crash from Baur himself. Kujau, on the other hand, alleged he had first learned of it from August Priesack, and Priesack, who knew of the crash from Baur's book, afterwards admitted that he could have been the one who first put the idea in Kujau's mind. Whichever version is the truth – and it should be remembered that in Baur's book the whole episode had been available in outline to anyone who was interested since 1955 – this was the decisive moment in the evolution of the fraud. Suddenly to produce a Hitler diary and claim it had been smuggled out of East Germany might be enough to satisfy collectors as gullible as Stiefel. To produce that diary and also to be able to point to Hitler's distress at the loss of valuable documents in a mysterious air crash – that suddenly made the story seem much more plausible.

At the end of the evening's festivities, Stiefel put his guests up for the night. The following day was a Sunday. After breakfast the industrialist unlocked the metal door to his collection and showed Tiefenthaeler the diary. A few weeks later, Tiefenthaeler told Gerd Heidemann what he had seen and at the beginning of 1980, Heidemann himself visited Stiefel, saw the diary and heard the story of the crashed Junkers 352.

What gives Kujau's fraud from this point onwards a touch of real genius is that having made the connection between the wrecked transport plane and the diaries, he left it to others to research the background. Never did the victim of a hoax work more assiduously towards his own entrapment than Gerd Heidemann. While Kujau shuttled between his two mistresses and tended his shop in Stuttgart, it was the reporter in Hamburg who worked long hours and even risked dismissal to make the story of the diaries credible. For Heidemann, each step in his attempts to prove that the diary he had seen at Stiefel's could be genuine represented an additional investment of time and effort. It is not surprising that by the end he *wanted* to believe in the existence of the diaries so desperately: by then he had put more work into them than Kujau. It took him a year, but gradually, in 1980, the two men's paths began to converge.

Stiefel still kept the 1935 diary in his safe, but his importance in the affair now lessened. He disapproved of *Stern*'s left-wing reputation and refused to help Heidemann by revealing the identity of the diary's supplier. Tiefenthaeler, who had already acted as Heidemann's agent in his attempts to sell *Carin II*, now supplanted him. His motive was almost certainly financial. He admitted that Heidemann told him it would 'not do him any harm' to help *Stern* find the diaries; in 1983 Kujau referred to him, with a laugh, as 'Mr Ten Percent'. It was in the summer of 1980 that Tiefenthaeler told Heidemann that the diary had been brought into the West by a Herr Fischer of Stuttgart. Heidemann and Walde had then spent hours trawling through the local telephone book. (The reason they never found him was that Kujau's home in Ditzingen was listed in the directory under Edith's surname, Lieblang.) A few months later, after their return from Boernersdorf in November, the *Stern* men had renewed their contact with Tiefenthaeler and asked him to transmit an offer to 'Herr Fischer' on their behalf. Tiefenthaeler did so in a letter to Kujau dated 29 November 1980:

Dear Conny,

I've got something to tell you which I don't think we should discuss on the telephone because you never know if the line is bugged or not. I assume that you'll be absolutely quiet about this matter and that you won't talk to anyone about it.

A large Hamburg publishing company has come to me with a request that I should establish contact between you and them. It's about the diaries of A.H. which you have or could obtain. I was quoted an offer of 2 million marks which would be paid [for the diaries]. In addition, these gentlemen were not so much interested in possessing the diaries as in taking photocopies. The diaries could stay, as before, in your possession. Should you indicate that you are interested in making contact, this would be done as quickly as possible. The whole thing would, of course, be handled in strict confidence and silence on both sides is a precondition. Should you prefer gold to currency, there would be an unlimited amount.

I would be very grateful if you could let me know as soon as possible what you decide – but please, not on the telephone.

Perhaps I should also mention that the wealthy company would take any risk entailed in publication as well as any legal consequences which publication might entail. The source of these volumes would never be named – in the case of a legal battle (the Federal Government versus the publishing company) the company would plead press confidentiality.

I have been officially assured of all these things and they are ready to conclude a contract with you in which all parties would be legally secure. Perhaps you would also allow me to point out, my dear Conny, that none of these gentlemen has been given your name by me. They know that a Herr Fischer is the key to these volumes, but they know neither your first name nor your address and they will not discover them from me, lest you take a negative view of this project. . .

Please don't even mention this to Fritz [Stiefel].

Kujau was already wealthier than he had ever been, thanks to his activities as a forger. But considering that 2 million marks represented almost *ten times* the amount he was to make from his best customer, Fritz Stiefel, it is scarcely surprising that he succumbed to this offer.

Even if this 'wealthy company' discovered that he was passing on fakes, he stood an excellent chance of getting away with something. His anonymity was guaranteed. If anything went wrong he could always fall back on the excuse that he was merely handling material which originated behind the Iron Curtain. Thus it was that at the beginning of 1981 he gave Tiefenthaeler permission to divulge his telephone number and his address in Aspergstrasse.

On 15 January a man calling himself Gerd Heidemann telephoned him in Ditzingen. They discussed the diaries. Kujau repeatedly stressed that he had to have a guarantee of absolute secrecy and that he would deal only with Heidemann personally. True to his past form he also embroidered the story, promising the reporter not simply diaries but a genuine Hitler opera and a third volume of *Mein Kampf*. Kujau knew that the more improbable his inventions sounded, the more likely people were to believe that he could not possibly be lying. He knew what he was doing. He knew Heidemann's type. He recognized beneath the affected calm the note of longing that signified the suspension of disbelief. It was all too easy.

Sure enough, on Wednesday 28 January, at about 7.15 in the evening, the telephone rang again. Kujau had a brief conversation, then turned to Edith. 'That was Heidemann,' he told her. 'He's on his way over.' Within five minutes he was opening the door to his latest, eager, moon-faced victim, who clutched in his hand a suitcase full of money.

PART THREE

'Swastikas sell – and they sell better and better.'

Sidney Mayer, publisher

II

This first encounter between Kujau and Heidemann lasted for more than seven hours. To begin with, Heidemann later testified, Kujau appeared reluctant to agree to a deal. He told the reporter that he had already had an offer of $2 million for the diaries from America and that the Hearst newspaper group was considering serializing them. According to Edith Lieblang, Heidemann then opened up the suitcase and displayed 'a huge amount of money'. He offered it to Kujau as a down payment for the diaries. He repeated that his company was willing to pay 2 million marks for all the volumes. As an added inducement, Heidemann also produced the Goering uniform, which appears to have excited Kujau even more than the money. 'I had to have it,' he said later. 'I had all the other uniforms – Hitler's, Himmler's, Rommel's. My one thought was: "How do I get this uniform off this man?"' Kujau, according to Lieblang, promised the reporter 'that he could provide the diaries'.

After that, the atmosphere relaxed somewhat. Heidemann, whisky in hand, boasted of his contacts with famous Nazis like Karl Wolff and Klaus Barbie. He described how he had tracked down the crash site in Boernersdorf. He then started recounting his experiences as a war correspondent. By about midnight Edith was beginning to fall asleep. She went off to bed. But Heidemann and Kujau stayed up talking until almost 3 a.m., when the reporter at last left to drive back to his hotel in Stuttgart.

After snatching a few hours' sleep, at 10 a.m., he was back with Kujau again, this time in the Aspergstrasse shop. His main concern was the diary held by Fritz Stiefel. He was worried that word of its existence would leak out to a rival newspaper. According to Edith, he was 'insistent' that they should go and retrieve it. Kujau, who was worried about souring his relations with Stiefel, managed to put him off by telling him that the industrialist was on holiday in Italy. Heidemann was anxious to conclude at least some sort of legal agreement with Kujau before he left. He suggested that he should make contact with Kujau's lawyer and arrange for him to come to Hamburg to sign an agreement with the Gruner and Jahr legal department – an offer which Kujau hastily declined. Instead, the two men parted with a tentative verbal understanding. Kujau would deliver the books, Heidemann the money. He would call the reporter when he heard from his brother in the East. As a gesture of good faith, they swapped gifts. Heidemann left his genuine Goering uniform behind and returned to Hamburg bearing a faked Hitler oil painting. The relationship had started on an appropriate note.

At 11.30 the following morning, in *Stern*'s elegant riverfront headquarters – known, irreverently, around Hamburg as 'the monkey cliff' – Heidemann went in to see Wilfried Sorge to report on the outcome of his trip to Stuttgart. The supplier of the diaries, he told Sorge, was a 'wealthy collector' of Nazi memorabilia whose brother was a general in East Germany. Some of Hitler's diaries were already in the West. Initially they had come over the border in ordinary travel luggage. Now they were being smuggled across hidden inside pianos (pianos being one of East Germany's main exports to the West). The general would at once cease supplying the diaries if he thought they were for publication in *Stern*. Heidemann was therefore posing as a Swiss collector. He repeated: it was imperative that the company maintain absolute secrecy.

In Stuttgart, meanwhile, Konrad Kujau was having to do some explaining to Fritz Stiefel, not about the Hitler diaries, but about the other pieces of so-called Hitler writing he had sold to the collector.

Eberhard Jaeckel and his co-editor, Axel Kuhn, had gone ahead and reprinted material from Stiefel's collection in their book of Hitler's writings from 1905 to 1924. The book had been published the previous autumn. To their embarrassment, Anton Hoch of the Institute of

Contemporary History in Munich had pointed out that some of Hitler's 'poetry' was obviously fake. In particular, 'Der Kamerad,' a poem supposedly written by Hitler in 1916, was actually lifted straight out of a book of verse entitled *Poems of the Old Comrades* by Herybert Menzel, published in 1936. It might have been possible to argue that Hitler himself had merely copied the poem from some earlier edition of Menzel's work. But unfortunately, as Hoch pointed out, Menzel was only ten years old in 1916. Jaeckel contacted Stiefel to demand an explanation. The outraged Stiefel contacted Kujau.

On 5 February, exactly a week after concluding his agreement with Heidemann, Kujau joined Stiefel and Jaeckel for an emergency meeting in the professor's office in Stuttgart University. What most perturbed him, said Jaeckel, was the fact that 'Der Kamerad' had been accompanied by a letter on official Nazi stationery, signed by a party official, stating that the poem was unquestionably genuine. The fact that 'Der Kamerad' was such an obvious forgery meant that the letter was also probably faked. And similar letters had been attached to dozens of pieces of Hitler writing belonging to Stiefel which Jaeckel had printed in his book. It had to be assumed that they were all forged.

This was a nasty moment for Kujau. According to Jaeckel he 'seemed very unsettled by my doubts'. But he handled the situation adroitly. In view of the aspersions which had been cast, he said, he was prepared to be more specific about the source of the material. He then proceeded, with considerable cheek, to recount to the two men the story of the crashed Hitler plane exactly as it had been described to him for the first time by Heidemann the previous week. Kujau, recalled Jaeckel,

> told me in detail what had only been suggested in general before: that the pieces came from a plane that had crashed near Boernersdorf in 1945 on its way from Berlin to Salzburg... To strengthen his case he said that the journalist Gerd Heidemann had seen the graves of the plane's crew in Boernersdorf.

Having used the evidence of one victim in an attempt to soothe the anxieties of another, Kujau then retreated to his customary last line of defence. According to Jaeckel 'he said he couldn't add very much more because he was only the middleman. He didn't really know much about the documents or their historical context.'

There was little more that could be done. Jaeckel had no alternative but to begin preparing an announcement to place in an academic journal admitting that he had been duped. He advised Stiefel in the meantime to submit his material for forensic examination. As for Kujau, he went home to Ditzingen to begin forging the first volume of Hitler diaries for Gerd Heidemann.

To sustain him through his labours over the next two years, Kujau, like any conscientious professional writer, established a regular routine. He would get up at 6 a.m. followed, half an hour later, by Edith Lieblang. The couple would have coffee together and then she would drive off to Stuttgart to her job in the Café Hochland. Kujau would cook himself a heavy breakfast of fried potatoes and two fried eggs and, thus fortified, retire to his studio where he would work right through the day, without even stopping for lunch. When the police raided his premises in 1983 they carried out ten cartons full of books and articles accumulated by Kujau to help him establish Hitler's daily activities. There were 515 books and newspapers in his workroom, 106 additional periodicals in his cellar. Stuffed into them were thousands of bookmarks – playing cards, blotting paper, old bills and tickets, visitors' cards and toilet paper – marking passages required for the concoction of the diaries. Kujau would write out a rough draft in pencil and then transfer it in ink into one of the school notebooks kept in his cellar. His work became more sophisticated with time. To start with, he confined himself to writing about Hitler's early years in power – years full of laws and decrees with which he could fill the Führer's empty days and which did not require much research into complex political issues. In the evening, when Edith returned from work, she would cook them both a meal. 'Conny would lie stretched out on the sofa,' recalled Edith. 'We'd watch television and often he'd fall asleep. I had no idea what he did during the day. We gave one another a lot of space.' This sedentary regime was to last until the spring of 1983.

According to Kujau, he finished the first three volumes about ten days after the meeting with Stiefel and Jaeckel. To dress them up, he stuck a red wax seal in the shape of a German eagle on the covers, together with a label, signed by Rudolf Hess, declaring them to be Hitler's property. He bashed them about for a while to age them, and sprinkled some tea over the pages. He then rang Heidemann to tell him he had the books. Walde said later that these early diaries were not supposed to have come from East Germany 'but from the United States, where "Fischer" had offered them through a lawyer to an interested party'. Kujau flew up from Stuttgart with the diaries to be entertained by Heidemann on board *Carin II*. To celebrate the arrival of the first books, the enthusiastic reporter opened a bottle of sparkling white wine.

Only five men at Gruner and Jahr knew the secret of the diaries' existence. For them, Wednesday 18 February was a memorable day. Shortly before 10 a.m., four of the initiated – Gerd Heidemann, Thomas Walde, Jan Hensmann and Wilfried Sorge – trooped into the office of the fifth, Manfred Fischer. The doors were closed, Fischer instructed his secretary to make sure they were not disturbed, and Heidemann laid the diaries before them.

It appears to have been a moment of almost religious solemnity. Hensmann picked up one of the diaries. It was 'bound in black', he recalled, '1.5 centimetres thick'. Like most of the others, he could not read the old Germanic script in which it was written, but it undoubtedly felt genuine. 'I held it with great care in my hands,' he said later. Manfred Fischer was also impressed by the slightly battered appearance of the books. 'They were a little bit damaged,' he remembered. 'The tops of the pages were bent.' For Fischer, the arrival of these first Hitler diaries was 'a great moment' in his life: 'It was a very special experience to hold such a thing in your hand. The certainty that this diary was written by *him* – and now I have it in my grasp...'

The diaries cast a spell over the room. The intense secrecy of the meeting; the thrill of handling contraband, smuggled at great cost and danger from the site of a wartime aircrash; above all, the presence of Adolf Hitler as contained in this unknown record of his intimate thoughts – all these elements combined to produce a highly charged atmosphere, a mood which in its turn created what Fischer subsequently called 'a sort of group psychosis'. The prospect of possessing something once owned by the Führer affected these cool, modern-minded North German businessmen just as it did the obsessive, ex-Nazi collectors in the south. 'We wanted to have them,' said Fischer of the diaries. 'Even if we'd only believed that there was a 10 per cent chance that they were genuine, we'd still have said, "Get them here."' Of all the figures in history, perhaps only Adolf Hitler could have exercised such an hypnotic fascination.

In this atmosphere, the five men now took a series of decisions which were to have profound consequences. Both Heidemann and Walde urged on the group the importance of maintaining absolute secrecy. If the slightest hint of the existence of the diaries leaked out, they told the three businessmen, the East German general would cease shipping the material. Heidemann, according to Hensmann, went further: 'He didn't merely warn of the need to protect his sources, but of the danger that human life itself might be threatened.' For this reason the two journalists argued strongly against bringing in any experts from outside to examine the diaries until the full set was in the company's possession. 'These reservations,' stated Sorge, 'were accepted. They led to the decision to obtain further volumes before authentication tests were carried out.' Not even Henri Nannen and the three editors-in-chief of *Stern* would be told what was going on until all the transactions had been completed; that would probably, said Heidemann, be in mid-May.

All these proposals were accepted. 'It was unanimously agreed,' stated Hensmann, 'that we should continue with the project.'

The five men were now effectively bound together in a conspiracy against *Stern*. Without consulting a handwriting expert, a forensic scientist or an historian, Fischer that day committed the company to the purchase of twenty-seven volumes of Hitler's diaries at a price of 85,000 marks each; plus a sum of 200,000 marks to be paid for the third volume of *Mein Kampf*. The total cost of the project would be 2.5 million marks. As the company's managing director, he signed a document authorizing the immediate transfer of 1 million marks from the company's main account for the obtaining of the diaries.

'We all had a kind of blackout,' he commented afterwards.

*

For all this talk of mental aberration, the businessmen's behaviour was not totally irrational. As publishers they knew the size of the potential market for any venture connected with the Third Reich. In Britain one publisher, Bison Books, had been built entirely on the strength of the public's fascination with the Nazis. *Hitler's Wartime Picture Magazine* was simply extracts from the Nazi propaganda magazine *Signal* stitched together in a single volume: it sold over a quarter of a million copies in Britain and the United States; between 1976 and 1978 it was reprinted eight times. Another picture book from the same publisher, *Der Führer*, edited by a former SS officer, Herbert Walther, was bought by more than 50,000 people. Bison's flamboyant founder, Sidney Mayer, was quite open about the reason for his success:

> I don't want to end up as Hitler's publisher. I would have thought the public was as sick of it as I am. But they are not. The booksellers always want more. Hitler sells. Nazis sell. Swastikas sell – and they sell better and better. It's the swastika on the cover that gets them. Nobody can out-swastika us. I've even thought of putting one on our vegetable cook book because Hitler was a vegetarian.

On the wall of his office, Mayer hung a large picture of himself with a small Hitler moustache and the caption 'Springtime For Mayer'.

If this was the market for what were basically retreads of material already seen, the marketing possibilities of Adolf Hitler's secret diaries were clearly stupendous. Gruner and Jahr was well placed to exploit it. The company owned a string of successful West German magazines, including *Stern* and *Geo*. It had outlets in Spain, France and the United States (where it owned *Parents* and *Young Miss*). Gruner and Jahr had a turnover of almost half a billion dollars and controlled a total of twenty periodicals across the world.

Since 1972, three-quarters of the company's shares had been held by the West German multinational, Bertelsmann AG, the country's largest publishing group. Founded in 1835 to produce religious tracts, by 1981 the company had 180 subsidiaries operating in twenty-five countries. In America it owned such well-known organizations as Bantam Books and Arista Records. Once this formidable publishing and marketing machine was thrown behind the Hitler diaries, profits could be expected which would easily recoup Fischer's initial investment of 2·5 million marks.

Hitler was going to make everybody rich, no one more so than Gerd Heidemann. Fischer accepted that the reporter had a special claim to the diaries project. He had pursued it in the face of outright opposition from the *Stern* editors. He was the only person with whom the supplier of the diaries would deal. Heidemann had already talked vaguely of taking over the project for himself. He could go into partnership with an American publisher. He could sell everything and try to finance the project himself. He could take up those job offers he claimed to have received from *Bunte* and *Quick*. He had even mentioned a Dutch oil millionaire named Heeremann, a former member of the SS, who was prepared to put up 1 million marks towards the purchase of the diaries, provided they proved that Hitler knew nothing of the extermination of the Jews. Fischer was understandably anxious to conclude an agreement with Heidemann. Immediately after the receipt of the first diaries negotiations began, and five days later, on 23 February, the two men signed a contract. Such was the secrecy of the project, the company's legal department was not told what was happening. Wilfried Sorge personally drafted the agreement in accordance with suggestions from Heidemann.

The first part of the contract set out the reporter's obligations:

> The author [Heidemann] will obtain for the publishing company from East Germany the original manuscripts of the diaries of Adolf Hitler from the years 1933 to 1945 as well as the handwritten manuscript of the third volume of *Mein Kampf*. The publishing company will place at the author's disposal for the obtaining of these manuscripts the sum of 85,000 marks per volume and 200,000 marks for *Mein Kampf*.
>
> The author will be of assistance to the publishing company in reaching a settlement with the heirs of Adolf Hitler. He will attempt to obtain the ownership of the rights and transfer them to the company. The company will compensate the heirs through the author.
>
> Together with Dr Thomas Walde, the author will work on the manuscript for a *Stern* series and for one, or perhaps several, *Stern* books. . . Other collaborators (for example, historians) will be engaged only with the agreement of the authors.

The authors give the company exclusive and unlimited publishing rights to this material in all its forms. They give over all their copyright and further rights to the publishing company. The publishing company will be able to decide to whom it will syndicate the material. The company will only transfer the rights to a third party for a fee, and any alterations to the material which make it substantially different to the original will require the approval of the authors.

The authors will not be given any special fees for the production of the *Stern* series. *Stern* will receive rights to the series for nothing. In return, it will release the authors for two years from their usual editorial work. Those two years will commence when all the original volumes have been obtained.

Next came details of his reward:

For the *Stern* books, the author will receive a royalty of 6 per cent of the cover price of every volume sold up to 10,000 copies. For sales in excess of 10,000 copies, up to a total of 50,000, the royalty will rise to 7.2 per cent. For sales above 50,000 copies, the royalty increases to 9 per cent.

As a share of the syndication sales made by the company, Heidemann will receive 36 per cent; Walde, 24 per cent.

Ten years after the start of publication, the company will return the original manuscripts to the author. When he dies, the author will bequeath them to the Federal Government. Before the expiry of the ten year deadline, the author will be allowed to use the material for his own researches...

As an advance against royalties, when eight volumes of the Hitler diaries have been delivered, the author will receive 300,000 marks...

If neither the publication of the books nor the syndication of the material covers the advance, nor the sale of the original material, the author will repay the difference within a year from the time when the last payment was made.

If for any reason the publishing company is prevented from publishing the work, it will be entitled to withdraw from this contract. In that case, all the payments due to the author will fall through, and if the author publishes the work with another company, he will be obliged to pay the money back.

Despite the caveat contained in the final two clauses, this contract represented a substantial victory for Heidemann. It was inconceivable that if the diaries were genuine they would fail to cover the cost of his advance. Even if *Stern* never published the material, Heidemann could keep the money, unless he took the diaries elsewhere: in other words, even if they were forged, Heidemann would not be obliged to pay back the advance. That fact alone gives some indication of the management's complete faith that the diaries were genuine. Assuming publication went ahead, the potential profit to Heidemann was enormous. Worldwide sales of Hitler's diaries would exceed 50,000 copies by a factor of ten, perhaps a hundred; the royalties that would yield, coupled with a third of world syndication rights, would make Heidemann financially secure for the rest of his life. To have such a golden vision of the future shimmering on the horizon would tend to make the most sceptical journalist incline to a belief in the diaries' authenticity. Heidemann was not one of the profession's natural sceptics. He had already shown himself capable of believing any amount of rubbish about the Third Reich. It is scarcely surprising that his attitude to the diaries from now on was one of blind faith. Gruner and Jahr had given the one man they had to trust an overwhelming financial incentive to deceive himself – and them.

12

Heidemann's advance of 300,000 marks was not due to be paid to him until he had delivered another five diaries. But Manfred Fischer knew of Heidemann's chronic financial difficulties (the reporter had taken out yet another company loan two months previously for 28,500 marks) and as a gesture of good faith he arranged to have the money paid into Heidemann's account the day after the conclusion of their agreement, Tuesday 24 February.

The following day, Heidemann rang Sorge to tell him that a new shipment of the diaries had arrived. He needed 480,000 marks. Sorge walked along the corridor to the office of Peter Kuehsel, the finance director, and asked for authorization to withdraw the money.

Kuehsel, a new arrival at Gruner and Jahr, must have wondered what sort of company he had joined. A month ago he had been ordered to find 200,000 marks in cash after the banks had shut; he had driven to the airport, stashed the money into a suitcase like a cashier for a Mafia family; then he had watched as Heidemann headed off into the night with it. Now he was supposed to hand over another 480,000 in cash with no explanation as to what it was for. He was an accountant. It offended his sense of business propriety. He sought out Manfred Fischer. 'I asked Dr Fischer what the money was for and why payments of this size had to be made in cash,' he recalled. 'I asked in order that I could make a proper entry in the company's accounts.' Fischer realized that the circle of the initiated would have to be widened from five to six. 'He swore me to secrecy,' said Kuehsel, 'and told me that Herr Heidemann was on the trail of the Hitler diaries.' Fischer warned Kuehsel that in all he would probably be called upon to hand over about 3 million marks. Kuehsel stared at his managing director in astonishment. 'I said it was a lot of money.' Fischer then asked him for some technical advice and the two men 'discussed how it could be dealt with from the point of view of tax'.

When Sorge had received the authorization, he drove to the main Deutsche Bank in (appropriately) Adolphsplatz. The money, in 500- and 1000-mark notes, was packed into a suitcase and given to Heidemann.

This established a routine which was to last for more than two years. Heidemann would hear from Kujau that a new consignment of books was ready for collection. He would then inform Sorge who would in turn approach Kuehsel. According to the accountant:

> Herr Sorge would tell me two days beforehand when money was to be handed out to Heidemann and how much was needed. I then made contact with the main branch of the Deutsche Bank in Adolphsplatz and asked them that same day to make arrangements to provide the money. Sometimes Sorge or sometimes Heidemann would decide the denominations of the notes. As far as I remember, it was mainly 500-mark notes; sometimes 1000-mark.

When Heidemann returned from Stuttgart with the new diaries he would make two photocopies on a machine installed in his private apartment, one for himself and one for the *Stern* history department. Crucial to the development of the whole affair was the fact that Heidemann was one of the few people at *Stern* who could decipher the handwriting and make sense of the obsolescent script in which they were written – a type of Gothic composition no longer taught in German schools. For most of those in the diaries' circle, Heidemann effectively became the Custodian of the Writ, the medium through whom the oracle of the diaries spoke. Once he had made the photocopies, he would take the originals to Sorge or Hensmann on the ninth floor of the *Stern* building. If those gentlemen had time they would listen while he read out passages to them. After this ritual, the diaries were put into brown envelopes, sealed, and placed in the management safe. The secrecy which surrounded this procedure was very tight. The *Stern Report* subsequently described how

The circle of those who knew about the diaries was carefully restricted. Written notes were avoided. If internal notes were required, they were supposed to be destroyed immediately. Those who knew about the project began to behave like a secret organization working underground.

Walde did not even tell his wife what he was working on.

This mania for secrecy makes it difficult to reconstruct some parts of the story. The only record of deliveries was kept by Sorge. It was handwritten and intelligible only to himself. On the left-hand side of a piece of paper he wrote the date and the amount of money paid to Heidemann. On the right he entered the number of volumes delivered. But, as the *Stern Report* noted, there was no record of 'the time lapses between the deliveries, nor the order in which they came: to this day nobody knows at what point a particular book arrived at *Stern*'. Heidemann was not expected to account for the money he received. 'It was quite clear to us,' explained Sorge, 'that in this sort of business, Heidemann wouldn't be bringing back receipts, nor would there be any indication of who the money was being paid to.' Having already given the reporter a personal payment of 300,000 marks, and promised him hundreds of thousands more when the diaries were published, the management reckoned they could count on Heidemann's integrity.

Whenever Kujau had finished forging a new batch of diaries he would telephone Heidemann at his home in Hamburg and tell him that a lorryload of pianos containing a fresh consignment of the books had arrived from East Germany. These telephone calls, according to the reporter, would generally come at about 8 a.m., when he was lying in his morning bath. Heidemann would then hasten down to the Aspergstrasse shop. Kujau would give him an A4-sized package, three or four inches thick, containing the latest instalments. Heidemann would give him a sealed envelope full of money to be passed on to 'General Fischer'. Sometimes Heidemann would open the package of diaries in Stuttgart and Kujau, pretending not to understand the old Germanic script, would ask him to read aloud from them. Heidemann would do so, a performance frequently interrupted by 'ahs' and 'oohs' from Kujau, as the forger feigned amazement at such an extraordinary historical document. After Heidemann had gone happily back to Hamburg, Kujau, equally happy, would open the packet of money, which – though he was not aware of it – held considerably less than it had when Heidemann took it from the safe in Hamburg.

Of the 680,000 marks which by the end of February had been paid to him for the acquisition of the diaries, the likelihood is that Heidemann stole almost half of it. It is impossible to be certain about this: it is Kujau's word against Heidemann's, the word of a compulsive liar against that of an inveterate fantast. Nevertheless, the balance of probability, for once, is on Kujau's side. According to both him and Edith Lieblang, the suitcase Heidemann opened up in their house on the night of 28 January contained 150,000 marks – not the 200,000 it had held when Heidemann had left Hamburg twenty-four hours earlier. In 1983, in a raid on Heidemann's home, the police found a note confirming the reporter's agreement with Kujau, but at a much lower cost than Manfred Fischer was aware of:

Private collection, Militaria, Stuttgart FA, E. Lieblang, 7000 Stuttgart 1, Aspergstrasse 20.

Documents and pictures	500,000 marks
27 diaries at 50,000 marks	1,350,000 marks
Mein Kampf	150,000 marks
Total	2,000,000 marks

Of the 85,000 marks being given to him for each volume in Hamburg, Heidemann was passing on at most 50,000 and keeping 35,000 for himself. In this way he pocketed 280,000 marks by the end of February alone.

The Hitler diaries project was less than one month old but already it had at least three layers of mendacity. Kujau was deceiving Heidemann; Heidemann was deceiving Kujau and the management of Gruner and Jahr; and the management of Gruner and Jahr was deceiving the editors of *Stern*.

*

On Monday 9 March, Manfred Fischer travelled to Guetersloh, 150 miles from Hamburg, for a meeting of the senior management of the Bertelsmann group. In his suitcase he had three of the Hitler diaries which he had removed from the ninth-floor safe the previous evening.

A full board meeting of the company on 11 February had confirmed Fischer as the next managing director of Bertelsmann. He was to take up his new job at the beginning of July, easing the workload presently being carried by Reinhard Mohn, head of the family which owned almost nine-tenths of the company. Mohn would shortly be reaching the firm's retirement age of sixty. Daily operating control of Bertelsmann would be relinquished to Fischer. Mohn would concentrate on broader policy issues as chairman of the company's board.

It would not be easy for Fischer to establish his authority, stepping straight into the place of such a powerful figure, especially as Mohn would also continue to oversee his work. The Hitler diaries were a means of establishing that he had vision, imagination, a capacity for taking decisive action – proof, in the words of the *Stern Report*, of 'his wide-ranging approach to the publishing business'.

At the Guetersloh headquarters, Fischer asked Mohn for a private meeting. The two men retreated to Mohn's inner office, his secretary was instructed not to let anyone pass, and Fischer brought out Heidemann's dossier. He handed it to Mohn and drew his attention to Baur's description of Hitler's distress at the loss of his valuable papers. 'We have now found them,' he said. With considerable pride he laid the diaries before Mohn. 'These are Hitler's diaries.'

Mohn leafed through them. His reaction was all that Fischer had hoped it would be. 'He was just as fascinated as we were,' he recalled. 'He thought it was just great.'

'Manfred,' said Mohn, 'this is the most important manuscript ever to have passed across my desk.'

His initiation brought the number within Bertelsmann who knew the secret of the Hitler diaries to seven.

Three days later, on 12 March, Fischer signed a contract with Thomas Walde similar to the one agreed with Gerd Heidemann. Walde's share of the profits would be a royalty of 4 per cent of book sales up to 10,000 copies, 4.8 per cent up to 50,000, and 6 per cent thereafter; from the sale of syndication rights he would receive 24 per cent of the gross revenue. His advance was 10,000 marks. Like Heidemann, he retained the right to veto the involvement of other historians on the project.

On 2 April, a small drinks party was held on board *Carin II* to celebrate the way things were going. Manfred Fischer and Jan Hensmann arrived at about 6 p.m. to find Heidemann, Walde and Sorge already waiting for them. For Fischer and Hensmann, this was their first visit to the yacht. Heidemann showed them around, pointing out his various treasures. 'He showed me Goering's shoehorn,' remembered Fischer, 'and the big loo, installed because Goering had such a big backside.' To Hensmann, the yacht 'gave the impression of being clean and cared for'. After the tour, the men sat around drinking whisky and soda for two hours discussing their triumph. Heidemann was particularly excited. His discovery, he said, would 'make the world hold its breath'.

But already the first doubts about the diaries were beginning to be expressed. Contrary to the agreed policy of strict secrecy, despite his repeated and melodramatic warnings that disclosure would jeopardize human life, Heidemann could not resist showing off his great scoop. Reading through one of the first volumes Kujau delivered, covering the first six months of 1933, he came across references to the Führer's élite troops, the SS *Leibstandarte Adolf Hitler*. Bursting with excitement he decided to contact a founder member of the *Leibstandarte* – his old friend Wilhelm Mohnke. In the spring of 1981 Heidemann rang the former SS general to tell him he had the first three diaries. 'I'll show you them,' he said to Mohnke. 'There are things about you in them.' Mohnke, who three months earlier, on the day of Doenitz's funeral, had disparaged the whole notion of 'Hitler diaries', hurried round to Heidemann's flat on the Elbchaussee where he was shown a 'black book'. He was unable to decipher the writing so Heidemann read out the relevant entries:

15 March 1933: Visit of the specially chosen men, and the plans for the new *Standarte* [unit] of the SS in Lichterfelde. These SS *Standarte* must carry my name.

17 March 1933: The Christian Unions are training themselves to be apolitical. From today an SS *Standarte* is in place in Lichterfelde. As from now all the relevant security measures will be taken by these people. These people are particularly good National Socialists. The *Standarte* are now carrying my name and are sworn in to me.

18 March 1933: Visit to these *Leibstandarte*. They are very fine men. Stayed up talking to members of the Cabinet until very late at night.

Heidemann recited these banalities – typical of the diaries as a whole – and asked Mohnke for his opinion. Mohnke was not impressed.

I said to Herr Heidemann that several things in these diaries were simply not true. First, the SS *Standarte* never had their barracks in Lichterfelde. I belonged to that troop and in March and April 1933 we were in the Friesenstrasse, in the police barracks. Secondly, at that time this troop of men did not have the name *Leibstandarte*. Thirdly, the entry for 18 March 1933 was false: Adolf Hitler never visited this troop in the Friesenstrasse.

Heidemann listened to this apparently devastating judgement with equanimity. He had long ceased operating on a rational wavelength: doubts about the diaries' authenticity were something he was not programmed to receive. 'Perhaps,' he suggested to Mohnke, 'Adolf Hitler *planned* all that and was putting his thoughts down on paper.'

He was equally unperturbed when, in the spring of 1981, Eberhard Jaeckel published his apology in Germany's leading historical journal, admitting that documents in his collected edition of Hitler's early writings were forged. Jaeckel kept his word and did not name Stiefel personally – he described the documents as having 'been in the hands of a private collector, totally unknown to the public' – but he conceded that the doubts which had been expressed about their authenticity were 'justified'. This was not only embarrassing to Jaeckel. It was also embarrassing to *Stern*. When Jaeckel's book had first appeared, the magazine had paid him 3000 marks to reprint the Hitler poems under the title *Rhymes from 'H'*: Kujau's handiwork had thus been published in the magazine for the first time two and a half years before the launch of the diaries. Was it possible, wondered Walde, that the diaries came from the same source as the poems? Heidemann was dispatched to the Institute of Contemporary History in Munich to copy the forged documents and check if they too had originated from the Boernersdorf crash. Heidemann did not bother to contact Jaeckel. Instead he sent the documents directly to Kujau for him to inspect, then rang him a few weeks later to ask if he had ever seen them before. Kujau, not surprisingly, said he hadn't and Heidemann reported back to Walde that there was no need for them to worry.

The publication of Jaeckel's apology stirred Kujau to another act of forgery. All the doubts about the authenticity of the poems stemmed from the fact that *'Der Kamerad'* was not the work of Hitler and could not have been copied by him because it was not written until 1936. Kujau attempted to calm the fears of Fritz Stiefel on this point by forging a letter, dated 18 May 1981, purportedly sent by a librarian at the East German 'State Archive for Literature' to his brother, 'General Fischer':

Comrade Fischer,

I inform you that the text of the document *'Der Kamerad'* was originally written, in a slightly different form, by Xaver Kern in the year 1871. This verse was published repeatedly under different titles until 1942, always with slight textual variations. It was also published in 1956 in *Volk und Wissen* (East Germany, volume nine). I will send you a photocopy of the original in the next couple of days.

(Signed) Schenk.

If Heidemann had bothered to check with Jaeckel, or if Jaeckel had troubled himself to speak to *Stern* about the forged poems, Kujau's activities would almost certainly have been exposed. As it was, his victims once again played into his hands and Kujau was allowed to carry on his lucrative business for another two years.

13

On 13 May 1981, Pope John Paul II was shot and wounded in an assassination attempt in St Peter's Square in Rome. When the news came through in the *Stern* building in Hamburg, there was an immediate editorial conference. This dramatic story had all the ingredients the magazine specialized in: violence, personal tragedy, conspiracy, espionage, international crisis, vivid pictures – *Stern* threw all its resources into reporting the event. Someone with experience of foreign investigations should go to Turkey, home of the would-be assassin. The ideal choice was Heidemann. Had anyone seen him? Where *was* Heidemann these days?

Henri Nannen had stepped down from the day-to-day editing of *Stern* at the beginning of the year to become the magazine's publisher. A triumvirate of editors-in-chief had replaced him: Peter Koch, responsible for politics, economics and foreign affairs; Felix Schmidt, in charge of the arts, entertainment and leisure sections; and a design expert, Rolf Gillhausen. Koch had already spent several fruitless sessions with Heidemann trying to force him to do some normal journalism for a change. Now, Schmidt undertook to track him down. He rang Thomas Walde, Heidemann's departmental head. Walde said the reporter was not available. 'I don't care where he is,' shouted Schmidt. 'Get him into my office.' In exasperation, he went to consult Nannen. 'Who is Heidemann working for?' he demanded. 'The editors or the publishing company?' Nannen said that obviously he worked for the editors and advised Schmidt and Koch to complain to the management.

Meanwhile, three floors above them, uncertain as to what he should do, Walde was speaking to Wilfried Sorge. Because Manfred Fischer was away the two men approached his deputy, Jan Hensmann, and explained the problem. Hensmann's objective was a quiet life. His advice was that Heidemann should feign illness; Walde could then lie to the editors and tell them that Heidemann was on sick leave. Neither of the journalists was enthusiastic about this idea. With great reluctance, Hensmann finally accepted that the time had come to inform the lucky editors of the scoop the management was acquiring for them. The diaries were fetched from the safe and arranged in a pile on a small table in the corner of his office. Hensmann then rang Koch, the most senior of the editors, and asked him to come upstairs.

Koch's first reaction on being shown the diaries was one of anger at having been deceived by the management. He rang down to Schmidt and Gillhausen in the *Stern* offices below and told them to come up and join him. Schmidt arrived a few minutes later to find his colleague 'bent over a pile of A4-sized books. Koch said to me that they were the diaries of Adolf Hitler and that Heidemann had got them.' Like almost everyone else in the company, they were unable to read the antiquated script. They could only concentrate on the diaries' external features. Gillhausen noted that most of the books had a 'black cover', 'a red cord and a red seal', and a note pasted on the front 'on which either Hess or Bormann had written that these books were the property of the Führer'. Hensmann said that Heidemann was not available for normal journalistic work because he was acquiring the books on the management's behalf. Large sums of money had been paid. Absolute secrecy was necessary.

The editors retreated to Koch's office to digest this information. Their reactions were mixed. There was unanimous resentment at the way they had been treated: five months into their new jobs it did not augur well for the future. On the other hand, the editors did not have the slightest doubt that the books were genuine. They had to be. Over half a million marks had already been spent. It was impossible to conceive of the shrewd, conservative, financially cautious managers of Gruner and Jahr investing in anything unless they were absolutely certain of its value. The three had to accept that if they rejected the diaries, they risked going down in history as the editors who threw away one of the biggest scoops since the war.

That point was made with brutal frankness a couple of days later, when Manfred Fischer returned and chaired a joint meeting of journalists and businessmen to review the whole project. Koch, Schmidt and Gillhausen faced Heidemann, Walde, Sorge and Hensmann. Fischer was not in the least apologetic for having circumvented the editors. As far as he was concerned their inept handling of Heidemann had almost lost the company this tremendous coup. He had no doubts about the authenticity of the diaries. 'Do you think,' he inquired, 'that I would have committed so much money if I were not convinced?' If *Stern* did not want the diaries, they could be marketed elsewhere: Bertelsmann could exploit the world rights; Bantam Books could handle the American publication. Heidemann scarcely opened his mouth. It was Fischer who explained the story of the East German general and his brother in the West whose identity could not be revealed. The three editors listened without enthusiasm. Humiliated and offended by the management's behaviour, their attitude to Heidemann's great scoop was, and would remain for many months, one of sullen acquiescence.

On 27 May, Heidemann crossed the border into East Germany and returned to Boernersdorf. This time he was on his own. He wanted to discover more about the crashed transport plane. He found some eyewitnesses to the disaster. Helda Fries, wife of a local hotel owner, described how the plane fell out of the sky, clipping the tops of the trees in the nearby Heidenholz forest. One of its three engines was wrenched off before it hit the ground. Richard Elbe, a local farmer who had been in the fields in charge of some Russian and French slave labourers, was the first to reach the burning wreck. Bullets were exploding, people trapped inside were screaming and hammering to get out. In front of them, one survivor, Franz Westermeier, crawled out of the chaos. 'Come here you cowardly dogs,' Elbe recalled him shouting. 'Come here. You are just too scared.' But the heat was too intense for the rescuers to get close. A farmworker, said Elbe, called Eduard Grimme later pulled the corpses from the wreckage. 'They didn't look like people any more. The arms were gone and the legs and everything else was charred.' The remains were examined in the local morgue by a German medical officer. On one body was a cigarette case embossed with the symbol of

Lufthansa and the words: 'In memory of 500,000 kilometres flying.' It had belonged to Gundlfinger. The remains of the plane were cordoned off by German police and SS men. But according to Erwin Goebel, son of the mayor at that time, 'many people managed to salvage parts from the aircraft and got richer for it, soldiers included'. Debris and pieces of luggage were scattered all over the forest. Richard Elbe had carried off two cockpit windows and used them to build part of a shed.

It was all very insubstantial – fragments of gossip, hazily recalled thirty-six years after the event. Nevertheless, it was something for Heidemann to grasp at. He bought the two old windows off Elbe and carted them back with him to Hamburg where he showed them off as further proof of the story.

On 1 June he received a further 225,000 marks. Shortly afterwards he returned from Stuttgart with more books. There were now twelve Hitler diaries in the management safe.

In May, Manfred Fischer had let another member of the publishing company's management into the secret of the diaries' existence. He was Dr Andreas Ruppert, Gruner and Jahr's legal adviser. Fischer wanted his opinion of the legality of the whole project. Would *Stern* be able to publish the diaries? Who owned the copyright?

Ruppert reported back that determining ownership of Hitler's estate was complex, indeed almost impossible. Hitler's property, together with 5 million marks owed to him by the publishers of *Mein Kampf*, was confiscated, after a court case, by the State of Bavaria in 1948. Hitler's will was declared invalid and in 1951, the Bavarian authorities seized personal objects bequeathed by Hitler to his housekeeper to prevent her selling them. But the following year they had been unable to prevent the appearance of *Hitler's Table Talk*: the state apparently owned rights in Hitler's literary estate only as far as published material was concerned; previously unpublished material fell outside their control. It was impossible to predict how the Bavarians or the Federal Government would react to news of the diaries' existence. The situation was further complicated by the fact that various private deals had been arranged with Hitler's descendants. François Genoud, the Swiss lawyer and ex-Nazi, had signed an agreement with Paula, Hitler's sister, shortly after the war. But Paula was long since dead. Meanwhile, the West German historian, Werner Maser, had a separate contract to act as a trustee for the Hitler family. It was decided, as a first step towards securing ownership of the diaries, to make a deal with Maser.

Maser was a controversial figure. Ten years previously he had written a bestselling biography of Hitler, translated into twenty languages, which was regarded as having dwelt, at suspicious length, on the positive aspects of Hitler's character and achievements. In 1977 he had written a book attacking the Allied handling of the Nuremberg trials, stating that, in many instances, the hanged war criminals were victims of a miscarriage of justice. His relations with the left-wing *Stern* were strained. The magazine therefore approached him through his former assistant, Michael Hepp. According to Maser:

> [Hepp] rang me in the summer of 1981 and asked me if I was inter-
> ested in talking to a journalist from *Stern*. I told him of my basic objec-
> tion to newspapers like *Stern*. . . Herr Hepp said that this journalist
> was a very sensible man who also had a large collection of Hitler
> memorabilia. We agreed a date and shortly afterwards Hepp and Hei-
> demann came to see me.

Heidemann arrived at Maser's home in Speyer, near Heidelberg, on 11 June. Without mentioning the diaries, he asked the historian to sell him the rights to any original Hitler material which he had already discovered or might discover in the future. After a week's haggling over terms, a handwritten contract was drawn up and signed on 18 June:

> Professor Dr Werner Maser receives, as the administrator of Hitler's
> will on behalf of Hitler's descendants, a fee of 20,000 marks, paid in
> cash. For this sum he allows Gerd Heidemann the rights to all the dis-
> covered or purchased documents or notes in the hand of Adolf Hitler,
> including transcribed telephone conversations and other conversations
> which have so far not been published and which could be used for
> publication. Professor Dr Werner Maser gives to Gerd Heidemann all
> the rights necessary for this, including personal rights and copyrights.
> Dr Maser affirms that he is empowered to do this on behalf of the

family. This document is completed in the legal department in Hamburg and is valid in German law.

Heidemann then opened a suitcase and pulled out a bundle of money. He counted out twenty-two 1000-mark notes and handed them to Maser.

After delivering the twelfth diary, Heidemann suddenly announced a price increase. Instead of costing 85,000 marks each, the books would now cost 100,000 marks. The East German general, he told the *Stern* management, was insisting on more money: to continue supplying the books, he was having to bribe an increasing number of corrupt communist officials. This news was a disappointment to the company. They had originally expected to have all the books in Hamburg by mid-May; instead, by mid-June, they had less than half. But they certainly did not want to jeopardize the project at such a late stage. They had no alternative but to agree to pay. Not once did they suspect where the additional cash was really going.

After years of living in debt, Heidemann was now awash with money. Over the following months he and Gina went on a spending spree impressive even by Hamburg's wealthy standards. In one of the city's department stores he bought 37,000 marks' worth of furnishings to renovate their flat; he produced the money from his jacket pocket with the bank's seal still on the bundles. At the Luehrs travel agency he put down 27,000 marks in cash on the counter and booked first-class cabins for himself and his family on the maiden voyage of the luxury liner *Astor*. The staff had no difficulty in describing the event to the police in 1983 – years later they could still remember the difficulty they had trying to stuff all Heidemann's money into the till. Gina got two cars – a convertible BMW 318 for 32,000 marks and a Porsche 911 for 26,000. The Heidemanns eventually moved into larger accommodation on the Elbchaussee, Hamburg's most exclusive street: not content with one, they rented two apartments. A fortune went on jewellery and carpets.

Inflated by *Stern*'s money, Heidemann's compulsion to collect Nazi memorabilia ballooned out of control. Some of it was presumably genuine, like Karl Wolff's SS honour dagger, for which Heidemann paid the old general 30,000 marks. Most of it, however, came from Konrad Kujau. It included a swastika banner which Kujau passed off as the 'Blood Flag', the famous symbol of Hitler's abortive beer hall *putsch* of 1923, preserved on Hitler's orders like a holy relic in honour of the sixteen Nazi 'martyrs' killed that day. In reality, Heidemann's 'Blood Flag' was simply an ordinary swastika banner – of which there are thousands in existence – to which Kujau had added his usual forged authentication. The swastika was in an old glass case upon which was glued a note: 'As the condition of the flag has suffered greatly in the years of confiscation it is shown in the flag hall of the Brownhouse behind glass. According to the wishes of the Führer.'

Heidemann also received from Kujau three hundred oil paintings, sketches and watercolours supposedly by Hitler; Nazi Party uniforms, flags and postcards; and 120 so-called Hitler documents. In addition, he acquired what he believed to be the actual revolver which Hitler had used to shoot himself. Attached to it was a label in Martin Bormann's handwriting stating that 'with this pistol, the Führer took his own life'. Heidemann proudly showed it to Wilhelm Mohnke and Otto Guensche. The gun was one of the most palpable fakes in his collection: it was a Belgian FN, whereas Hitler was known to have used a much heavier weapon, a 7.65 millimetre Walther. Both men said as much to Heidemann. Guensche, in particular, was in a position to know. He had helped carry the bodies of Hitler and Eva Braun out of the bunker. Indeed he had actually picked up the suicide weapon from the bunker floor where it had slipped from Hitler's fingers. But as with the diaries, Heidemann could not be swayed from his belief in its authenticity. He seemed to read great significance into the fact that only one of the revolver's bullets had been fired.

Heidemann felt that such treasures should be exhibited in a setting worthy of their value. During his meetings with Werner Maser in June he raised the possibility of buying Hitler's childhood home in Leonding. Maser, who knew the area well from his earlier researches, offered to help. On 1 July, the historian and his wife, together with Heidemann and Gina, drove into Austria where Maser had arranged a meeting with the *Bürgermeister* and town council of Leonding. According to Maser:

Heidemann offered to buy Hitler's parental home. A large sum was mentioned as the purchase price – I think it was 270,000 marks, I'm not sure exactly. Heidemann said that money was no problem and patted his wallet. It seemed to the gentlemen of the town council of Leonding rather dubious that a journalist from Germany should be travelling around with so much of his own money in his pocket. . . I asked Herr Heidemann on this occasion where he got the money from. He insisted it wasn't money from *Stern* but from his wife who had sold two hotels for about 9 million marks.

From Leonding we drove on together to Braunau. Heidemann wanted to look at Hitler's birthplace and possibly even to buy that. For my part, I declined to put Heidemann in touch with the town authorities there. I had slight doubts about Heidemann. For a start, I was worried by the fact that he was wandering around with so much money and saying that the price was no object. The other thing was that the behaviour of Herr and Frau Heidemann rather repelled me when they talked about Hitler.

As part of their tour that summer, the Heidemanns and the Masers also visited Berchtesgaden where they spent a while poking around in the rubble.

The idea of buying the house in Leonding was not a mere whim. Heidemann was serious. After his return to Hamburg, on 13 July, he wrote to the town council to repeat his proposal 'once again in writing'. Hitler's childhood home, said Heidemann, 'always meant more to him than his birthplace in Braunau':

Adolf Hitler had a decisive influence on the history of our century. The world and the events of today are a consequence of his politics and his war. A complete knowledge of all the threads in his life and the politics of this man is the basic precondition for the understanding of history. In my opinion, the house of Hitler's parents is an ideal site for an historical museum, to be supervised by a trustee from your town to ensure that the presentation is strictly factual.

If the town authorities agree, I will purchase from the town, for an agreed sum, the relevant house and land. I accept the conditions this would entail – for example, not altering the use to which the property is put without the express approval of the town authorities.

Should there be any complications in selling this piece of land to me as a citizen of West Germany, an Austrian historical institute could be found who would become the legal owner of the land and museum.

I ask you to consider this offer in a positive way. I await your answer and remain yours, etc, etc.

The town council met to discuss Heidemann's offer three days later. Despite his assurances that his Hitler museum would be 'strictly factual' there was something about the reporter and his proposal which the burghers of Leonding found faintly sinister. Heidemann's scheme was rejected.

Thwarted in his plan to install his collection in Leonding, Heidemann had a new idea. He decided to investigate the possibility of moving his Hitler memorabilia to South America and in the summer of 1981, he sought the advice of Klaus Barbie.

Heidemann had met Barbie in Bolivia two years previously, during his honeymoon tour with Gina and General Wolff. The two men had enjoyed a friendly relationship. Unfortunately, from Heidemann's point of view, a year after his return, in October 1980, *Stern* had decided to salvage at least something from the trip which they had financed. There had been a military coup in Bolivia in which Barbie, correctly, was suspected of having played a part. Despite strong opposition from Heidemann, the transcript of his interview with 'the Butcher of Lyons' had been used by another reporter as the basis for an article entitled 'New Power for Old Nazis'. The piece depicted Barbie as a brutal SS torturer. Barbie had not been pleased.

Hoping for a reconciliation, Heidemann wrote to him on 22 August 1981. He sent his condolences on the recent death of Barbie's son. 'I am very sorry,' he added, 'that I have also caused you some sorrow.' He then explained how the transcript of their interview had been taken off him by *Stern*'s editors and given 'a completely different slant':

Of course I tried with all the means at my disposal to prevent publication – sadly, in vain. For me, the matter has been a continuing source of embarrassment and my wife reproached me for it for months. If she could not understand my dilemma, I can, of course, expect even less understanding from you and your wife. I can only ask for your forgiveness. I regret very much the loss of your friendship as a result of this stupid affair.

Nevertheless I would like to entrust you with an important matter, and seek your advice on it.

I have succeeded in securing a large part of Hitler's property – extremely interesting notes, watercolours and oil paintings executed in his own hand; the pistol with which the Führer killed himself in the bunker (a handwritten letter from Bormann guarantees it); crates with documents from the Reich Chancellery; and, above all, the Blood Flag, still in its original case with the memorial plaque to the fallen of 1923. In my view, these relics of the National Socialist movement should, at the very least, be kept in a safe place by reliable men. You will understand that I do not want to store the flag for too long in Germany: here, the relevant laws and statutes are always getting tighter and tighter and there are frequent house searches for Nazi relics. Perhaps you can advise me where I could place these relics for safety?

In the hope that you will still be prepared to have anything to do with me, I await your answer and will then give you more details about my finds. With best wishes to your wife from my wife and myself;

Yours,
Gerd Heidemann.

There is no record of Barbie's reply.

14

On 1 July Manfred Fischer left Hamburg to take up his new appointment in Guetersloh as managing director of Bertelsmann. He was now in the first rank of European executives, controlling a company with an annual turnover of more than $2 billion. Bertelsmann had expanded so rapidly during the 1970s, growing by as much as 15 per cent a year, that its capital base had become thin; a period of retrenchment was required. Mohn had decided that Fischer was the best man to oversee this new policy: he did so on the basis of Fischer's reputation as a cost cutter. Similarly, to replace Fischer at Gruner and Jahr, Mohn chose another businessman supposedly with an ability to enforce stringent economy.

Gerd Schulte-Hillen was only forty years old. After leaving school he had spent a year in the Bundeswehr, then qualified as an engineer, joining Bertelsmann in 1969. He was promoted rapidly, from assistant manager in Germany, to technical manager of printing plants in Spain and Portugal. He was put in charge of printing for the whole of Gruner and Jahr and built a huge new factory for the group in the United States. Schulte-Hillen's appointment as managing director came as something of a surprise. He was a highly respected technician, but he had little experience of handling journalists, of whom he was felt to be slightly in awe. He was quickly initiated into Gruner and Jahr's great secret. 'I think it was in June 1981,' he recalled, 'that Dr Manfred Fischer swore me to secrecy and then told me that the Hitler diaries were being bought by the company.'

He was soon deeply involved in the operation. On 29 July, Heidemann received 345,000 marks for the next batch of diaries. A week later, on 5 August, he picked up another 220,000 marks. This meant that since January he had removed a total of six suitcases full of cash from the Deutsche Bank, containing 1.81 million marks. There were now eighteen diaries in the management safe.

The next day, Hensmann and Sorge went to see the new managing director in his office. Before any further payments could be made, they explained, Schulte-Hillen had to sign a fresh authorization for the transfer of the company's funds. Without hesitation, he signed a document endorsing Sorge to use another 1 million marks of the company's money. According to Schulte-Hillen:

> Somehow I thought – oh, you don't have to worry too much about that. I was still feeling my way into the job. I said to myself – well, 2 million has already been spent, it must be OK. Fischer himself did it, and now he's on the overall board of the company and is my boss. Who was I to question it? That was a mistake. The next time I was asked to give my approval for the payment of another million, the room for manoeuvre was even smaller.

Manfred Fischer, the man who had initiated the operation, was 150 miles away, grappling with the day-to-day running of a multinational company. Schulte-Hillen, a relatively inexperienced businessman in a new job with little experience of journalism, was merely carrying on what Fischer had started. Hensmann was a weak man. The finance director, Kuehsel, did what he was told. Sorge's objectivity was compromised by his friendship with Thomas Walde. Walde and Heidemann, both expecting to make a fortune when the books were published, were the last men to call a halt to the delivery of the diaries. The editors were sulkily refusing to show much interest in the management's scoop.

The whole project was out of control.

The only person who seemed to be showing any financial sense was Edith Lieblang in Stuttgart. She took charge of the envelopes full of cash which Heidemann was delivering and invested them in bricks and mortar. When it came to money, she said firmly, 'We didn't have "mine" and "yours".' In May the couple bought a new apartment in Wolfschlugen for 235,000 marks, together with a garage for 18,000 marks. In July she paid 230,000 marks for a flat in Schreiberstrasse.

This was on the ground floor of a substantial, heavy masonried, four-storey block, tucked away at the end of a quiet street near the centre of Stuttgart. Schreiberstrasse became Kujau's new shop. He bought a large building at the back for 120,000 marks, installed heavy steel shutters and a security camera to scan the courtyard, and transferred to it his entire collection from Aspergstrasse. He hired a local taxi company to do the removals.

Kujau continued to work on the diaries during the day at home. Edith knew he was supplying Hitler diaries to *Stern* but claimed, somewhat implausibly, that she thought they were genuine: she did not know, she said, what Kujau was up to during the day when she was out working at the Café Hochland. 'I don't know what he did in my absence. I rarely went into his workroom. He used to clean it himself.'

Once he had done the research, it took Kujau, on average, only four and a half hours to forge a complete diary. His favourite source was a weighty, two-volume edition of *Hitler's Speeches and Proclamations 1932–45*, a daily chronology of the Führer's activities, compiled in 1962 by the German historian Max Domarus. Working against the clock to satisfy Heidemann's demand for diaries, Kujau resorted to wholesale plagiarism, copying out page after page from Domarus. The Hitler diaries – the object of one of the most extravagant 'hypes' in the history of journalism – were for the most part nothing more interesting than a tedious recital of official engagements and Nazi Party announcements. Nine-tenths of the material being so carefully hoarded in the Gruner and Jahr safe was unpublishable. These, for example, are the entries for the first seven days of September 1938 – a typically uninspired week in the life of the Führer, as recorded by Konrad Kujau:

1) The Reich Air Defence Federation received its own insignia and flag. The founding of the 'Federation for the unity of Germany and Poland' was today announced by the Polish Prime Minister.
2) Opening of the exhibition 'Great Germany' in Japan (telegram). A youth delegation from Japan is received in Munich by Schirach (telegram). Reception at the Berghof for Henlein. Conference.

4) Admiral Horthy has kept his word. As from today there is compulsory military service in Hungary.

5) Opening of the Party Rally 'Great Germany'. Reception in the Nuremberg town hall.

6) Opening of the Party Congress. Proclamation. Handing over of Reich insignia to the mayor of the town of Nuremberg. A cultural meeting.

7) Call to the Reichs Labour Service. Diplomatic reception in the Hotel Deutscher Hof.

The bulk of the diaries, especially the early ones, consisted of padding of this sort – a technique which reached a pinnacle of improbability in the entry for 19 July 1940, when Hitler was supposed to have devoted five pages to copying out the entire list of senior promotions in the German armed forces following the fall of France.

At the end of each month's entries, Kujau had 'Hitler' write a set of more general notes headed 'Personal'. It was in these sections of the diary, unfettered by chronology and so less vulnerable to checks for accuracy, that Kujau allowed the Führer to think aloud about the state of his affairs. There were occasional revelations: that the burning of the books in May 1933 'was not a good idea of Goebbels''; that some of 'the measures against the Jews were too strong for me'. But overall, the tone remained relentlessly trivial. Health was one recurrent theme: 'My health is poorly – the result of too little sleep' (April 1933); 'I suffer much from sleeplessness and stomach pains' (June 1934); 'My stomach makes it difficult to sleep, my left leg is often numb' (July 1934). Eva Braun was another regular source of concern: 'Although I have become Reichs Chancellor, I have not forgotten E's birthday' (January 1933); 'She is the sporty type – it has helped her very much to be in the fresh air' (October 1934). Occasionally, as in June 1941, these twin preoccupations met: 'On Eva's wishes, I am thoroughly examined by my doctors. Because of the new pills, I have violent flatulence, and – says Eva – bad breath.' It was for material of this sort that *Stern* was to end up paying roughly £50 per word.

Kujau turned out the diaries so quickly that he had soon exhausted the stock of school notebooks in his cellar. In the summer of 1981 he flew to West Berlin, crossed into the East, and in a taxi travelled from shop to shop, buying up the old-fashioned, black-bound volumes. He returned home the same day bearing twenty-two of them. The whole lot cost him 77 marks.

Shortly afterwards Kujau passed on to Heidemann some wonderful news from his brother in East Germany. Contrary to their initial estimate, it now appeared that there were more than twenty-seven diaries. The haul of Hitler writings salvaged from the Boernersdorf crash was much larger than had been thought.

Heidemann returned to Hamburg to tell Gruner and Jahr of this latest development.

On 23 August, less than two and a half weeks after he had been asked to authorize payment of 1 million marks, Schulte-Hillen had to sanction a second transfer of money, this time of 600,000 marks. Heidemann reported that the price of the diaries had shot up to 200,000 marks each. The East German general, he said, was now having to pay money to members of the Communist government as well as to other corrupt officials. The company once again felt that it had no option but to pay up. Indeed, perversely, the price rise increased the company's confidence that the diaries were genuine. 'We weren't surprised,' said one of the managers later. 'In fact, we expected it. Once you've bought part of a collection, you naturally want the rest. It's worth that much more to you. The seller knows that and takes advantage of it. It's normal commercial practice.'

Schulte-Hillen was hopelessly out of his depth. Every so often, Heidemann would come into his office, escorted by Sorge, and read extracts from the latest diaries out loud to him. The banality of the content meant nothing to the technically minded managing director. 'I didn't concern myself with the question of whether they were sensational or not. That wasn't my affair.' For Schulte-Hillen, struggling to read himself into his new job, the diaries were an exotic project bequeathed to him by his predecessor. 'I didn't really worry about the details,' he confessed. 'Sorge and Walde were Heidemann's principal points of reference.'

Heidemann now began fantasizing about his role as middleman between *Stern* and the diaries' supplier. Simply flying down to Stuttgart, handing over the money and picking up the diaries did not accord with his vision of himself as a sleuth reporter. He decided to glamorize the story. 'I remember a very hot day in the summer,' said Walde later. 'Gerd Heidemann arrived in the office in a blue suit looking unusually worked-up.' According to Heidemann, the lorry driver who used to bring the diaries out of East Germany had been replaced. Heidemann said he was now having to drive into the East himself and smuggle the documents illegally over the border. 'The whole thing seemed very dangerous to him,' said Walde. 'He didn't know what to do when he got to the frontier. He just put the envelope containing the diary under the car's mat.'

For the benefit of Schulte-Hillen, Heidemann further elaborated on the story. He told the managing director that he would drive down the autobahn to Berlin. At an agreed point on the journey, another car would draw alongside him with its passenger window open. With both cars travelling at the same speed, Heidemann would toss the packet of money through the open window. The vehicles would then exchange positions and the driver of the other car would throw him the diaries. The managing director had never heard anything like it. He told Heidemann he was 'crazy': 'I said he shouldn't do it, especially in view of his family responsibilities.' 'Don't worry,' Schulte-Hillen remembers Heidemann telling him, 'I'll do it.'

Despite his misgivings for Heidemann's safety, Schulte-Hillen was impressed, and now treated the reporter with even greater respect. He would not hear a word said against him. He would rebuke anyone who expressed doubts about Heidemann's heroism: 'When a colleague puts himself in personal danger in order to obtain things,' he used to say, 'he should be entitled to the trust of others.' When Heidemann complained to Sorge that his own car was too dilapidated for this kind of work and that he was having to use Gina's, Schulte-Hillen arranged for him to be given a brand new company Mercedes.

In fact, Gruner and Jahr had a strong motive for believing Heidemann's story. If they could swear on oath that the money for the diaries had been paid outside West Germany, they would enjoy substantial tax concessions. In November, there was a month-long series of negotiations to provide Heidemann with a special life insurance policy at Gruner and Jahr's expense. Heidemann insisted on a clause providing for the payment of ransom money in case they should have to buy him out of an East German jail. In the event of his death, his share in the profits from Hitler's diaries was to be given to his heirs. Heidemann joked that this generous policy might induce his wife to 'separation, Italian style'. This farce carried on until the first week of December, when Heidemann announced that the piano shipments had resumed.

Around this time Heidemann also complained to Schulte-Hillen that he had not received a salary increase for several years. He hinted that he might be forced to leave the company unless something was done. The managing director immediately called in Peter Koch, Felix Schmidt and Rolf Gillhausen and instructed them, in Koch's words, 'to take better care of Heidemann, to motivate him more'. The editors had not recommended Heidemann for a rise because they had not thought his work merited one. Now, under pressure, they once again started paying him regular annual increments. Schmidt was also told by Schulte-Hillen to give Heidemann a special bonus payment of 20,000 marks. 'The man needs recognition,' Schulte-Hillen told him, 'and he needs to be treated with special care.' Schmidt gritted his teeth and arranged this reward for the reporter who had spent a whole year deceiving his editors. '*Recognition . . . special care. . .*' 'These words of the management,' said Schmidt two years later, 'still ring in my ears.'

Heidemann's fiftieth birthday coincided with a call from Kujau to tell him that more diaries were ready for collection. Heidemann decided to take Gina down to Stuttgart with him and the couple spent the evening of 3 December having a celebration dinner with Kujau and Edith in the local Holiday Inn, close to the Munich motorway exit. It was the first time all four of them had been together. They got on well; Gina particularly liked Edith – 'a very nice lady,' she called her, 'very bourgeois'. There was champagne, and at midnight the gregarious 'Dr Fischer' led them in the singing of 'Happy Birthday'. Amid warm embraces, Gina presented her husband with a solid gold Rolex watch.

It had been a good year for the couple. Heidemann had at last found the recognition he craved so desperately. Soon he would be able to present the world with his magnificent story and he and Gina would be wealthy for life. The Heidemanns beamed at Kujau, the source of their good fortune. 'We owe you so much,' said Gina. Kujau grinned.

15

The New Year of 1982 witnessed further large withdrawals of cash from the Adolphsplatz bank by Gerd Heidemann: 400,000 marks on 14 January; 200,000 on 27 January; 200,000 on 17 February. On 1 March, after picking up another 400,000 marks, he and Walde were taken out to dine at Hamburg's Coelln Oyster Restaurant by Gerd Schulte-Hillen.

According to Walde, the purpose of the meal was for Schulte-Hillen 'to show some recognition to Heidemann and to get to know me better'. Between mouthfuls of oysters, the three men discussed the Hitler diaries. There were already more than two dozen volumes in the management safe. There seemed no sign of an end to the stream of books emanating from behind the Iron Curtain. Even so, the time was approaching when decisions would have to be taken about the form of publication. Obviously there would be those who would seek to denigrate *Stern*'s scoop. Some form of independent authentication would have to be obtained – not because there were any doubts about the material in the management's mind, merely to ensure there was a weapon available with which critics could be silenced.

Walde had already made contact with West Germany's two main police organizations, the *Bundeskriminalamt* (BKA) and the *Zollkriminalinstitut*. Without mentioning the Hitler diaries specifically, he asked them in general terms what sort of tests had to be done to determine the age of documents and the authenticity of handwriting; who could do such tests; how much they might cost; what materials the experts would require for testing. 'Because neither of these two authorities does work for private individuals, I tried to arrange for people who work there to do tests for us in a private capacity.' He had then rung the Institute of Contemporary History in Munich and the Federal Archives – the Bundesarchiv – in Koblenz, to make arrangements to collect copies of Hitler's handwriting; this could then be sent to the experts for comparison with *Stern*'s material. It should be possible to organize such tests within the next few weeks.

Assuming, as they all did, that the Hitler diaries would quickly pass through the formality of authentication, Walde, Heidemann and Schulte-Hillen discussed how the books might be marketed. Their discovery was a scoop, but their content, it had to be admitted, was meagre. Each diary contained an average of only 1000 words. Added together, Gruner and Jahr's two dozen volumes scarcely added up to a couple of chapters, never mind a book. The three men agreed that the material could not be printed as it stood. It would have to be 'journalistically worked on', setting quotations from the diary in their historical context. This would have to be done whilst the diaries were still arriving, in complete secrecy and without outside help – an enormous undertaking, especially since neither Heidemann nor Walde was a qualified historian.

Two days after the meeting with Schulte-Hillen, on Wednesday 3 March, Walde and Wilfried Sorge were invited round for the evening to Heidemann's flat. The reporter wanted them to meet an important contact of his who could provide *Stern* with important Nazi documents. According to Sorge, Heidemann said 'he needed our presence if he was to appear to be negotiating seriously on *Stern*'s behalf'. That night in the elegant Elbchaussee apartment they were confronted by a seedy and furtive character in his mid-fifties, whom Heidemann introduced as Medard Klapper.

Medardus Leopold Karl Klapper exerted a hold over Heidemann similar to that exercised by Konrad Kujau. He spun large and elaborate fantasies about the Third Reich in which Heidemann believed and in which he invested large sums of *Stern*'s money. Klapper claimed to have joined the SS in 1944 at the age of seventeen and to have been one of Hitler's bodyguards in the final days of the war. He was now an arms dealer in Karlsruhe in southern Germany. Apart from the Nazis,

Klapper's other obsession was with cowboys and Indians: his shop in Karlsruhe, called The General Gun Store, was designed to look as if it belonged in the American wild west. Heidemann had made his acquaintance in 1971 when he was working on crime stories for *Stern*. Klapper was a police informer. Like Kujau, Klapper dealt in Nazi memorabilia and occasionally ran a stall selling militaria in the Flea Market in Konstanz. When Heidemann was short of money in the late 1970s Klapper had sold a few Goering mementoes on his behalf: a French collector bought a silver cigarette case and some silver picture frames for 20,000 francs.

Klapper's speciality was buried Nazi treasure. He promised Heidemann he could lead him to a hoard of enormous value. It would not only provide the reporter with a great story for *Stern*, it would also make him rich. On 19 August 1981 – shortly after the collapse of his attempts to buy Hitler's childhood home – Heidemann opened up his suitcase to Klapper, paying him 25,000 marks in cash. 'He said he now had money "like it was growing on trees",' recalled Klapper. 'He showed me his pocket which was stuffed with 1000-mark notes.' In return for the money, Klapper provided Heidemann with a photocopy of a map, purporting to show the whereabouts of 450 kilos of gold and platinum, dumped by the Nazis at the end of the war in the Stolpsee, a lake in East Germany. A few weeks later, Heidemann signed an agreement with some East German representatives. He put up an undisclosed amount of money in return for which the East Germans promised to provide the manpower to search the Stolpsee; the proceeds would be split fifty-fifty. Eventually forty engineers from the East German army equipped with tons of dredging machinery were involved in searching the lake; all they sucked out of the water, Heidemann later complained to Klapper, was 350 cubic metres of mud.

Undeterred, Heidemann continued to believe the arms dealer's stories. Confiscated receipts suggest that over the next eighteen months he paid him almost 450,000 marks. In particular, he believed the gun salesman's claim that Martin Bormann was still alive: this story, after all, accorded with his own, earlier obsession of 1979. Klapper played on Heidemann's gullibility, assuring him that eventually he would take him to 'Martin'. According to him, Bormann led a nomadic existence, shuttling between hideouts in Argentina, Paraguay, Spain, Egypt and Zurich (where he was being watched by the Israeli secret service). Klapper told Heidemann that if he was willing to undergo a secret ceremony called a '*Sippung*', he would be admitted to Martin's inner circle. As far as Heidemann was concerned, Klapper was clearly a very important individual indeed, which was why he wanted to introduce him to Herr Walde and Herr Sorge, his colleagues from *Stern*.

Klapper was more restrained in his storytelling when there were others present than he was when he had Heidemann on his own. He told Sorge and Walde that Bormann had set up a secret Nazi archive in Madrid, administered by a Spanish lawyer named Dr Iquisabel. Among other things, these documents allegedly proved that the Germans had built three atomic bombs by the end of the war. These documents could be made available to *Stern*, free of charge, provided the magazine agreed to deal with the material 'objectively'. Walde and Heidemann signed a contract promising to abide by this undertaking and in return Klapper pledged to deliver the documents from 'Dr Iquisabel' by the end of the month.

Needless to say, nothing came of this agreement. But Klapper maintained contact with Heidemann and the reporter continued to believe his stories: for example, that he had met Bormann and Josef Mengele at Madrid airport and that Bormann lived in a big house with a garden and a car park in Zurich. Heidemann gradually became certain that through Klapper he was talking to Bormann, and that 'Martin' had chosen him to be his intermediary with the outside world. This fantasy became inextricably linked in Heidemann's mind with the discovery of the Hitler diaries until, by April 1983, when *Stern* eventually launched its scoop, Heidemann confidently believed that Bormann himself would appear at the magazine's press conference to authenticate them.

While Heidemann pursued these shadows from the Third Reich, Thomas Walde organized the submission of the diaries for expert analysis.

This should have been the moment at which Kujau's fraud was exposed. The forger, after all, had failed to take even the most rudimentary precautions. The diaries were written in ordinary school notebooks stained with tea. The initials on the front of at least one volume were made of plastic. The labels, signed by Bormann and Hess, stating that the books were 'the property of the Führer' were supposed to span thirteen years but were all typed on the same machine. The diaries' pages were made of paper manufactured after 1945. The binding, glue and thread which held them together all contained chemicals which proved them to be postwar. The entries themselves, dashed off by a man with no academic training, were pitted with inaccuracies. The ink in which they were written was bought from an ordinary artists' shop. Logically, the Hitler diaries hoax should have collapsed in the spring of 1982, the moment the experts started work. Instead, Kujau was once again saved from exposure by the behaviour of his victims.

Inside *Stern*, the idea that the diaries might be forgeries was unthinkable. The project had been allowed to reach a stage where cancellation would ruin careers and cost millions of marks; successful completion, on the other hand, would bring the participants enormous financial and professional rewards. From the start the *Stern* men had been prepared to suspend disbelief, to have faith that the books were genuine. Now, subconsciously, their minds had become closed to any other possibility. All of them, from Manfred Fischer and Gerd Schulte-Hillen downwards, had a vested interest in the diaries passing the experts' scrutiny as great as Konrad Kujau's: the trickster and his dupes were on the same side.

If *Stern* had been properly sceptical, the magazine would have commissioned a thorough forensic examination of a complete diary volume. Instead, they concentrated on securing the bare minimum of authentication felt necessary to satisfy the rest of the world. The process, consequently, was flawed from the start.

'The security precautions surrounding the authentication had to be very tight,' recalled Walde. 'We had to prevent word leaking out and jeopardizing the life of "Fischer's" brother in East Germany.' It was considered too risky to part with an entire book. A single page was cut out of the special volume devoted to the flight of Rudolf Hess which had been delivered to *Stern* the previous November. The page consisted of a draft, supposedly in Hitler's hand, of the Nazi Party's official announcement of Hess's flight to Scotland. This tiny sample was considered sufficient to determine the authenticity of the entire hoard of diaries. The text of the Hess statement was selected for analysis because it was already well known; the diary page on which it was copied out was to be passed off simply as a hitherto undiscovered Hitler document, part of a larger find which the magazine wanted checked. None of the experts was told that what they were actually authenticating were Hitler's diaries. This duplicity on *Stern*'s part, the product of its anxiety to safeguard its scoop, was to lead it to disaster.

On Monday 5 April, Heidemann and Walde visited the Bundesarchiv in Koblenz to meet two of the archive's senior officials, Dr Josef Henke and Dr Klaus Oldenhage. They gave them what purported to be a handwritten draft by Hitler of a New Year greetings telegram, dated 1 January 1940, addressed to General Franco: this was one of the documents Kujau had supplied to Heidemann along with the diaries. The two journalists told the archivists that it was one of a set of documents which *Stern* believed it could obtain from sources outside the Federal Republic. In return for an assurance that after *Stern* had finished with it the material would eventually be donated to the Bundesarchiv, Dr Henke agreed to submit the telegram to the West German police for an official handwriting and forensic analysis. The following day, Walde sent the archivists two further original documents: a speech draft dated 29 December 1934 and a letter to Hermann Goering dated 17 October 1940. These too were drawn from the archive accompanying the diaries. In a covering note, Walde stressed the need for secrecy:

> Once again we ask you to treat the enclosed documents with absolute discretion and not to reveal the source. Your report should be completed as soon as possible in order to enable us to secure the other material should it prove genuine. Otherwise, we must assume that the documents which are still abroad will be sold to collectors in the United States.

Only on 7 April, in a postscript to his letter, did Walde announce that 'Herr Heidemann and I have decided to give you a copy of a further document'. *This* was the Hess statement, slipped in casually among the other papers, with no suggestion that it had been cut out of a diary. Two weeks later, on 21 April, the Bundesarchiv sent all the *Stern* documents (three originals and one photocopy) to the regional police headquarters in Rhineland-Pfalz for a handwriting analysis. For comparison purposes, they enclosed five authentic examples of Hitler writing from their own archives. They would have to wait a month for the results.

Walde, meanwhile, had embarked on a 7000-mile round trip to commission additional experts to give their opinions. On Tuesday 13 April, accompanied by Wilfried Sorge, he flew to Switzerland to see Dr Max Frei-Sulzer, former head of the forensic department of the Zurich police. Frei-Sulzer was living in retirement in the small lakeside town of Thalwil, but was always willing to undertake freelance work. According to Walde, he advised them not to bother with a paper test: 'With today's technology it is possible to make paper look any age you choose.' He agreed to conduct a handwriting analysis. Walde, swearing him to secrecy, provided him with two photocopies of documents from the *Stern* hoard: the Hess statement and a draft telegram to the Hungarian ruler, Admiral Horthy. As comparison material, Frei-Sulzer was supplied with the same copies of authentic Hitler writing that the Bundesarchiv had given to the Rhineland-Pfalz police. A third set of documents for comparison was provided by Gerd Heidemann from his private collection: a paper from 1943 recording the promotion of General Ewald von Kleist to the rank of Field Marshal, along with three signed Hitler photographs. Unfortunately for Frei-Sulzer, these supposedly genuine examples of the Führer's writings were also the work of Konrad Kujau, a confusion which meant that the scientist in some instances would be comparing Kujau's hand with Kujau's, rather than with Hitler's.

The following day, leaving Frei-Sulzer to begin his examination, Walde and Sorge flew from Switzerland to the United States to see a second freelance expert. They spent the night of 15 April in the Hyatt Hotel in Greenville, South Carolina, and early the following morning headed off to their final destination: the town of Landrum, an hour's drive to the north.

Ordway Hilton, like Max Frei-Sulzer, was an elderly man, living in retirement, happy to undertake freelance work. He had been employed by the New York Police Department for almost thirty years and was a distinguished member of his own particular fraternity – a contributor to the proceedings of the American Board of Forensic Document Examiners, the American Academy of Forensic Science and the American Society of Questioned Document Examiners. Hilton now operated from his house in Landrum to which, at 10 a.m. on Friday 16 April, he welcomed his two visitors from Germany.

The American was handed the originals of the two documents copied for Frei-Sulzer: the page from the Hess volume and the telegram for Horthy, together with an accompanying folder of 'authentic' Hitler writing for comparison, part of which was genuine and part from Heidemann's collection of forgeries. 'Some bore signatures that were his or that they told me were his,' he later recalled. 'Some were photocopies they said came from their archives.' Hilton promised to keep their visit secret and to deliver his verdict as quickly as possible.

Walde and Sorge began the long journey back to Hamburg unaware that the only result of their four-day mission was to botch one of *Stern*'s last chances of avoiding catastrophe. If only they had taken the Hess page to a practising forensic expert – for example, Dr Julius Grant, a freelance consultant based in London – they would have discovered within five hours that it contained chemicals of postwar origin and therefore had to be forged. But in their ignorance they chose to depend on the much less reliable and slower process of handwriting analysis. They compounded this error by selecting as experts two men unsuited to the task. True, Frei-Sulzer and Hilton both had international reputations – they were chosen because it was felt their approval would be an advantage in syndication negotiations in Europe and America. But Frei-Sulzer's speciality was investigating biological microtraces, not handwriting; and Ordway Hilton was handicapped by the fact that he could not even understand the language in which the diaries were written. Neither man was a specialist in Nazi documents. In 1983, an expert who was – Charles Hamilton, a New York autograph dealer – estimated that on the American market only Abraham Lincoln's signature commands a greater price than Hitler's. A page of the Führer's writing might fetch $15,000 and no man's autograph is more commonly forged: Hamilton reckoned to see a dozen forgeries a year. If Hilton and Frei-Sulzer had been aware of the extent of the market in Hitler fakes they might have been more suspicious of the gentlemen from Hamburg. And as if all this were not enough, Walde and Sorge had crowned the confusion by unwittingly introducing forgeries from Heidemann's collection into the process of authentication.

Little suspecting the potential for chaos they had left behind them, the two Germans returned to Hamburg. They remained supremely confident that within a month they would have proof that the diaries were genuine. Once that was in their hands, plans could at last be drawn up for publication.

16

At the same time as Walde and Sorge were landing in Hamburg, August Priesack and Billy F. Price arrived in London. They made an odd couple: the impoverished, white-haired Nazi 'professor', and the rich, barrel-chested, aggressive Texan, drawn together by a shared obsession for the paintings of Adolf Hitler.

When Price was not in Europe, searching salerooms and private collections for Hitler's art, he could generally be found in his native city of Houston, pounding round the artificial-grass running track in the grounds of the Houstonian Country Club, or driving across his farm taking pot shots at squirrels with a Magnum from his convertible Cadillac El Dorado, 'custom built for Mr Billy F. Price'. ('Did you give them your design?' 'Hell no, boy, I gave them my cheque.')

At first sight, Price seems a bizarre figure, but he is not unique. It has been estimated that there are 50,000 collectors of Nazi memorabilia throughout the world, of whom most are Americans, involved in a business which is said to have an annual turnover of $50 million. In the United States a monthly newsletter, *Der Gauleiter*, published from Mount Ida in Arkansas, keeps 5000 serious connoisseurs and dealers informed of the latest trade shows and auctions. Prices increase by 20 per cent a year. 'In the States,' according to Charles Hamilton, 'the collectors of Hitler memorabilia are 40 per cent Jewish, 50 per cent old soldiers like me and 10 per cent of them are young, fascinated by people like Rudel,' In Los Angeles, a collector enjoys himself in private by donning Ribbentrop's overcoat. In Kansas City, a local government official serves drinks from Hitler's punch bowl. In Chicago, a family doctor has installed a reinforced concrete vault beneath his house where he keeps a collection of Nazi weapons, including Hermann Goering's ceremonial, jewel-encrusted hunting dagger. In Arizona, a used-car salesman drives his family around in the 1938 Mercedes which Hitler presented to Eva Braun; it cost him $150,000 to buy and he expects to sell it for $350,000.

In 1982 Billy Price was fifty-two and a multi-millionaire. ('Hell, if you can't become a millionaire in Houston, you're an asshole, boy.') His money was derived from his ownership of the Price Compressor Company Incorporated, manufacturers of nine-tenths of all compressors used in undersea oil exploration. Like Fritz Stiefel – whom he had met in Stuttgart – Price was a wealthy engineer, no scholar, whose success had given him the means to indulge his interest in Adolf Hitler. He had first become fascinated by the Nazis in the 1950s during his service with the US Army in Germany. While he was stationed in Europe he sought out former Nazis and witnesses from the Third Reich, including Rommel's widow. In the early 1970s, having made his fortune, he returned to begin buying memorabilia, particularly Hitler paintings, paying between $2000 and $12,000 for each one.

Hitler seems to hold a special interest for businessmen, particularly when – as in the case of Billy Price and Fritz Stiefel – they are self-made men. Hitler's career represented the most extreme, as well as the most monstrous, example of what an individual can do if he dedicates himself to the exertion of his will. 'People say Hitler couldn't have kept diaries,' said Price after the forgery had been exposed. 'They say he couldn't have done this, he couldn't have done that – shit, Hitler could paint paintings, he could write operas. Hell, he controlled more real estate than the Roman Empire within three years. There's nothing Hitler couldn't have done if he set his mind to it.' The years of Hitler's 'Triumph of the Will' coincided with the years when the philosophy of self-help was at its height – the Depression was an era of personal improvement courses and guides to success which culminated in 1938 with the appearance of Dale Carnegie's *How to Win Friends and Influence People*. Everything was possible, given the drive to achieve it. 'A man is not what he thinks he is,' wrote the American clergyman Norman Vincent Peale, 'but what he *thinks* he is.' 'My whole life,' said Hitler in 1942, 'can be summed up as this ceaseless effort of mine to persuade other people.' With his studied mannerisms, his cultivated habit of staring into people's eyes, his hunger to read manuals and absorb technical data, Hitler was self-help run riot. 'I look at that picture,' said Price, staring at one of his Hitler paintings, of flowers in a vase, 'and I just can't imagine *what was going through the man's mind when he did it.*'

The gates to Price's farm are thirty feet high and topped by stone eagles – scale replicas of a set of gates designed for Hitler by Albert Speer. Beyond them, on the lawn outside his house, stand a tank and a piece of field artillery. The bulk of his collection is housed in his company's headquarters close to Houston's Hobby Airport. On one wall is a portrait of Rudolf Hess in Nazi uniform. In the lavatory is a painting of Hitler. In glass frames are a few small souvenirs – the bill of sale for the first automobile Hitler bought for the Nazi Party; a laundry note in Hitler's handwriting; a letter, on prison stationery, from Goering to his wife at the time of the Nuremberg trial; and a letter from Goering to Field Marshal Milch. On a side table stands a large picture of Goering in a swastika-decorated silver frame. Next to it is a heavy, vulgar birthday card sent by Hitler to SS General Sepp Dietrich. There are busts of Hitler. There are two of Hitler's wartime photograph albums – silver-bound with SS flashes and swastikas in the corners and a large eagle on the cover; as one opens a bookplate flutters to the floor: *'Ex Libris Adolf Hitler'*. An ornate cabinet houses Hitler's cutlery and napkins. Price likes showing off his souvenirs but is anxious not to offend visitors. 'I do a lot of business with Jews,' he says. 'When Jews come I put it all away.'

The pride of Price's collection, the fruit of a decade's labour, takes up an entire wall at the end of his conference room: thirty-three Hitler paintings, insured for more than $4 million, arranged in an illuminated display behind armour-plated glass, protected by a sophisticated array of burglar alarms. The pictures are lifeless and uninspired: clumsy landscapes, fussy reproductions of Viennese buildings, a couple of paintings of flowers, two crude architectural sketches, scrawled in pencil, bought by Price from Albert Speer. The Texan's favourite is a watercolour of the Vienna City Hall, completed in 1911. 'Most knowledgeable people say he was not the best artist in the world, but I think he was certainly a good artist considering the amount of training he had.' Price claims to have bought the paintings 'in the interests of history': one day, he thinks, given current advances in technology, 'it might be possible to feed them into a computer to get a read-out on Hitler's brain'.

Price's dream, for the sake of which he had gone into partnership with August Priesack, was to track down every extant Hitler painting and drawing in order to catalogue them in a book which he would publish himself. Price had no personal liking for his companion: it was a relationship founded on necessity. 'Sure, I know Priesack's a Nazi. But if you want to know about Hitler, you have to hire Nazis. Hell, if I was going to investigate cancer, you wouldn't start saying to me, "Why are you hanging around all those cancer victims?" would you?' Together the two men had done the rounds of the private collectors in America and Germany. It was this mission which in the spring of 1982 brought them to Britain.

In the final week of April they drove down to the West Country, to Longleat, one of the finest stately homes in England, ancestral seat of Sir Henry Frederick Thynne, sixth Marquess of Bath. Lord Bath, seventy-seven years old and deaf in one ear, but otherwise remarkably sprightly, took them up in his ancient lift to the third floor, a part of the house closed to the public. He unlocked a door next to the library and led Price and Priesack into a long, narrow room, cluttered with Nazi memorabilia. Dominating the scene at the far end was a life-size wax model of Hitler wearing a black leather overcoat and a swastika armband. But neither this, nor Himmler's spectacles, nor the Commandant of Belsen's tablecloth interested Price. What he had come to see was Lord Bath's private exhibition of Hitler paintings. It ran all along one wall, the finest collection in the world: sixty paintings – worth, in Price's opinion, $10 million.

A few days later, back in London, on the afternoon of Thursday 22 April, August Priesack telephoned David Irving in his flat in Duke Street, Mayfair. Priesack explained why he and Price were in Britain and asked him if he would like to come round to their hotel for dinner that night. Irving agreed.

Priesack had been looking forward to meeting the British historian for a long time. Of all Hitler's biographers, Irving was the most controversial. In *Hitler's War*, published in 1977, he had quoted one of the Führer's doctors, who described how Hitler had expressed his admiration for an 'objective' biography of the Kaiser written by an Englishman. According to the doctor:

> Hitler then said that for some time now he had gone over to having all important discussions and military conferences recorded for posterity by shorthand writers. And perhaps one day after he is dead and buried an objective Englishman will come and give him the same kind of treatment. The present generation neither can nor will.

Irving was in no doubt that he was the man the Führer had in mind. *Hitler's War*, ten years in the making, had been based on a wealth of previously unpublished documents, letters and diaries. Irving's aim was to rewrite the history of the war 'as far as possible through Hitler's eyes, from behind his desk'. This made for a gripping book, but one which was, by its nature, unbalanced. However 'objectively' he might piece together the unpublished recollections of Hitler's subordinates, they were still the words of men and women who admired their ruler. And confined to Hitler's daily routine, the biography had a curiously unreal quality: the death camps, the atrocities, the sufferings of millions of people which were the result of Hitler's war were not to be found in *Hitler's War* as it was reconstructed by David Irving.

Irving's stated purpose was to portray Hitler as an ordinary human being rather than as a diabolical figure of monstrous evil. It was an aim which was bound to arouse offence: 'If you think of him as a man,' says one of the Jewish characters in George Steiner's *The Portage to San Cristobal of A.H.*, 'you will grow uncertain. You will think him a man and no longer believe what he did.' Irving pilloried earlier biographers who had depicted Hitler as a demon: 'Confronted by the phenomenon of Hitler himself, they cannot grasp that he was an ordinary, walking, talking human weighing some 155 pounds, with greying hair, largely false teeth, and chronic digestive ailments. He is to them the Devil incarnate.' Central to Irving's thesis 'that Hitler was a less than omnipotent Führer' was his argument that Hitler did not order, indeed did not even know of, the Holocaust. It was an assertion which provoked uproar. In Germany, after a dispute with his publishers, the book was withdrawn from sale. In Britain, he became involved in a furious row with a panel of academics during a live edition of David Frost's television chat show. In America, the book was savaged by Walter Laqueur in the *New York Review of Books* and boycotted by the major US paperback publishers. Irving revelled in the publicity, aggressively offering to pay $1000 to anyone who could produce a document proving that Hitler was aware of what was happening in the extermination camps. He claimed that the book upset Jews only 'because I have detracted from the romance of the notion of the Holocaust – that six million people were killed by one man'.

Irving admitted that in writing *Hitler's War* he had 'identified' with the Führer. Looking down upon him as he worked, from the wall above his desk, was a self-portrait of Hitler, presented to him by Christa Schroeder. He did not smoke or touch alcohol. ('I don't drink,' he would say. 'Adolf didn't drink you know.') He shared Hitler's view of women, believing that they were put on the earth in order to procreate and provide men with something to look at: 'They haven't got the physical capacity for producing something creative.' He had married and had four daughters, but wished he had remained single: his marriage had been 'my one cardinal mistake . . . an unnecessary deviation'. In 1981, at the age of forty-three, he had founded his own right-wing political group, built around his own belief in his 'destiny' as a future British leader. With his black hair slanting across his forehead, and a dark cleft, shadowed like a moustache between the bottom of his nose and the top of his upper lip, there were times, in the right light, when Irving looked alarmingly like the subject of his notorious biography.

When Priesack rang he was hard at work on his latest project: a vastly detailed account of Churchill's war years, designed to prove his contention that Britain's decision to go to war with Nazi Germany had been a disastrous mistake. But by 1982, though Irving still had his smart home and his Rolls-Royce he was going through a hard time. He was in the middle of a rancorous and expensive divorce. He was short of money, and smarting from the reception given to his last two books – one of which, *Uprising*, had been dismissed by a reviewer in the *Observer* as 'a bucketful of slime'.

Irving arrived for dinner at the Royal Lancaster Hotel, overlooking Hyde Park, at 9.45 p.m. Billy Price and his wife were unable to join them, so he and Priesack dined alone. Priesack told Irving that he was in difficulties and needed his help. In October of the previous year he had at last brought out his book of unpublished pictures of the Nuremberg rallies. But on 27 November, the Bavarian authorities had decreed that the book contravened anti-Nazi legislation. They ordered that every one of the 5000 copies printed should be confiscated. 'The printers and every bookshop in Germany were raided in a dawn swoop,' noted Irving in his diary. 'On 31 December the order was revoked and the books were returned. On 11 January this year the whole silly confiscation procedure was repeated.' Priesack asked Irving if he would be willing to appear as a character witness at his forthcoming trial. Irving agreed. 'It is difficult,' he wrote, 'to distinguish between these practices and the book burnings of the thirties.'

But sympathetic as he was to Priesack's problems, it was another of the 'professor's' stories which most interested Irving that night:

He is in touch [he wrote in his diary] with a mystery man in Stuttgart whose brother is a major general in the East German People's Army and about to retire to take over a military museum in Germany.

They have a nice racket going: Stuttgart man has acquired from his East German sources loads of Hitler memorabilia, for cash. These include the Führer's *Ahnenpass* [proof of ancestry], bound in green leather, and revealing that his paternal great-grandfather was identical with his maternal grandfather, 27 half-annual volumes of Hitler's diary, tooled in silver, including a reference to the 1934 Night of the Long Knives ('I have dealt with the traitorous swine'), oil and watercolour paintings by Hitler, medals, photographs, letters, etc. In return for this, 'hard' West German currency, Saxon and Thuringian medals have been bought for the military collection in East Germany.

Problem is that the Bavarian state might try to seize this hoard if they knew where in the Federal Republic it is now located, as they have laid claim to all Hitler's properties by means of a spurious postwar ruling setting aside the personal testament signed and witnessed in the Berlin bunker. Therefore nobody on our side is saying where this Stuttgart man is, or who.

Irving was always interested in documents. Documents were the life-blood of his career. Probably no other historian in the world had spent as long as he had trawling through the wartime archives in Europe and America. He had tried to track down Eva Braun's diary in New Mexico. He had spent weeks fruitlessly searching an East German forest with a proton-magnetometer, trying to find the glass jar containing the final entries in Goebbels's diaries. Over the past twenty years, like the Zero Mostel character in *The Producers* with his constant trips into 'little old lady land', Irving had visited countless lonely old widows in small German towns, perched on countless sofas drinking cups of tea, made hours of polite conversation, waiting for the moment when they would invite him to look at 'a few pieces of paper my husband left behind'. In this way he obtained a mass of new material, including the diaries of Walther Hewel, Ribbentrop's liaison officer on Hitler's staff, and the unpublished memoirs of Field Marshal Richthofen. Priesack's story of the 'mystery man in Stuttgart' naturally intrigued him, and when he returned home to Duke Street that night he made a careful note of the conversation. He decided that when he was next in Germany he would make a few inquiries about these 'Hitler diaries'.

17

Spread before him in his office in South Carolina, Ordway Hilton had nine samples of writing for analysis. His task was to determine whether two of them – the Hess document and the Horthy telegram – were genuine. The other seven pieces of material were supposedly authentic 'standards' which he understood had been 'identified as being in the handwriting of Adolf Hitler'. There were three photocopies from the Bundesarchiv: a short postscript signed 'Adolf H' at the end of a typewritten letter dated 1933; a handwritten letter to a party official dated 1936; and copies of eleven Hitler signatures, also from 1936. The other four samples were originals from Heidemann's collection: a handwritten note recording the promotion of General von Kleist dated February 1943 ('In the name of the German people as Reichs Chancellor and Supreme Commander, I award Colonel-General Ewald von Kleist the rank, dignity and protection of a Field Marshal of the German Reich . . . '); and three signed photographs showing, respectively, Hitler with Goering, Schaub and Bormann, Hitler with Konstantin Hierl, leader of the Reich Labour Service, in May 1940, and Hitler standing with a group in front of the Eiffel Tower in Paris after the fall of France.

Hilton quickly noticed a puzzling discrepancy in this comparison material. Using a binocular microscope he could see that in the photocopies, Hitler signed the 'A' in Adolf with a cross-stroke 'slanting downward'. In the originals, this stroke was horizontal. Unfortunately for him and for *Stern*, he did not pay much attention to this seemingly trivial detail: signatures, after all, often vary over the years and the original documents were all dated at least four years after the photocopies.

Three and a half weeks after Walde's and Sorge's visit, on Tuesday 11 May, Hilton completed what he described as 'an extensive examination' of the documents he had been given. His findings were exactly what *Stern* had hoped and expected. The Hess document, he wrote in his report, 'reveals a free, natural form of writing':

> Letters which should have looped enclosures below the line are more commonly a simple long curving stroke. The legibility and details of the single space letters are poor due to the compression of their vertical height. Variable forms are present such as the 't' with a separate cross stroke and with the closing made by a triangular movement at the letter base to connect the cross stroke to the body of the letter.
>
> These same habits are found in the known Hitler writing. . . The lack of lower loop, the flattened single space letters, the variable use of letter forms, and the interruptions in the words especially at points when the letter forms are connected in other instances are all common to both the known and this page of writing under investigation. The combination of all these factors establishes in my opinion adequate proof that this document was written by the same person who prepared all of the known writings. Further there is no evidence within this writing which suggests in any way that this page was prepared by another person in imitation of the writing of Adolf Hitler, and consequently I must conclude that he prepared the document.

After studying the Horthy telegram he reached a similar conclusion. He was particularly impressed by the signature. 'The name Adolf has been condensed to a capital "A" followed by a straight crossed downstroke'; whilst in the signature of the surname:

> The H-form is rotated to the right so that it lies almost horizontal, and the balance of the signature projects downward at a steep angle. This form is typical of the 1940 signatures as can be seen on the photographs and on the von Kleist appointment. Thus all the elements of the signature to the Horthy telegram are consistent with Adolf Hitler's signature and must have been signed by him.

Hilton's report, couched in five pages of professional gobbledegook, was conclusive. But, based as it was on the assumption that all the documents he had been given for comparison were authentic, it was also completely wrong. It was scarcely surprising that the signatures in the Kleist document, the Horthy telegram and the photographs proved 'consistent': they were all forged by Kujau.

At first sight, this mingling of genuine and false material would seem to suggest that Hilton was deliberately misled by the *Stern* men. In fact, neither the police nor *Stern*'s own subsequent internal inquiry found this to be the case. According to the *Stern Report*: 'Heidemann cannot be accused of imposing material on [the experts]. Walde and Sorge asked him for it.' Walde confirmed this. 'Heidemann,' he told the police, 'left the organization of the authentication tests completely to me and Sorge. I have no reason to believe that he wanted to obstruct or twist the authentication of the documents.' The bungling of the tests was the result of straightforward incompetence, typical of the negligence with which the whole diaries affair was handled. Walde and Sorge, in commissioning Hilton, failed to differentiate between documents from the Bundesarchiv and material from Heidemann's collection. And Hilton, working in isolation 3000 miles away, unfamiliar with the script in which the documents were written, did not bother to check.

The American could at least plead in mitigation that his mistake was based on an initial error by *Stern*. The police department of Rhineland-Pfalz had no such excuse.

The police were busy. A routine request from the Bundesarchiv was low on their list of priorities. It was a month before one of their handwriting experts, Herr Huebner, was able to look at the material they had been sent. Huebner had four samples to check: a photocopy of the Hess announcement and originals of a message to General Franco, some speech notes and a letter to Goering. His comparison material, five original Hitler documents from the Bundesarchiv, was unpolluted by Heidemann's fakes. Nevertheless, in a brief report submitted on 25 May, Huebner declared 'with a probability bordering on certainty', that three of the *Stern* documents were genuine. He could not be quite so positive about the Hess communiqué because he had not seen the original, but in his opinion it was 'highly probable' that it was in Hitler's hand.

When this news was relayed to the *Stern* offices in Hamburg, champagne was opened in the history department. The fact that an official government agency had certified that the papers were genuine was an occasion which called for a celebration. There could be no doubt now. The world would have to accept that the magazine had obtained one of the greatest scoops in history. Only Heidemann seemed unaffected by the general jubilation. 'Aren't you pleased?' asked Walde. Heidemann replied that he saw no reason to celebrate: he had known all along that the diaries were genuine.

On 2 June, Walde wrote to Dr Henke at the Bundesarchiv to thank him for sending them the police report. 'Its result greatly pleased us. With the certainty that it has given us, we are going to intensify our efforts to obtain further original material.' Walde added that 'to thank you, and as a gesture to the Bundesarchiv' Gerd Heidemann would like to make them a gift of the originals of Hitler's speech notes and of the Franco telegram.

Nine days later came the third and final handwriting report.

The meticulous Max Frei-Sulzer had been determined not to rush to a premature conclusion. On 4 June, unwilling to make a judgement on the basis of photocopies, he travelled from Zurich to Koblenz where he was met by Dr Henke and shown original Hitler material from the vaults of the Bundesarchiv. After Hilton had finished his report, Frei-Sulzer was given the originals of the Hess statement and the Horthy telegram, along with the photographs and Kleist document from Heidemann's collection. He also received a dossier containing copies of Hitler's writing from 1906 to 1945, pieced together by Heidemann to show how the Führer's writing had changed over the years; and a guide to the old-fashioned script in which the documents were written. By the time he had finished assimilating all this, he had been working on the project for two months and his analysis ran to seventeen pages.

'The script of Adolf Hitler,' wrote Frei-Sulzer, 'is highly individualistic and offers a good basis for the examination of questionable handwriting.' He singled out fourteen special characteristics, analysed the *i*s, the *h*s and the *t*s, the gaps between the letters and the pressure that had been applied to the pen. He made large photographic blow-ups of individual passages, and at the end of it all his conclusion on the Hess communiqué and the Horthy telegram was unequivocal: 'There can be no doubt that both these documents were written by Adolf Hitler.'

What had gone wrong? The police report certainly appears to have been rushed. The Bundesarchiv's request had been treated as relatively trivial in comparison with the police department's real task of dealing with criminals. Their analyst had been provided with only a relatively small sample of handwriting to work on, and in the case of the longest document, the Hess statement, he had only had access to a photocopy. He had no idea that he was putting a seal of approval to what ultimately would be an archive of sixty volumes of Hitler diaries. How was Herr Huebner to know that so much rested on his findings?

Of the two private experts, one was unable to understand the language in which the documents were written; the other was operating outside his specialist field. Both were misled by the introduction of fakes into supposedly genuine Hitler writing.

But even after allowance has been made for all these factors, it has to be said that the success of Konrad Kujau's forgeries casts serious doubts on the 'science' of handwriting analysis – or 'holography' as its practitioners prefer to call it. Freelance analysts are always under pressure to reach a definite conclusion. Their clients want to hear 'yes' or 'no', not 'maybe'. Hilton and Frei-Sulzer were not the first experts to fall into the trap of committing themselves to rash overstatements on the basis of flimsy evidence. In 1971, when Clifford Irving faked his notorious 'autobiography' of Howard Hughes, one 'holographer' gave odds of a million to one against the possibility that it could be anything other than genuine. The reputable New York firm of Osborn, Osborn and Osborn, specialists in handwriting analysis since 1905, declared that it would have been 'beyond human ability' to have forged the entire autobiography.

The Hitler diaries fiasco has close parallels with the Hughes case. Like *Stern*, McGraw-Hill, publishers of the autobiography, were obsessed with leaks and failed to commission a handwriting analysis until late in the project: when they finally did so, they allowed the experts to see only a fraction of the material. The tests were not ordered in a spirit of impartial inquiry: they were required as ammunition to fight off the attacks of sceptical outsiders. Kujau and Clifford Irving were both fluent forgers. They did not give themselves away by being over-cautious, copying out words in the slow and tedious manner which produces telltale tremors: Irving, like Kujau, could write in another person's hand at almost the same speed as he could write in his own. When the discovery of the Hitler diaries was announced by *Stern*, Irving recognized at once that they were probably the work of a forger like himself. 'Once you have the mood,' he commented, 'you can go on forever. I know that from personal experience. I could write sixty volumes of Howard Hughes autobiography and they would pass. Once you can do one page, you can do twenty. Once you can do twenty, you can do a book.' Handwriting experts were useless: 'Nine times out of ten they come out with judgements their clients expect. . . They're hired by people who want an affirmative answer.'

Clifford Irving and Konrad Kujau succeeded in the same way that most confidence tricksters succeed: by playing on two of the most ancient of human weaknesses – vanity and greed. There came a point during the duping of McGraw-Hill when one of Irving's confederates found it impossible to accept that a powerful company led by intelligent men could be stupid enough to accept their often ludicrous forgery. 'It's got to occur to them,' he said. 'How can they be so naïve?' In his account of the hoax, Irving recalled his answer:

Because they *believe*. First they wanted to believe and now they have to believe. They want to believe because it's such a coup for them. . . Can't you see what an ego trip it is? The secrecy part – the thing that protects you and me – is what they love the most. That takes them out of the humdrum into another world, the world we all dream of living in, only we really don't want to because we know it's mad. And the greatest thing for them is that this way they can live in it part time. They're participating but they're protected by an intermediary. I'm their buffer between reality and fantasy. It's a fairy tale, a dream. And the beauty part for them is that they'll make money out of it, too. Corporate profit justifies any form of lunacy. There's been no other hoax like it in modern times. . .

Twelve years later, the analysis fitted *Stern*'s behaviour to perfection.

18

With the diaries' handwriting now apparently authenticated as Adolf Hitler's, work on the project within *Stern* intensified. Five people were now engaged virtually full time on the operation: Thomas Walde; Walde's thirty-five-year-old assistant, Leo Pesch; two secretaries; and Gerd Heidemann. To safeguard the secret of the diaries' existence, the group moved out of the main *Stern* building to new offices a few minutes' walk away. The diaries were also moved. Every few weeks, Manfred Fischer would empty the management safe of the latest volumes and take them back with him to his own office at Bertelsmann's headquarters in Guetersloh. Eventually, fearful of a robbery, Fischer and Schulte-Hillen decided to transfer them out of the country altogether, to a bank vault in Switzerland. Not for the first time, the saga of the diaries assumed the trappings of a cheap thriller. Safe deposit box number 390 was rented from the Handelsbank in Talstrasse, Zurich. Periodically Fischer himself would board Bertelsmann's private jet carrying a suitcase containing the diaries and fly to Switzerland. Herr Bluhm, director of the Handelsbank, would meet him and the two men would descend into the vaults. Bluhm would unlock two steel mesh doors, retrieve the large metal box, and discreetly turn his back while Fischer filled it with the latest diaries. One key to the box stayed with the bank. The other was taken back to Germany by Fischer and locked in the safe in Hamburg.

Gradually, a publication strategy for the diaries began to evolve. On Tuesday 25 May – the day on which the Rhineland-Pfalz police expert concluded that the writing he had been given was Hitler's – a conference was called to discuss the marketing of the material. Present were Wilfried Sorge, Thomas Walde, Peter Koch, Felix Schmidt, Leo Pesch,

Henri Nannen and Gerd Heidemann; Schulte-Hillen presided. Neither of the two editors said very much. Their status within the company had recently been eroded still further, when *Stern*, humiliatingly, was scooped by its rival, *Der Spiegel*, over a trade union scandal. Peter Koch, who had originally turned down the story, had offered to resign. He had been allowed to stay on, but in the aftermath of the affair, neither he nor Schmidt was in a position to argue with the management. The fact that their mishandling of Heidemann had almost cost the company the diaries scoop as well hung, unspoken, over the entire proceedings.

Thomas Walde put forward the plan which he had discussed with Pesch and Heidemann. One of the most interesting documents so far delivered to Hamburg was the special diary volume Hitler had devoted to the Hess affair. This had been with the history department since November. Entitled 'The Hess Case', it consisted of a few pages of notes scrawled in the early summer of 1941, proving that the Führer had known all along of his deputy's flight to Britain. 'From November 1940,' Hitler had supposedly written, 'Hess was whispering in my ear that he thought as I did that England and Germany could live together in peace, that the sufferings of our two peoples could bring satisfaction to one person, namely the old fox in Moscow, Stalin.' The content was sketchy – little more than 1000 words – describing how Hess had evolved his plan, how Hitler had been 'kept informed about preparations' and how he had been forced to deny all knowledge of the mission when the British had imprisoned Hess.

> Now [concluded 'Hitler'] the last attempt to reach an understanding with England has failed.
>
> The English people perhaps understand what the flight of Hess signified, but the ossified old men in London don't. If Providence does not help our two peoples, the fight will go on until one people is totally destroyed, the English people.
>
> After the victory, the German people will also be ready to understand the flight of Party Comrade Hess and this will be appreciated for its worth.
>
> 16 May 1941
> Adolf Hitler

Walde's proposal was that this material should be used as the basis for a sensational story to be published in January, the fiftieth anniversary of Hitler's accession to power. The Hess volume stood on its own. There was no need to refer to the actual diaries, whose existence could be kept secret for a few more months. The advantage of Walde's idea was that it would give the magazine a good cover story whilst also enabling it to test the water prior to the launch of the main diary hoard. The plan was accepted by the conference. The only mildly dissenting voice was Henri Nannen's. Would it not, he suggested, be a good idea to bring in Sebastian Haffner or Joachim Fest, recognized authorities on the Third Reich, to work on the material? The idea was angrily slapped down. This was *Stern*'s story, and *Stern*'s men should take all the credit. Neither Nannen nor the editors were aware that Heidemann and Walde had contracts with the management which enabled them to veto the involvement of outside historians.

Ten days later, on Friday 4 June, Manfred Fischer, Gerd Schulte-Hillen and Jan Hensmann flew down to Munich to meet Olaf Paeschke, the head of Bertelsmann's international publishing division. It was agreed, without reference to the *Stern* editors, that Walde and Pesch would first turn the Hess material into a book, provisionally entitled *Plan 3*. This would then be serialized in the magazine. The idea of marketing the Hess scoop through the book publishing industry was attractive to the businessmen. It would enable Bertelsmann to bring its foreign companies into the action and take control of the syndication negotiations. Shortly afterwards, Paeschke briefed Louis Wolfe, President of Bantam Books in New York, on the contents of the forthcoming manuscript. Wolfe was a lucky man, said Paeschke. *Plan 3* would be 'the publishing event of the century'.

On 5 July, Leo Pesch went down to Koblenz to hand the Bundesarchiv the original of the Hess announcement and the Horthy telegram which had now been returned to *Stern* by Frei-Sulzer. These, together with the original documents already in the archive's possession, were then forwarded to the West German Federal Police for a final forensic examination to confirm the age of the paper and the ink. *Stern* had hoped for a quick result. But the police laboratories were involved in anti-terrorist investigations and were swamped with work. Weeks passed and despite occasional reminders from Walde, nothing was done. There was no particular sense of urgency in Hamburg. The documents had, after all, been authenticated by three different handwriting experts: the forensic tests were only a safety check.

Meanwhile, Heidemann carried on draining the company's special diaries account – 200,000 marks was withdrawn on 29 March, 600,000 marks on 21 May, 400,000 marks on 2 June, 200,000 marks on 10 June – and the Heidemann family spending spree continued. Precise details of what was bought and when will probably never be known. More than 80,000 marks was spent in auction houses, mainly to buy Third Reich memorabilia. Ninety thousand marks went on jewellery and carpets; 37,000 on furniture. A futile attempt to recover Mussolini's treasure, supposedly dumped in Lake Como at the end of the war, swallowed 185,000 marks. At least a quarter of a million marks was paid into one or another of Heidemann's six known bank accounts. To house his Nazi relics, the reporter rented a gallery in Milchstrasse, in the heart of one of Hamburg's most expensive shopping areas. In the middle of April, Gina visited an estate agent. 'She said she was interested in buying a large house with a view over the Elbe,' recalled the agent, Peter Moller. 'The price was no object.' Over the next year they maintained contact and he sent her details of property costing in the region of 1–2 million marks.

On 14 July, after Heidemann received the largest single payment for the diaries to date – 900,000 marks – contracts were signed to start the long-awaited renovation of *Carin II* 's hull. The yacht alone cost Heidemann a fortune. Experts were flown in from England. New engines were installed. The boat was rewired. The interior was refurbished. The total cost exceeded 500,000 marks. To restore the woodwork, Gunther Lutje, a Hungarian boatyard owner who had known Heidemann and *Carin II* for almost a decade, was paid 300,000 marks.

In his prosperity, Heidemann did not forget those who had helped him in the past. In June, Axel Thomsen, the young seaman who had sailed *Carin II* from Bonn to Hamburg, rang Heidemann to ask for a loan. He had heard that the reporter now had plenty of money. 'He

said immediately that he was perfectly willing to lend me 6000 marks,'
recalled Thomsen. 'Two or three days later he came to my house and
gave me the money, in 500-mark notes. It was lying around in his briefcase.' Encouraged by Heidemann's readiness to help, Thomsen rang
him again two months later to ask for a further 13,000 marks. 'From
his reaction, I could see that he was slightly hesitant, but he said he
was willing to lend me the money. He said he felt duty bound to assist
me. He said I could have it and that I should go round to his flat in
the Elbchaussee to collect it.' When Thomsen appeared, Heidemann
handed him an envelope containing 13,000 marks in cash. Thomsen
put the money in his pocket. Heidemann asked him to make sure that
Gina did not get to hear about it. Heidemann also remembered Hannelore Schustermann, the secretary from whom, in his hard-pressed
days, he had been forced to scrounge money to go to the canteen. She
was let into the secret of the Hitler diaries and went to work for Heidemann in his special suite of offices. The diaries, he confided to her,
were going to make him a millionaire.

On 29 July, Heidemann flew to Spain and arranged to buy two holiday villas in the Mediterranean town of Denia, midway between the
resorts of Valencia and Alicante. The two houses, which stood next to
one another, cost him 390,000 marks in cash. In August, he suggested
to Kujau that he should buy one of them. The two villas, he said, both
had spacious cellars which could be knocked together to make a large
underground vault. Heidemann proposed that they should each move
their Nazi collections there. Together they would create the biggest
museum of Third Reich memorabilia in the world. The plan came to
nothing the moment Edith Lieblang got to hear of it. She told Kujau,
in forceful tones, that she was 'absolutely against' it. 'It seemed to me
completely worthless,' she recalled, 'owning it and only spending a
couple of weeks a year in it. For 200,000 marks, I could go on holiday around the world until the end of my life.' Edith's word was final
and Heidemann's dream of erecting a monument to the Führer amid
the haciendas and cicadas of the Costa Blanca evaporated.

Not all the money Heidemann spent at this time belonged to *Stern*;
at least some of it was his own. He was now drawing a salary of over

100,000 marks a year. He had received a bonus of 20,000 marks. He had already been given an advance of 300,000 marks by Manfred Fischer and his position as the sole contact between Gruner and Jahr and the 'antiques dealer' in Stuttgart meant that he found no difficulty in extracting more. His moodiness and periodic threats to take his great scoop elsewhere were guaranteed to throw the *Stern* management into a panic. Without him, the flow of diaries from East Germany would dry up. Like wealthy drug addicts, they were prepared to pamper their supplier: to ensure he continued to deal with them, they were willing to give him whatever he asked.

In June 1982 Heidemann told the company that in order to keep up the pretence of being a Swiss collector, he was having to buy additional material from the communist general: Nazi documents and paintings and drawings by Adolf Hitler. Although as a collector he was naturally interested in obtaining such items, he did not see why he should have to go on paying for them out of his own pocket. Gerd Schulte-Hillen accepted Heidemann's argument and on 11 June concluded a new contract with him, by which the reporter was to be paid a 'loan' of 25,000 marks for each volume of diaries he delivered. To date, there were thirty-five books in the company's possession. Heidemann was therefore entitled to receive 875,000 marks, minus the 300,000 marks advance paid to him in February 1981, and the 80,000 marks still outstanding for his unwritten books – *Bord Gespräche* and *My African Wars*. The money was described, for tax purposes, as an 'interest-free loan' to be recovered through 'profit-sharing and royalty fees' following 'the commercial exploitation of the diaries'.

But Heidemann wanted more than mere money. Incapable of writing up the stories he researched, he had, throughout his career, suffered from an inferiority complex. Now, as he watched Walde and Pesch start putting together a book based on the material he had gathered, his resentment welled up in a demand for praise for his achievement. He craved respect and recognition. It was like dealing with a child. Gerd Schulte-Hillen had already had to cope with one of these bouts. On that occasion, at the end of 1981, he had forced the editors to give Heidemann a salary increase. In the summer of 1982, Wilfried Sorge warned him once again that the company's ageing prima donna was proving difficult. 'He was portrayed to me,' remembered the managing director, 'as being rather like a circus horse: because he'd made this find, you had to say "hello" to him and pat him on the head from time to time.'

Acting on Sorge's advice, on Monday 28 June, Schulte-Hillen took Heidemann out 'for a meal on expenses'. They met in the Ovelgonne, a restaurant in a picturesque street overlooking the Elbe. For three courses, Schulte-Hillen listened patiently to Heidemann's stories. He heard of the reporter's adventures in Africa and the Middle East, of his experiences with the white mercenaries in the Congo, of his long search for Traven. Finally, over dessert, Heidemann invited him back to his home in the Elbchaussee to see part of his collection. 'He showed me drawings by Hitler,' said Schulte-Hillen, 'and the pistol with which Hitler was supposed to have shot himself.' The businessman inspected Heidemann's archive: the shelves full of history books and folders crammed with documents, all neatly arranged and catalogued. He congratulated Heidemann on his professionalism and, after a couple of hours, the two men parted on excellent terms.

Heidemann was given another opportunity to show off a few weeks later, when Henri Nannen also decided to visit him at home. Nannen had retired from daily involvement in *Stern* to devote himself to the erection of his own memorial: an art gallery in his home town of Emden, to house his collection of German Expressionist paintings. But to Heidemann – as to most West German journalists – Nannen, despite his retirement, *was Stern*, and he was determined to impress his old employer. Nannen parked his car beside the Elbe and got out to see Heidemann on his balcony, waving at him with one hand, and raising a glass of iced champagne to him with the other. Climbing the stairs, he suddenly realized that Heidemann not only had the top floor apartment, but the one underneath as well. Inside, the impression of luxury continued. 'The place was decorated in the very best taste,' recalled Nannen. 'There were some superb pieces of furniture – Queen Anne, I think – and on the walls were drawings. The first thing that hit me was the original manuscript of *'Deutschland über Alles'* by Hoffman. He also had the autographs of Bismark and Moltke, along with other historical documents under glass and in frames. I was astonished. Where has he got all this from? I thought.' Heidemann told him he had been forced to buy it from the supplier of the Hitler diaries in order to disguise the fact that he was interested only in the diaries themselves. 'He gave me some convoluted story and showed me thirty or forty Hitler drawings,' said Nannen. 'I'm something of an art historian. They seemed to me to be perfectly genuine.'

After seeing Hitler's suicide weapon, and a pair of busts supposedly sculpted by the Führer, Nannen inquired about the diaries.

Heidemann crossed the room, pulled a cord, and a pair of black curtains slid back to reveal a bookcase full of files. These were Heidemann's private photocopies of the diaries, each sheet protected by a transparent plastic cover.

'What do you want to see?' asked Heidemann.

'The Roehm *putsch*,' replied Nannen.

He was handed the relevant volumes and read a few pages. He found them 'unbelievably boring' – a fact which further convinced him that they must be genuine: 'I couldn't believe that anyone would have gone to the trouble of forging something so banal.'

But although Nannen had no doubts that the diaries were authentic, his visit convinced him that Heidemann was a crook. Unlike Schulte-Hillen – who had known Heidemann for only a year – Nannen had been his employer since the 1950s. The change in the man's fortunes was startling. It was inconceivable that he could have moved from near bankruptcy to such affluence without robbing the company. Nannen left the Elbchaussee and immediately drove to the *Stern* building. Within ninety minutes he was in Schulte-Hillen's office. 'I've just come from Heidemann's,' he told him, 'and he's shitting on us – from a great height.' Schulte-Hillen asked if he meant that the diaries were forgeries. 'No,' said Nannen, 'but he's clearly pocketing our money.' Privately, *Stern*'s editors thought the same: Peter Koch had been in no doubt ever since he learned of the expensive renovation work being carried out on *Carin II*. But they could have warned Nannen that to raise such suspicions with Schulte-Hillen was useless. The managing director regarded himself as a good judge of character; he was convinced of the reporter's integrity; and having made up his mind, he was unshakeable. He reacted, in Koch's words, 'like a man with an allergy' whenever Heidemann's honesty was questioned. That afternoon, when

Nannen told him of his fears, Schulte-Hillen stared at him with contempt. Heidemann, he said, was being well rewarded for his work: the only sort of person who would think that he was robbing the company was someone who was capable of committing such a crime himself.

Meanwhile, as the summer wore on, Thomas Walde and Leo Pesch worked hard on the manuscript of *Plan 3*. Heidemann appeared in the offices occasionally and continued to deliver new volumes of diaries, but they had no time to look at them. To help them with the background for the Hess book, the two would-be historians hired a team of freelance researchers. 'We employed them without telling them the context in which they were working,' said Walde. 'We simply asked them to do some research in certain areas.' At the beginning of September, after three months' intensive work, more than half the book was completed. On Monday 6 September, chapters 2–7 were submitted to the editors of *Stern*. Walde explained in a memorandum to Felix Schmidt how the book would be structured. The first chapter would be an account of Hess's life in Spandau and of his relations with his family. 'We have already won over Hess's son,' confided Walde, 'but not yet Frau Ilse Hess.' Not until chapter 8 – which had still to be written – did the authors intend to introduce quotations from the Hitler notebook on the Hess affair. Then would come an account of Hess's experiences in Britain, the Nuremberg trial, and his sentencing to life imprisonment. There was to be no mention of the existence of the diaries.

Schmidt later described himself as 'amazed' at Walde's proposed treatment. He was a journalist. It was ridiculous, in his opinion, to start publication of the documents with a history lesson on Rudolf Hess. *Stern* should launch its scoop with an account of the discovery of Hitler's diaries. Once again the editors realized that decisions had been taken behind their backs. *Plan 3* was the child of the Bertelsmann marketing division, not the company's journalists, part of a long-term commercial scheme to exploit the diaries.

The sales strategy was based on two premisses. First, to enable the company to recoup its investment, publication would have to be spread over as long a period as possible – somewhere between eighteen months and two years. Secondly, the company would have to find reliable foreign partners to syndicate the material. *Plan 3* would enable Bertelsmann to begin earning money, whilst leaving the bulk of the diaries untouched. The manuscript would be sold to news organizations all over the world. Only if they paid promptly, adhered to *Stern*'s publishing timetable, and generally behaved 'correctly', would they be told of the existence of the real prize – Hitler's diaries – and be offered a share in its exploitation.

The moment Walde and Pesch had finished the first part of the manuscript, Wilfried Sorge and Olaf Paeschke flew to New York to hold discussions with the management of Bantam Books. The talks took place on Friday 10 September. They did not go well. The Germans wanted to draw on Bantam's experience of the American and British markets. They wanted to know which would be the best magazines and newspapers to approach. As far as Bantam was concerned, their interest was in a book, not a newspaper serial – especially as the two Germans were insistent that they should retain the syndication rights. As paranoid as ever, Sorge and Paeschke refused to reveal the secret of the diaries, leaving the American publishers with a feeling that they were being used. The talks ended, according to one of the participants, with a 'bitter feeling' on both sides.

Sorge flew back to Hamburg over the weekend. On Monday he went in to see Schulte-Hillen to brief him on his trip. The managing director wanted to know how much the diaries were likely to fetch on the world market. This was a difficult question to answer. Sorge had no idea of the total sales potential. The project was unprecedented. After the discussions in New York, it was clear that the only author who might remotely be compared to Adolf Hitler was Henry Kissinger. His memoirs had been syndicated across the globe in 1979 in an intricate network of deals, simultaneous release dates and subsidiary rights, which was a wonder to behold. Hitler was probably bigger than Kissinger – 'hotter', as the Americans put it. Certainly, the company was looking at an income of upwards of $2 million.

Sorge's report did not please Schulte-Hillen. The company had already paid out 7 million marks – roughly $2 million – to obtain the diaries. Under the terms of the contracts agreed with Heidemann and Walde in 1981, Gruner and Jahr was entitled to only 40 per cent of the revenue from syndication sales. That figure made sense when there were only twenty-seven diaries; but now there were more than forty, the tally was still rising and the costs were going to be more than four times the amount originally predicted. Unless something was done, the company was going to end up making a loss. During a business trip to Majorca, Schulte-Hillen took the opportunity to tell Manfred Fischer that he had decided to renegotiate the original contracts. On 14 October, he summoned Heidemann and Walde to a meeting in a Cologne hotel and explained the problem.

Legally, both men would have been entitled to reject Schulte-Hillen's proposal. Nevertheless, they were forced to accept the logic of what he said. A new, handwritten contract was drawn up, under which both men would be entitled to the same percentage of the syndication revenue – but only after Gruner and Jahr had cleared its costs. Walde signed, reluctantly. Heidemann, characteristically, demanded something in return. He pointed out that he was giving up a probable income of 2.3 million marks. Schulte-Hillen had no alternative but to agree to pay him yet more 'compensation'. Under the terms of the contracts of February 1981 and June 1982, he had already received 1.1 million marks in advances and 'loans'. Schulte-Hillen arranged for that sum to be converted into a once-and-for-all 'fee' of 1.5 million marks.

Heidemann also extracted another concession. From now on, it was written into his contract that he was 'not obliged to reveal in fine detail the method by which the diaries were acquired, nor the names of his sources'. Schulte-Hillen took this as further evidence of Heidemann's integrity – of his determination to protect the lives of his suppliers. In reality, Heidemann's manoeuvre was almost certainly designed to cover up his own fraudulent activities: if he could prevent the company checking with Kujau, no one would ever know precisely how much he had paid for the diaries. Schulte-Hillen's concession, seemingly trivial at the time, was to have important consequences.

The day after the meeting in Cologne, Heidemann withdrew another 450,000 marks from the bank in Adolphsplatz.

19

On Saturday 20 November, the German People's Union (DVU), a right-wing political group, organized a meeting in the Westphalian village of Hoffnungsthal. The speaker – a regular favourite among DVU audiences, with his stirring denunciations of communists and socialists – was David Irving.

Irving arrived at the hall to be met by the unmistakable figure of Otto Guensche. The devoted SS major, whose claim to fame was that he had burned Hitler's body, was a local DVU supporter. 'He talks to nobody,' noted Irving in his diary, 'but has been an informant of mine for twelve years or more.' After a few pleasantries, Guensche abruptly asked the historian: 'What's your view of the Rudolf Hess affair?' According to Irving:

> I did not know what he was getting at. He continued, 'Do you think the Chief knew about it in advance or not?' I said I thought there were signs that Hitler approved of the idea in the autumn of 1940, but unless it was discussed by Hitler with Hess when they met briefly after the Reichstag session of 4 May 1941, Hitler was probably taken by surprise. Guensche said: 'He knew about it. I know.' I asked how. Guensche: 'I've seen the proof.'

Suddenly, Irving remembered his dinner with Priesack in London back in April.

> Acting on a hunch I said, 'You've seen the Stuttgart diaries too?' He said he had, that they were beyond doubt authentic, and that in this particular case they reveal Hitler as deliberating different courses of

action: what to do if Hess's mission succeeded, what if it failed, etc.
The diaries also contain Hitler's character assessments of his contemporaries, showing him a better judge than has hitherto been supposed,
etc. Guensche implied that he has seen the originals.

The conversation ended when Irving had to go up on to the platform
to deliver his speech. Afterwards, hoping to pick up more information, he went back to Guensche's house for tea. But Guensche had not
withstood ten years of interrogation in the Soviet Union in order to be
tricked into disclosure in his own home. He refused to say any more
about the diaries and Irving left frustrated.

Despite his elaborate show of concern for secrecy, Heidemann had
always been remarkably indiscreet about the diaries. He had shown
original volumes to former Nazis like Guensche, Mohnke and Wolff
and to such shady contacts as Medard Klapper. On several occasions,
Walde and Pesch had been forced to restrain him from boasting openly
about his discovery to colleagues in the corridor at *Stern*. In 1981, he
had sat his old friend Randolph Braumann down on the sofa in his
apartment. According to Braumann: 'He said: "Are you sitting comfortably?" and then from under the sofa he pulled out a plastic bag
stuffed with bundles of money. He said it was for the diaries and asked
me not to tell anybody.' The following year, meeting Braumann in
the *Stern* canteen, Heidemann had taken him outside to his car 'and
produced a packet containing seven or eight books. He seemed very
proud, positively euphoric.' Now *Stern* was to pay the price for Heidemann's showing off.

Returning to London twelve days later, Irving telephoned Phillip
Knightley, the senior reporter on the *Sunday Times*, and told him of
the existence of the Hitler diaries. 'He is interested,' wrote Irving in his
diary. 'I said I'd let him have a note about it at his private address.' That
same afternoon, Irving wrote to him, enclosing an account of his conversations with Priesack and Guensche, and stressing the usefulness of
his reputation as a right winger: 'I would be prepared to set up or conduct such negotiations with traditionally awkward German personalities as might prove necessary in an attempt to secure this material.' In
return, he made it clear that he expected a 'finder's fee' of 10 per cent

of the cost of the diaries. Knightley – who was about to return to his native Australia for four months – passed Irving's offer on to Magnus Linklater, the features editor of the *Sunday Times*. On Wednesday 8 December, Linklater telephoned Irving to confirm that the paper was interested. At 9.15 that night, Irving rang August Priesack in Munich to try to extract more information from him. The first part of the conversation concerned itself with the old man's forthcoming trial for 'propagating the swastika' in his book about the Nazi Party rallies.

'*You* promised to provide a reference for me,' said Priesack, reproachfully.

'Yes,' lied Irving, 'that's why I'm calling.' (He had found the old man, frankly, to be rather a bore and had never had any intention of allowing his name to be associated with such an obvious crank.) He then had to endure five minutes of Priesack alternately moaning about his persecution and bragging about the book on Hitler's art he was working on with Billy Price. ('The book is written by *me* in every way. But it can't be put out like that because the American has paid 400,000 marks for it – so he has to appear as the author.') At last, after a number of false starts, Irving managed to turn the conversation to the diaries. According to Priesack 'six or seven' were already in America, where they were to be published. 'That's interesting,' said Irving.

PRIESACK: They're just headlines from the *Völkischer Beobachter*.
IRVING: The whole twenty-seven volumes?
PRIESACK: Yes. He wrote them as something to jog his memory. . . I've only seen a half-yearly volume from 1935, and there were in total only six interesting pages. You can read them in Hitler's handwriting here [i.e. in Priesack's apartment].
IRVING: Good. When I'm there, I'll—
PRIESACK: But I've also got *Mein Kampf*. The third volume.
IRVING: [*emits stifled cry*]
PRIESACK: Haven't you heard about that?
IRVING: When did he write *that*?
PRIESACK: He started that on the day after the seizure of power. *Mein Kampf Three*. I've got a few pages. They've not been sold. They'll probably end up in America because America pays better.

1   A large Junkers 352 transport aircraft of the type which crashed in
April 1945 ferrying some of Hitler's property to safety. 'In that plane,'
exclaimed Hitler, when told of its disappearance, 'were all my private
archives, that I had intended as a testament to posterity. It is a catastrophe.'
(DPA)

2   In November 1980, *Stern*'s 'Bloodhound', reporter Gerd Heidemann,
discovered the village in East Germany where the Junkers 352 had crashed.
He posed for a photograph by the graves of the victims. (DPA)

3 Konrad Kujau, alias Konrad Fischer, universally known as 'Conny', graduated from forging luncheon vouchers to copying out sixty volumes of Hitler's diaries – the most well-publicized and costly fraud in publishing history. (DPA)

4 A page from one of the forged diaries. The books were written in an antiquated German script which made them difficult to read. This extract – supposedly Hitler's draft for the announcement of Rudolf Hess's flight to Britain in 1941 – fooled three handwriting experts and convinced *Stern* that the diaries were genuine.

Plakatentwurf: Das Hakenkreuz marschiert unaufhaltsam! 29

Plakatentwurf: Ende des alten Systems! 29

5, 6, 7 In addition to the diaries, Kujau also forged more than 300 Hitler paintings and drawings. These three sketches were supposedly designs by Hitler for early Nazi party posters.

Plakatentwurf: Es werde Licht! 1929

8, 9, 10   Three key figures in the diaries affair: Fritz Stiefel (*top left*), a collector of Nazi memorabilia, received the first Hitler diary in 1978; August Priesack (*top right*), ex-Nazi and self-styled 'Hitler expert' was shown the diary by Stiefel and was convinced it was genuine; SS General Karl Wolff (*left*) was a witness at the Heidemanns' wedding and accompanied them on their honeymoon to South America to look for old Nazis. He encouraged Heidemann's obsession with the Third Reich. (DPA)

11   The launching of a book of Hitler's paintings, by the Texan millionaire Billy F. Price, brought together four people with a passion for the Führer's art: Heidemann and Price, together with Christa Schroeder and Gerda Christian, two of Hitler's devoted private secretaries. (Price)

12   Gina Heidemann. (DPA)

13   Edith Lieblang, Kujau's common-law wife. (DPA)

14 Manfred Fischer, the
businessman who ferried the
Hitler diaries from Hamburg to a
Swiss bank. (DPA)

15 Gerd Schulte-Hillen, who
personally authorized payments
for the diaries of more than 7
million marks – £2 million. (DPA)

16 Henri Nannen, founder and
publisher of *Stern*. (DPA)

17 Dr Thomas Walde, the head
of *Stern*'s history department.
(DPA)

18 Peter Koch, chief editor of *Stern*. (DPA)

19 Eberhard Jaeckel, Professor of History at the University of Stuttgart, the first academic to be taken in by Kujau's forgeries. (DPA)

20 Hugh Trevor-Roper (Lord Dacre), former Regius Professor of History at Oxford, who authenticated the diaries for Times Newspapers. (DPA)

21 Gerhard Weinberg, Professor of History at the University of North Carolina, who inspected the diaries for *Newsweek*. (DPA)

22 'Torpedo running': the right-wing British historian David Irving caused uproar at the *Stern* press conference which launched the diaries, when he produced sheets of Hitler diaries which he claimed were forged. (*Stern*)

23 End of an obsession: Gerd Heidemann, with prison beard, stands trial with Kujau, accused of fraud. He stole *Stern*'s money but was convinced to the end that the diaries were genuine. (DPA)

IRVING: Do you know where all this is? Can you find that out?
PRIESACK: Up to a point, yes.
IRVING: You are a real gold mine.
PRIESACK: [*laughs*]

After promising to send Priesack a character reference (describing him as 'a well-known scientist'), and suggesting he might come and see him in Munich in a few days' time, Irving hung up and switched off his tape recorder.

The following day in Hamburg, the Hitler diaries team received an unpleasant surprise. In the belief that it might shake loose some information from someone, somewhere in Germany, Irving had written letters to dozens of West German newspapers to alert their readers to the existence of the diaries. On Thursday 9 December, these seeds of mischief began sprouting in news columns and letters pages across the country:

> I am of the opinion that German historians are guilty of failing to explain to the German public the facts behind the Nazi crimes against the Jews. We know that Adolf Hitler's own diaries – 27 half-yearly volumes, including the first six months of 1945 – have entered the Federal Republic as a result of horse-trading with a major-general in the East German Army. They are however in private hands in Baden Wuerttemberg [the area of Germany which includes Stuttgart] and German historians are taking no notice of them. The Hitler diaries would surely clear up any doubts about whether he knew or did not know of Auschwitz, Treblinka and Majdanek.

Among the thirteen West German newspapers which eventually carried Irving's letter was Kujau's and Stiefel's daily paper, the *Stuttgarter Zeitung*.

The effect of this burst of publicity on the furtive circle of South German collectors was dramatic. Like insects whose stone had been kicked away, they scurried for cover. Kujau rang Heidemann to warn him that Irving was on their trail. The reporter told him to put as much pressure as he could on Stiefel to ensure he kept quiet: above all, Irving must not get to see the 1935 diary which Stiefel still had in his safe.

Kujau contacted the industrialist and warned him that he had heard from his brother that sixty-four East German generals had been summoned to Berlin in an effort to flush out whoever was supplying the diaries. Stiefel panicked. Convinced that he would be raided by the police at any moment, he packed his entire collection – his medals, papers, paintings and concentration camp china – and shipped it out of the country to his holiday home in Italy. He also wrote to Priesack. 'I must ask you,' he told him, 'under the terms of our agreement, to return to me all the copies and photographs which are in your possession and which come from us.'

At four o'clock in the afternoon, Heidemann spoke to Irving on the telephone. He pleaded with him to keep quiet about the diaries. Not all the material, he said, was in the West: he was having to make repeated trips into East Germany and his life would be in danger if there were any more publicity. Irving replied that Priesack had told him that most of the material had already been smuggled out. 'What has Priesack got?' asked Heidemann. For a moment, Irving – who had not yet seen any of the material – was stumped for an answer. Recalling his conversation with Guensche he replied that Priesack had a letter from Hess to Hitler dated May 1941. As the conversation went on, Heidemann began to realize that Irving was bluffing. He did not know the scale of the archive in *Stern*'s possession. He thought that some of the books were still in America. He did not know about Hitler's special volume on Hess. Almost all his information was either two years old or based on nothing more than regurgitated gossip. 'Priesack,' he warned Irving, 'is talking about things of which he knows nothing.'

At the end of the conversation, Heidemann reassured his colleagues in the history department that the leak was not as serious as it appeared. He played them a tape recording of his telephone call from Kujau during which 'Conny' told him not to worry about Irving. According to Leo Pesch, Heidemann told them that ' "Conny" was putting so much pressure on Stiefel, there was no way he would hand over his diary volume to Irving.'

That same day, Heidemann collected another 450,000 marks from Sorge.

*

In London, Irving began transcribing the tape of his telephone call to Priesack. It was a laborious task and took him until after midnight to complete. At 2 a.m. he drove round to the offices of the *Sunday Times* in Gray's Inn Road and left a copy of the transcript in reception addressed to Magnus Linklater. He fell into bed, exhausted, half an hour later.

Linklater found Irving's envelope when he came into the office the next day. He was in a dilemma. Obviously he wanted to pursue the story. On the other hand, it was not wise, in his opinion, for the *Sunday Times* to become involved with a man of Irving's reputation. Irving's suggestion – that he should fly out to Hamburg and Munich at the paper's expense in order 'to identify and talk with the Stuttgart source' – filled him with unease. Instead, he decided to do some checking of his own. He rang the German historian Hermann Weiss at the Institute of Contemporary History in Munich and explained what Irving had told him. Weiss's reaction was that the story was rubbish: it was inconceivable that there were any such 'Hitler diaries'. The *Sunday Times* also contacted Gerd Heidemann, whose name had been given to them by Irving. Heidemann, according to Linklater, confirmed he was involved in trying to obtain Hitler material, but said that as a result of recent publicity much of it had 'gone back' over the border to East Germany.

Early in the morning on Wednesday 15 December, five days after receiving Irving's transcript of his conversation with Priesack, Linklater rang Irving at home. He told him that the *Sunday Times* could not afford to fly him to Germany: 'We don't have the large sums of money to throw around that we used to have.' They would much prefer to send Hermann Weiss or one of their own reporters down to see Priesack. The paper wanted to involve someone who was 'neutral'. Apologetic for the obvious inference in this remark, Linklater offered to pay Irving £250 for having given them the information in the first place. 'We don't want you to think we are trying to go behind your back,' he said. He offered to give him time to think it over. Irving thanked him for his honesty and said he felt inclined to accept his offer.

As soon as Linklater had hung up, Irving telephoned a contact at the German publishing company Langen Mueller. He told them that if they wanted to secure Hitler's diaries they should move fast because the *Sunday Times* was on to them. By mid-afternoon, the publishers had called him back and offered to pay his air fare if he would inspect the material on their behalf. Irving immediately booked seats on a flight to Munich. He had no intention of being double-crossed by the *Sunday Times*.

At the same time in Hamburg, Heidemann and Walde were being presented with a formal copy of the agreement sketched out in Cologne in October with Gerd Schulte-Hillen. Once the company had recovered its costs, the revenue generated by the diaries would be divided up between the journalists and Gruner and Jahr – and for the first time, in recognition of his work on the Hess manuscript, Leo Pesch was to be given a slice of the cake. Heidemann would receive 36 per cent of the money; Walde, 16 per cent; Pesch, 8 per cent; the company would take the remaining 40 per cent. These percentages would apply both to the sale of the syndication rights and to the sale of the actual diaries themselves.

An appendix to the contract set out in detail exactly how the agreement might work in practice. Supposing syndication sales brought in 10 million marks: the company would immediately claim 9 million to defray its own costs; of the remainder, Heidemann would receive 360,000 marks, Walde 160,000 and Pesch 80,000 – Gruner and Jahr's 40 per cent share would yield it 400,000 marks. If the books were sold – say, to an archive or a collector – for an additional 5 million marks, the company would immediately take half to cover its initial outlay. Of the remaining 2.5 million marks, Heidemann would then take 900,000, Walde 400,000 and Pesch 200,000; again, the company's share would be 40 per cent – 1 million marks. In other words, despite the readjustment insisted upon by Schulte-Hillen, the journalists still stood to become rich men as a result of the diaries' publication.

Although individual volumes, mainly from the war years, were continuing to come in, the Hess manuscript was now finished. The most difficult task had been securing the cooperation of Frau Hess, from whom Walde and Pesch had wanted information about her visits to see her husband in Spandau. The Hess family had called in a lawyer who had insisted on payment of a fee of 5000 marks as well as a guarantee that the family's 'political standpoint' would be represented when the story appeared in *Stern*. It had finally been agreed that this would be done in the form of an interview.

A copy of the manuscript of *Plan 3* was sent to Henri Nannen for his approval while Felix Schmidt briefed the head of *Stern*'s serialization department, Horst Treuke. Schmidt told Treuke to begin planning on the assumption that they would be running the Hess story in the summer of 1983. He also let him into the secret of the existence of the diaries. Treuke, startled by the news, asked if they were sure they were genuine. Schmidt reassured him. Did he seriously think that Schulte-Hillen would have paid out 9 million marks to buy a set of forgeries?

David Irving arrived at August Priesack's apartment at 8.30 a.m. on Saturday morning. The much-vaunted 'archive' was spread out on the floor. 'It consisted,' recalled Irving, 'of some twenty folders, A3-sized, with photographs stuck on the front and photocopies of documents of the entire Hitler period, from his birth to the end of his life. A special folder covered the years from 1939 to 1945.' When Stiefel had called Priesack in to look at his collection in 1979, he had rashly provided the 'professor' with photocopies of much of his Hitler material, including half a dozen sheets covering the most interesting entries from the 1935 diary. Several times, while Irving was skimming through the material, the telephone rang with urgent messages. The caller was Fritz Stiefel, but despite pressure from Irving, Priesack refused to identify him. He referred to him either as 'Fritz' or 'the client'. He said that he was in trouble for having said as much as he had, that according to 'Fritz' the entire higher command of the East German Army had been summoned to Berlin for an inquiry into the rumours that one general was smuggling Hitler's diaries to the West.

If he was ever to get to the diaries, Irving knew that he needed to speak to this mysterious 'client'. He decided to trick his doddering old host. 'I persuaded Priesack – who would not give me Fritz's other name however hard I tried – to telephone him reassuringly from the neighbouring room.' Irving crept across to the door and counted the clicks as Priesack dialled the number. In this way he managed to make out the prefix code. ('It's easy. You know the first number is "0" and you can work out the rest from that.')

Making an excuse that he had to go out for a while, Irving left Priesack's apartment and found a neighbouring telephone office. 'I checked all the phone books and found that the area code was for Waiblingen, and the number was for one Fritz Stiefel, whose address I thus obtained.'

The search took Irving several hours. By the time he returned at 5.30 p.m., Priesack had already finished entertaining another visitor. Wolf Rudiger Hess, son of Rudolf Hess, had called to inspect the letter supposedly sent by his father to Hitler in May 1941. 'He had roundly denounced the handwriting as a forgery,' noted Irving. 'If that is faked, what else might not be too?'

Promising to try to arrange a publisher for him, Irving managed to persuade Priesack to part with his precious folders.

Next morning, Irving left Munich for Stuttgart. He caught a train to Waiblingen and marched, unannounced, up to Fritz Stiefel's front door. 'Reluctantly, he appeared,' recalled Irving, 'and reluctantly invited me in.' The historian explained that he had not telephoned because 'one never knew who was listening in'. Stiefel said that if he had phoned him, he would have told him there was no point in coming. 'He approved my method of gaining entry this way and congratulated me.' To thaw the atmosphere further, Irving produced from his inside pocket one of his most valuable possessions: one of Adolf Hitler's monogrammed teaspoons from the Berghof. Whenever Irving was researching in Germany, he carried it with him, a talisman to charm reluctant old Nazis into helping him. 'That spoon,' says Irving, 'has opened a lot of doors.' Stiefel examined it and then went and fetched one of his own to show Irving.

Having compared cutlery the two men settled to business. Irving asked about the Hitler diaries and Stiefel – as Heidemann had predicted – proceeded to lie. A local dealer, he said, had been to see him a few years earlier and shown him a diary. He had kept it for one or two weeks and then given it back. Irving asked if there was any way of finding out where the other volumes were. Stiefel 'answered that he'd heard they'd all been sold to an American'. The industrialist would not reveal the American's name, nor would he identify the diaries' supplier.

All Irving's hard work and cunning appeared to have been in vain. His only consolation was that he had managed to get hold of Priesack's photocopies.

On Tuesday 21 December he flew back to London. He rang Alan Samson, his publisher at Macmillan, and told him about the diaries. Samson was interested and they arranged an appointment for the following day.

Irving did not begin a detailed examination of the Priesack material until 8.30 the next morning. He sat in his first-floor study, pulled out his own folder of authenticated Hitler writing and then began indexing Priesack's papers 'to try to get an impression of their value'.

Whatever allegations may be levelled at Irving as an historian – and there have been many – there is no doubting his ability to sniff out original documents. Over the past twenty years he had become only too familiar with the scale of the trade in forgeries. He had himself almost been fooled by a faked 'diary' of the German intelligence chief, Wilhelm Canaris. He therefore approached Priesack's papers critically – and almost at once he began finding discrepancies. The writing of words like 'Deutsch', 'Nation' and 'NSDAP' which recurred regularly varied in style from document to document. The most damning piece of evidence as far as he was concerned was a letter purporting to have been written by Goering in 1944. The word 'Reichsmarschall' in the printed letter-heading was misspelt *'Reichsmarsall'*. 'By lunchtime,' he wrote in his diary, 'I was unfortunately satisfied that the Priesack collection is stuffed with fake documents.' He cancelled his appointment with Macmillan and rang Priesack. 'There are such huge variances,' he told him, 'that the documents cannot be genuine.' Priesack, according to Irving, 'gasped'. If Stiefel's documents were fakes, how reliable was the rest of the businessman's memorabilia? At that moment, one of the largest printing companies in Italy was busy producing several thousand copies of Billy Price's book, *Adolf Hitler as Painter and Draughtsman*, which was full of pictures from Stiefel's collection.

'Does this mean,' asked Priesack, 'that the watercolours are also forged? They come from the same source.'

Irving replied that he was no art expert. He could not answer that question. He did however say that in his opinion 'the entire story about East German involvement' was 'part of an elaborate *Schwindel* to prevent the purchasers from showing their acquisitions around... I urged him to advise Fritz Stiefel to buy nothing more from this source.'

According to Irving's diary, Priesack was fawning in his gratitude. There were those, he said, who believed that Irving should be given the title 'doctor'. He disagreed: in Germany, the name 'David Irving' was honour enough. To which Irving, angry at having wasted his time, and weary of this tiresome old man, added in his diary the single word: *schmarm*.

But if Irving's visit to Germany had done little to restore his own fortunes, it did at least bring profit to August Priesack.

So far, using Kujau to pressure Fritz Stiefel into keeping quiet, Heidemann had been able to contain the damage done by Priesack's disclosure. Now, the reporter acted to seal the leak altogether. Hard on the heels of David Irving, Heidemann travelled down to Munich to see Priesack. He offered him 30,000 marks in cash for his archive – a sum which Priesack, scraping a living on a school teacher's pension, was happy to accept. 'This is worth a lot to me,' Heidemann told him. 'Now I will own everything Stiefel has.' He did not mention *Stern*'s diaries: Priesack assumed that he and Stiefel were simply rival collectors. Anyway, the reason for the offer was of less interest to him at that moment than the 500- and 1000-mark notes his visitor now pulled out of his briefcase. If Heidemann wanted to throw his money about buying up photocopies, who was he to complain?

20

Nineteen eighty-three was going to be a big year for Gerd Heidemann and he and Gina were determined to greet it in style. At a cost of more than 5000 marks, the couple flew to New York to attend the annual New Year's Eve Ball at the Waldorf Astoria.

As 1982 came to an end, Gerd Heidemann's behaviour was – if anything – even odder than usual. Two-and-a-half years after his honeymoon visit to South America, he was once more obsessed by Martin Bormann, gripped as if by a bout of some recurrent tropical fever. He was utterly convinced by Medard Klapper's stories that Bormann was still alive, presiding over a circle of old Nazis, shuttling between various countries in Europe and the Middle East. Klapper gave Heidemann Bormann's telephone number in Spain and Bormann's Spanish cover name, 'Martin di Calde Villa'. He showed him a house in Zurich where the 'Bormann Group' had its headquarters and allowed Heidemann to photograph the building. He was always on the point of taking the reporter to meet Bormann – only to have to tell him, regretfully, a few days later, that 'Martin' couldn't make the appointment. Heidemann commissioned one of his oldest colleagues, a photographer named Helmut Jabusch, to fly to Zurich to take pictures of 'one of the most prominent Nazis': he even booked airline tickets, but once again, the assignment fell through.

In November 1982, Klapper gave Heidemann six Polaroid photographs of an old man whom he claimed was Bormann. The reporter paid him 25,000 marks for the pictures which he then began showing to colleagues. He pointed out to Felix Schmidt that the man in the photograph – who wore, as Schmidt recalled, 'a Basque cap' – had a birth mark on the left side of his forehead, exactly as Bormann had.

According to Schmidt: 'Heidemann explained that it was possible to make contact with Bormann. Everything had to go through a middle-man but he was sure he would meet Bormann shortly, either in Zurich or in Cairo. The Nazis who surrounded Bormann were going to allow him to meet him. Heidemann always spoke of Bormann as "Martin".' Schmidt was incredulous: not least, because it was *Stern* that had actu-ally proved that Bormann was dead. He began to have doubts about Heidemann's mental health and confided his worries to Peter Koch. Koch shook his head. 'With Heidemann,' he said, 'anything's possible.' Heidemann sent one of the photographs to Max Frei-Sulzer, who was commissioned to investigate it for fingerprints. The versatile Frei-Sulzer reported back on 21 November that he could not reach a positive con-clusion: 'Unfortunately, at the critical place there are several prints on top of one another which cannot be separated. The others are so frag-mented, there is no question of being able to evaluate them.' There was only one clear print, said Frei-Sulzer: its owner was unknown.

His colleagues at *Stern* treated Heidemann's behaviour at this time as if it were no more than a minor eccentricity. It does not seem to have occurred to any of them that a man capable of such obvious self-delusion over Martin Bormann might be equally unreliable on other matters. Leo Pesch recalled that Heidemann now seldom came into the office. When he did so, it was to show them the photograph and to 'talk very intently about Bormann'. Pesch and Walde regarded it as a 'half-crazy story' and used to have 'teasing conversations' with him about it. It was another example of Heidemann showing off, trying to convince people of his importance. 'My impression was that Heidemann had lost more and more contact with reality through his success,' Pesch said afterwards. 'In my view, Heidemann had a great deal of vanity. Again and again, quite unprompted, he would tell colleagues stories about the diaries and about Martin Bormann.' The general view was that funny old Heidemann was up to his usual tricks; as long as it didn't interfere with his real work, the best thing was to humour him. 'Our main con-cern,' admitted Walde, 'was that Heidemann might be diverted by this myth about Bormann from the task of obtaining the diaries.'

Was there a connection between the two stories? Heidemann cer-tainly acted as though there were. Whenever he came across a flattering reference to Bormann in the diaries, he photocopied it and gave it to Klapper to pass on to Bormann. Klapper reported back that 'Martin' was so pleased, he had hung an enlargement of one extract on his study wall in Madrid. Heidemann also talked about Bormann to Kujau. During one of these conversations, the forger told Heidemann that his East German brother could obtain Hitler's gold party insignia, allegedly given to Bormann at the end of the war. Heidemann reported this to Klapper who subsequently passed on 'Martin's' confirmation that the story was indeed correct. Heidemann told Kujau and shortly afterwards, a reference to the decoration appeared in the final volume of the diaries.

Further evidence of possible collusion between Kujau and Klapper surfaced at the beginning of December 1982. Every reference in the Hess special volume was being checked methodically against published sources to make certain it contained no errors. The name of one SS captain, supposedly appointed by Hitler to watch over Hess, proved to be almost indecipherable. Even Wilfried Sorge was called in to give an opinion. Lautman? Lausserman? Eventually, the consensus was that the name was Laackman. Because Walde and Pesch could find no mention of the name in any of their reference books, they asked Josef Henke of the Bundesarchiv to undertake a search on their behalf in the closed records of the Berlin Document Centre. Three weeks later, Henke sent them thirty photocopied pages of SS Captain Anton Laackman's military record. Heidemann also asked Klapper to check with Bormann. In January, Klapper returned with three *original* pages from Laackman's personnel file which he told Heidemann he had removed from Bormann's office in Spain. There was no question but that the documents were authentic. Once again, the Bormann story and the Hitler diaries appeared to be substantiating one another.

Naturally, the Laackman papers did *not* come from Bormann. They were stolen, at Klapper's request, along with other Nazi documents, by a corrupt employee of the West German state archives named Rainer Hess. But Heidemann was not aware of that. For him, the production of the papers was the clinching proof that Bormann was still alive.

Months later, after the diaries were exposed as forgeries, the *Sunday Times* used this episode as the basis for its assertion that 'Klapper played a pivotal role – perhaps the central role – in the diary fraud'.

The kindest thing that can be said about the *Sunday Times* investigation is that it overstated its case. If Laackman's name had not appeared in any book, and Kujau could have forged the diary entry only on the basis of documents supplied by Klapper, the evidence that the two men were working together to trick Heidemann would be conclusive. But Laackman's name *does* appear in a book. It occurs – as the *Sunday Times* was forced to admit – on page 221 of the Nazi Party's Yearbook for 1941: police discovered it, carefully marked by Kujau, when they raided his home in 1983. Moreover, the Hess volume was forged by Kujau in 1981. If the planting of Laackman's name was part of a carefully laid plot, it is hard to see how he could have known fourteen months in advance that *Stern* would fail to spot the reference in the 1941 Yearbook and ask Klapper to obtain the documents.

It is possible there was a link between Kujau and Klapper. The fact that both men, proven liars, deny knowing one another, is no proof to the contrary. But if they were working together, they have covered their tracks with great care. The only place in which the Bormann story, the hunt for secret Nazi treasure and the discovery of Hitler's diaries all came together with any certainty was in the overwrought imagination of Gerd Heidemann.

Now that *Plan 3* had been completed, sale of the syndication rights could begin in earnest. On Wednesday 5 January, Manfred Fischer turned over control of the safe-deposit box in Zurich to Dr Jan Hensmann, deputy managing director of Gruner and Jahr. The following day, Hensmann, Wilfried Sorge and Gerd Schulte-Hillen, accompanied by Olaf Paeschke representing Bertelsmann, flew back to New York for a second round of negotiations with Bantam Books.

Knowing the extent of the market for books on the Second World War, Bantam was enthusiastic about the project. *Plan 3*, based on new writings by Hitler, with its revelation that the Führer authorized Hess's peace mission, would make headlines all over the world. If the hardback edition appeared that autumn, the paperback could tie in with Hess's ninetieth birthday in April 1984. But once again, the discussions foundered. Bantam's President, Louis Wolfe, wanted to involve expert historians in the project. He also demanded extensive guarantees of compensation should the book's authenticity be called into question – an open-ended commitment which the Germans were reluctant to make. A more serious problem concerned newspaper rights. Bantam was prepared to offer $50,000, but their visitors were insistent on retaining syndication rights for themselves. Wolfe 'found it difficult to grasp what Schulte-Hillen and Hensmann actually wanted'. He was not aware that *Plan 3* was regarded in Hamburg merely as a trial balloon for a much bigger scoop. Wolfe could not understand it. He thought that 'the whole thing was being handled in an amateurish way'.

While the businessmen were arguing in the United States, David Irving was preparing to speak to a packed meeting in West Germany. At noon on 9 January, 2000 supporters of the DVU jammed into one of Munich's enormous beer cellars to listen to Irving speak at a memorial meeting for Hans-Ulrich Rudel, the highly decorated fighter pilot who had lived in exile in Brazil and Paraguay, an unrepentant admirer of Adolf Hitler until the end of his life. 'I spoke first,' noted Irving, 'and was interrupted by a huge roar of applause as I called the Bonn politicians *Charakterschweine* for not allowing military representation at the Rudel funeral.'

At the end of the meeting, Irving drove across town to see August Priesack to return his Hitler documents. The material was so riddled with fakes, he told him, he was not going to waste any more time trying to sort it out. He showed Priesack the misspelt Goering notepaper. 'He indicated by his manner that he had already noticed that, but did not consider it important. At this I mildly exploded: "If even the printed letter head of the second most important man in Germany contains a printing error, how can the document be anything other than a fake?" He implied that in 1944 even Goering would be happy to have headed notepaper, printing error or not. I did not even bother to discuss that remark.' Priesack said that he thought he should contact Gerd Heidemann. 'Why contact him?' asked Irving. 'It is quite obvious from these documents that they are fakes.' He told Priesack that he suspected Fritz Stiefel had a hand in the forgeries. Priesack flushed and insisted that was not the case. 'Throughout the half hour conversation he kept putting his hand on my shoulder,' noted Irving, who was as fastidious as the Führer about physical contact. 'At one stage he even held my hand, which was not pleasant.'

Priesack accompanied Irving out to his car. 'I don't suppose I shall be seeing you again?' he said. 'He seemed sad about that,' recalled Irving in his diary, 'though not at all about the prospect of the money he had lost.' (Irving did not know that Priesack's apparent stoicism was that of a man who had sold his collection – fakes and all – to Heidemann for 30,000 marks.) The historian drove off in a bad mood. *He*, at any rate, had lost money. Even allowing for the expenses paid to him by Langen Mueller, he reckoned he had spent 2000 marks he could ill afford. 'But,' he wrote that evening, 'I do not regret that as it would have been much worse if I had proceeded any further before realizing that his files of documents were largely forgeries.'

'I suspect,' he added, 'that Heidemann has also been tricked.'

The following day in New York the negotiations between Gruner and Jahr and Bantam Books finally broke down. In their hotel suite that evening, the Germans discussed what they should do next. The English language market was largely a mystery to them. Clearly, if they were to exploit their property to the full, they would need some professional advice. Sticking to their original model of the Kissinger memoirs, they decided to enlist the help of Kissinger's agent, Marvin Josephson. Josephson was the head of International Creative Management (ICM), the largest artistic agency in the world. Josephson did not handle their business personally. Instead, the *Stern* men were referred to Lynn Nesbit, Senior Vice-President of ICM, whom they were told was the company's expert on magazine rights.

According to Ms Nesbit, at a meeting with Sorge, she undertook to handle 'the North American serial rights to a document called *Plan 3* ', based on original, unpublished notes written by Adolf Hitler. She did not bother to check its authenticity herself. Sorge told her that *Stern* had a series of expert reports which proved that the Hitler material was genuine. The magazine would be willing to show these reports to potential purchasers. 'The word "diary" was never mentioned to me,' she recalled. If she had known she was actually representing sixty volumes of Hitler's diaries, she would have been 'much more sceptical':

It seemed totally plausible that a 4000-word [*sic*] document could have been hidden all these years. *Stern* has a reputation for reliability and they were putting their own reputation on the boards with this. If it had been just a person with no journalistic credibility and nothing at stake, I would have been much more suspicious.

Sorge was insistent that the material should be offered only to 'reputable' organizations. *Time*, *Newsweek* and the *New York Times* were the obvious candidates. Ms Nesbit promised to arrange a series of meetings at which Sorge could meet potential clients. Her tentative estimate of the market value of *Plan 3* in the United States was $250,000.

The next week in Hamburg was a busy one for Gerd Heidemann. On Tuesday 18 January he finally signed the revised contract, drafted in October, finalized in December, guaranteeing him 36 per cent of the syndication revenue once the company had cleared its costs. This immediately entitled him to claim 300,000 marks – the balance owing on his 'compensation' settlement of 1.5 million. On Wednesday, he withdrew 150,000 marks in cash from the Adolphsplatz bank, telling Sorge he needed it for the next batch of diaries. On Saturday he was in Munich with Gina, at the invitation of August Priesack, for the launching party of Billy F. Price's book, *Adolf Hitler as Painter and Draughtsman*.

For Mr Price, millionaire compressor manufacturer and connoisseur of the Führer's art, Saturday 22 January was a great day. He had already spent at least $100,000 on producing his book and to celebrate its publication he spared no expense. A room was booked at the Four Seasons, one of the most expensive hotels in Munich. There was plenty of fine wine and food. The guest list read like a Berghof reception.

There was Frau Henriette Hoffmann von Schirach – daughter of Hitler's photographer, Heinrich Hoffmann and widow of Baldur von Schirach, leader of the Hitler Youth and Gauleiter of Vienna. When she was a young girl, Hitler had taught Henriette to play the piano; when she was a bride, he had been best man at her wedding. She was suing the United States Government for the return of two Hitler paintings, allegedly stolen from her house at the end of the war and now hanging in the National Army museum in Washington. Price was paying her legal fees.

There was Frau Gerda Christian, most dedicated of Hitler's secretaries. Next to her was her old colleague, Christa Schroeder, seventy-five years old and ill with a kidney complaint. She had helped Price with his book and sold him some pictures from her own collection. In return, Price was paying her medical bills.

There was Frau Schmidt-Ehmen, wife of one of Hitler's favourite sculptors, and Eva Wagner, descendant of his favourite composer. There was Peter Jahn, the Viennese 'art expert', who had worked with Priesack cataloguing Hitler's paintings in the 1930s and who had helped the Marquess of Bath acquire much of his collection. There was one of Hitler's doctors. There was Bormann's adjutant. . .

Price moved among them, proud and prosperous, in a dark three-piece suit, signing copies of his book. He realized, he said later, that the only reason most of his guests wanted to know him was that he was rich – 'but what the hell?' He felt he was performing a service to history by gathering together Hitler's art. What he did not know was that of the 725 pictures in his book, at least 170 were the work of Konrad Kujau. At one point, Fritz Stiefel – who had supplied the pictures to Price – approached the Texan and asked him actually to autograph a copy of the book for his 'good friend Conny Fischer'. But for some reason, Price never signed the book. 'God,' he declared afterwards, with revivalist fervour, 'stayed mah hand.'

For Gerd and Gina Heidemann, the reception was filled with familiar faces and when the time came to leave, a tipsy Frau Heidemann thanked their host for 'a wonderful party'. Gerd Heidemann invited Price to come to Hamburg to see his own collection of Hitler's art. He confided to his fellow devotee that he had 'something big' himself coming out in a few months' time. 'He couldn't tell me what it was,' recalled Price, 'and I didn't question him too much about it.'

A few days after the party, Price took up Heidemann's offer and visited him at his home in the Elbchaussee. The Texan had met plenty of Hitler obsessives, but seldom anyone as far gone as Heidemann: 'Priesack's in love with Hitler. But Heidemann's more in love with Hitler than anyone I've ever met in my life.' He was impressed by much of the reporter's collection, but even he – who had been taken in by Stiefel's pictures – found some of it 'ridiculously fake'. Heidemann showed him one painting (admittedly, one of Kujau's more exuberant efforts) which almost made him burst out laughing: a portrait, supposedly by Hitler, of King Farouk of Egypt. Price was still shaking his head about the episode a year later. 'Hell, man. *King Farouk*. No *way* would I accept that.'

Another foreign visitor entertained by Heidemann in the two Elbchaussee apartments at this time was Gitta Sereny of the *Sunday Times*.

According to David Irving, he had warned the *Sunday Times* in a telephone call on 30 December that the material he had seen was 'dangerously polluted with fakes'. But the newspaper was not inclined to take his word for anything, let alone the authenticity of Adolf Hitler's diaries. They decided to send a reporter of their own to make contact with Heidemann, and Gitta Sereny was the obvious choice. Brought up in Austria before the war, she was trilingual in English, French and German, and a regular contributor on Nazi subjects. In 1974 she had written *Into that Darkness*, an examination of Franz Stangl, Commandant of the Treblinka extermination camp. She was also, as it happened, a personal enemy of Irving's, having published a damning attack on *Hitler's War* in the *Sunday Times* when it first appeared in 1977.

Over the course of two days, Heidemann and Sereny spoke for about eight hours. He took her on a tour of his archive. She found his collection 'breathtaking'. Filed away, protected by clear plastic covers, was a series of what appeared to be 'extraordinary' documents, including the original of Hitler's order to liquidate the Soviet commissars. He showed her a letter from Karl Wolff in which the general appointed him his literary heir and executor. He showed her his library of negatives from the Hoffmann photographic archive. The walls of the Heidemanns' two flats were crammed with Hitler paintings. 'I was stunned,' she recalled, 'absolutely stunned.'

> I had seen examples of Hitler's painting before at Albert Speer's. These things looked exactly the same. There were about three dozen hanging round the Heidemanns' bed. I said: 'Jesus Christ, doesn't this stuff give you nightmares?' Gina said: 'Oh no, we couldn't possibly sleep without them.'

Heidemann told Sereny that he was making regular, clandestine trips to East Germany. He assured her that the Hitler diaries existed. He was not, however, prepared to say whether they were in his possession. Although Heidemann struck her as a man obsessed by the Nazis, characterized by 'an extraordinary political and intellectual naivety', she believed he was telling the truth. If anyone could obtain the diaries, he could.

Inadvertently, despite his concern not to give anything away, Heidemann also provided her with a clue to the origin of the diaries' trail. He mentioned Professor Eberhard Jaeckel as an historian who knew something about the East German material. From her hotel in Hamburg, Sereny telephoned Jaeckel who confirmed that some years previously he *had* seen something: not a diary exactly, but a 'yearbook'. Sereny asked him if he thought it was authentic. He said it was 'interesting'. He would not go any further on the telephone. 'Come down to Stuttgart,' he said. Sereny asked if he could introduce her to the person who obtained the diary. Jaeckel replied that if she came down, it might be possible for them to go and see some people. Sereny telephoned Magnus Linklater in the *Sunday Times* office with this exciting news. But to her amazement, he refused to authorize a trip to South Germany. The paper's new owner, Rupert Murdoch, had demanded that the editorial department reduce its costs: the *Sunday Times* was gripped by what Sereny later called 'a rabid economy drive'. Even in sending her to Hamburg for two nights, Linklater had risked incurring the wrath of the editor, Frank Giles. She had to return to London at once.

If the *Sunday Times* had not decided on this false economy, the events of the next three months would probably have developed very differently. Sereny would have met Jaeckel and learned of the forgeries printed in his book of Hitler's writings. She would probably have met Stiefel. She might even have met 'Herr Fischer'. 'I could have stopped the whole goddam thing right there,' she complained later. As it was, the *Sunday Times* passed up one of the few remaining chances of uncovering the hoax. The impending fiasco, swollen by the profligacy of West Germany's journalism, was abetted by the parsimony of Great Britain's.

21

On Wednesday 16 February, Wilfried Sorge arrived in the international departure lounge of Hamburg airport to catch a flight to Denmark. It was almost two and a half years since that stroll in the Black Forest when Walde had first told him of the hunt for Hitler's diaries. Now, with a copy of *Plan 3* in his luggage, he was about to depart on the first stage of a three-week odyssey to sell the story to the world. In terms of his career, Sorge – like Walde and Heidemann – had a great deal staked on the Hitler diaries. To have been entrusted with such an important mission, six weeks short of his fortieth birthday, was a clear sign of the young executive's growing stature within the company. Gruner and Jahr were counting upon him. Schulte-Hillen personally was watching the way he handled things.

Sorge was well equipped for his mission. Immaculately tailored, endlessly charming, permanently tanned, he was the epitome of expense-account smoothness. The strategy which he was about to put into action had been agreed in Hamburg after consultations with Bertelsmann and ICM. A list of foreign companies had been compiled to whom the Hess story would be offered. In some countries – the United States and Spain for example – several news organizations would be approached at the same time, in order to encourage competition and push up the price. In others, such as France and Italy, Sorge would deal with one company exclusively.

Sorge flew first to Copenhagen for discussions with Bertelsmann's agent in Scandinavia. From there he caught a transatlantic flight to New York. Lynn Nesbit had arranged three interviews for him. At the offices of *Newsweek* he met the magazine's editor-in-chief, William Broyles, and its managing editor, Maynard Parker. Peter Koch had mentioned the project to Parker during a visit to America shortly before Christmas. At the time he had been rebuked for his indiscretion, but Sorge found that the notion of publishing original Hitler material had taken hold at *Newsweek*. Broyles and Parker told him they were very interested and would probably be submitting an offer. At *Time*, the response of William Mador, former Bonn correspondent, also sounded promising. The only person who did not seem enthusiastic was the woman who represented the *New York Times*. After a few days in the United States, Sorge flew back to Europe – to Amsterdam, where he discussed the prospects for Holland and Belgium with the Bertelsmann people. Then it was on to France, to make a sales pitch to *Paris Match*. From there, Sorge flew south to Madrid to see representatives from the magazine *Cambio 16* and the newspaper *El Pais*. Leaving Spain, he headed east: first to Milan for a meeting with the publishing group Mondadori, then on again for the longest leg of the journey so far – to Tokyo, and the ancient mysteries of the Far Eastern market. . .

It was during one lunchtime the following week, while Sorge was midway through his sales trip, that Heidemann met Henri Nannen and Peter Koch in the street near the *Stern* building. They passed on some devastating news. It had been decided to abandon the current publishing plan in favour of launching the scoop with the story of the diaries' discovery. Heidemann hurried back to the special office to tell Leo Pesch and Thomas Walde. In the afternoon, Heidemann and Walde went over to see Koch to find out what was going on.

Neither Koch nor Schmidt had ever been happy with the idea of starting with the serialization of the Hess scoop. It might make sense commercially, but from a journalistic point of view it was ridiculous. The sensation was in the fact of the diaries' existence, not in the single revelation of Hitler's knowledge of Hess's flight, buried in the biographical detail of *Plan 3*. Alone, Koch and Schmidt had been unable to convince Schulte-Hillen and the *Stern* management. But now they had a powerful ally. Henri Nannen had taken the manuscript of *Plan 3* home to read over Christmas. 'I was amazed to find that it was simply the Hess story with Hitler quotations in it,' he recalled. He gave the book to a girlfriend for her opinion. She was forty-two. What did she think her generation would make of it? 'She found the story interesting, but she didn't appreciate its historical importance, and she didn't grasp at all that she was looking at part of a sensational find of Hitler's diaries.' When Nannen returned from his holiday in January he told Schulte-Hillen that he was in danger of squandering his investment by being overcautious: 'If one had Hitler diaries, one should start the story with this announcement, and with the story of the find.' Henri Nannen was one of the most successful journalists in West Germany. Schulte-Hillen listened to him with respect. He endorsed Nannen's decision.

The meeting in Koch's office that afternoon was noisy. Heidemann was horrified by the new idea. He returned to his old argument that premature publication would endanger lives and jeopardize the supply of the remaining diaries. Koch was sarcastic: the reporter had already spent more than two years bringing in the books; how many more were there? Schmidt and Gillhausen also arrived to add their support to Koch. Schmidt was worried that if they delayed much longer, David Irving or some rival organization would obtain photocopies of the diaries. Gillhausen – the most junior of the editors, but nevertheless respected as a man with a 'nose' for a good story – added his opinion. 'His feeling,' recalled Walde, 'was that the newsworthy part came in three little paragraphs before the end. The whole story should be published the other way round, starting with the story of the find.'

Walde shared Heidemann's fears. He also had two additional concerns: he did not want to see his book swamped by the controversy which would be aroused by the announcement of the diaries' discovery; and secondly, he wanted to write the story of the find himself – something which would be impossible if he had to prepare extracts from the diaries as well. Suddenly, he saw his dreams of becoming an authority on Hitler disappearing into the maw of *Stern*'s accelerating timetable. But Koch had been pushed around by his own staff for long enough. According to Walde he 'threatened' him. He said that 'he would take the work on the diaries out of my hands if I persisted in obstructing publication by my "inflexible" behaviour'.

'Despite my huge reservations about whether publication was possible in the time allowed,' said Walde, 'I gave in. That was my big mistake.'

*

Walde had one particularly good reason for being alarmed by the decision to speed up publication. Although the company had obtained three reports authenticating the handwriting of its Hitler archive, no part of it had yet been subjected to forensic tests. If he had contacted a freelance chemical analyst, these could have been performed in a matter of days. Walde's mistake had been to rely upon the West German Federal Police, the *Bundeskriminalamt* (BKA). On 5 July 1982, under the auspices of the Bundesarchiv, the BKA had been sent the originals of the material studied by the handwriting experts – the Hess statement and the Horthy telegram – with a request that they conduct tests to determine the age of the paper. Later, they had also been sent the various signed Hitler photographs and the Kleist document. Nothing happened. Despite occasional reminders from Walde, the BKA forensic experts continued to concentrate on their official police work. In December, *Stern* had asked for their request to be given 'the highest priority'. Still nothing had been done. Now the unpleasant meeting with Koch galvanized the history department into making a new approach, this time enlisting the help of the Bundesarchiv. On Tuesday 1 March, Leo Pesch telexed Dr Oldenhage, pleading with him to contact *Stern* as quickly as possible: 'We have some urgent deadline problems regarding the expert reports.'

On Friday 4 March, Wilfried Sorge, jet-lagged in his bedroom in a hotel in Tokyo, was telephoned by Peter Hess, Gruner and Jahr's publishing director, and summoned back to Hamburg. 'What's happened?' he asked. 'The whole publishing concept has been changed,' he was told: he must return immediately 'in order to pitch the sales strategy in line with the new plan'. Sorge was bitter at this news. In the space of a single telephone call, thousands of miles of air travel and days of meetings and planning had been ruined. He had no choice but to book himself on the first available flight back to Germany.

In New York, Lynn Nesbit's contract to sell *Plan 3* was terminated. She received a fee of $10,000 for her efforts. *Newsweek*, which had already submitted a tentative offer of $150,000 for the serial rights to the Hess book, was told that *Stern* had changed its mind. From

Hamburg, telexes were dispatched to all Sorge's potential customers informing them that they 'could no longer be offered the material'.

The following Tuesday, Gerd Schulte-Hillen convened a meeting in a conference room on the ninth floor of the *Stern* building. It was attended by all those involved in the diaries project: Nannen, Gill-hausen, Koch, Schmidt, Walde, Heidemann, Pesch, Sorge, Hess and Hensmann. The history department's flickering hope that the new publication plan might be abandoned was crushed by Schulte-Hillen's opening words. 'Gentlemen,' announced the managing director, 'the time has come. We intend to publish.' Nevertheless, Walde, Pesch and Heidemann were determined to make one last stand. The source of the diaries, they warned, would be threatened, and important volumes had yet to be delivered. Walde reported that they had no books from the year 1944: 'If we did not get hold of those volumes . . . we would be unable to settle some very important questions about the Third Reich.' Imagine what Hitler might have written about the German response to D-Day or the July bomb plot. Sorge supported his old schoolfriend. Speaking as a salesman, he would find it much easier to offer the diary archive in its entirety, rather than having to tell customers that part of it had not yet arrived.

Schulte-Hillen was not convinced. He accepted the argument of Nannen and the editors: to start with the Hess story and not to men-tion the diaries was the wrong way of doing things. If they delayed any longer there was a danger of leaks. They should go ahead and begin printing the story in May.

That settled, the conference went on to take a series of decisions on the timetable for publication. The existence of the diaries would be revealed in eight weeks' time, in *Stern*'s issue of 5 May. To wring the last ounce of sensation and profitability out of the diaries, serialization would be divided into three separate periods, spaced out over a period of eighteen months. In May and June, the magazine would run eight weekly instalments, covering the story of the diaries' discovery, the Hess flight and the Nazis' rise to power. There would then be a break over the summer. In the autumn they would relaunch the scoop with a ten-part series based on the pre-war diaries. This would be followed by a second and much longer interruption while the final extracts were prepared. Finally, in the autumn of 1984, *Stern* would publish another ten extracts based on the diaries from the war years. Heidemann was instructed to deliver the missing volumes by 31 March. Another *Stern* reporter, Wolf Thieme, was given the task of putting together the story of how the diaries were found – once again, Heidemann was expected to turn over all his information for someone else to write up.

The magazine, concluded Schulte-Hillen, had less than a month to produce the first eight-part series: it would need to be shown to potential foreign customers during syndication negotiations at the beginning of April.

Early the next morning, the peripatetic Sorge was back at Hamburg airport to catch the first flight to London. He had already scheduled meetings with potential British customers before *Stern* changed its publication strategy. In view of the importance of the British market, it was decided to go ahead with the London sales trip as planned. At Heathrow, Sorge was met by *Stern*'s bureau chief in London, Peter Wickman, and the two men drove to their first appointment: with Sir David English of Lord Rothermere's Associated Newspapers group.

English, editor-in-chief of the *Daily Mail* and the *Mail on Sunday*, listened to Sorge's presentation of the Hess story. His immediate worry was the possibility that the Hitler document might be a fake. He had been caught himself, when editor of the *Daily Mail*, by forged correspondence supposedly originating from Lord Ryder. Another worry was the reputation of the *Mail on Sunday*, to whom the Hess scoop would be given as ammunition in its circulation battle with the *Sunday Express*. The *Mail on Sunday*'s editor, Stewart Steven, was the man who had helped Ladislas Farago track down Martin Bormann for the *Daily Express* in 1972 only to discover, too late, that 'Bormann' was actually an innocent Argentine high school teacher. English told Sorge he was interested in *Stern*'s story, but he would require absolute guarantees of authenticity before going any further.

In the afternoon, Sorge and Wickman went to see their other possible client, Times Newspapers. Colin Webb and Charles Wilson attended the meeting on behalf of *The Times*, Brian MacArthur for the *Sunday Times*. Before revealing what he had to offer, Sorge made the three men sign a pledge of secrecy. They were more interested in the story than David English, but before they could make any commitment, they would have to consult the editors of the two papers and their proprietor, Rupert Murdoch. The secrecy pledge was amended to allow these three gentlemen to be informed of *Stern*'s scoop.

Sorge spent the night in the Savoy Hotel and the following morning returned to Hamburg.

Heidemann dreaded the impending launch of the diaries. His comfortable existence of the last two years – the suitcases full of money, the flattery of his superiors – was bound to come to an end. He would cease to have a hold over the company. He would suffer the humiliation of watching while the diaries were passed to other writers for exploitation. Already, he had been forced to entertain Wolf Thieme in his gallery in Milchstrasse and tell him the story of the diaries' discovery. This meeting had posed another problem for Heidemann. It was safe for him to talk about the evacuation of documents from Berlin and the loss of the plane. He could describe how he had located the crash site using Gundlfinger's name. He could talk of the local peasants who had salvaged material from the wrecked aircraft. But then, of necessity, there was a gap of more than thirty years, until the books started accumulating in the management's safe in Hamburg. Heidemann explained to Thieme that he could not say any more without jeopardizing the lives of his informants. Naturally, he did not tell Thieme the other reason for his reticence: that if Kujau's identity were ever disclosed, and if the garrulous relics dealer ever spoke to anyone else from *Stern*, it would only be a matter of time before the company discovered he had been defrauding them for the past two years.

To try to ward off publication, with all its attendant hazards, Heidemann used every argument, cajolement and threat at his disposal in a desperate attempt to make the company change its mind. On Thursday 17 March he went to see Schulte-Hillen and handed him a closely typed two-page memorandum 'for his eyes only'. The managing director, said Heidemann, must destroy it as soon as he had read it. 'Dear Herr Schulte-Hillen,' it began,

Before you reach any irrevocable decisions, I would like once again to put my reservations on paper. I cannot guarantee that the missing diaries will be in Hamburg by the beginning of May 1983. There is no way that they will be with us by the beginning of April. How are the sales negotiations to proceed if we cannot offer those who are interested a complete set of diaries? Are we to answer questions by admitting that we have not had the nerve to wait as long as it takes to have the last diary in our hands? Are we to say to those interested that we are worried there might be photocopies of the diaries on the market? What do we do when the main protagonists [in the negotiations – i.e. Sorge] are insisting that the diaries can only be sold as a complete package and we should wait until the autumn? Of course I am of the opinion that we should have the complete story of the find and several issues prepared and ready to go in order to be able to begin publishing immediately should any photocopies surface. But this danger is very slight: my business partner in East Germany is counting on the fact that the 'Swiss collector' will eventually buy other things from him. . .

Heidemann went on to list fourteen separate sets of Hitler documents which his 'business partner' had told him were on offer:

1   Six diary-like volumes which Hitler wrote alongside the diaries which are known to us.

2   Adolf Hitler's handwritten memoirs, *My Life and Struggle for Germany*, written in the years 1942–44.

3   Hitler's book about women, in which there are said to be descriptions of his experiences with women.

4   Hitler's plan for the solution of the Jewish question, written after the Wannsee Conference on 28 January 1942, in which he gives Himmler precise orders as to what is to happen to the Jews (eighteen handwritten pages).

5   Hitler's handwritten *Documents about Himmler, Ley and Others*, including notes about the Jewish origins of those concerned.

6   Hitler's notes from 18 April until his death on 30 April 1945.

7   Goebbels's notes following Hitler's suicide.

8   Hitler's handwritten testament and marriage documents (twenty-one pages).

9 Hitler's documents about his supposed son in France.
10 Hitler's documents about his origins and relatives.
11 *Secret Thoughts about Different Military and Political Problems*.
12 Hitler's book about Frederick the Great.
13 Hitler's book about King Ludwig II of Bavaria.
14 Hitler's opera, *Wieland the Blacksmith*.

Heidemann added that there were 'three hundred other drawings and watercolours by Hitler' also available in East Germany.

Heidemann was not necessarily lying when he outlined this fantastic catalogue to Schulte-Hillen. He appears to have genuinely believed what Kujau told him: that these documents could be rescued from behind the Iron Curtain and that premature disclosure might lose *Stern* the chance of obtaining them. Not all the items were new to *Stern*. For example, Kujau had first offered to sell *Wieland the Blacksmith* to Heidemann at the beginning of 1981. The forger had hit on the idea after reading the memoirs of August Kubizek. In *The Young Hitler I Knew*, published in 1955, Kubizek described how Hitler set about writing an opera, a sub-Wagnerian epic of rape and murder, set in the rugged wastes of Iceland, complete with flaming volcanoes, icy glaciers and winged Valkyries in shining helmets rising from the waters of 'Wolf Lake'. In the end, *Wieland the Blacksmith* was too much even for Hitler, and he abandoned it, after a few weeks' work, in 1907. The incident provided Kujau with a perfect cover story for another fake, and for more than two years he kept promising to supply the opera to Heidemann. The imagination recoils at the thought of what Bertelsmann's marketing department might have done with a Hitler opera – especially as one of the company's American subsidiaries was Arista Records. Mercifully, *Wieland the Blacksmith* was one piece of Hitleriana that Kujau never got round to forging. (He would have done it, he said later, but for the fact that he did not read music.)

Another of the new documents – the biography of King Ludwig II of Bavaria – was also familiar to Heidemann. One of the first diaries the reporter delivered to Hamburg contained a description of a visit supposedly made by Hitler to the town of Hohenschwangau. 'During my address,' noted 'Hitler' on 12 August 1933, 'I mention that in earlier years I once wrote a small book about Ludwig II. This must be in Munich.' Thus Kujau, with characteristic cheek, used one forgery to prepare the way for another.

In his memorandum, Heidemann warned Schulte-Hillen that it would be impossible to obtain all these treasures by 31 March – the managing director's 'target date' for the completion of *Stern*'s archive. Therefore, said Heidemann, he proposed to deliver the material to 'other interested parties', and asked to be released from his contract with Gruner and Jahr.

Schulte-Hillen was not impressed by Heidemann's bluster. The reporter had threatened to resign so often over the past few years, the bluff no longer carried any conviction. It was not that Schulte-Hillen saw anything inherently implausible in such documents as Hitler's 'book about women', it was simply that the time had passed when he was prepared to tolerate this sort of procrastination. Besides, the company already had enough Hitler material to fill *Stern* for the next eighteen months. He was a stubborn man, and he had made up his mind. They would begin publishing the diaries in May.

Schulte-Hillen also ignored Heidemann's request that he should burn the memo. When he had finished reading it, he locked it away in the same file as Heidemann's various contracts. Afterwards he mentioned the episode during a conversation with Henri Nannen. To Nannen, Heidemann's determination to try to postpone publication was further evidence of fraud. 'Heidemann,' he thought, 'was only really interested in providing further material in order to obtain further payments.' But recalling Schulte-Hillen's reaction the last time he had aired his suspicions, he said nothing.

Three days later, Sorge announced to his clients that in addition to the Hess story, *Stern* was now offering to sell syndication rights in Adolf Hitler's diaries. Interested organizations were invited to send representatives to inspect the material in Zurich at the end of the first week of April.

22

The first intimation that there might be something seriously wrong with *Stern*'s great scoop came a week and a half later. Walde had at last succeeded in persuading the West German Federal Police to carry out the long-awaited forensic tests. On Tuesday 22 March he telexed Dr Henke and Dr Oldenhage at the Bundesarchiv to tell them he had fixed an appointment to hear the results the following Monday morning. He hoped they could both make it: 'Colleague Heidemann will attend for us.'

At 10 a.m. on 28 March, Heidemann, Henke and Oldenhage duly assembled at the police headquarters at Wiesbaden. It was assumed that the meeting would be a formality. The material had, after all, been authenticated by three different handwriting analysts. The police expert, Dr Louis Werner, appeared. He had been given nine samples to examine: the Hess statement, the Horthy telegram, the Kleist document, the draft telegram to Franco, some speech notes, a letter to Goering and the three signed Hitler photographs. His conclusion: of the nine documents, he thought at least six were forgeries.

To begin with, Heidemann could not believe what he was hearing. He asked Dr Werner to elaborate. Werner explained that under ultraviolet light, six of the samples, including all the signed photographs and the Horthy telegram, appeared to contain a substance called 'Blankophor', a paper-whitening agent which as far as he was aware had not come into use until after the Second World War. In his opinion, it was therefore impossible that they could have been written at the time their dates indicated. He proposed to consult an expert from the Bayer chemical company for confirmation. In addition, the Kleist document contained glue of recent manufacture, and one of the letters had been typed on a machine built after 1956.

Heidemann asked about the other three samples, which included the Hess statement, the only page to come from the actual diaries. They, at least, were definitely genuine? Not necessarily, replied Werner. He could not be sure until he had carried out further tests.

How long would that take?

A week.

Heidemann asked if he could borrow the telephone. Werner told him to go ahead. In the scientist's presence, he rang Walde and repeated what he had just heard. He handed the receiver to Werner.

Walde asked the expert if he could absolutely guarantee that the Hess document was a fake. Werner said he couldn't: he would have to carry out further tests. These would necessitate damaging the page by cutting away part of it which could then be broken down into its separate components.

Greatly relieved, Walde thanked him and asked him to put Heidemann back on the line. Walde told Heidemann to retrieve the material and return with it to Hamburg immediately.

The two men discussed this unexpected setback the next day. There was no question in their minds that the material was genuine. They had three handwriting reports to prove it. Clearly, there had been a misunderstanding somewhere. Perhaps the documents had become contaminated with whitener in the course of their travels around Europe and North America during the previous year. Perhaps Werner had made a mistake. Or perhaps somehow a few dubious papers *had* been mixed up with the genuine material.

Heidemann rang Kujau and explained what had happened. 'Oh, don't worry about the BKA,' Kujau assured him. 'They're all mad there.' He told Heidemann that he had encountered this problem before. According to a police official *he* knew, paper whitener had been in use since 1915. Werner was talking nonsense.

Heidemann relayed this conversation to Walde. They agreed, as a safety check, to arrange further forensic tests, this time specifically concentrating on material from the diaries. They did not bother to tell *Stern*'s editors or management of Werner's preliminary assessment.

To launch Hitler's diaries, *Stern* was planning the biggest publicity campaign in its history. There would be a press conference in Hamburg. There would be advertisements in all West Germany's leading newspapers. There would also be a special television documentary, packaged and ready to sell to networks throughout the world.

On Thursday 31 March, Wilfried Sorge called in the head of *Stern*'s TV subsidiary, Herr Zeisberg, and briefed him on the story of the diaries' discovery. Could he have a forty-minute film ready by 3 May, to coincide with the launch? Zeisberg said it was possible. They discussed who they might commission to make it. The obvious choice as producer was Klaus Harpprecht: he had made programmes on historical subjects, he had an excellent reputation, and he had worked extensively in America – an important qualification, as Sorge wanted to include an American element to help US sales. As presenter, they picked Barbara Dickmann, an experienced journalist, occasionally tipped as a potential German equivalent of ABC's Barbara Walters.

Peter Koch approved their choices. He called Dickmann at her office in Bonn that afternoon. Would she come to a confidential meeting at his home in Hamburg next Monday? She asked him what it was about. He refused to tell her over the telephone. Intrigued by Koch's secretive manner, she agreed.

In America, Maynard Parker of *Newsweek* telephoned Gordon Craig, Professor of History at Stanford University. Swearing him to secrecy, Parker told him about the Hitler diaries and asked if he would be willing to advise *Newsweek* on their authenticity. Craig, author of *The Germans*, was not an expert on Hitler: his speciality was the eighteenth and nineteenth centuries. He advised Parker to ask someone else. Parker asked him if he could recommend anyone. Craig suggested Gerhard Weinberg of the University of North Carolina. Parker said he would try him.

Craig promptly rang his old friend Weinberg. He could not go into details, he said, but 'off the record' *Newsweek* would be getting in touch with him very shortly. Weinberg, fifty-five years old, quiet and punctilious, had managed to pursue his profession in peace for more than three decades and had only limited experience of journalists. 'I don't think that's very likely, Gordon,' he said.

'You'll see,' insisted Craig. 'They'll be in touch.'

In London, Peter Wickman spoke with Sir Edward Pickering, executive vice-chairman of Times Newspapers. Pickering said the company wanted to send a historian out to Zurich to give them an opinion on the diaries: 'We thought we'd ask Trevor-Roper.' He was not only considered an authority on Hitler, he was also one of the company's five Independent National Directors. Wickman said that *Stern* did not mind who Times Newspapers nominated as long as it was someone discreet. The next day – Friday 1 April – Colin Webb, assistant editor of *The Times*, tried to contact Trevor-Roper.

For the 'Sleuth of Oxford', the years since the publication of *The Last Days of Hitler* had been filled with honours and success. In 1957, his friendship with one Conservative prime minister, Harold Macmillan, had helped bring him the post of Regius Professor of Modern History at Oxford University; and in 1979 Margaret Thatcher granted him a peerage. He was an honorary fellow of two Oxford colleges, a member of three London clubs, and a Chevalier of the Legion of Honour. In 1954 he had married Lady Alexandra Howard-Johnston, elder daughter of Field Marshal Earl Haig, and the couple had become renowned for grand dinner parties at which Trevor-Roper would occasionally appear in velvet smoking jacket and embroidered slippers. His friend, the philosopher A. J. Ayer, 'admired his intellectual elegance' and 'appreciated his malice'.

Intellectually, even in private, Trevor-Roper could be faintly menacing; in print, he was devastating. An attack on one historian's work (on the Elizabethan aristocracy) was described as 'a magnificent if terrifying work of destruction' and brought him a rebuke from the venerable R. H. Tawney: 'An erring colleague is not an Amalekite, to be smitten hip and thigh.' In the course of one intellectual dogfight with Evelyn Waugh on the subject of the Catholic church, Waugh advised him to 'change his name and seek a livelihood at Cambridge'. Trevor-Roper did so in 1980, taking the title Lord Dacre of Glanton and becoming Master of Peterhouse, the oldest and most conservative college in Cambridge. Since then, anecdotes of the running battle between the college's High Church fellows and their anti-clerical Master had reached mythical proportions within the university. At his first dinner on High Table, Trevor-Roper was said to have objected to the consistency of the soup. '*Gentlemen*,' he announced, 'only have *clear* soup at dinner.' The following evening's menu began with *Potage de Gentilhomme*, a soup thick enough for the Master to stand his spoon in.

Trevor-Roper was not at home in Peterhouse when Webb tried to reach him on the telephone. It was Good Friday, and he and Lady Alexandra had retired for Easter to Chiefswood, their country house in Scotland, once the property of the novelist, Sir Walter Scott. Here, Trevor-Roper was able to escape the in-fighting of Oxbridge and affect the habits and costume of a laird of the Scottish borders; and it was here, on 1 April, that Webb tracked him down, told him of Hitler's diaries, and asked him to fly to Zurich the following week.

On Easter Sunday, Peter Koch made several trips to Heidemann's home on the Elbchaussee to pick up drawings and paintings from the reporter's collection. The idea was to take them to Zurich and exhibit them alongside the diaries to create the right atmosphere for the negotiations. It was the first time Koch had seen Heidemann's lifestyle at first hand, and he was shocked by its luxuriousness. As he was led from room to room he tried to reckon up in his mind how much this would cost in rent. Ten thousand marks a month at least, he thought. Heidemann said he found it rather cramped. 'He told me he was thinking of buying a *house* on the Elbchaussee,' recalled Koch. 'It was a place with a view of the Elbe.' A house like that would cost over a million marks.

Heidemann pointed out some of his treasures. 'There was a whole pile of antiques,' said Koch. 'There were some old walking sticks, drawings by Rembrandt and Dürer, a memento of Napoleon. . . He also told me he had about three hundred paintings by Hitler.' Heidemann produced Hitler's suicide weapon, with Bormann's note attached to it. 'There was also a ladies' pistol, which was supposed to have been

Eva Braun's.' Heidemann told him it had all come from the Boernersdorf crash. Koch asked him how he had paid for it. The reporter told
him the company had compensated him for buying it with a payment
of 1.5 million marks.

Heidemann mentioned this quite casually, apparently assuming that
Koch already knew of it. It was the first Koch had heard of any special payment and he confronted Schulte-Hillen with the story at one
of the company's routine financial meetings the following week. 'He
behaved as if he didn't know anything,' Koch remembered. 'Then he
asked his deputy, Hensmann, if he knew anything. They both looked
very embarrassed, running their hands through their hair and behaving as if they had great difficulty in remembering. They hesitated and
then they said they had made a special payment of 1.5 million marks
to Heidemann.'

Koch told Felix Schmidt what the management had done. They
were both angry. Money had been paid out to a member of their staff
behind their backs, and they had learned of it only by accident. But
they were not surprised. The longer the affair went on, the more private deals they seemed to discover. What might they stumble on next?

For all those involved in the Hitler diaries project, the pace of events
now began to accelerate.

On Monday 4 April, Klaus Harpprecht and Barbara Dickmann,
together with executives from *Stern*'s television company, arrived at
Peter Koch's apartment to meet Sorge, Walde, Pesch and Heidemann.
The two television journalists were informed of the existence of the
Hitler diaries. Koch said that *Stern* wanted a film ready to launch the
scoop. It would almost certainly be bought by one of the West German
networks, and probably by foreign stations as well. It would have a
budget of 160,000 marks. Harpprecht and Dickmann were worried
about their reputations as impartial reporters. To avoid being seen to
be making a publicity puff for *Stern*, they asked for editorial freedom
to make the film as they wished. Sorge and Koch readily agreed to
their demands: all the information contained in the film would have
to come from *Stern*, and most of the potential interviewees – old Nazis
like Karl Wolff and Hans Baur – were acquaintances of Heidemann's;

in the time available, there was no chance of the television team carrying out independent investigations of their own.

On Tuesday, Heidemann withdrew another 300,000 marks from the diaries account.

On Wednesday, Walde telexed Dr Werner at the police headquarters in Wiesbaden: 'I cannot yet give you our company's decision regarding the material for authentication. We will ring you or your colleague on Monday 11 April to inform you what material can be given to you, and when.'

On Thursday, Dr Klaus Oldenhage of the Bundesarchiv drove up from Koblenz to the Gruner and Jahr offices for a meeting with the company's lawyers.

In March, Gerd Schulte-Hillen had suddenly learned some shocking news. After more than two years of paying out money for the diaries, he was informed by the Gruner and Jahr legal department that the company did not actually own the diaries. The lawyers had revised their earlier opinion; the agreement with Werner Maser, they warned him, was probably worthless. It was impossible to say with certainty who held the copyright on the diaries: it could be the Federal Government; it could be the State of Bavaria; it might even be some distant relative of Hitler's of whose existence no one was aware; at any rate, it was not Gruner and Jahr. Schulte-Hillen found himself preparing to hold syndication negotiations which technically involved the handling of stolen property. There was only one hope: an agreement with the Bundesarchiv.

The Federal Archives had known of the existence of *Stern*'s hoard of Hitler's writings for more than a year, ever since Walde had sent them samples for handwriting analysis. Legally, they were aware that ownership of the material might well be theirs anyway, as the archive's lawyers thought that the copyright was vested in the West German Government. On the other hand, it was undeniable that without *Stern*'s expertise and money, the documents would never have come to light. At his meeting with the lawyers in Hamburg on Thursday, Oldenhage therefore announced that the Bundesarchiv was prepared to do a deal with the magazine, allowing them exclusive rights to the material for a limited period – on condition that eventually the originals would all be deposited in the Bundesarchiv. A contract was drawn up. To avoid accusations that the authorities were giving special treatment to *Stern*, the agreement was in Heidemann's name.

'Herr Gerd Heidemann,' stated the contract, 'has access to unpublished written and typed documents belonging to Adolf Hitler.' The material came from 'outside the Federal Republic of Germany' and was 'of political and historical significance'. (Oldenhage still had no idea that the documents in question were Hitler's diaries.) The Bundesarchiv agreed to give Heidemann 'unlimited newspaper, book, film, TV and audio-visual rights in the material for him to dispose of as he thinks fit'. The rights would remain his for 'as long as the material has a marketable value', a period which was not to exceed ten years. At that point, the documents would revert to the Bundesarchiv 'in order to preserve them and allow them to be used in a proper historical context'.

For *Stern*'s lawyers, the agreement was a triumph. It was, of course, still possible that when the diaries were launched, some unknown descendant of Adolf Hitler would step out of the shadows to claim his inheritance. But now the magazine would have the West German authorities on its side. The contract also gave the company's salesmen a legal document to wave at potential purchasers in the syndication talks. Gruner and Jahr had secured ownership in its scoop a bare twenty-four hours before the sales negotiations began.

That night, the principal figures in the first stage of those negotiations began moving into position. Sorge, Hensmann and Koch flew from Hamburg to Zurich, while Hugh Trevor-Roper travelled south from Scotland to London to be ready to catch a flight to Switzerland the next morning.

Trevor-Roper had finished breakfast and was preparing to leave for Heathrow on Friday when the telephone rang. It was Charles Douglas-Home, the editor of *The Times*.

The grandson of an earl, the nephew of a prime minister, educated at Eton, commissioned in the Royal Scots Greys, a dedicated hunter of the English fox – Douglas-Home's qualifications to edit *The Times* were perfect to the point of caricature. Trevor-Roper knew him well, and liked him: as one of the five independent directors of the paper he had supported his candidature for the editorship on the grounds that he was 'more academic' than his rival, Harold Evans. Nevertheless, he was not pleased at being bothered by Douglas-Home that morning.

In the course of the previous week, Trevor-Roper had had several conversations with *The Times*. He had told them that it would be impossible for him to reach an instant decision about the diaries' authenticity. He had been assured that he would not be required to do so. He should get a feel of the diaries in Zurich, and on his return to London he would be given a typed transcript of the material up to 1941. Only after he had studied that would he be required to deliver a verdict. The purpose of Douglas-Home's call ran contrary to that understanding. The editor of *The Times* told Trevor-Roper that Rupert Murdoch was taking a personal interest in the project, that he was determined to secure serial rights in the diaries, that there were rival news organizations equally determined, and that Murdoch wanted to be in a position to make his bid quickly. He could not afford to sit around while transcripts were studied; if he did, he would lose the deal. Douglas-Home therefore asked Trevor-Roper if he would ring London from Zurich *that same afternoon* with a preliminary assessment of the diaries' authenticity.

Trevor-Roper was 'very irritated' and 'surprised' by the request. It was ridiculous to expect him to reach a conclusion so quickly. But, 'under the pressure of events' and with assurances from Douglas-Home that this would only be an interim opinion, he agreed.

The next four hours were a blur of taxis and airports. Shortly after 9.30 a.m. he was picked up by car and driven to Heathrow. At 10.30 a.m. he met Peter Wickman. At 11.15 a.m. he took off on a Swissair flight to Zurich. He read the outline of *Plan 3* on the aircraft and thought it so phoney that his entire journey was wasted. At 1.50 p.m., Swiss time, he landed in Zurich. Wickman hurried him through immigration and customs. At 2.30 p.m. they dropped their luggage off at their hotel. At 3 p.m. he was led into the entrance hall of the Handelsbank, taken through a door immediately to his left, and found himself staring – 'astonished' – at fifty-eight volumes of Hitler's diaries.

*

This was the first occasion on which a trained historian had seen their treasure and the *Stern* men had prepared for it thoroughly. The diaries had been brought up from the vault and arranged in a neat pile on a table at the end of the room, embellished by other Hitler documents, paintings, drawings and memorabilia, including a First World War helmet, supposedly authenticated as Hitler's by a note from Rudolf Hess. Seen in its entirety, the archive looked stunning in its scope and variety. As Trevor-Roper bent over the stack of books, Sorge, Koch and Hensmann swiftly surrounded the elderly gentleman.

Trevor-Roper's specialist field – *The Last Days of Hitler* notwithstanding – was the sixteenth and seventeenth centuries. He was not a German scholar. He was not fluent in the language and had admitted as much in a review of *Mein Kampf* published a decade earlier: 'I do not read German,' he confessed, 'with great ease or pleasure.' Written in an archaic script, impenetrable even to most Germans, the diaries might as well have been composed of Egyptian hieroglyphics for all the sense Trevor-Roper could make of them. He had to rely on the *Stern* men for translation. The conversation was entirely in English.

Sorge, who had spent three months perfecting his sales patter, did most of the talking. He showed Trevor-Roper Heidemann's dossier of how Hitler's handwriting had changed over the years. He showed him the extract in Baur's book in which the pilot referred to the Führer's anguish at the loss of Gundlfinger's plane. He showed him photographs of the graves in Boernersdorf. He talked of their 'star reporter', Heidemann. He gave him the reports of three independent handwriting experts who all confirmed that the writing they had seen was Hitler's. He pointed out that the diaries were not the only cargo salvaged from the plane. He handed him a box full of drawings and paintings. As Trevor-Roper leafed through the books, listening to Sorge, his doubts 'gradually dissolved'.

Recollections of the meeting vary between the participants, but on at least two points it would seem that Trevor-Roper was deliberately misled. He was told that the age of the paper had been chemically tested and found to come from the right period. This was not true. He was also told by Peter Koch that *Stern* knew the identity of the 'Wehrmacht officer' who had originally kept the material in East Germany, and that this same individual was the supplier of the diaries. This, too, was false. Heidemann was the only man who had dealt with Kujau and knew the route by which the diaries had supposedly reached the West.

Trevor-Roper has never been renowned as a trusting and simple soul. Nevertheless, it does not seem to have occurred to him that his hosts might lie to him. *Stern* stood to gain a fortune if the syndication negotiations proved successful: for that reason alone, their statements should have been treated with scepticism. But Trevor-Roper trusted them. He could see no reason why *Stern* should choose to sell forgeries. They might not be a particularly reputable organization, but he believed them to have high professional standards. As he put it afterwards in characteristic terms: 'I took the *bona fides* of the editor as a *datum*.'

'I was also impressed,' he said, 'by the sheer bulk of the diaries. Who, I asked myself, would forge sixty volumes when six would have served his purpose?'

He was struck by *Stern*'s 'almost neurotic fear of leakage'. At one point, Koch produced a sheet of paper and wrote out in longhand a pledge of secrecy which he asked Trevor-Roper to sign. He was not to discuss what he had seen with anyone except those authorized to discuss the project on *The Times*. Trevor-Roper asked why he had to give such an undertaking. 'In case *The Times* doesn't buy the diaries,' replied Koch. 'It seemed a reasonable request,' recalled Trevor-Roper, 'so without thinking any more about it, I signed.'

By the time Trevor-Roper left the bank, he was convinced that the diaries were genuine. He did not like the fact that *Stern* had refused to tell him the name of its supplier, but then, in his experience, an insistence on anonymity was not unusual: 'Both the papers of Bormann and the diaries of Goebbels have come to publication through persons who have never been identified; and no one doubts that they are genuine.' He went straight back to his hotel, the Baur au Lac, and from his bedroom telephoned Charles Douglas-Home. 'I think they're genuine,' he told him. Douglas-Home, excited, thanked him for calling and said he would ring him back in an hour.

Believing that he would have an opportunity to study a transcript of the diaries on his return to Britain, Trevor-Roper had done no preparation for his visit to Zurich. He had not brought out a sample of Hitler's writing or any kind of chronology of the dictator's life with which to carry out a random check of the diaries' contents. The only thing he had brought, jotted on a scrap of paper, was the telephone number of a German historian he knew and respected – someone with whom he had planned to discuss the diaries. The historian whose name he had written down was Eberhard Jaeckel.

'If I had rung him,' lamented Trevor-Roper afterwards, 'he would have told me of his experience. He would have warned me.'

But it was not until Trevor-Roper was back in his hotel that he remembered the pledge of secrecy he had signed at the bank. He did not dare break it. He decided not to call Jaeckel.

The telephone rang. Trevor-Roper answered it, and a voice announced: 'Rupert Murdoch's office. I have Mr Douglas-Home on the line for you.' Trevor-Roper realized at once that the editor of *The Times* must have gone straight from speaking to him to see the proprietor.

'I've spoken to Rupert,' said Douglas-Home. 'We're both coming out to Zurich tomorrow.'

Trevor-Roper said that he was in a hurry to get back to Britain. He wanted to resume his holiday in Scotland. What flight were they coming on?

Douglas-Home told him not to worry. They were coming in a private plane.

Months later, the historian looked back and saw this as the decisive moment in the developing disaster:

> What I should have done was insist on waiting for a transcript before giving my verdict. I should have said that in my view the diaries were *superficially* genuine. I should not have been so enthusiastic on the telephone.
>
> If I'd refused to commit myself and reserved my position, then I'm quite sure Murdoch would have insisted on an answer. But I would have stood my ground. As it was, I lost the initiative. And I never regained it.

There was no liking between Murdoch and Trevor-Roper. The Australian tycoon regarded the Master of Peterhouse as a typical English establishment waxwork of the type he had been forced to acknowledge in order to purchase *The Times*. He was also 'too clever by half': Harold Evans described the historian at board meetings of Times Newspapers, sitting with 'eyes screwed up behind pebble glasses ... permanently sniffing the air for *non sequiturs*'. For his part, Trevor-Roper thought Murdoch 'an awful cad'.

When the millionaire bought *The Times* and *Sunday Times* in 1981, he had been obliged to sign an agreement designed to safeguard the integrity of the papers. The undertakings subsequently proved a feeble restraint, but at the time they had seemed to promise a curb on Murdoch's legendary ruthlessness. According to Evans, Trevor-Roper had boasted that 'we have Leviathan by the nose'. He was about to discover, as scores of others had done before him, that Leviathan was not so easily restrained.

23

On Friday night, the *Stern* team took Trevor-Roper out for a meal in one of Zurich's most expensive restaurants. The following morning, he flew back to Britain.

As Trevor-Roper left Switzerland, Murdoch arrived. With him on board his private jet he brought his tough Australian lawyer and business adviser, Richard Searby, along with Sir Edward Pickering and Charles Douglas-Home. Gerald Long, the former chief executive of Reuters and deputy chairman of News International, flew in to join them on a separate flight from Paris. Peter Wickman met them in the lobby of the Baur au Lac and took them through to a private dining room for lunch.

Around the table, there was an unmistakable feeling of anticipation. Murdoch sat next to the senior *Stern* negotiator, Jan Hensmann. Wickman sat beside Douglas-Home. Koch talked with Maynard Parker and William Broyles who had flown in from New York to make an offer on behalf of *Newsweek*.

Murdoch seemed particularly excited. In the spring of 1983, his corporation News International controlled more than thirty newspapers and magazines, four book publishers, three television companies and a variety of firms specializing in transport, energy and leisure. He ruled his empire in a manner not dissimilar to that which Hitler employed to run the Third Reich. His theory of management was Darwinian. His subordinates were left alone to run their various outposts of the company. Ruthlessness and drive were encouraged, slackness and inefficiency punished. Occasionally, Murdoch would swoop in to tackle a problem or exploit an opportunity; then he would disappear. He was, depending on your standing at any given moment, inspiring, friendly, disinterested or terrifying. He never tired of expansion, of pushing out the frontiers of his operation. 'Fundamentally,' Richard Searby, his closest adviser, was fond of remarking, 'Rupert's a fidget.'

The sudden decision to buy the Hitler diaries was a perfect example of Murdoch in action. He loved the concept of The Deal – spotting the opening, plotting the strategy, securing the prize. Already, in Zurich, he had his eyes on more than simply the British rights, which were all that *Stern* had originally offered him. Sure, the diaries could run in *The Times* or the *Sunday Times* (he would work out which later). But they could also run in the *New York Post* and the *Boston Herald* and *The Australian* and in one of the outlets of New Zealand's Independent Newspapers group (of which he owned 22 per cent). He had also recently acquired a 42 per cent stake in the Collins publishing company: he was aiming to buy the book rights to the Hitler diaries as well. It was this ability to spread the cost of his purchases throughout his many holdings which made Murdoch such a formidable force in international publishing. The Hitler diaries deal was exactly what he was looking for: he would publish the book, serialize it in three continents, and – given that he had recently joined forces with Robert Stigwood to produce Associated R & R Films – he might even make the movie which he could eventually show on Channel Ten, his television station in Sydney. The Hitler diaries potentially were a model for the internationally integrated media package.

After lunch, the *Stern* men took Murdoch and his entourage over to the bank. Seated around the table in the ground floor conference room, Sorge read out extracts from a typed transcript, Gerald Long provided a simultaneous translation, while Murdoch skimmed through a handful of diaries, nodding intently. He had no doubts that Hitler would help sell his papers. The diaries were sensational. At one point, he asked the Germans if they were sure their security was good enough: in his view it was possible that the Israeli secret service might try to seize the material.

A couple of hours later, back in *Stern*'s suite at the Baur au Lac, Murdoch made Hensmann an offer. He told him he wanted to bid for syndication and book rights. Hensmann said he could not discuss a book deal – Bertelsmann was insisting that Bantam retained the first option.

Disappointed, Murdoch submitted an opening bid for American, British and Commonwealth serial rights. Hensmann considered it too low. Murdoch and his team retired to confer and to make some telephone calls. Shortly afterwards, they returned. News International, announced Murdoch, was willing to offer $2.5 million for the American rights, plus an additional $750,000 for serialization in Britain and the Commonwealth.

Three and a quarter million dollars. It was a good offer. It would clear Gruner and Jahr's costs and still leave them European and Asian serial rights and a percentage of the book sales. Hensmann, provisionally, agreed. He said he would give Murdoch a final answer at 5 p.m. on Monday. The two men shook hands and the News International team returned to London.

Meanwhile, Broyles and Parker were inspecting the books for *Newsweek*. They too considered the diaries a wonderful story. Serialization would attract tens of thousands of readers and give them a coveted boost in their ceaseless circulation battle with *Time*: whereas *Newsweek* sold roughly 3.5 million copies around the world each week, its rival had sales of almost 6 million.

The Hitler diaries appealed to Broyles in particular. A Texan, a former marine, only thirty-eight years old, he had been appointed editor the previous September. It had been a surprising choice. Broyles's background had been in glossy magazines – *Texas Monthly* and *California*. He had no background in immediate news coverage. Announcing his arrival, *Newsweek*'s owner, Katherine Graham, had declared: 'He will add a whole new dimension.' He had, and *Newsweek*'s staff did not like it. He appeared to be more interested in features than news. Fashion, show business and social trends seemed to be his priorities. When *Time* led on the massacre of hundreds of Palestinians in the Lebanon, *Newsweek*'s cover story was the death of Princess Grace of Monaco. Broyles's editorial standards were attacked, but he tried to keep above the intrigue. He saw it as his task to provide long-range direction; he did not bother with the day-to-day running of the magazine. Just as the Hitler diaries suited Murdoch's style of running his company, so they fitted Broyles's approach to editing *Newsweek*.

Returning from the bank at about 8 p.m., the Americans offered Hensmann $500,000 for serialization rights in the diaries. Hensmann, sitting on Murdoch's offer of $3.25 million, found this 'totally unacceptable'. *Newsweek* doubled its offer to $1 million. Hensmann told them he wanted $3 million for the American rights. He would not take less. Broyles and Parker said they would have to return to New York. They would telephone him on Monday with an answer.

Back at the bank, Wilfried Sorge supervised as a guard carried the diaries down from the negotiating room to the vault. He watched to make sure the volumes were safely stowed, locked the deposit box, and took a taxi to the airport. He managed to catch the last flight home. It was his fortieth birthday party in Hamburg that night and he had no intention of missing it.

At his house in Chapel Hill, North Carolina, Gerhard Weinberg was telephoned by Maynard Parker.

Weinberg was fifty-five, a neat and bespectacled man, fastidious in his personal and professional habits. His origins were German Jewish. His family had fled the Third Reich when he was twelve and he now spoke in a broad New York accent which gave no hint of his German background. His name was not generally well known like Trevor-Roper's, but among professional historians he was respected as a careful scholar. In 1952 he had helped compile the US armed forces' *Guide to Captured German Documents*. He was the author of a two-volume study of Hitler's pre-war foreign policy that had taken him more than a decade to complete. He did not like to be hurried and he did not care for journalists – their sloppiness, their deadlines, their assumption that one was willing to drop everything 'to jump to their tune'.

Weinberg's first reaction to the alleged discovery of Hitler's diaries was the same as Trevor-Roper's: he thought it was improbable but was reluctant to dismiss it out of hand. It was true that there were no references to diaries in any of the reminiscences of Hitler's subordinates. It was also well known that Hitler had a strong personal aversion to writing in his own hand. (Weinberg knew this well, having enjoyed a minor historical scoop himself in the 1950s when he discovered the Führer's private testament of 1938 – the longest passage of Hitler's handwriting in existence; after drafting the will, Hitler had told his associates that the task had demanded 'a quite special effort on my part, since for years I've had the habit of writing directly on the machine or dictating what I have to say'.) However, Weinberg – professionally cautious – considered that 'too many things turn up which are not supposed to exist'; if the entries were short enough, the discovery of a diary might not be too far fetched.

The fact that Murdoch had already had *his* expert over to Zurich put added pressure on *Newsweek*. Parker said he wanted Weinberg to fly to Switzerland to look at the diaries. How soon could he go? Weinberg replied that he was going to work as a visiting professor at Bonn University for three months over the summer. He was flying out to Germany on 22 April – what if he was to go early and inspect the diaries then? No use, said Parker: he wanted Weinberg in Zurich next week. The historian protested that he had classes in North Carolina on Monday, Wednesday and Friday. Cancel them, said Parker. Weinberg refused. He consulted his diary. 'I could go after my last class on Monday,' he said, 'as long as you can guarantee to get me back in time for my next one on Wednesday. Talk to your travel people.'

The morning of Monday 11 April found Sorge back in Zurich, exhausted after having snatched only four hours' sleep in the past two days. At the bank he met the television presenter Barbara Dickmann, Heidemann and the *Stern* film crew who had arrived to shoot the opening sequence of the documentary; Sorge's attendance was required because he was the only person with keys to the safety deposit box.

The lights were set up outside the vault, the camera began turning, and Heidemann self-consciously walked into shot. He plodded woodenly over to the deposit box, opened it, pulled out one of the diaries and began reading.

By mid-afternoon, the filming was finished, and for the second or third time that day Heidemann took the opportunity to slip out to attend to some mysterious 'business' in Zurich. Barbara Dickmann asked him what he was doing. Heidemann replied that he was trying to make arrangements to drop in and see Martin Bormann who lived nearby.

*

Meanwhile, in Hamburg, London and New York, the negotiations to buy the diaries continued.

For *Newsweek* it was clear that to stay in the game they would have to match the News International offer. On Monday, back in the Gruner and Jahr headquarters, Hensmann received a telephone call from the United States informing him that the magazine was now prepared to offer $3 million for the American serialization rights. The deal was conditional on their being satisfied that the diaries were genuine. Broyles and Parker wanted to return to Zurich the following day and show the books to their nominated expert, Gerhard Weinberg. Hensmann agreed. This opened up the enticing prospect for Gruner and Jahr of pushing up the price by playing off *Newsweek* and News International against one another.

In London, Rupert Murdoch had already become suspicious that something was going on behind his back. Throughout the day, he made a number of attempts to ring Hensmann, without success. Each time he was told that Hensmann could not be reached. Finally, towards the end of the afternoon, the German rang him.

The deal was off, said Hensmann. *Newsweek* had made him a very attractive offer for the American rights. Murdoch could still have serial rights in the diaries in Britain and the Commonwealth for $750,000, but if he wanted the complete package, including United States rights, he would have to pay $3.75 million – $500,000 more than Murdoch had originally offered in Zurich on Saturday.

Murdoch was furious. He understood that the handshake had clinched the deal. He unleashed a torrent of invective down the telephone which a shaken Hensmann was later to describe as 'bitter'.

Wilfried Sorge was at Zurich airport to catch the evening flight to Hamburg when he was paged over the public address system. It was Hensmann. 'I don't want you to come back. I want you to stay there,' said the deputy managing director. '*Newsweek* are coming to see the diaries tomorrow.'

Wearily, Sorge returned to the Baur au Lac.

Across the Atlantic, Gerhard Weinberg's last class at the University of North Carolina – a two-hour seminar on Nazi Germany – was coming to an end. At 4.15 p.m. Weinberg dismissed his students, drove twenty miles to the local airport, Raleigh-Durham, and caught a flight to New York. There was a limousine waiting at La Guardia airport to rush him through the heavy evening traffic to the inter-continental terminal at JFK. Maynard Parker and William Broyles were already there waiting for him. Half an hour later, the three men boarded the overnight Swissair flight to Zurich.

Settled into their seats in the first-class section, the *Newsweek* men handed Weinberg the reports of the three handwriting experts. He read them carefully. 'It looks good,' he said when he had finished. 'If these people say the handwriting is correct, that's fine by me.' Only one thing puzzled him: nowhere in the report was there any mention of diaries. He told Broyles and Parker that before they bought the books, they ought to have a specific volume checked. He also raised the question of copyright.

'We'll buy that off *Stern*,' replied Parker.

Weinberg shook his head. 'Mr Parker, it's not as easy as that.'

In the course of his work with original documents, Weinberg had acquired some understanding of the complexities of West German copyright law. As he understood it, literary rights in *unpublished* papers could not be confiscated. Although the State of Bavaria claimed ownership of *Mein Kampf*, it had no jurisdiction over Hitler's private diaries.

'I tell you what will happen,' warned Weinberg. 'Hitler's heirs will wait until you've printed millions of copies – and then they'll sue you.'

Weinberg, Broyles and Parker landed in Zurich shortly after 9 a.m. on Tuesday morning and went directly to the Handelsbank. They had no time to waste: the professor's irritating insistence on being back in North Carolina in time to take his next class had forced *Newsweek* to book him on a 3 p.m. flight to New York out of Amsterdam. At the bank they were met by Sorge and also by Heidemann who had stayed overnight in Zurich after the previous day's filming. The introductions were friendly. Heidemann especially struck Weinberg as charming and anxious to help.

The session began with Heidemann reading aloud extracts from the diaries for 1940 and 1945. Sorge then invited the Americans to help themselves to whatever volumes they wanted from the stack in front of them.

Weinberg had brought with him a copy of the diary of Hitler's valet, Heinz Linge, covering the second part of 1943. Linge's daily notes of Hitler's activities were available for inspection in the National Archives in Washington but had never been published: if the *Stern* diaries were poor quality fakes, discrepancies with the Linge record would swiftly expose them. Unfortunately, the entries in the *Stern* diary covering the last three months of 1943 were so sketchy, Weinberg was unable to make an adequate comparison. He then asked to see the volumes covering the battle for Stalingrad. These were no use either. There was no typed transcript available and the handwriting was so bad that Weinberg was unable to decipher it. He pulled out a few other volumes at random. Nothing in them struck him as false. He noted that there was a page missing from the volume devoted to the Hess affair, and a statement witnessed by a notary indicating that it had been sent away for analysis. He looked up the entry for the Munich conference in 1938 and found a startling tribute from Hitler to the British prime minister, Neville Chamberlain:

> He almost outwitted me. This smoothie Englishman... I would have imposed quite different conditions on Mussolini and Daladier [the French prime minister], but I couldn't do so with this cunning fox, Chamberlain.

The entry impressed Weinberg, who nodded sagely as he read it. 'This accords with my own theories,' he announced.

Half-way through the examination, a third *Newsweek* journalist arrived. He was Milan Kubik, the magazine's bureau chief in Jerusalem, flown in by the Americans to inspect the Jewish angle. Broyles and Parker introduced him and explained his presence on the grounds that the magazine expected there to be 'enormous interest' in the Hitler diaries in Israel. Throughout the meeting, the *Newsweek* editors kept probing the material for information which would appeal to their American readership. At one stage, Parker asked to see the volume covering the Battle of the Bulge in the winter of 1944, but Heidemann told him it was one of the four books which had yet to be delivered from East Germany.

Two things, meanwhile, had struck Weinberg, who was carefully reading through the diaries. One was the fact that almost every page carried Hitler's signature. No one in his right mind, he thought, would have risked forging hundreds of signatures; it seemed a strong argument in favour of authenticity.

He also pointed out to Broyles and Parker that most of the diaries began with a handwritten note stating that if anything happened to him, Hitler wanted the books to be given to his sister Paula. This could pose further copyright problems, said Weinberg, strengthening the case of any heirs of Hitler who cared to argue that the diaries were actually their property. Sorge and Heidemann, already aware of the problems over copyright, looked at one another in embarrassment: that had not occurred to them, they said.

Weinberg also wanted to know why no German scholar had been shown any of this material. Sorge replied that they were worried about leaks. He asked who Weinberg would recommend. Weinberg said he was thinking of a very reliable historian – Eberhard Jaeckel of Stuttgart. Had they heard of him? The *Stern* men replied that they had. 'It was clear to me,' recalled Weinberg, 'that they didn't want to involve Jaeckel.'

At 2 p.m., Weinberg's self-imposed deadline expired and the *Newsweek* party had to leave. In order to obtain Weinberg's assessment, Broyles, Parker and Kubik had to fly with him to Amsterdam. The historian admitted he was 'astonished' by what he had seen. He had not been able to find fault with the diaries. On balance, he inclined to the view that they were authentic.

This was what *Newsweek* wanted to hear. At Amsterdam airport, Weinberg caught his flight to New York. The three *Newsweek* journalists boarded a flight to Hamburg to clinch the deal.

Stern's London office was based in Peter Wickman's house in Barnet, miles out of town in the northernmost fringe of the capital. On Tuesday morning, as the *Newsweek* contingent sifted through the diaries in Zurich, Wickman's telex machine suddenly clattered into life with an urgent message from the Gruner and Jahr headquarters. It was a contract requiring Rupert Murdoch's agreement, offering him the

British and Commonwealth rights in the Hitler diaries for $750,000. It included a 25 per cent penalty clause should News International default on the deal.

Following Hensmann's instructions, Wickman delivered the contract to Murdoch personally in his office in *The Times* building in Gray's Inn Road. Murdoch scarcely glanced at it before handing Wickman his own version – roughly twenty pages long, drawn up by his lawyers, reiterating the terms he understood had been agreed in Switzerland on Saturday.

Wickman made his way back up to High Barnet and began feeding the pages into a telecopier, transmitting Murdoch's counter offer back to Hamburg.

The next day, Wednesday 13 April, Heidemann and Barbara Dickmann continued their work on the *Stern* television film, driving to Herrsching, near Munich, to interview Hans Baur.

The Baur family detested the media, even when it came in the friendly and uncritical form of Gerd Heidemann. The eighty-five-year-old ex-Nazi hobbled over to them on his wooden leg and stared at the camera with undisguised hostility. Then a former Munich policeman arrived, 'in a state of extreme agitation', according to Dickmann, claiming he had been summoned by Baur to protect the family. On his advice, Frau Baur went round the house taking down photographs of her husband with Hitler and packing away various Nazi mementoes. Heidemann, the Baurs and the ex-policeman then disappeared into another room while Dickmann and the crew waited to hear whether they would be allowed to film.

After twenty minutes, the group reappeared. According to Baur, Heidemann had shown him one of the diaries: 'a black book with a red cord and a red seal . . . I was of the opinion that it was Hitler's writing.' The camera was set up and Baur described the plane crash and Hitler's distress.

When the interview was over, the atmosphere relaxed. The retired policeman, who came from Luxembourg, turned out to be a collector of Nazi relics. He told Heidemann, in Dickmann's presence, that 'his circle of friends was almost exclusively composed of prominent ex-Nazis'.

He suggested that they should 'set up an agency for Hitler relics in Munich'. Heidemann told him about the Blood Flag and offered to sell it to him. When the time came to leave, the two men made an appointment to have dinner together.

Listening to this conversation merely served to confirm Barbara Dickmann's feelings about Heidemann. The man was 'unable to distance himself professionally from the events of the Nazi era'. Although she had known him for little more than a week, she had already spent many hours with him, driving between locations. Being trapped in a car with Heidemann had not proved a pleasant experience. 'I couldn't avoid having to listen to his stories,' she recalled.

> He talked to me constantly about his friend 'Martin'. He told me incredible stories about 'Martin's' life after the collapse of the Third Reich. He said that 'Martin' was in Switzerland, that he was being watched over by the Israeli secret service.
>
> Heidemann also indicated that he had original material belonging to Hitler supposedly containing the 'ten theses' of Hitler's Final Solution.

He had told her during filming in Zurich on Monday that he was trying to arrange a meeting with Bormann. Later, he showed her his set of Polaroid pictures and confided to her that he was going to meet him on 20 April, Hitler's birthday, when he would be given important documents. (Martin subsequently cancelled the meeting.) He showed her his collection of relics: 'several glass cases in which he had helmets, uniforms, a brown shirt, a pair of trousers, a damaged watch, weapons, drawings allegedly by Hitler, a swastika flag, a Party book of Hitler's, his passport and all sorts of other things'.

Dickmann was shocked by Heidemann's behaviour. He seemed 'euphoric' about his access to senior Nazis, gripped by 'sick fantasies'. Their relationship became 'increasingly cool'. When the television team returned to Hamburg, she was worried enough to seek out Peter Koch and tell him what his reporter was up to. Koch reassured her: Heidemann always immersed himself in whatever he was researching – it was part of his technique for gaining access to circles which were normally impossible to penetrate. She could rely, said Koch, on the fact that Heidemann 'was not a Nazi and that once he'd finished his researches he'd be normal again'.

Meanwhile, as Heidemann and Dickmann were leaving Hans Baur in Herrsching, Rupert Murdoch's draft contract was arriving on Jan Hensmann's desk in Hamburg. *Stern*'s chief negotiator regarded it as 'completely unacceptable'. News International had refused to improve its offer in the face of *Newsweek*'s bid. Hensmann decided to sign a deal with the Americans.

Broyles, Parker and Kubik, who had arrived in Hamburg the previous night, were informed that their offer of $3 million for the American serial rights had been accepted. The *Newsweek* representatives were taken to the special suite of offices occupied by the diaries team. As a gesture of good faith, Peter Koch was authorized to give them the story of the find as it had been written by Wolf Thieme, together with the rough text for the first four instalments of the *Stern* serialization.

It was at this point that word came from the nearby Four Seasons Hotel that two emissaries from Rupert Murdoch – Richard Searby and Gerald Long – had arrived to discuss the News International offer. They wanted to come over to the *Stern* building straight away.

Confronted by this embarrassing situation, Hensmann dispatched Wilfried Sorge to the Four Seasons. He was to tell them to go home – the deal with Murdoch was off.

Sorge relayed the message.

He had often seen negotiators lose their tempers, but he had never before witnessed anything to compare with the reaction of the two Murdoch men. Searby was normally smooth and urbane; Long, beetle-browed and pugnacious, looked, even in his lighter moments, as if he would enjoy nothing more than a good Victorian eviction, preferably involving widows, orphans and a tied cottage. When Sorge told them that the diaries had been sold to *Newsweek*, both men blew up in anger. 'They were beside themselves with rage,' he recalled: as close as men could come to physical violence without actually resorting to it. But despite the threats and accusations of bad faith, Sorge refused to yield.

Later that night, after he had calmed down, Searby rang Sorge at home to ask him what the hell was going on. Privately, Sorge was beginning to have doubts himself about the way Hensmann was handling the negotiations, but in his conversation with Searby he remained loyal to his superior.

'Murdoch's people,' he recalled, 'went away with nothing.'

In London, Peter Wickman received another urgent communication from Hamburg. *Stern* wanted to use three quotations from Trevor-Roper to launch the diaries. The quotes they had in mind were, first, that the discovery of the diaries 'was the most important historical event of the last ten years'; secondly, that 'it was a scoop to equal Watergate'; and thirdly, that it would 'make it necessary, at least in part, to rewrite the history of the Third Reich'. All three lines were actually the work of Peter Koch, but he instructed Wickman to ask Trevor-Roper if he would allow them to be attributed to him.

For Wickman, this was the latest in a series of bizarre requests from Hamburg. *Stern*'s mania for secrecy was such that he now had to make any telephone calls connected with the diaries from a public call box in case MI6 had bugged his phone. He was also sick of having to shuttle back and forth between Hensmann and Murdoch. It was with some embarrassment that he rang Trevor-Roper and relayed Koch's request.

Trevor-Roper was not enthusiastic. 'I didn't like any of the quotes,' he recalled, 'and said so to Wickman.' Nevertheless, reluctantly, he agreed to put his name to the statements that the diaries represented the most important historical discovery of the decade and a scoop of Watergate proportions. He rejected the third one about the rewriting of history – he had yet to see the promised transcript of the diaries.

Wickman telexed Trevor-Roper's reply to Germany.

On the morning of Thursday 14 April, Gerd Schulte-Hillen arrived back in Hamburg from his trip to the United States. He had barely walked through the front door of his house when the telephone rang.

It was Rupert Murdoch.

It is a measure of Murdoch's tenacity as a businessman, and also of his determination to secure the Hitler diaries, that even after Long and

Searby had been sent back empty-handed, he still believed he could salvage his deal with Gruner and Jahr. He subjected Schulte-Hillen to an harangue about the behaviour of Jan Hensmann. He complained that he had been double-crossed, his associates insulted. What was going to be done about it?

Schulte-Hillen apologized. He said he had only just returned from abroad.

Murdoch wanted to know whether the negotiations could be reopened. He was now willing, he said, to pay $3.75 million for the English language world rights, matching *Newsweek*'s latest offer.

Schulte-Hillen now made the first of what was to prove a succession of extremely costly mistakes. He noted Murdoch's offer and promptly invited him to attend a new round of negotiations in Hamburg the following day. He then drove over to the Gruner and Jahr office and, overruling Hensmann's objections, instructed him to issue a similar invitation to *Newsweek*.

Broyles and Parker had made two round trips to Europe in six days. They had assumed that an agreement had been reached. Hensmann's call to New York to tell them that the deal was off and that they had to come back a third time produced an outraged response. 'They were not pleased,' said Sorge. But if *Newsweek* wanted the diaries they had no alternative. They agreed to come.

A few hundred yards away, in the headquarters of the diaries team, Thomas Walde was at last getting round to sending a fresh sample of the diaries for forensic analysis. Under the supervision of a Hamburg notary, blank pages had been cut out of two of the books – one was removed from the Hess volume, one from a volume covering 1933. The two sheets of paper, marked 'Hess' and 'August 1933', together with another of the Hitler documents accompanying the diaries – a draft telegram to Mussolini – were parcelled up and given to Walde's secretary, Hannelore Schustermann, to take down to the Bundesarchiv in Koblenz. 'It is urgent,' wrote Walde in a covering letter to Dr Henke, 'and a particular priority should be given to the two blank sheets. A thousand thanks and best wishes.'

Henke, still ignorant of the diaries' existence, forwarded the material to a forensic chemist named Arnold Rentz who lived a few miles outside Koblenz. Rentz undertook to deliver his verdict within the next week.

Shortly before noon on Friday 15 April, representatives of *Newsweek* and News International arrived at the Gruner and Jahr headquarters. There was an immediate shock for the Germans. The two organizations – which Schulte-Hillen had eagerly expected to come ready to bid against one another, pushing the price still higher – arrived *together*. Rupert Murdoch headed the News International delegation; Mark Edmiston, President of *Newsweek* Inc., led the Americans. Tired of *Stern*'s sloppy and amateur tactics, the two men had decided to join forces. They would share the costs and split the diaries between them. The details had yet to be worked out, but considering there were supposed to be twenty-eight separate instalments, there was plenty of Hitler material to go around. Extracts of particular interest to the Americans could run in *Newsweek*, those relevant to Britain could go to Murdoch. The rest could be carved up between them at a later date. For now, the first priority was to end the uncertainty and reach a final agreement. Watching the supposed rivals conferring together, Sorge was deeply disappointed. They would be able to set their own price. There was no chance now that *Stern* would get the $3.75 million which up until yesterday had been on offer.

The negotiations took place around the large conference table in the managing director's office, with its imposing view out over the Elbe. Schulte-Hillen, Murdoch and Edmiston did most of the talking, turning occasionally to their advisers for clarification on particular points. The number of men present at any one time varied between ten and twenty – lawyers, journalists, accountants and executives, neatly dressed in two and three-piece suits, briefcases full of circulation figures, memoranda, balance sheets and legal opinions. For the next eleven hours they haggled over simultaneous release dates and standard extracts as if *Stern* was offering nothing more unusual than franchises in a new kind of fast food.

The two biggest sources of contention were the order in which the diaries were to be serialized and the time scale over which they would be published. Edmiston maintained that the American public didn't give a damn about Rudolf Hess and his peace mission to Britain. They wanted to know about the murder of the Jews. The whole series, as far as *Newsweek* was concerned, should begin with the Holocaust. Schulte-Hillen rejected that. Many of the diaries had not yet been transcribed. The only section which had been properly checked was that relating to Hess. With publication less than a month away, it was too late to change. To maximize revenue, *Stern* wanted to tease out the diaries for as long as possible: the only way to do that was to publish the books in chronological order. Again, Edmiston objected. As one of the Americans put it afterwards: 'We were especially bothered by the idea that *Stern* was trying to drag this out for almost thirty instalments. If it were 500,000 words, that's one thing, but it's only 50,000 words. We thought they were trying to slice the salami very thin.'

Eventually, after some hours of discussion, the meeting began to grope towards a compromise. Perhaps the diaries could be published grouped under themes: 'Hitler and the Jews', 'Hitler and his Women', 'Stalingrad' and so on.

After dinner, the conference moved on to copyright. This was the most worrying area for *Stern* and the company fielded three lawyers to try to handle it. Schulte-Hillen and his colleagues were acutely aware of the fact that if anyone pirated the diaries, it might well prove impossible to stop them. Indeed, if a rival organization could somehow get hold of a descendant of Hitler, they might be able to sue Gruner and Jahr for the return of the diaries. Thankfully, *Stern* could at least fall back on the agreement between Heidemann and the Bundesarchiv – this, they claimed, would be enough to prevent any breaches of copyright.

Edmiston and Murdoch agreed to have their lawyers check over that aspect of the contract the following morning.

At 10.30 p.m. the main outstanding issue was the money. Schulte-Hillen suggested they should reconvene the following day. The News International and *Newsweek* people shook their heads. It was essential that this was finally straightened out tonight. Schulte-Hillen again suggested a postponement. Edmiston was sarcastic. Was Schulte-Hillen, he asked, planning to fix the price on his own?

There was an uneasy shifting around the table.

Very well, said Schulte-Hillen. How much would they offer?

Surprisingly, Murdoch and Edmiston had not planned to take advantage of their alliance to reduce the price. They were confident that the diaries would easily generate enough extra revenue to recoup the cost.

The original offer stayed on the table, announced Edmiston. 'We'll stick to $3.75 million.'

To Sorge, who had been expecting the worst, this was an enormous relief. He was therefore startled to hear Schulte-Hillen's reply:

'We no longer think that is enough. We want $4.25 million.'

There was a moment's pause, and then an explosion of exasperation. Both Edmiston and Murdoch said that they had never encountered such bad faith in the course of negotiations. They stood up, and like courtiers to a pair of princes, all the lawyers, journalists, accountants and executives immediately followed suit. Jackets were taken off the backs of chairs, cigarettes were stubbed out, papers were shovelled into briefcases, and in a dramatic display of contempt, the Americans, British and Australians filed out of the room without another word.

The *Stern* team was left alone.

Hensmann had slipped out earlier in the evening. Only Schulte-Hillen, Sorge and the three lawyers were left. Beneath them, the eight floors of offices and corridors were dark and deserted. Schulte-Hillen began shuffling the documents in front of him. He suggested they prepare for the following day's talks. The other four looked at him incredulously. It was obvious to all of them there were not going to *be* any more talks. After a week of intensive negotiations, 'the deal', as the *Stern Report* later put it, 'which had once seemed so certain for $3.75 million, had burst like a bubble'.

24

Early the next morning, Schulte-Hillen and Sorge tried ringing Murdoch and Edmiston in their hotel suites. It was, as Sorge had feared, hopeless. Edmiston said that he had no further interest in the diaries: Gruner and Jahr should pretend that he was no longer in Hamburg. Murdoch refused even to come to the telephone. A few hours later, the *Newsweek* and News International teams flew home.

It was a decisive turning point in the development of the diaries affair. The initiative had passed out of *Stern*'s hands. From self-confident salesmen they had, overnight, been reduced to anxious supplicants. There were no other potential clients to turn to who were in the same league as Murdoch and *Newsweek*. *Time*'s interest had always been lukewarm. The *New York Times* had turned down the Hess story within six hours of being told about it. Associated Newspapers had only offered £50,000 for *Plan 3*, and had made that conditional on the most stringent guarantees of authenticity. Even more worrying for the *Stern* men was the realization that *Newsweek* and Times Newspapers between them now knew an enormous amount about the diaries. Each organization had been allowed to send in an expert to read through the material; journalists from both groups had had extracts read out to them; and *Newsweek* had actually been handed the complete story of the find and the first four instalments of the *Stern* series.

It was the thought of what *Newsweek* might do, with its worldwide sales of more than 3 million copies, which most terrified the Germans. There was nothing to stop Broyles and Parker breaking the news of the diaries' existence and running pirated extracts. They could have their story on the news stands by Tuesday 26 April – in less than ten days' time.

Over the weekend, an emergency meeting of *Stern*'s editors and management reviewed the situation and concluded that they had only one option. Their next issue was due out on Thursday 21 April – there was no way they would be ready to run the diaries by then. The following week, 28 April, would be too late to beat *Newsweek*. Accordingly, they would have to change their publication date. Monday 25 April would give them the maximum amount of time, while still allowing them to head off the Americans. In the meantime, it was decided that Schulte-Hillen and Peter Koch should fly to New York to try to salvage some sort of agreement.

On Sunday 17 April, Hugh Trevor-Roper came south from Scotland to Cambridge, ready for the start of the University's summer term. On Monday he was telephoned at the Peterhouse Master's Lodge by Colin Webb of *The Times* who told him of the collapse of the negotiations.

The news came as a surprise to Trevor-Roper. The *Stern* television people had asked him to give them an interview for their documentary. He had agreed. They had offered to come to Cambridge, but he had insisted on flying to Hamburg: he wanted to meet this 'star reporter' Heidemann and see what else he had in his collection. He was supposed to be going the next day. What should he do now?

Webb said that *The Times* would still like him to go. Murdoch, now in New York, was confident he would soon be in a position to buy the diaries – on his terms; the Germans had nowhere else to go.

Schulte-Hillen and Koch arrived in New York on Monday evening. They began telephoning around town, trying to speak to *Newsweek* and Murdoch. No one would return their calls.

In Zurich, the diaries were removed from the Handelsbank and locked in a safe in the Schweizer Bankgesellschaft, where security was much tighter. After Murdoch's warning about the Israeli secret service, the Germans were determined not to take any chances.

On Tuesday, a conference of *Stern*'s senior editors and heads of department met to discuss their special Hitler edition. It would be the biggest in the magazine's history: 356 pages thick, with a 48-page supplement devoted to the diaries – half in colour, half in black and white. The print run would be increased to 2.3 million copies. The expected boost in sales would cover the additional production costs, estimated at 720,000 marks. The meeting was secret. Only those staff who needed to know were to be told that *Stern* was about to publish Hitler's diaries.

Trevor-Roper came through customs at Hamburg airport on Tuesday and was met by a fat, pale man in glasses. There was a brief period of pantomime thanks to Trevor-Roper's assumption that he was merely the chauffeur sent by *Stern* to collect him. Eventually, Heidemann made himself understood: *he* was the Bloodhound, the German equivalent of Woodward and Bernstein, the man responsible, in Trevor-Roper's reluctant words, for 'the greatest scoop since Watergate'. The historian apologized and said he was very pleased to meet him.

It took fifteen minutes for Heidemann to drive Trevor-Roper from the airport to his archive in Milchstrasse. Before the television interview he wanted to show off his collection to the famous historian – it satisfied the same craving for recognition which Nannen and Schulte-Hillen had found it politic to feed. Trevor-Roper found himself conducted down a quaint, narrow street of small boutiques and art galleries, into a curiously arranged apartment. It consisted, he recalled, of four corridors laid out in the shape of a 'hollow square'. There were no sleeping or washing facilities. Heidemann explained that he used it solely as a museum.

Trevor-Roper found the contents 'staggering'. There were hundreds of folders full of documents and photographs from the Third Reich. Some had been sold to Heidemann by Karl Wolff and Heinrich Hoffmann and were unquestionably authentic. There was, for example, an SS file on an expedition to Tibet organized by Himmler, part of the

Reichsführer's crackpot research into 'Aryan bloodlines'. The file contained carbon copies of the outgoing correspondence and originals of the incoming. Trevor-Roper was in no doubt that it was genuine.

At least two of the corridors were crammed with Nazi memorabilia. Then, turning the corner, came a section devoted to Mussolini. Finally, Heidemann conducted Trevor-Roper into an area with a few mementoes of Idi Amin. 'Those,' he said, pointing to a pair of voluminous white cotton drawers, 'are Idi Amin's underpants.'

For the first time, the former Regius Professor of Modern History began to eye his host uneasily. Until now, he had assumed that Heidemann was simply a thorough journalist. Suddenly it occurred to him that the reporter was slightly odd. He seemed to have an obsession with dictators. Trevor-Roper started to dislike him. The more he talked, the more phoney he seemed. Like Koch and Nannen before him, Trevor-Roper found himself wondering how Heidemann could afford such an obviously expensive collection.

After this guided tour, Heidemann took his guest over to the Atlantic – one of the most imposing and luxurious hotels in Hamburg, looking out across the Alster to the *Stern* building. *Stern* had reserved Trevor-Roper a room for the night. In another part of the hotel, the film crew was waiting. Trevor-Roper took his place in front of the camera and recorded a brief interview. Despite his personal misgivings about Heidemann, he was still convinced that the diaries were genuine and he said so. Heidemann was delighted.

Trevor-Roper had been looking forward to a quiet meal alone with a book followed by an early night before his flight back to London. But Heidemann insisted that they dined together. He led the protesting historian into the bar.

Heidemann ordered meals for them both and began drinking heavily. He became loquacious. Trevor-Roper experienced the sequence of emotions familiar to those who had had the misfortune to be trapped in a conversation with Heidemann: bewilderment, disbelief, distaste and an overwhelming sense of claustrophobia.

He told Trevor-Roper that he had access to an important archive of Nazi documents which Martin Bormann had deposited in Madrid in 1938.

Trevor-Roper pointed out that such an action by Bormann was rather unlikely – Madrid was in Republican hands in 1938.

Perhaps it was somewhere outside Madrid, said Heidemann. Or perhaps it was 1939. Anyway, it was certainly true; he had been told the story personally – by Martin Bormann.

Trevor-Roper smiled, assuming that Heidemann was making a joke. But the reporter was serious. He pulled out his wallet and produced a photograph. 'This is a picture of Martin, taken recently.'

The historian studied the photograph. It showed a man in his mid-sixties – an obvious impostor, considering that Bormann would by then have been eighty-three.

Heidemann would not be dissuaded. Martin, he insisted, was alive and living in Switzerland. . .

The evening crept by with more stories of Heidemann's Nazi contacts, until Trevor-Roper at last felt able to make a polite excuse and escape to his bedroom.

In retrospect it is difficult to understand why Trevor-Roper's uneasiness and scepticism about Heidemann did not begin now to extend to the diaries he had seen in the Swiss bank. In fact, his reaction was almost exactly the opposite. He reasoned that if he, after half a day's acquaintance, found Heidemann unreliable, *Stern*, after employing him for thirty years, must surely have known what he was like and been all the more careful about checking his stories. He was under the impression that this had been done. As far as he was concerned, the diaries had been authenticated by three handwriting experts and by forensic analysis; their provenance in the Boernersdorf air crash was entirely credible; their contents had been thoroughly investigated by *Stern* over a period of several years; and the magazine's editor had assured him that the supplier of the diaries was known to them and had also been checked.

Heidemann reminded Trevor-Roper of the late Ladislas Farago, the American writer who claimed he had seen a decrepit Bormann propped up in a large bed in 1973 surrounded by Bolivian nuns. Farago had visited Trevor-Roper in Oxford and had exhibited a similar naivety and readiness to believe whatever he was told, combined with a genuine talent for unearthing documents and information.

With these complacent thoughts, the historian retired to his bed, his belief in the Hitler diaries unshaken.

Murdoch's handling of the negotiations had been masterful. By Tuesday, isolated in New York, Koch and Schulte-Hillen found themselves effectively reduced to begging the Australian to buy the syndication rights. When he finally consented to resume negotiations, he was able to dictate his own price. His original offer for the British and Commonwealth rights had been $750,000. Now, he picked them up for little more than half that sum – $400,000. The money was to be paid over the next two years. The first instalment of $200,000 was handed over on signature of the contract. (Shortly afterwards, Murdoch also acquired the American rights for a bargain price of $800,000.)

The continuing silence from *Newsweek* convinced the Germans that the magazine was indeed going to steal their story. Further negotiations were useless. The pair had the feeling that they were being deliberately kept waiting around in a New York hotel in order to hold up publication in Hamburg.

On Wednesday, Schulte-Hillen telephoned Reinhard Mohn and confessed to the Bertelsmann owner that he had made a mess of the negotiations – in his words, he had 'over-pokered' his hand. He also rang Hensmann and issued orders confirming that *Stern* would publish its scoop the following Monday. The discovery of the diaries would be announced in a statement on Friday.

Koch and Schulte-Hillen caught the next plane back to Germany.

In the offices of *The Times* and *Sunday Times* that Wednesday, very few people knew of the impending acquisition of the Hitler diaries. Those who did were mostly confused or apprehensive.

Phillip Knightley had arrived back at the *Sunday Times* on Tuesday after four months in Australia. That night he had gone out for a drink with Eric Jacobs, the editor responsible for commissioning the long articles on the front of the paper's *Review* section. He wouldn't be requiring anything for a while, he told Knightley. He understood he was going to be running the Hitler diaries in that space.

The next day, Knightley went in to see Magnus Linklater, the features editor. 'These Hitler diaries,' he asked, 'they're not the ones that David Irving put us on to in December, are they?' Linklater said they weren't – they'd been offered to the paper by *Stern*. A few minutes later, Knightley bumped into the *Sunday Times* editor, Frank Giles, in the lavatory. He told him he was worried about the rumours he was picking up regarding the diaries. It all sounded very suspicious.

'You're right to be cautious,' replied Giles. 'But don't worry. It doesn't concern us. Murdoch's going to run them in *The Times*.'

Knightley was still anxious. He asked if he could submit a memorandum setting out his reservations.

By all means, said Giles, but keep it to one page. Murdoch's attention span was notoriously short; there was no point in giving him anything longer than a few hundred words to read.

What was nagging away at the back of Knightley's mind was the memory of another set of wartime documents which had been bought for the *Sunday Times* fifteen years earlier – the diaries of Benito Mussolini. These had been offered to the Thomson Organization, at that time the owners of the *Sunday Times*, for £250,000. A series of expert examinations had failed to find anything wrong with them, and £100,000 had been handed over as a down payment to a Polish-born arms dealer who was acting as middle man. Further large sums had been paid out in expenses – for example, Vittorio Mussolini, the dictator's son, had been given £3500 in cash in a brown paper bag in order to buy himself a sports car in return for agreeing to renounce his claim on the diaries. In the end, the books had turned out to be the work of an Italian woman called Amalia Panvini and her eighty-four-year-old mother, Rosa. The affair had cost Thomsons a fortune and made the *Sunday Times* a temporary laughing-stock in Fleet Street. Knightley – one of the few reporters left on the paper who remembered the affair – had been cautious of so-called 'finds' of wartime papers ever since.

It took him the rest of Wednesday to write his memorandum. Point by point, he drew attention to the similarities between the forgery of 1968 and the 'scoop' of 1983. The Mussolini fiasco should have taught the *Sunday Times* some lessons:

1   You cannot rely on expert authentication. Thomson engaged five
    experts, including the author of the standard work on Mussolini,
    the world's greatest authority on paper, a famous handwriting
    expert, an internationally known palaeographer and an academic
    who authenticated the Casement Diaries. *Not one expert said that
    they were fake.*

2   You cannot rely on people close to the subject. Vittorio Mussolini,
    Mussolini's son, said that the diaries were definitely his father's.

3   You cannot rely on legal protection. Slaughter and May [a firm of
    solicitors] did the negotiations for Thomson. They did not succeed
    in recovering a single penny when the diaries turned out to be
    fakes.

4   Beware of secrecy and being pressed to make a quick decision. The
    Mussolini con men were able to bring off their sting by pressing
    Thomson to make a quick deal. Absolute secrecy was essential,
    they said, to prevent the Italian government from stepping in. Both
    manoeuvres prevented proper examination of the background of
    the salesmen and the provenance of the diaries.

Questions to consider:

1   What German academic experts have seen all the diaries? Has, for
    instance, the Institute of Contemporary History seen them?

2   What non-academic British experts have seen all the diaries? Has
    David Irving seen them?

3   How thoroughly has the vendor explained where the diaries have
    been all these years and why they have surfaced *now*: the fiftieth
    anniversary of Hitler's accession to power?

The crux of the matter is that secrecy and speed work for the con man.
To mount a proper check would protect us but would not be accept-
able to the vendor. *We should insist on doing our own checks* and not
accept the checks of any other publishing organization.

Knightley's intuition was subsequently proved correct in almost every
detail: the authentication had been inadequate; the supposed involvement of East German officials and the fear that the copyright might
not be secure had fostered a climate of secrecy, bordering on paranoia;

no German historians had been allowed to see the diaries; no explanation had been given as to where the diaries had been kept for more than thirty years; and Times Newspapers had not carried out its own checks, apart from sending Trevor-Roper on his brief expedition into the Swiss bank.

Knightley sent his memorandum to Frank Giles to be forwarded to Murdoch. He never heard another word about it. It was too late. Murdoch had bought the diaries and now his priority, like *Stern*'s, was to beat *Newsweek* into print.

Trevor-Roper arrived home in Cambridge late on Wednesday night. He was talking to his wife in her sitting-room at about midnight when he received a transatlantic telephone call from Murdoch and Charles Douglas-Home in New York. Murdoch told him that *Stern* was bringing forward its publication date to Monday. News International had acquired syndication rights in the diaries. 'I think we'll put them in the *Sunday Times*,' he said. The announcement of the discovery would be made on Friday morning, in less than thirty-six hours' time. Douglas-Home cut in. 'We want a piece from you for Saturday's *Times*. Can you do it?' Trevor-Roper said he thought he could, if he wrote 'flat out'. It was agreed that the article would be picked up from Peterhouse by dispatch rider on Friday morning.

In Hamburg on Thursday, Sorge and Hensmann tied up the loose ends with *Stern*'s smaller, European syndication partners. *Paris Match* bought the diaries for $400,000. The Spanish company Grupo Zeta paid $150,000. Geillustreerde Pers of the Netherlands handed over $125,000 for serial rights in Belgium and Holland. Norshe Presse of Norway bought the diaries for $50,000. The Italian rights went to Mondadori, publishers of the magazine *Panorama*, although as a precaution they decided at this stage to buy only the first four instalments for $50,000. Added together with the $1.2 million paid by News International for the English language serialization, this meant that the Hitler diaries had so far realized $1.975 million – less than *Stern* had originally hoped for, but still one of the largest syndication deals in history. And, of course, there were still the world book rights to come.

*

The Peterhouse Master's Lodge is a large and stately Queen Anne house on the eastern side of Trumpington Street, opposite the college. This spacious and well-proportioned home was regarded by Trevor-Roper as one of the more attractive aspects of being Master of Peterhouse. ('The only drawback,' he remarked, 'is that the college comes with it.')

Throughout Thursday 21 April, Trevor-Roper sat in his first-floor study, trying to write his article for *The Times*. Although justifiably renowned for his literary style (A. J. P. Taylor called him 'an incomparable essayist'), he had always found writing 'terribly painful'. Deadlines especially were a torture to him. He never used a typewriter, always a fountain pen, and liked to 'write, sleep on it, and then rewrite'. Today he had no time for such luxuries. At length, having sorted through his notes and cleared his mind, he set to work.

'A new document' – he began – 'or rather, a whole new archive of documents – has recently come to light in Germany. It is an archive of great historical significance. When it is available to historians, it will occupy them for some time. It may also disconcert them. It is Hitler's private diary, kept by him, in his own hand, throughout almost the whole of his reign . . .'

On Thursday night in his laboratory in the small town of Bad Ems outside Koblenz, Dr Arnold Rentz completed his analysis of the three sheets of paper *Stern* had sent to the Bundesarchiv the previous week.

When he had commissioned him, Dr Josef Henke had told Rentz that the tests were a matter of the utmost urgency. The chemist therefore worked late in order to be able to give Henke the results the following day. He had some good news, and some bad.

PART FOUR

'After all, we are in the entertainment business.'
Rupert Murdoch on the Hitler diaries

25

Friday 22 April.

At 9 a.m. a motorcycle dispatch-rider from *The Times* arrived at the Peterhouse Master's Lodge.

Trevor-Roper was entitled to feel a certain professional pride as he handed over his article. It was long – over 3000 words – and had been difficult to write, but he had finished it in a day and submitted it on time. It was an impressive piece of journalism, if not of scholarship.

His career had always been marked by a curious dichotomy. There was Hugh Trevor-Roper, patient historian, author of learned works on such *esoterica* as the sixteenth-century European witch craze, the ancient Scottish constitution and the life of the fraudulent Sinologist, Edmund Backhouse, 'the Hermit of Peking'. And then there was Lord Dacre, man of public affairs, newspaper director, pundit, MI5 officer and Hitler expert. His article for *The Times* represented the triumph of the intelligence officer over the scholar. His authentication of the Hitler diaries was not based on a careful analysis of their content – it could not be, he had scarcely bothered to read a single entry. It was based almost entirely on circumstantial evidence.

He confessed that to start with he had been sceptical ('the very idea of Hitler as a methodical diarist is new'). But then he had 'entered the back room in the Swiss bank, and turned the pages of those volumes, and learned the extraordinary story of their discovery' and his doubts had 'gradually dissolved'. What most impressed him, he wrote, were the other parts of the Hitler archive shown to him by *Stern* in Zurich and by Heidemann in Hamburg:

... it is these other documents – letters, notes, notices of meetings, mementoes, and, above all, signed paintings and drawings by Hitler, all covering several decades – which convinced me of the authenticity of the diaries. For all belong to the same archive, and whereas signatures, single documents, or even groups of documents can be skilfully forged, a whole coherent archive covering 35 years is far less easily manufactured.

Such a disproportionate and indeed extravagant effort offers too large and vulnerable a flank to the critics who will undoubtedly assail it... The archive, in fact, is not only a collection of documents which can be individually tested: it coheres as a whole and the diaries are an integral part of it.

That is the internal evidence of authenticity...

Trevor-Roper's entire misjudgement was founded upon the *non sequitur* contained in that last, fatally confident sentence. The fact that the archive spanned thirty-five years and included paintings and other documents did not, except in the most superficial sense, provide 'internal evidence of authenticity'. If such internal evidence existed, it was to be found in the detailed content of the diaries themselves. But no German scholar had even been allowed to see them, let alone check every entry; at least twenty volumes had not yet been transcribed into typescript; and Walde and Pesch, the only journalists apart from Heidemann who had access to the diaries, had thoroughly examined only one volume: that devoted to the flight of Rudolf Hess. (Ironically, the authenticity of the Hess book was the one feature of the diaries which still worried Trevor-Roper. 'We must not jump to premature conclusions,' he wrote. 'There are many mysteries in the case of Hess.')

The 'external fact' which impressed Trevor-Roper was the plane crash and Hitler's reaction to it: 'a clue which connects him, by a thin but direct line, with this archive'. The outburst in the bunker, together with the extent of the material accompanying the diaries, 'seems to me to constitute clear proof of their authenticity'.

The world, he concluded, would have to revise its opinion of Hitler to take account of the fact that he was 'a compulsive diarist'.

In fact, we must envisage him, every night, after he had apparently gone to bed ... sitting down to write his daily record: and perhaps more too,

for the archive contains not only the diaries but whole books by Hitler –
books on Jesus Christ, on Frederick the Great, on himself (the three subjects which seem equally to fascinate megalomaniac Germans) – and a
third volume of *Mein Kampf*. If Hitler (as he said in 1942) had long ago
found writing by hand a great effort, that may be not so much because
he was out of practice as because he already suffered from writer's cramp.

*

As this hasty compilation of donnish jokes and misunderstanding sped
down the M11 to London, Felix Schmidt opened the regular *Stern* editorial conference in Hamburg. It was 11 a.m., German time.

He had a brief announcement to make, he said. His statement was
simple and to the point. Over the past few days, colleagues had probably heard rumours of an impending scoop of great importance. He
was now pleased to be able to let them in on a secret which had been
kept by the magazine for the past two years. *Stern* had acquired the
diaries of Adolf Hitler and would begin publishing them on Monday.

The news was met with gasps and whistles of astonishment.

Simultaneously, the magazine was issuing a public statement
announcing its discovery to the world. 'Following evaluation of the
diaries,' it claimed, 'the biography of the dictator, and with it the history of the Nazi state, will have to be written in large part anew.'

At 11.15 a.m., *Stern*'s news department began sending out the
telexed message – to the German press agency, DPA, to Associated
Press, to Reuters, to United Press International, to West German radio
and television. . .

It was at this point, with the juggernaut already beginning to roll,
that Thomas Walde received a telephone call from Dr Josef Henke at
the Bundesarchiv. Henke had received the results of Rentz's forensic
analysis. The two blank pages which had been cut from the diaries
did not contain paper whitener and therefore could have been manufactured either before or during the Second World War. The Mussolini telegram, however, *did* contain whitener and Rentz was convinced
the paper was made after 1945. Rentz's findings supported those of
the West German police in March: while the diaries might be genuine,

much of the accompanying archive (whose existence had done so much to convince Trevor-Roper) was faked.

Walde thanked Rentz for his help and asked him to rush Rentz's written report to Hamburg as quickly as possible.

At first sight, this news was not too disturbing for *Stern*: the diaries, after all, were what mattered, and Heidemann had already told Walde that, according to 'Fischer', the other material did not necessarily come from the Boernersdorf crash. But considered more carefully, the implications of the Rentz report were frightening. Three handwriting experts had concluded that the draft telegrams to Admiral Horthy and General Franco (similar to, and from the same source as, the Mussolini telegram) were written by the same person as the author of the page from the Hess special volume. If they were fakes, how much reliance could be placed on the handwriting authentication? And Rentz had been able to establish, by the apparent absence of whitener, only that the two diary pages *might* be from the right period: they could still be made of paper manufactured after 1945 by an old-fashioned process (as indeed eventually proved to be the case). Thus, at the very moment that news of *Stern*'s scoop was being flashed around the world, the magazine received indications about its authenticity which were, at best, ambiguous.

As soon as Walde had finished speaking to Henke, he went off to find Peter Koch to tell him the news. Koch, newly returned from America, was understandably alarmed. Walde tried to reassure him: according to Heidemann, he said, whitener was in use before the war; and even if the Mussolini telegram was a fake, it did not originate from the same source as the diaries.

Koch was still not happy. He told Walde that they must inform the management at once. They collected Felix Schmidt on the way, briefed him on what had happened, and together all three went up to the ninth floor to see Schulte-Hillen.

Koch explained the situation and made a short speech. At any moment, he declared, a wave of scepticism was going to descend upon them. They were going to be attacked by academics and newspapers all over the world. They had to be absolutely confident that the story was watertight. There was only one way they could be sure. Heidemann must be made to divulge the name of his source. Koch was worried. 'I told Schulte-Hillen,' he recalled, '"Heidemann has greater trust in you than in me. Please ask him to write down the exact course of events. You can then read the piece of paper and lock it away in a safe. You don't even need to give it to me to read. Just tell me that the source is OK."'

Schulte-Hillen agreed. He asked his secretary to get Gerd Heidemann on the telephone.

The reporter was not in Hamburg. He was eventually traced to the Bayerischer Hof, an expensive hotel in the centre of Munich.

Schulte-Hillen explained the problem and asked him to write down, in confidence, the complete story of how he had obtained the diaries. Heidemann refused. 'I asked him again,' recalled Schulte-Hillen, 'emphatically.' It was no use. According to the managing director:

> He told me that as an experienced journalist he knew that anything that was written down could also be copied and anything that was said could be passed on to other people. He was not so unscrupulous that he would endanger the life of his informant. He could not live with his conscience if he put someone else's life in danger.
>
> When I tried to pressurize him further, he became quite irritated and said: 'What is it that you want of me? I won't tell you. I swear to you on the lives of my children that everything is in order. It has all been properly researched. The books are genuine. What more can you ask of me?'

Schulte-Hillen was once more struck by what seemed to him Heidemann's obvious sincerity. 'I too have children,' he said afterwards. 'Heidemann's oath impressed me.' He let the matter drop. In any case, under the terms of his contract, Heidemann had the right to keep the identity of his supplier secret. The managing director told the editors that there was nothing he could do. They would all have to trust Heidemann.

In London, Frank Giles, editor of the *Sunday Times*, summoned two of his senior colleagues, Hugo Young and Magnus Linklater, to his office. He was, recalled Linklater, 'obviously very flustered'.

Giles was not a member of Murdoch's inner circle. He had been only on the fringes of the group which negotiated to buy the diaries – vaguely aware of what was going on, unenthusiastic, yet comforted by his belief that they would be running in *The Times*. His *sang froid* had been shattered the previous day by a brisk, transatlantic announcement from Murdoch that the Hitler diaries were going to be serialized in the *Sunday Times* after all: now that *Stern* would be appearing on Monday, Sunday had become the perfect day to print the extracts. It would enable the paper to avoid the risk of rivals getting hold of advance copies of the German magazine and printing pirated extracts from the diaries twenty-four hours ahead of them.

Murdoch was not a proprietor who encouraged dissent. Even strong editors found it hard to stand up to him. Giles was not a strong editor. He was sixty-four years old, sleek and aristocratic, a lover of Glyndebourne, fine French wines and classical music which he listened to on his Sony Walkman. His relationship with Murdoch was akin to that between a rabbit and a stoat. The proprietor made no secret of his habit of ripping into Giles's editorial decisions. He once announced jauntily to Harold Evans that he was 'just going over to terrorize Frank'. Murdoch's office on the sixth floor of *The Times* building looked directly across into Giles's at the *Sunday Times*. Evans recalled how the Australian tycoon 'would stand up with a big grin and with his fingers pointed like a pistol fire bang! bang!' at Giles working with his back to the window. The subject of this imaginary target practice was in no position to stop Murdoch from doing what he wanted with his newspaper.

Giles told Young and Linklater that the *Sunday Times* would be serializing the Hitler diaries. They would prepare the ground on Sunday with extensive coverage of their discovery. The two men were 'aghast'. How could Giles countenance something as irresponsible as running the diaries without allowing the paper's own journalists to make independent checks? Had he not seen Knightley's memorandum? Had he forgotten the Mussolini diaries?

Giles, according to Linklater, raised his hands to his ears.

'I know, I know,' he said. 'But I don't want to hear about all that. The deal's been signed and we're going to have to do it.'

Minutes later, Arthur Brittenden, Times Newspapers' Director of Corporate Relations (their press officer), announced that the Hitler diaries would be running in the *Sunday Times*. 'It's not been decided how many Sundays,' he told the *New York Times*, 'because the complete translation is not yet finished. But I think we'll run it for two or three weeks, then there will be a gap and we'll pick it up again.'

By coincidence, many of the leading characters in the British subplot of the affair came together for lunch on Friday at the Dorchester Hotel. The Dorchester was hosting the UK Press Awards, an annual ceremony at which Britain's journalists present prizes to one another in recognition of their professional skill. Charles Douglas-Home was holding forth to a woman sitting next to him. 'It's just been announced,' he told her. 'It's the greatest historical find of the century.'

Sitting at the table, Gitta Sereny of the *Sunday Times* asked what he was talking about.

'The Hitler diaries,' said Douglas-Home.

'Are you running them?' she asked.

'No. You are.'

Sereny relayed the gist of this conversation to Phillip Knightley, sitting a few yards away. Knightley hurried back to the office and sought out Magnus Linklater. Linklater gloomily confirmed that the news was true. '*The Times* is running an article by Trevor-Roper tomorrow saying they're genuine. Why don't you talk to him?'

It was 3 p.m. In the Master's Lodge, Trevor-Roper was preparing for a visit to the opera when Knightley called him. The historian's tone was confident and reassuring.

'The one thing that impressed me most,' he told Knightley, 'was the volume of the material. I asked myself whether it all could have been constructed out of the imagination and incidental sources. I decided that it could not.'

Knightley reminded him that there had been thirty volumes of the purported Mussolini diaries. Trevor-Roper was unperturbed: 'I *know* Hitler's handwriting. I *know* his signature. I *know* the changes in it between 1908 and his death. It seemed to me that an operation of forgery on that scale was heroic and unnecessary.' He pointed out that they were not dealing with some shady characters operating on the fringes of the law, but with one of the wealthiest and most widely read magazines in Europe: 'The directors of *Stern*, one must assume, do not engage in forgery.'

By the time he hung up, Knightley – who recorded the call – felt much happier. Trevor-Roper's reputation was impeccable. It was inconceivable that he could be so emphatic about the diaries' authenticity without good cause. 'I must say,' Knightley recalled, 'he went a long way to convincing me.'

Trevor-Roper and his wife left the Master's Lodge shortly after 3.30 p.m. to join a party of Cambridge dons and their families on an excursion to the Royal Opera House at Covent Garden. The historian still felt fairly confident about his judgement of the diaries. But the conversation with Knightley had been vaguely disconcerting and as he settled down in his seat on the party's private coach, somewhere in the recesses of his mind, something began to stir.

Three thousand miles away, America was waking up to the news of the diaries' discovery. All the major US wire services were running the *Stern* announcement, and across New York, in the offices of publishers, agents and newspapers, telephones were ringing with demands for information.

At Bantam Books, Louis Wolfe confirmed to the *New York Times* that he had heard of the Hitler diaries. 'An offer was made,' he admitted, 'but we were never sure exactly what was being offered, so it seemed much simpler to have our parent company handle it out of its group office in Munich. To the best of my knowledge no one in the United States has signed a contract to publish a book based on Hitler's diaries.' Wolfe's Vice-President, Stuart Applebaum, was also fielding calls. 'We have a great interest in the possibility of doing a book someday related to the diaries,' he told the *Washington Post*, 'but at this time we have no plans to publish one. Nor do we have any deal to do one.'

At ICM, Lynn Nesbit struggled to answer a deluge of questions. Yes, she had been hired to represent *Stern*. No, she was no longer their agent. Yes, she was paid a commission. No, she wouldn't disclose the amount...

Almost every big American magazine found itself pressed to issue a statement. *Time*'s was terse ('We have had an interest'); *Life*'s was baffled ('We haven't been involved at all; we just heard about it today'); the *National Enquirer* tried to pretend it was on the point of clinching a deal ('right now we are involved in negotiations with *Stern*'). The longest came from *Newsweek*, read out by the magazine's publicity director, Gary Gerard: '*Newsweek* does not have an agreement with *Stern* for publishing rights to the Adolf Hitler diaries. We are covering the story as news.'

Newsweek's behaviour went much further than merely 'covering the story as news'. At a morning editorial conference it was decided to ransack the material handed over in Hamburg. Hitler would go on the cover. Inside the magazine, thirteen pages would be devoted to the diaries (as opposed to four for the week's main story, the bombing of the US embassy in Beirut which left forty-seven dead). The advertising department was instructed to prepare an extensive publicity campaign. Full-page advertisements were taken out in six major US newspapers, including the *New York Times* and the *Washington Post*; these were to be backed up by thirty-second television commercials in twelve American cities.

As it happened, this was the day on which *Newsweek*'s nominated expert, Gerhard Weinberg, was due to fly to Germany to take up a temporary teaching post in Bonn. Maynard Parker was nevertheless determined to extract an article from him. Weinberg dismissed his last class on the campus at Chapel Hill at 11 a.m. He and his wife caught a flight to New York and at 3 p.m. were met at La Guardia airport by two *Newsweek* reporters and a photographer. The journalists steered the professor into a corner of the arrivals lounge and thrust a copy of Trevor-Roper's *Times* article into his hands – the text had just been wired over from London. Weinberg skimmed through it: '*doubts dissolved . . . satisfied documents authentic . . . standard accounts Hitler's personality have to be revised . . . astonishing archive . . .*' Weinberg, who had always respected Trevor-Roper's scholarship, was startled by the lack of equivocation. Such a ringing endorsement seemed to him 'in itself to be a strong argument in favour of the diaries' authenticity'. Trevor-Roper, he reasoned, must know something he didn't. He told the *Newsweek* reporters that in view of the article, the diaries, in his opinion, were now more likely to be genuine than not.

The *Newsweek* men still needed more information to complete their coverage. Weinberg was equally determined to catch his flight to Germany. The only solution was for one of the journalists, Steven Strasser, to fly out with him, interview him on the plane, and file a piece by telephone from Germany. The photographer stood Professor Weinberg against a wall and took a few hasty pictures. Then Weinberg, his wife, and Mr Strasser left to catch the afternoon flight to Frankfurt.

Peter Koch's prediction of the hostility the diaries would arouse was already coming true.

In Stuttgart, Eberhard Jaeckel – although, like Weinberg, 'shaken by Trevor-Roper's position' – declared himself 'extremely sceptical'. He had seen a so-called 'Hitler diary' some years before, he said, and decided it was forged.

'I have not seen their evidence, but everything speaks against it,' Werner Maser told Reuters. 'It smacks of pure sensationalism.'

'I am extraordinarily sceptical,' announced Karl-Dietrich Bracher of Bonn University. 'It would be a total surprise and I consider it highly unlikely.'

A spokesman for the Federal Archives in Koblenz confirmed that they had arranged for the examination of 'about ten pages' of Hitler's handwriting for *Stern*, but denied having authenticated any diaries.

The loudest condemnations of all were emanating from London.

David Irving reckoned he was due for some luck. For two years, everything had gone wrong for him. His marriage had ended in an acrimonious divorce. He was being pursued by the Inland Revenue. His political activities had collapsed due to lack of funds. He was on the point of being evicted from his flat. Most of the furniture had been taken by his wife and entire rooms were left stripped and abandoned while he was reduced to squatting in one corner. By the spring of 1983, he was in desperate need of money and a boost for his flagging career. And now, as if in answer to a prayer, Adolf Hitler came to his rescue.

Ever since 10 a.m., when a reporter from *Der Spiegel* had called to tell him of *Stern*'s impending announcement, he had been inundated with inquiries from around the world – Reuters, *Newsweek*, the

New York Times, the *Observer*, the *Sunday Mirror, Bild Zeitung*, Independent Radio News, the BBC. . . 'As soon as I rang off, the phone rang again,' he noted in his diary. 'Quite extraordinary.' His answer to all of them was the same: the Hitler diaries were fakes, and he had the evidence to prove it.

He was 'shocked' by *Stern*'s decision to publish. He was certain that the forgeries he had received from Priesack in December originated from the same source as Heidemann's diaries. Thankfully, he still had photocopies of the material – letters, drawings, a few pages from the original volume for 1935 (the one Kujau had forged in 1978 and given to Fritz Stiefel). With the Hitler diaries fast becoming the hottest news story in the world, these worthless scraps had suddenly become a potential gold mine. Irving's priority now was to make money as quickly as possible.

In between constant interruptions from the telephone, he wrote to the *Sunday Times* drawing their attention to the fact that he had given them an 'exclusive lead to these documents' before Christmas and demanding as commission a percentage of the price paid for the diaries. He then set about marketing his information. *Der Spiegel* offered to pay him for his photocopies. *Bild Zeitung*, a mass-circulation West German paper, promised to meet his expenses and provide a fee if he would fly out to Hamburg to confront *Stern* at its press conference on Monday. One of the *Sunday Times*'s main rivals, the *Observer*, paid him £1000 for his help in compiling an article which derided the diaries' authenticity; another, the *Mail on Sunday*, gave him £5000 for his documents and a statement that the diaries were forged.

This was only the beginning of an extraordinary resurgence in Irving's fortunes. No one now cared about his reputation as a right-wing maverick. Seeing their circulations threatened by the Hitler scoop, newspapers and magazines which would have treated him as a pariah twenty-four hours earlier queued up for quotes. By the end of the afternoon Irving had emerged as *Stern*'s most vociferous and dangerous assailant.

At 9.30 p.m., a BBC taxi picked him up and took him to Television Centre where he appeared in a live studio confrontation with Charles Douglas-Home. Irving waved his fakes at the camera. Douglas-Home was unperturbed. 'I have smelt them,' he said of the diaries. 'I'm a minor historian and we know about the smell of old documents. They certainly smelt.'

At that moment, sitting in the audience at the Royal Opera House, Covent Garden, Times Newspapers' star witness was beginning to have second thoughts. Borne along by the momentum of deadlines, midnight phone calls and departure times, infected by the pervading atmosphere of excitement and secrecy, he had scarcely had time for an hour's calm reflection all week. Now, as the other academics and their wives concentrated on the music of Verdi's *Don Carlos*, Trevor-Roper's thoughts were elsewhere, ranging back over his experiences in Hamburg and Zurich, with one incident in particular gnawing at his mind.

On Tuesday, Heidemann had shown him a letter, supposedly by Hitler. It was dated 1908 and addressed to a girl with whom Hitler was supposed to have been infatuated during his days in Vienna. The incident had been described by August Kubizek in *The Young Hitler I Knew*. In retrospect, this letter 'disquieted' Trevor-Roper. It fitted in 'just a little too neatly' with the known historical record. 'Could this letter have been forged for this purpose?' he wondered. And why was it with Hitler's papers? Why wasn't it with the girl's? Until this moment he had taken the existence of such supplementary material, which helped to make up the sheer bulk of the archive, as an almost unanswerable argument in favour of the diaries' authenticity. Suddenly he saw the flaw in this logic. For the first time since leaving the Swiss bank, he allowed his mind to approach the *Stern* find from a different angle.

> I began to consider the whole archive with the mind of a forger. How would a forger of Hitler's diaries proceed? I decided that he would concentrate on a period when Hitler's movements were well documented, and, outside that period, select only detached episodes for which public evidence was accessible. He would also, since his main material would be derivative or trivial, vary it where he safely could with interesting deviations. The diaries, I noted, had a discomforting correspondence with this model. They were continuous from 1932; before that there were isolated episodes; and an interesting variation was suggested in the affair of Rudolf Hess.

Trevor-Roper had always had doubts about the Hess book: 'That Hitler, with his political brain, should have sanctioned such a mission – it was insane.' Now, these doubts and his reservations about the 1908 letter, began to set off a fearful chain reaction in his mind. Why hadn't any German experts seen the material? And Heidemann – the memory of that awful evening at the Atlantic swam back into his memory – Heidemann could so easily have been deceived; 'he was not a critical spirit'. Trevor-Roper's confidence in his judgement began rapidly unravelling.

'If at that moment,' he said later, 'I could have stopped the course of events, I would have done so.'

He briefly considered groping his way out of the dimly lit auditorium to find a telephone. He rejected the idea. He knew the workings of a modern newspaper sufficiently well to appreciate that there was no chance of stopping his article now. At that moment, less than a mile away, in the print-room of Times Newspapers, twelve hours after it had been picked up from his home, 400,000 copies of it were coming off the presses.

26

Hugh Trevor-Roper arrived home in Cambridge in the early hours of Saturday morning. He went to bed but was soon up again. Shortly after 7 a.m. he went down to collect the morning's edition of *The Times*. The story dominated the front page:

38 Years after Bunker suicide
Hitler's secret diaries to be published

- Hitler approved the 'peace' flight to Scotland in 1941 by his deputy, Rudolf Hess, but then declared him insane.
- He ordered his troops not to destroy the British Expeditionary Force trapped at Dunkirk in 1940 in the hope that he could conclude a negotiated peace.
- He thought Neville Chamberlain, whom history has judged harshly, was a skilled negotiator and admired his toughness.

Trevor-Roper opened the paper. His own article was spread across an entire page:

'When I had entered the back room in the Swiss bank, and turned the pages of those volumes, my doubts gradually dissolved. I am now satisfied they are authentic.'

Secrets that survived the Bunker
BY HUGH TREVOR-ROPER

Reading the article spurred Trevor-Roper into action. At 8 a.m. he began making a series of telephone calls.

He rang Charles Douglas-Home and told him he now had 'some doubts' about the authenticity of the diaries. 'They were not doubts such that I could say I disbelieved in the diaries,' he recalled – but they were serious reservations. Douglas-Home took the news with remarkable calmness. He told the historian that there had been a good deal of publicity on television the previous evening, with David Irving emerging as 'prosecuting counsel'. He said that he, too, personally regretted the deal with *Stern* – the Germans were unpleasant to deal with, arrogant and paranoid. They still hadn't supplied a complete transcript of the material. The conditions they had imposed were 'insulting'. They would have to see what developed over the next few days.

Trevor-Roper also spoke of his doubts to Colin Webb. Next, he rang Peter Wickman. *Stern* wanted him to attend the press conference to launch the diaries on Monday. Trevor-Roper told Wickman he would take part only if he were given an opportunity to put some questions to Gerd Heidemann beforehand. In addition, he wanted to see a typed transcript of the Hess volume. Wickman promised to see what he could do.

One good reason for Douglas-Home's stoicism in the face of Trevor-Roper's sudden nervousness was the fact that he was no longer responsible for the diaries. That burden had passed on Thursday to Frank Giles at the *Sunday Times*. A fatal breakdown in communication now occurred. Douglas-Home believed that Trevor-Roper's doubts were relatively minor; if they were serious, he assumed the historian would pass them on to the *Sunday Times*. But Trevor-Roper was relying on Douglas-Home to spread the word of his unease around Gray's Inn Road. He did not think of calling them direct. 'I had had no dealings with the *Sunday Times* myself,' he explained. 'I had been employed solely by *The Times*.' He sat at home in Cambridge and waited for Knightley or Giles to ring him. He was 'surprised that they didn't call; it would seem the thing to do'.

Meanwhile, happily ignorant of Trevor-Roper's change of heart, the staff of the *Sunday Times* were racing against the paper's deadline to do justice to a story endorsed by the historian as the greatest scoop since Watergate. Professional instincts were now overriding natural scepticism. Magnus Linklater (co-author of *Hoax*, the story of the faked Howard Hughes autobiography) and Paul Eddy, the head of the paper's Insight team, were responsible for putting together the coverage. *Stern* would not allow them to talk to Heidemann directly. Quotations from the diaries were having to be extracted from the Germans by Anthony Terry, the *Sunday Times* representative in Hamburg, who translated them and telexed them to London. Even as they worked, Linklater and Eddy were conscious of how phoney they sounded. According to the telexes, Hitler had written some peculiar entries.

[*On Goebbels's affair with a Czech actress*]
The little Dr Goebbels is up to his old tricks again with women.

[*On Himmler*]
I shall show this deceitful small animal breeder with his lust for power; this unfathomable little penny-pincher will find out what I am about.

[*On the July 1944 bomb plot*]
Ha, ha, isn't it laughable? This scum, these loafers and good-for-nothings. These people were bunglers.

The two journalists discussed what they should do. 'We agreed,' said Linklater afterwards, 'that the honourable course would have been to have refused to touch it. But as Paul said, if we did that, we would have to resign. We both laughed about that, so we carried on – like a couple of hacks.'

Phillip Knightley was also searching his conscience. His task was to write an article setting out the reasons for the diaries' authenticity and their importance as an historical source. 'I agreed to do it on the understanding that my name wasn't to be attached to it. Then someone pointed out that it would look odd if the article appeared anonymously and I was asked to reconsider.' Knightley went off to consult John Whale, the *Sunday Times*'s religious correspondent, 'a great moral force on the paper'. Knightley showed him what he had written and asked him what he should do. Whale advised him to agree to the request – he had been sufficiently detached in the piece to cover himself against the possibility that the material was fraudulent. (Only one sentence – the first – later returned to haunt Knightley: 'Hitler's diaries,' he wrote, 'have been submitted to the most rigorous tests to establish their authenticity.')

The edition of the paper which emerged after all this agonizing was extraordinary: a testament to the skill of the journalists and the old rule that anything about the Nazis, once embellished with swastikas and pictures of Hitler, has a quality of compulsion. 'We did a hell of a good job on it,' said Linklater. 'It was gripping stuff. Professionally, we were all very pleased with it.'

Dominating the front page, spread over eight columns, headed 'WORLD EXCLUSIVE', was an article promising the reader 'The secrets of Hitler's War'. There was a superimposed picture of Gerd Heidemann holding the diaries; behind him, looking out over his shoulder, staring hypnotically at the potential purchaser, was an enormous close-up of Hitler's face. The story spilled over on to page two and was backed up by articles on pages sixteen, seventeen and eighteen. The centre spread announced 'HITLER'S SECRET DIARIES' in letters almost two inches high. There were photographs of Hitler and Eva Braun, of extracts from the diaries, of Goebbels, Himmler and Bormann, of the graves in Boern-ersdorf and of Heidemann solemnly holding up the salvaged window from the crashed plane. 'Look at that,' said Brian MacArthur, the deputy editor, when the first proofs arrived in the newsroom. 'You will never see another front page like that as long as you live. It is sensational.'

It is a tradition on the *Sunday Times* that, as the presses begin to turn, the senior members of the staff gather in the editor's office for a drink. Shortly after 7 p.m., Linklater, Eddy, MacArthur, Knightley and their colleagues trooped in to see Giles. There was a mood of self-congratulation. The paper looked so good, it almost convinced the people who had written it. Over a glass of wine, the conversation turned to the following week's paper: who would attend the *Stern* press conference, who would handle the serialization. . . Giles suggested they should invite Trevor-Roper to write an article demolishing 'all these carping criticisms' about the diaries' authenticity. This was considered a good idea. Giles picked up the telephone. What followed has entered the mythology of Fleet Street, a scene etched in the memory of the witnesses, 'told and retold over the milk-bars of Fleet Street', as Evelyn Waugh once wrote of a similar moment in *Scoop*, 'perennially fresh in the jaded memories of a hundred editors. . .'

'Hugh? . . . Frank Giles. . . Very well, thank you. . .'

There had been a murmur of conversation in the room, but this gradually died away as more of the *Sunday Times* men began listening to one side of the telephone conversation.

'. . . I think we'd like just a quiet, scholarly, detailed piece, rebutting. . .'

There was a pause. 'Frank didn't go white exactly,' recalled Knightley, 'but his tone suddenly changed.'

'Well, naturally, Hugh, one has doubts. There are no certainties in this life. But these doubts aren't strong enough to make you do a complete 180-degree turn on that? . . . Oh. I see. You *are* doing a 180-degree turn. . .'

The editorial conference froze into a tableau of despair: MacArthur, who had slumped against the wall, now slid gently to the floor; Linklater sat with his head between his knees; Knightley silently pounded the table; nobody spoke.

After Giles had hung up there was, according to one participant, 'a tense fifteen-minute conversation'. Should the presses be stopped? That would require Murdoch's agreement. He was in New York. Someone went off to try to reach him. It was decided that Giles should ring Trevor-Roper back and insist that if he had doubts, he should not air them in public at *Stern*'s press conference but should reveal them exclusively in the following week's *Sunday Times*. Everyone left to enable the editor to make the call in peace; as they did so, his ebullient wife, Lady Katherine Giles, burst through the door carrying her husband's supper in a hamper. She stayed with him while he made the call and emerged a few minutes later to reassure everyone: 'Frank was *marvellous*.' Meanwhile, Brian MacArthur was speaking to Rupert Murdoch who had been tracked down in the United States. MacArthur outlined the problem caused by Lord Dacre's change of heart. Should they stop the print run and remake the paper?

'Fuck Dacre,' replied Murdoch. 'Publish.'

Sunday 24 April.

As 1.4 million copies of the *Sunday Times* were distributed across Great Britain, the assault on the diaries' authenticity intensified. Lord Bullock, author of *Hitler: A Study in Tyranny*, made the same point as a number of critics of the scoop: how could Hitler have written about the attempt on his life in July 1944, when his right arm was known to have been damaged in the blast? Bullock called for an international commission of French, British, American and Jewish historians to be appointed to examine the diaries. The *Sunday Times*'s rivals, using the information bought from Irving, were having a field day. 'Serious doubts cast on Hitler's "secret diaries",' claimed the *Observer*. 'THE DAMNING FLAWS IN THE HITLER DIARY', alleged the *Mail on Sunday*. 'All too splendid, too neat, too pat to be anything but a gigantic hoax.' In Germany, a succession of Hitler's former aides, few of them under seventy, was wheeled out for comment. 'We often used to eat at about three or four o'clock in the morning,' said Nicolaus von Below, the Führer's air force adjutant, 'and only after that did Hitler go to bed. He had no time to write anything. It's all a complete lie.' Richard Schulze-Kossens echoed von Below: Hitler 'never had time' to keep a diary. 'The Führer never made notes by hand,' insisted Christa Schroeder.

At 8.30 a.m., David Irving was picked up by a *Mail on Sunday* car and driven to the airport to catch the 10.35 a.m. flight to Hamburg. He was met at the other end by Jochen Kummer, a senior reporter on the mass-circulation *Bild Zeitung*. Irving was to be their 'torpedo' at the *Stern* press conference the following day. 'We agreed a fee of £1000 plus expenses,' noted Irving in his diary.

A couple of hours later, Trevor-Roper also arrived at Heathrow, accompanied by two minders from the *Sunday Times*, Paul Eddy and Brian MacArthur. At the airport he found himself 'pursued by massed cameras'. 'The whole story had been blown up into a sensation,' recalled Trevor-Roper. Microphones were thrust at his face. 'I do believe the diaries are genuine,' he said, 'but there are complications. I will not put a percentage figure on my belief. I admit there are problems...'

In Hamburg the three men met Anthony Terry, and Trevor-Roper once again checked into the Atlantic Hotel to await the arrival of Gerd Heidemann.

It was late afternoon by the time Heidemann arrived. He apologized for having kept Trevor-Roper waiting. He had just flown in from Munich, he said, where he had been talking to Frau Ilse Hess. Trevor-Roper told him there were certain points he wanted clarified before he was prepared to endorse the diaries at the press conference. Would Heidemann tell him, once again, how the diaries came into *Stern*'s possession?

This posed a problem for Heidemann. Since he had last spoken with Trevor-Roper, *Stern* had received the results of the Rentz forensic investigation. Heidemann was now aware that although the diaries might still be genuine, the accompanying archive was probably forged. Kujau had assured him that the two sets of material came from different sources. But how could Heidemann square that with his original assertion that there was one plane crash, one salvaged cargo, and one supplier? His solution was to add a new twist to his story. Heidemann now told Trevor-Roper that the diaries had been brought out of the East by a former Wehrmacht officer currently living in West Germany. The reporter said he had collected the first diaries from Switzerland. *Other material had been delivered to him in Hamburg by the Boernersdorf peasants.*

Trevor-Roper was immediately suspicious. This was the third version of the story he had heard, he said. Originally, in Zurich, he had been told by Peter Koch that the diaries' supplier lived in East Germany: that was why his name could not be disclosed. Then, in Hamburg last week, Heidemann had told him that the so-called 'Wehrmacht officer' lived in Switzerland and could not be identified for tax reasons. Now he was supposed to live in West Germany and only to have supplied the diaries, not the additional material. Which version was correct?

Heidemann blustered. He was not responsible for anything Koch said. Koch knew nothing. Koch knew only as much as he, Heidemann, chose to tell him.

The historian was insistent. He would not authenticate the diaries unless Heidemann gave him the full story of their discovery. They should start again from the beginning. How had the diaries come into *Stern*'s possession?

'In interrogation,' Trevor-Roper once observed, 'pressure must be uninterrupted.' That afternoon in the Atlantic Hotel he drew on the skills he had learned in the prisoner of war cages of Germany in the autumn of 1945. Remorselessly, he battered away at Heidemann's story in a way that no one had done since the diaries had first begun to emerge in Hamburg. Heidemann pulled out document after document from his briefcase. 'I'll produce anything if you just won't put me through the mincing machine.'

Trevor-Roper read through the Hess special volume. It was ludicrously superficial. He had no doubts now. It was a forgery.

'Can you give me,' he demanded, 'any reason why I should believe in this Wehrmacht officer?'

'No,' said Heidemann. 'Why should I?'

'Well, then, why should I believe?' retorted Trevor-Roper.

There was real anger in the exchanges; old resentments flared. 'You are behaving exactly like an officer of the British secret service,' shouted Heidemann. 'We are no longer in 1945.' After putting up a stubborn resistance for more than an hour, the reporter declared that he had had enough and stalked out of the room, refusing to attend a dinner that *Stern* was supposed to be giving in Trevor-Roper's honour that evening.

Trevor-Roper, too, considered boycotting the meal. In the end he agreed to attend only in the hope of extracting the name of the diaries' supplier from Peter Koch. But to the historian's astonishment, Koch, when confronted with his earlier assertion that *Stern* knew the identity of the 'Wehrmacht officer', calmly denied ever having made such a claim. Trevor-Roper threatened to stay away from the following morning's press conference. The *Stern* men were unmoved. The dinner ended, according to the subsequent *Stern Report*, with 'an icy atmosphere around the table'.

After the meal, Trevor-Roper discussed his dilemma with Paul Eddy, Brian MacArthur and Anthony Terry. They urged him not to recant in public at the press conference. He should at least wait until he had returned to Britain. The three *Sunday Times* men were persuasive, and by the time they left him at midnight, the historian was half convinced. He was crossing the lobby of the hotel on his way up to bed when he unexpectedly ran into an old friend – Sir Nicholas Henderson, Britain's former ambassador in Washington and Bonn. The two men retreated to the bar and drank beer until 2 a.m. Henderson's advice was unequivocal. Trevor-Roper should state his reservations as quickly and publicly as possible. He would not have a better opportunity than the *Stern* press conference in a few hours' time. Trevor-Roper decided 'to sleep on the matter'.

Monday 25 April.

'The big day,' wrote Irving in his diary.

The special issue of *Stern* was already piled up on the news stands to greet the early morning commuters. More than two and a quarter million copies had been printed over the weekend. 'Hitler's Diary Discovered', proclaimed the cover, displaying a stack of black-bound volumes, topped by one bearing the Gothic initials 'FH' (the 'F' still assumed by *Stern* to be an 'A'). Coverage of the diaries sprawled across more than forty pages, with extracts blown up to three or four times their original size. There was Hitler on Ernst Roehm:

> I gave him the chance to draw the consequences, but he was too cowardly to do so. On my orders he was later shot.

Hitler on the *Kristallnacht*, the 'Night of Broken Glass' in 1938, when Jewish shops and synagogues were smashed and thousands of Jews sent to concentration camps:

> Report brought to me of some ugly attacks by people in uniform in various places, also of Jews beaten to death and Jewish suicides. What will they say abroad? The necessary orders will be given immediately.

Hitler on the Russian attack on Berlin in April 1945:

> The long-awaited offensive has begun. May the Lord God stand by us.

There were pictures of Hitler in the Reichschancellery in 1945, Hitler with Mussolini, Hitler writing at his desk, Hitler holding a bunch of flowers, Hitler with Hess; the only other person shown as often was

Gerd Heidemann: Heidemann on *Carin II*, Heidemann with the diaries, Heidemann in Boernersdorf, Heidemann with Wolff, Heidemann with Guensche and Mohnke – the entire issue was a monument to one man's obsession, a tasteless and hysterical trampling over thirty-eight years of post-war German sensitivity about the Nazis. *Stern* was already under attack for its handling of the diaries; this tactless treatment was to earn the magazine the odium of almost the entire West German press.

In the Four Seasons Hotel, Irving was up early. He prepared for the morning's combat with a haircut in the hotel barber's followed by a heavy German breakfast. The restaurant, he found, was 'packed with journalists and television teams, poring over this morning's *Stern*'.

Trevor-Roper woke at 8 a.m. to a telephone call from Charles Douglas-Home. How was he feeling? Trevor-Roper said that he had talked to Heidemann, that his doubts had not been assuaged, that they had, in fact, increased. Douglas-Home urged him not to 'burn his boats' at the press conference.

By 10.30 a.m., the *Stern* canteen was packed with journalists. More than two hundred had converged on Hamburg from all over the world. There were twenty-seven television crews. All the seats were taken and reporters and photographers squeezed into every corner, squatting, and in some cases lying full-length, beneath the platform at the far end of the room. Incongruous yet unnoticed, in the centre of it all, sat General Wilhelm Mohnke, attending by special invitation of Gerd Heidemann. Each of the journalists was issued with a press kit: twenty pages of information about the diaries and a set of seven photographs. Also included were copies of the Rentz forensic reports on the two diary pages; the Rentz finding on the Mussolini telegram was omitted, giving the impression that his tests had been a hundred per cent in favour of the authenticity of the *Stern* material.

At 11 a.m., the stars of the conference filed in to a battery of flashes from the photographers: Peter Koch, Felix Schmidt, Thomas Walde, Gerd Heidemann and Hugh Trevor-Roper. The professor was startled by the size of the audience, the hot and noisy atmosphere, the brilliance of the television lights. It looked, wrote one journalist afterwards, like 'a Sadler's Wells set for hell'.

Peter Koch's introduction was aggressive. He denounced the attacks on the diaries' authenticity. Eberhard Jaeckel was making assertions about material he had not even seen. 'If we as journalists behaved in such a manner,' said Koch, 'we would be accused of superficiality.' David Irving – sitting half-way down the room – he dismissed as an historian 'with no reputation to lose'. 'I am a hundred per cent convinced that Hitler wrote every single word in those books,' insisted Koch. 'We paid a lot of money for the diaries, but when it comes to informing the reader, nothing is too expensive.'

The press was then shown the *Stern* documentary film, *The Find*. Trevor-Roper watched his own endorsement of the diaries, recorded the previous week, with his head in his hand. When the programme finished, a young woman pushed her way through the cameras to the tables at the end of the canteen and tipped out the contents of two parcels: a dozen volumes of the Hitler diaries. It was a *coup de théâtre* – 'as if,' said Brian James of the *Daily Mail*, 'Hitler had suddenly thrust an arm out of the grave'. The photographers scrambled for close-ups. The *Stern* men tried to shield the contents to prevent any premature disclosure. Koch thrust a handful of diaries at Gerd Heidemann who was persuaded to stand up, with great reluctance, and pose with them for the cameras. Koch invited questions. Almost all of them were directed at Trevor-Roper.

In his own mind, the historian had already concluded that the diaries could well be false. 'Having once admitted it to myself,' he said later, 'I felt I must attend the press conference and admit it to others.' With head tilted back, eyes focused on some indeterminate point in the middle distance, he began to recant. 'The question of the authenticity of the diaries is inseparable from the history of the diaries. The question is: are these documents linked necessarily to that aeroplane? When I saw the documents in Zurich, I understood – or, er, misunderstood – that that link was absolutely established. . .' The diaries 'might' be genuine, he said, but 'the thing looks more shaky' – there was, after all, 'such a thing as a perfect forgery'. He ended with a swipe at *Stern* and Times Newspapers:

> As a historian, I regret that the, er, normal method of historical verification, er, has, perhaps necessarily, been to some extent sacrificed to the requirements of a journalistic scoop.

One of Trevor-Roper's Oxford pupils, Timothy Garton Ash, covering the press conference for the *New Republic*, described the performance as 'rather like watching a Victorian gentleman trying to back-pedal on a penny farthing'.

Someone asked the historian about the damage the affair had done to his reputation. Trevor-Roper took a meditative sip from a glass of water. 'I suppose my personal reputation is linked to anything I say. I am prepared to express my opinion, and if I am wrong I am wrong, and if I am right I am right. I don't worry about these things.'

Until Trevor-Roper's contribution, the press conference had been going well for the *Stern* men. Now they sat, stony-faced, with arms folded, as the proceedings began to disintegrate around them. David Irving leapt to the microphone in the centre of the hall, incensed at Koch's description of him as a man without any reputation. 'I decided to play hardball,' he wrote in his diary afterwards. 'I am the British historian David Irving,' he declared. 'I may not have a doctorate, or a professorship, or even the title "Lord", but I believe I have a reputation in Germany nevertheless.' He demanded to know how Hitler could have written of the July bomb plot in his diary, when *Stern*'s own film had just shown the dictator meeting Mussolini a few hours after the explosion, and having to shake hands with him with his left hand. He brandished his photocopies. 'I know the collection from which these diaries come. It is an old collection, full of forgeries. I have some here.' The television cameras swung away from the *Stern* dignitaries and on to the gesticulating figure in the middle of the room. 'Reporters stormed towards me,' recalled Irving, 'lights blazing, and microphones were thrust at me.' A Japanese film crew was trampled in the rush and a fist fight broke out. Chairs and lights were scattered as chaos rippled across the crowded floor. From the platform, Koch shouted that Irving should ask questions, not make speeches. Irving's microphone was switched off. But it was too late. Irving challenged *Stern* to say whether the diaries' ink had been tested for its age. There was no answer. 'Ink! Ink!' shouted some of the reporters. 'Torpedo running,' whispered Irving to one of the journalists sitting next to him as he sat down. The local NBC correspondent approached and asked if he would leave immediately to take part in a live link-up with the

Today show, now on the air in America. Irving agreed. 'All most exhilarating,' he noted, 'and I left a trail of chaos behind me.'

As Irving was going out of the *Stern* building, Gerhard Weinberg was coming in. The American academic had been unpacking in Bonn on Saturday, finishing off his interview with Steven Strasser of *Newsweek*, when Peter Koch telephoned him. Koch had pleaded with him to attend the press conference. Weinberg had told him that it was impossible – he had his first class in Bonn at 10 a.m. on Monday; he wouldn't cancel it. ('It took him some time to realize I wasn't being difficult,' said Weinberg. 'I was just being me.') But Koch was persistent: he would fix the travel arrangements to ensure that the professor did not miss his class. Accordingly, the instant his lecture finished, at 11 a.m. on Monday, a *Stern* driver rushed Weinberg from the university campus to the airport. From Bonn he was flown in the company's private plane to Hamburg, then driven straight to the *Stern* office. At 12.30 p.m. he took his place on the platform.

Weinberg repaid *Stern* for its trouble and expense by raising fresh doubts about its scoop. 'All the handwriting authentication I have seen,' he told the world's press, 'pertains to documents other than the diaries, except one page said to have been cut out of one diary. In other words, the memorandum from the American handwriting expert and the German police handwriting expert refer to Hitler's handwriting, but not to Hitler's handwriting in the diaries. In fact, they probably didn't know the diaries existed when shown this evidence.' It was 'inappropriate' to cite the analysis of one set of documents and apply it to another.

Koch stared at Weinberg in horror, but the professor had not finished yet. In his careful, pedantic manner, he continued: 'One question has troubled me from the outset – that no knowledgeable expert on the Third Reich has been allowed to study the whole text to see if there are any textual absurdities. I mean, we're not living on a South Sea island here, they wouldn't have had to have gone outside the Hamburg city limits to find experts who would know. It is vital now that a group of experts from all over the world should be given the chance to test these manuscripts.' Koch cut in to say that, of course, experts would be given the opportunity to study the diaries. There were shouts of 'When?' and 'Set a date.' 'When the journalistic evaluation has been completed,' replied Koch.

The news conference, which had begun so well for *Stern*, broke up after more than two hours in complete disarray. It was not merely a public relations disaster; the failure to produce convincing evidence for the diaries' authenticity also had legal implications. One of *Stern*'s lawyers, Herr Hagen, had warned Schulte-Hillen on Friday in a confidential memorandum that the magazine's coverage was such that the company risked prosecution for disseminating Nazi propaganda. *Stern*'s defence, obviously, would be that it was furthering historical research. But that argument could collapse if historians regarded the diaries as being of dubious value. The State of Bavaria could use the uncertainty as a pretext to withdraw the publishing rights it had conceded through the agreement with the Bundesarchiv. Watching as the press conference disintegrated, Hagen decided that 'only a quick and definitive judgement on the diaries' authenticity could save the situation'. With the consent of the *Stern* management, he arranged for three of the diaries – the Hess special volume and books from 1934 and 1943 – to be handed over immediately to Dr Henke of the Bundesarchiv, who had attended the conference. Henke promised to deliver a judgement to Hagen swiftly and privately. The lawyer was relieved. The prospect of a court battle to try to establish that *Stern* was not sympathetic to the Nazis, with Gerd Heidemann possibly called as a witness, did not bear contemplating.

Trevor-Roper felt a sense of relief as he left the *Stern* building. His action might have come as 'a painful surprise' to his hosts, but he had done as his conscience dictated. After a light lunch with the three *Sunday Times* journalists, he caught an afternoon flight back to London.

Trevor-Roper hoped he might now begin putting the whole affair behind him. He was over-optimistic. One of the first things he saw on his arrival at Heathrow was a placard advertising the London *Standard*. Its front-page banner headline was 'HITLER DIARIES: DACRE DOUBTS'. 'My heart sank,' he recalled.

At home in Cambridge the telephone had scarcely stopped ringing since his departure for Germany on Sunday. He found his wife deeply upset. Reporters were camped on his doorstep. His first act was to instruct the Porter's Lodge not to put through any more calls. It was impossible to stroll across the road to Peterhouse without running the gauntlet of journalists in the street outside. Instead, he had to leave through his garden, shin a back wall, cut through a car park and sneak into the college a few yards further up the street. He had to keep up this performance for the rest of the week.

Pictures of the *Stern* press conference were carried on all the evening news bulletins and dominated the following morning's papers. The stories all focused on Trevor-Roper: 'I'M NOT SURE NOW CONFESSES HITLER DIARY PROFESSOR', 'HITLER: THE GREAT RETREAT', 'BOFFINS' BATTLE ON NAZI "DIARIES"', 'FISTS FLY IN HITLER UPROAR', 'I'M NOT QUITE SO SURE, SAYS DACRE'. The *Guardian* wanted to know why he had decided to 'risk his reputation by pronouncing the diaries genuine after only the most cursory examination?' His former colleague at Oxford, A. L. Rowse, wrote an article headed 'The trial of Lord Dacre' describing him, at the age of nearly seventy, as 'a young man in a hurry'. 'I have always had reservations about him,' said Rowse, 'since he started writing at Oxford as my protégé.' A limerick did the rounds of Cambridge senior common rooms:

> There once was a fellow named Dacre,
> Who was God in his own little acre,
> But in the matter of diaries,
> He was quite *ultra vires*,
> And unable to spot an old faker.

The final insult came in a solicitor's letter sent on behalf of Rachel, Lady Dacre. She was a distant cousin who had arranged for the ancient Barony of Dacre to be called out of abeyance in her favour in 1970; she had strongly objected to Trevor-Roper's decision to use the same name when he was awarded a life peerage in 1979. Now she had her lawyers warn him always to use his full title – Lord Dacre of Glanton – so as not to embarrass her side of the family in the light of his action over the Hitler diaries.

'Life,' said Trevor-Roper, subsequently reflecting on the period, 'was torture.'

27

But what was torture to one historian was food and drink to another. After his triumph at the press conference, David Irving spent the rest of Monday writing articles and giving interviews. 'Adolf Hitler is still big box office, from Hamburg to Harlem,' he wrote in the *Daily Mail*. He described Heidemann as 'a typical nice guy. He does not believe that villains exist in this world; he is the kind of man who believes the claims of tyre advertisements.' For the readers of *Bild Zeitung* he outlined seven reasons why the diaries had to be forgeries. He was inexhaustible. At 3.30 a.m. on Tuesday morning, he was roused in his hotel room in Hamburg and rushed to a local television studio for a live link-up with the ABC programme *Nightline*. 'Twenty million viewers again,' recorded Irving gleefully in his diary. 'Paid 700 marks in cash as requested.' From the studio he was taken back to his hotel. He grabbed another two hours' sleep and after breakfast heard from *Der Spiegel* that they were willing to pay him 20,000 marks for his photocopies and his story. '*Very* satisfactory,' he noted. 'That brings the total up to about £15,000 in three days.' In the afternoon, he flew to Frankfurt to take part in a West German television debate on the diaries' authenticity.

Meanwhile, in the United States, the full extent of *Newsweek*'s alleged perfidy was at last apparent. Monday had seen the airing of the magazine's television commercials, none of which made any mention of doubts about whether the diaries might be genuine. Casual readers of the accompanying newspaper advertisements would also have had the impression that *Newsweek* had bought the diaries and that there was no question surrounding their authenticity:

These controversial papers could rewrite the history of the Third Reich from Hitler's rise to power to his suicide in the ruins of Berlin.

They shed new light on his character, his plans for war, Munich, the miracle of Dunkirk, the flight of Rudolf Hess, his military campaigns, his relations to his lover, Eva Braun.

The patient reader had to wade through to the fifth paragraph before coming to the throwaway question 'Are they real?' Maynard Parker, responsible for putting together the *Newsweek* treatment, was subsequently unrepentant about this aggressive salesmanship: 'The advertising department had earlier deadlines than ours, but I do not feel that the ads misrepresent what is in the magazine.'

This was true. Although *Newsweek* gave some space to the views of the sceptics, the overwhelming impression left by its extensive coverage was that the diaries were genuine. The magazine actually ran more extracts than *Stern* – seventeen individual quotations, culled during the course of the syndication negotiations. Here was an 'awestruck' Hitler on Josef Stalin ('How on earth does Stalin manage it?'); Hitler on Mussolini ('He does not have the courtesy to face me'); on the Wehrmacht High Command ('These old officers let themselves be hung with titles, decorations and property, but they don't obey my orders'); and a 'tender and sentimental' Hitler on Eva Braun ('Eva had to endure much suffering'). The Germans were predictably outraged. 'That was a nice dirty trick,' Peter Koch complained in an interview with *Time*. 'We would like to sue. We were cheated and I guarantee *Newsweek* will regret what they did.' There was a separate article on the forensic and handwriting examinations commissioned by *Stern*, there was 'A Scholar's Appraisal' by Gerhard Weinberg and a piece on 'Hitler and the Holocaust'. The magazine concluded with a prediction that the discovery of the diaries would force the world 'to deal, once again, with the fact of Hitler himself'.

Germans will have to wonder anew about their collective, inherited guilt. Jews will have to face their fears again. All of us will have to ask once more whether Hitler's evil was unique, or whether it lurks somewhere in everyone. Those speculations have been trivialized for years in gaudy paperback thrillers and made-for-television movies. Now the appearance of Hitler's diaries – genuine or not, it almost doesn't matter in the end – reminds us of the horrible reality on which our doubts about ourselves, and each other, are based.

Newsweek's behaviour over the Hitler diaries was widely criticized in the United States. An editorial in the *New York Times* entitled 'Heil History' poured particular scorn on the magazine's assertion that the question of whether or not the diaries were genuine 'almost doesn't matter':

> Almost doesn't matter? Almost doesn't matter what really drove the century's most diabolic tyranny? Almost doesn't matter whether Hitler is reincarnated, perhaps redefined, by fact or forgery?
>
> Journalism should take no solace from the customary excuse that it must deal with history in a hurry. And scholars in such a hurry, their second thoughts notwithstanding, can hardly be called historians.

Newsweek gave enormous play to the diaries, but the magazine was not alone in seeing it as the most important story of the moment: the *New York Times* itself ran it on its front page on Saturday, Sunday, Monday and Tuesday; the mass-circulation tabloids gave it even greater space. By the fifth day the Hitler diaries affair had turned into a kind of giant soap opera – an international entertainment playing on almost every radio and television network and newspaper front page in the world. And what a story it was – Hitler's bunker, old Nazis, a wartime plane crash, a trail across the Iron Curtain, millions of dollars, Swiss bank vaults, secret documents, a punch-up in front of the cameras, dramatic changes of heart, the Rewriting of History, Lord Dacre, David Irving, Rupert Murdoch, Gerd Heidemann. . .

It seemed that every academic who had ever written about Hitler was at some stage called upon to comment. Professor Donald Watt, the editor of the most recent English language edition of *Mein Kampf*, thought the diaries 'odd'. John Kenneth Galbraith called them 'impossible'. William L. Shirer said they were 'outlandish . . . a hoax'. 'I don't think serious historians will touch these things for a long time,' said J. P. Stern, the author of *The Führer and the People*. Professor Gordon A. Craig called it 'one of the most sensational finds of the century'.

'The question is of little importance,' was A. J. P. Taylor's characteristic comment. 'Who cares about Hitler nowadays?'

There was a section of opinion which held that the material, even if genuine, should not be published. What had caught the popular imagination was the fact that these were Hitler's *diaries*. A diary was something intimate and human. How could a figure who had caused so much suffering be allowed to speak in ordinary language, to justify what he did? It directly touched the point George Steiner had made: 'You will think him a man and no longer believe what he did.' The Chief Rabbi of Great Britain, Immanuel Jakobovits, put this argument in a letter to *The Times* which was extensively quoted around the world, especially in West Germany:

> As a human being – victim and survivor of history's most monstrous tyranny – I protest vehemently against the publication of the so-called Hitler diaries. Whether they are authentic or not is quite immaterial to the outrage of resurrecting the incarnation of evil and his propaganda, rehabilitating him for a generation which knew not this master gangster ... Hailing this find as 'the biggest literary discovery since the Dead Sea Scrolls' is a sacrilege which only compounds the insult to the millions who perished and suffered under this tyranny.

Nineteen eighty-three marked the fiftieth anniversary of the Nazis' rise to power. But although more than a generation had passed since the end of the war, the reaction aroused by the diaries showed how potent a symbol Hitler remained. It was not simply fresh proof of the accuracy of the old cliché about the fascination of evil; the comments also revealed how little attitudes towards Hitler had changed. In the communist world, the Hitler portrayed in the diaries was denounced as an agent of capitalism. Similarly, some conservatives in the West, in their comments on *Stern*'s Hitler, were blinded to any other consideration by their overwhelming mistrust of the Soviet Union. Both responses were a curious echo of those of the 1930s.

On the day of the *Stern* press conference, Professor Karl-Dietrich Bracher of Bonn University dismissed the diaries as forgeries and speculated as to who might be responsible. He noted that this was a Hitler who was supposed to have expressed admiration for the shrewdness of the arch-appeaser, Neville Chamberlain; who had allowed the British Army to escape at Dunkirk; who had sanctioned Hess's peace mission in 1941. Perversely, it was Hitler's enemies in the West, Churchill and Roosevelt, who were portrayed as the warmongers. Bracher suggested that the diaries were 'an attempt to manipulate German history at a politically sensitive moment'. Perhaps the diaries were the work of a foreign power? The 1980s, after all, were 'a time of intense debate about the deployment of new NATO missiles in West Germany' – at such a moment 'there was a growing audience for history unfavourable to the United States and Britain'. Werner Maser alleged the diaries were the work of an official 'forgery factory' in Potsdam in East Germany 'where Hitler letters and Hitler notes are produced to earn hard currency for the East Germans'. This theme was developed in Britain in a radio interview by George Young, a former deputy director of MI6 and a noted cold warrior. Without any evidence – without even having seen the diaries – he alleged the affair might be part of 'an East German official disinformation effort':

> The East German security and intelligence service has a document-faking or disinformation section. No doubt they would be capable of doing this... It would suit the Russians' book to sow mistrust in any shape or form, particularly among the West Germans. NATO croaks and groans quite a bit these days and anything that sows doubts about the past may create mistrust about the present.

At a press luncheon in New York on Tuesday, the American Ambassador to the United Nations, Mrs Jeanne Kirkpatrick, also detected in the diaries the hand of an Eastern intelligence agency. 'I have no doubt,' she claimed, 'that there are those in central Europe today who would, and indeed do, attempt to sow distrust between the United States and its German friends.'

The communists nurtured suspicions of their own. The Soviet Union lost 20 million dead in Hitler's war; the memory was still a decisive influence on Russia's foreign policy. Moscow had not officially confirmed Hitler's death until 1968 and remained acutely sensitive to what it saw as any attempt to rehabilitate the Nazis. On Monday, Professor Sergei Tikhvinski, a leading Russian historian and a member of the Soviet Academy of Science, denounced the Hitler diaries as 'a most obvious act of political sabotage'. At 6.30 on Wednesday evening, Soviet television described the diaries' publication as 'an attempt to whitewash the chief fascist criminal'. Ninety minutes later, Radio Moscow International broadcast a similar opinion to its listeners in France, where *Paris Match* had just begun its serialization:

> The phantom of the human Führer ... is an attempt to make allowances in advance in the eyes of public opinion for those in the USA and in NATO headquarters who are working out new versions of limited warfare, or other wars for Europe, using the pretext of the old myth of the threat from the East – the one that allowed Hitler to unleash the Second World War.

'These "diaries",' claimed the official news agency Tass, 'are intended to propagandize Nazism among the young generation, to distract them from the fight for peace and put them on the path of right-wing nationalist forces in the Federal Republic.'

In Berlin, the East German Foreign Ministry issued an official statement: 'The German Democratic Republic regards the publication of the Hitler diaries in *Stern* as a belated attempt to rehabilitate Hitler.' Western journalists who applied for permission to visit the site of the crashed plane in Boernersdorf found that visas were granted with unusual speed. The East Germans were eager to allow foreigners to speak to the local farmers who, virtually without exception, derided the idea that documents could have been salvaged from the burning wreck. Suddenly, after centuries of calm, the peaceful village was invaded by the western media. Ignorant of the furore about the diaries, a rumour went round Boernersdorf that the reason for the influx of cameramen and reporters was that two of the graves in the churchyard, marked 'Unknown man' and 'Unknown woman', contained the remains of Hitler and Eva Braun.

On the night of Tuesday 26 April the leading western protagonists in the controversy were brought together on West German television. ZDF, one of the country's two national networks, cleared its evening schedules to mount a debate on the diaries' authenticity. Peter

Koch and Gerd Heidemann flew down from Hamburg to the television studios in Wiesbaden. At Frankfurt airport they ran into another participant on his way to ZDF, David Irving. The three men shook hands – 'Koch unwillingly', wrote Irving in his diary.

The programme began with the screening of *The Find*, which ZDF had bought off *Stern* for 175,000 marks. The film was followed by an interminable and crowded discussion of the sort beloved by West German television. Four historians – Walther Hofer, Andreas Hillgruber, Eberhard Jaeckel and David Irving – faced Peter Koch in Wiesbaden. Gerhard Weinberg took part down the line from Bonn. Trevor-Roper was persuaded to sit in a studio in London – an isolated figure who spoke throughout in English (evidence of his unease with the German language which did not go unnoticed in the West German newspapers the following day). Gerd Heidemann was prevented from taking part by Peter Koch: his belief that the diaries had been authenticated by Martin Bormann would not have enhanced *Stern*'s credibility.

Trevor-Roper went further than he had done at the press conference. The burden of proof once again rested with *Stern*, he said. 'I also believe that some of the other documents which I have seen in Mr Heidemann's house and which come from the same source are forgeries.'

Koch, undeterred, put up a spirited defence of the diaries. There was no question but that they were genuine, he insisted. They had been tested by handwriting and forensic experts and most of *Stern*'s critics were motivated by commercial jealousy. Even Irving, a master at hijacking the medium for his own purposes, was impressed by his 'manful' performance. 'At the end he put his Hitler diary on the table and challenged me: "Now, Herr Irving, put your 'diary page' next to it and let's see which is genuine." Fortunately, the cameras were off or it would have been difficult: the pages were clearly different. . .'

The debate was a victory for *Stern*. Afterwards, at about midnight, as Koch and Heidemann were driving back to the airport, they passed Irving and Jaeckel walking down the hill from the studio to their hotel. They pulled alongside and asked the two historians if they wanted a drink. Irving and Jaeckel agreed.

In this private conversation Koch gave vent to his bitterness about *Newsweek*. It was only because of the Americans, he complained, that

Stern had been forced to rush into print so precipitately. But for *Newsweek*, they would have had more time to check the documents and could have prevented the damaging publicity which now surrounded the diaries. Irving said *Stern* had been foolish to trust *The Times* and *Newsweek* while refusing to take a West German historian into its confidence. 'I suggested he should show [the diaries] to a *sceptical* historian like Jaeckel. Jaeckel nodded, puffed his pipe sagely, and was staggered when Koch then turned to him and asked if he would, in principle, agree to assess all sixty diaries, after signing an undertaking incorporating a savage financial penalty if he revealed the contents.' The idea was discussed for a while, but by the time the drinking session broke up at 2 a.m., it was obvious there was no room for agreement: Jaeckel was 'too fixed in his hostility' to the diaries.

When Peter Koch walked into the *Stern* editorial meeting in Hamburg a few hours later, he was greeted by a round of applause from his colleagues for his 'valiant defence' of the diaries on television the previous night. Emboldened by this success, *Stern* now planned a counter-attack on its critics. They would take the fight into the heart of the enemy camp with a lightning campaign on American television. Koch would fly over to New York the next day with one of the diaries and offer himself for interview on every available US television and radio network.

That same afternoon, *Stern* recruited a valuable new ally to its cause. Wolf Hess emerged from a two-hour meeting with Koch and the other editors to announce to reporters that he had no doubts that the magazine's scoop was genuine. 'I will ask the Allied authorities to allow my father to comment on the diaries.'

Rudolf Hess had celebrated his eighty-ninth birthday in Spandau prison on Tuesday. The family had been trying to secure his release for years. The appearance of the diaries now offered them a fresh chance to focus attention on his plight. Wolf Hess agreed to accompany Koch, at *Stern*'s expense, on his American tour. He also sent a telegram to the American, British, French and Soviet Ambassadors appealing to them to let his father examine and authenticate the diaries 'as the sole living and direct eyewitness'.

*

David Irving arrived back in London on Wednesday afternoon and rushed straight round to see his bank manager, arriving late and perspiring for his appointment. To his surprise, he found him 'very friendly': he had followed his client's progress over the past few days with great interest. That did not, however, lessen his distress at the fact that Irving's overdraft stood at £26,700, unchanged since January; it must come down. Irving, as he noted in his diary, was at last able to give him some good news. 'I said I have earned about £15,000 since Friday in various ways (TV, newspaper articles and contracts, etc.) and this money is due *now*; I guarantee to let him have £6000 in two weeks. He is very happy. God knows what I would have had to offer at the interview without the happy events since Friday.'

Despite the scepticism being heaped upon the diaries by experts from West Germany and abroad, Gerd Heidemann betrayed no trace of anxiety. He was undoubtedly aware by now that there were some problems with his material: both the police and Arnold Rentz had found that part of the archive he had obtained from Kujau was false; he also knew that the faked diary pages which Irving was hawking around Europe came from the original Fritz Stiefel diary, a volume which had finally come into his possession at the end of March. But self-deception was one of the strongest traits of Heidemann's character. He had no difficulty in accepting Kujau's excuses – that the dubious telegrams came from a different source, that paper whitener was in existence before the Nazis came to power, that the Stiefel diary was a 'party yearbook' and not part of the main diary archive. Nor was his delusion that the diaries were genuine entirely without foundation. He could point to the three handwriting analyses which had found that the page cut from the Hess special volume was in Hitler's hand. He could also call in support the two forensic tests, neither of which had established that the diary's paper was of the wrong date. He exuded confidence. When the Austrian magazine *Profil* asked him whether he was alarmed by David Irving's claim that he had a sample of the diaries, Heidemann's answer was that Irving was bluffing – he 'has no original and has never seen an original'. Was he, at least, concerned by Trevor-Roper's change of heart? 'Of course not,' he replied. 'I know where the diaries come from. . . My informant is neither an old Nazi nor a wanted war criminal, but he won't go public because he doesn't want huge press attention and I won't name him because I promised not to.'

Heidemann's unshakeable conviction that the diaries were authentic soothed the worries of his colleagues. Throughout the week which followed the press conference, *Stern* presented a united front to the world. Brian MacArthur, the head of the *Sunday Times* team staying at the Four Seasons Hotel, shared the doubts of his British colleagues. 'But when you see their absolute confidence,' he said to Gitta Sereny after one meeting with the *Stern* men, 'their total calm in the face of this almost universal disbelief, then all one can think is that they know something they are not telling; that they have something up their sleeves, some sort of absolutely reliable confirmation of authenticity.'

On Thursday 28 April Heidemann announced that the missing diaries had at last arrived in a consignment of pianos delivered to Saarbruecken. He visited Peter Kuehsel in his office and arranged to pick up the final instalment of 300,000 marks at 9.30 a.m. the next morning.

On Friday, he met Konrad Kujau in Hamburg and took delivery of the last four volumes.

Kujau had been watching events unfold from Stuttgart with some interest. On Friday, when the evening news had announced the diaries' discovery, he had telephoned Maria Modritsch and told her to switch on her television. He had viewed the coverage of Monday's press conference and found it 'unbelievable'. Could he get away with it? He was confident enough to believe that he could: he had, after all, been forging Nazi documents for the best part of a decade and had so far managed to avoid detection. Surely *Stern* would not be publishing the material unless it had already succeeded in fooling enough experts to put him in the clear? When Ulli Blaschke, his friend in the police force, saw him in the Beer Bar in Stuttgart at the height of the controversy, he brought up the subject of the diaries and asked Conny whether he thought they were genuine. Kujau solemnly assured him that in his opinion they were.

The forger has provided a colourful account of his final transaction with Heidemann that Friday. According to him, they met in the archive in Milchstrasse. Outside, the public debate about the diaries was still raging; inside, the telephone scarcely stopped ringing. Heidemann received the diaries and handed him in return 12,000 marks and an IOU for a further 100,000. He then told Kujau that he had a plan showing the location of a hoard of Nazi treasure in East Berlin, buried 'two spades deep'. Heidemann suggested that Conny and Edith should go over together and dig it up. He would pay them 20,000 marks as a reward. 'Oh yes?' replied Kujau. 'You'll be coming to hold the lamp, will you?' The reporter said he couldn't: it was impossible for him to cross the border at the moment. Kujau immediately suspected that Heidemann planned to tip off the East German police and arrange for him to disappear into a communist jail. He declined the offer and returned to Stuttgart.

A few hours after saying goodbye to Kujau, Heidemann rang David Irving in London.

Since his return to Duke Street, Irving had been pondering the events of the past few days. He was forced to admit that as far as attacking the authenticity of *Stern*'s diaries went, he had 'squeezed the lemon dry'. He asked himself what he could do to recapture the initiative, and he came up with one answer: he could announce that he had changed his mind and declare the diaries genuine.

There were a number of factors which made this an attractive idea, apart from the obvious injection of fresh publicity it would provide. One was temperamental. Irving had always relished his role as an *enfant terrible*. He liked being outrageous, making liberal flesh creep. Now, for the first time in his career, his stand on the diaries had put him on the side of conventional opinion. It was not his style and he found it disconcerting.

He had also begun to have genuine doubts about the wisdom of the uncompromising line he had adopted. He had been shaken by the sheer quantity of *Stern*'s archive when he had seen it in the ZDF studio on Tuesday night. Perhaps there *was* a genuine set of Hitler diaries somewhere, which had served as a model for the forgery in his possession? One of his objections to the *Stern* material had been that Hitler had suffered from Parkinson's Disease in the final weeks of his life. Now he had to admit, having seen them, that the final entries did slant sharply to the right, as if oblivious to the lines on the page – a classic symptom of Parkinsonism. And finally, there was the fact that the diaries did not contain any evidence to suggest that Hitler was aware of the Holocaust – *Stern* might help substantiate the thesis of *Hitler's* War.

Irving told Heidemann that he was on the point of changing his mind. He had given an interview to the BBC that morning announcing his reservations. Heidemann asked him when it would be broadcast. Next Wednesday, replied Irving. 'Heidemann,' he wrote in his diary, 'urged me to say it *now* as Peter Koch is going on television in New York on *Monday* with his counter-attack.' Irving promised to think it over.

Meanwhile, that afternoon, Radio Moscow had resumed its attack on the diaries with a heavy-handed 'satirical broadcast' to West Germany. Its target was a new one: not *Stern*, but the rest of the republic's press, at that moment filling its pages with reports of the affair. The broadcast took the form of a story set in the office of the editor of *Die Welt*. The editor wants to know what he should put in the paper over the next few weeks. The home editor suggests unemployment, which is about to reach three million. The foreign editor suggests the deployment of American missiles. The editor-in-chief 'explodes':

> 'You are quitters. The hit of the coming months is the diaries of our Führer. Granted, the copyright is in the hands of our business rivals. To hell with them. Nobody can stop us discussing the authenticity of the diaries. We shall quote from the diaries in every edition and in every column. You [he says to one reporter] will have to take care of statements by historians from abroad. You [to another] provide interviews on the subject with comrades-in-arms of the Führer. What is important is to make the Führer appear as respectable as possible. And you, well you go to Berchtesgaden, to the former residence of the Führer. He says in his diary that his favourite alsatian, Blondi, always stopped at the gate during walks. You take samples of the soil there and give them to the laboratory. If these soil tests are compatible, then . . . ?'
>
> 'The diaries are authentic,' the reporter bursts out.

'That's right,' the boss says, grinning. 'Let's get to work now. And don't say a word about missiles or unemployment.'

For once, Hugh Trevor-Roper had other things on his mind apart from the Hitler diaries. Friday 29 April was an important occasion in the life of Peterhouse – the day of the annual college Feast, an ancient ritual of good food and fine wine. The guest of honour was the Lord Chancellor, Lord Hailsham, who arrived in mid-afternoon to take tea with Trevor-Roper and his wife in the Master's Lodge.

It was now four days since the historian had given orders to have all telephone calls to the Lodge stopped at the porter's switchboard. It was inconvenient, particularly with a member of the Cabinet in the house. In some trepidation, Trevor-Roper decided to rescind the instruction. The telephone rang almost immediately. 'I'll answer it,' said Hailsham.

It was the *Observer*.

'I'm afraid Lord Dacre is not at home at present,' said the seventy-five-year-old Lord Chancellor. 'May I take a message? I'm his butler.'

It was an amusing end to what was otherwise one of the more unpleasant weeks of Trevor-Roper's career.

28

As the crisis over the Hitler diaries worsened, Rupert Murdoch flew back from New York to London. The *Sunday Times*'s reputation was clearly in jeopardy, but Magnus Linklater was struck by Murdoch's apparent lack of concern. He seemed almost bored by the diaries: they were yesterday's deal; his restless mind had already moved on to other matters. In commercial terms, the question of whether or not the diaries were genuine was of only minor importance. In the past week, sales of the *Sunday Times* had increased by 60,000 copies. As long as the controversy continued, circulation was likely to remain buoyant. Besides, under the terms of News International's agreement with Gruner and Jahr, his money would be refunded if the diaries proved to be fakes. Whatever the final verdict on authenticity, Murdoch would not suffer. At a meeting with the journalists involved in the project he readily agreed that if the situation worsened, he would suspend publication. They wanted to know how much worse things had to get. Murdoch said he would pull out of the deal only if there was a 55 per cent chance that the diaries were forged – in other words, the onus was on the sceptics to substantiate their doubts, not on *Stern* to justify its faith. This irresponsible formula was, none the less, regarded at the time as a major concession on Murdoch's part.

The psychology which was leading *Stern* to disaster now began to operate on the *Sunday Times*. The reporters involved on the story had no desire to see their paper humiliated; they *wanted* to believe that the diaries were genuine and set out to find evidence to keep their hopes alive. Brian Moynahan was dispatched to Boernersdorf where he managed to find a fifty-one-year-old quarryman named Helmut Schmidt who had been thirteen when the Junkers 352 had crashed. Schmidt told

Moynahan that he had seen one of the survivors sitting dazed on the ground clutching a wooden case more than two feet long and eighteen inches wide. 'He hung on to it like this,' he claimed, at which point, according to Moynahan, 'Schmidt, working on his allotment, gripped his hoe until his veins rose.'

While Moynahan tramped round Boernersdorf, in London, Elaine Potter ploughed through some of the US Counter-Intelligence Corps files. She extracted the story of how the CIC picked up rumours of a 'Hitler diary' during its investigations in the Berchtesgaden area in 1945.

In Hamburg, Gitta Sereny interviewed Heidemann. The reporter gave her the variation on his original story which he had given to Trevor-Roper on Sunday: the diaries had stayed in the hayloft in Boernersdorf for only a few days; they had been brought to the West by an officer in 1945; this officer was now over seventy and had given Heidemann the documents on condition his name should never be divulged; Heidemann claimed to have talked to him only 'two days ago'. 'Here,' wrote Sereny, 'is one of the indispensable links demanded by critics who have questioned the authenticity of the diaries.'

Frank Giles presided over this rearguard action with his customary diffluence. When the *Sunday Times* journalists in London expressed their concern about the affair and asked him to address a union meeting, he turned them down. He told them he was going away on holiday to Corfu. 'Even if I were here,' he added, 'I must tell you that I do not think that this matter is appropriate for the chapel.' Publication of the diaries would go ahead in his absence, he informed the editorial conference, and would stop only if the diaries were conclusively proved to be forgeries.

On Sunday, the paper appeared with a somewhat more muted front page than it had presented the previous week:

Hitler's Diaries – the trail from the hayloft
Stern challenges David Irving
'No shred of doubt,' says Heidemann

The editor of the *Sunday Times* then left the country.

*

David Irving spent the day sending out invoices to newspapers and magazines, billing them for his work attacking the diaries' authenticity. Shortly before noon, a reporter from the *Daily Express* rang to ask if it was true that he was suing the *Sunday Times* for failing to pay him his commission for putting them on to the Hitler diaries. 'Not suing,' replied Irving, 'just asking.' He then told him to 'hold on to his hat' and gave him what he modestly described as 'the story of the day': that he now believed the diaries were genuine.

The *Express* ran the story in its early editions, and at 11 p.m. a sub-editor from *The Times* rang to ask if the report in the *Express* was correct. Irving said it was.

The Times immediately put it on its front page.

The following morning, as *The Times* in Britain announced Irving's belief that the diaries were genuine, *Der Spiegel* appeared in Germany carrying his assertion that they were fakes. 'Hitler's Diary: Find or Forgery?' was the title on the magazine's cover; the contents left little doubt of *Der Spiegel*'s opinion as to the correct answer. It was a devastating assault, attacking the *Stern* scoop for 'bad German, bad punctuation and banality'. *Der Spiegel*'s reporters had tracked down the SS man who discovered the Boernersdorf crash and using his testimony they picked Heidemann's research apart. The Junkers' fuselage had been made of metal, not canvas, as *Stern* had claimed; the plane had ploughed straight into the ground, not ended up on its roof; gold bars, pistols and ammunition had been salvaged, but no papers. In contrast to the carefully cultivated image of 'the Bloodhound' which *Stern*'s public relations department had built up of Heidemann, the reporter was depicted as an obsessive friend of old Nazis, whose discovery had been inadequately checked and blown up into an international sensation. 'If it all goes wrong,' Peter Koch was quoted as saying, 'the editors will charter Heidemann's boat, sail it to Helgoland and pull out the plugs.' Much of the information had been provided by Irving and the centrepiece of the attack was a reproduction of a page from his fake diary.

Der Spiegel's attack was bad enough news for one day, but worse was to come when the company's lawyer, Dr Hagen, arrived at the Bundesarchiv.

Josef Henke had handed the three diary volumes given to him after the *Stern* press conference to the Federal Institute for Forensic Investigation in Berlin. On Monday, he was able to give Hagen the scientists' preliminary findings. All three volumes contained traces of polyamid 6, a synthetic textile invented in 1938 but not manufactured in bulk until 1943. The binding of the Hess special volume – supposedly written in 1941 – included polyester which had not been made until 1953. Ultraviolet light had also shown up fluorescent material in the paper. These results had yet to be confirmed in writing, said Henke, but *Stern*'s scoop was beginning to look extremely dubious. In addition, although the archive's researchers had had time for only a brief check of the diaries' written content, they had already found a couple of textual errors: two laws relating to agriculture and student organizations were not passed on the dates given in the diaries.

Hagen hurried back to Hamburg to pass on this information.

At about 6 p.m. Schulte-Hillen convened a crisis meeting in his office on the ninth floor of the *Stern* building. Wilfried Sorge did not attend (he was on holiday in Italy), nor did Koch, who was in the United States preparing his media campaign, but all the other leading figures in the affair were present: Jan Hensmann, Felix Schmidt, Rolf Gillhausen, Henri Nannen, Gerd Heidemann and Thomas Walde.

As Hagen reported the Bundesarchiv's findings an atmosphere of barely suppressed panic spread through the room. Only Heidemann seemed unmoved, sitting wrapped in his own private world as the others began shouting at him. Felix Schmidt was enraged by his calmness. How could he sit there, he demanded, and act as if none of this concerned him? It was imperative that he reveal the name of his source; otherwise, publication of the diaries should be stopped. Heidemann remained silent. 'You either belong in a madhouse or a prison,' Nannen told him. He added that in his opinion, the magazine's editors could not be allowed 'to dangle like this any longer'.

Schulte-Hillen now spoke up, and for the first time he addressed Heidemann sharply: he wanted to speak to the reporter alone – immediately. The two men left the room.

Before the emergency meeting began, the managing director had been approached in private by Felix Schmidt who had suggested that

Heidemann might be keeping the identity of his supplier secret because he had stolen some of the money. As far as Schmidt was concerned, that no longer mattered: the important thing was to find out whether the diaries were genuine. He had pleaded with Schulte-Hillen to try once more to persuade Heidemann to tell him the whole story, if necessary by promising him 'that if he has pocketed some of the money, it will not be held against him'.

In another office, away from the others, Schulte-Hillen confronted Heidemann. 'I asked him to tell me the whole story,' he recalled, 'leaving nothing out.' Heidemann, reluctantly, agreed. According to Schulte-Hillen:

> Heidemann told me that the South German collector was called Fischer. This was the first time I had heard the name. Herr Fischer was supposed to have a sister in East Germany who was married to a museum director called Krebs. For a long time, Frau Krebs had been putting advertisements in East German newspapers asking for militaria. One day, an old man from the Boernersdorf area had contacted Frau Krebs and asked if she was interested in handwritten documents belonging to Adolf Hitler. Frau Krebs had been so taken aback by this offer that she had told her brother, an army general. . .

At last, Heidemann was telling Schulte-Hillen the truth – or, at least, the truth as he had been given it by Kujau. 'General Fischer' had been to see the old man and obtained the names of peasants in the Boernersdorf area who had hidden material salvaged from the plane crash. The documents turned out to be the Hitler diaries. The general had kept them hidden for some years, before offering them for sale through his brother in South Germany. Heidemann said that at least three other communist generals were involved in smuggling them out of the East, including one from the Ministry of State Security; he added that he knew their names. 'I asked him to tell me them,' recalled Schulte-Hillen. 'He said he would have to check in his archive, then he could show me them in writing.'

Heidemann disappeared for two hours and returned at about 11 p.m. His 'evidence' turned out to be two letters addressed to an East German general, whose name had been blacked out. Schulte-Hillen was disappointed. 'What am I supposed to make of this?' he asked. The letters proved nothing. Heidemann said he was sorry, but 'the originals were in a safe place to which he had no access'.

Schulte-Hillen reported back to the group assembled in his office. The story of the diaries' discovery, as Heidemann had explained it, seemed plausible to him. But he still did not have a full account, and given Heidemann's insistence that it was a matter of life and death for people in East Germany, he did not feel able to put any more pressure on the reporter.

What has frequently – and accurately – been described as a 'bunker mentality' now descended on the headquarters of *Stern*. Surrounded by enemies, cut off from reality, the leaders of the magazine began deploying phantom divisions in a frantic attempt to stave off the impending disaster.

Surely they could somehow prove that paper whitener had been in use before the war? Henri Nannen spent the night reading through chemistry books. In an old dictionary he came across a pre-war entry for a substance called 'blankit'. Wolf Thieme spoke to a contact of his in the Bayer chemical company who told him that the paper whitener 'Blankophor' might have been used on an experimental basis in the 1930s. Early on Tuesday morning, Hans Shuh, the head of *Stern*'s business section, was summoned to Nannen's office and instructed to write a detailed article on the history of the paper industry. Meanwhile, a statement, resonant with hollow bravado, was issued to the news agencies, signed jointly by Nannen, Schmidt and Schulte-Hillen:

> For a week *Stern* has been accused, with ever-increasing shrillness, of publishing forged Hitler diaries. Professor Werner Maser spoke in detail of an East German forgery factory near Potsdam. In spite of repeated demands, Maser could not provide any proof of this.
>
> Professor Broszat, the director of the Institute of Contemporary History in Munich, demanded that all the diaries be laid before an international historical commission. *Stern* immediately turned down this demand. Historians, like doctors, diverge in their diagnoses. One day the English historian Trevor-Roper confirms the authenticity of the diary and the next day doubts it. The writer David Irving behaves in an opposite manner.

But at least doctors are bound by an oath of confidentiality. Historians, it is now clear, are under no such obligation. Laying all the documents before an historical commission would, as Henri Nannen, *Stern*'s publisher, has pointed out, compromise the exclusivity of the material.

Even the handwriting and forensic tests, commissioned by *Stern* before publication from well-known experts, have been misinterpreted by the press, television and radio, and partly pronounced false. Certain newspapers have not hesitated even to raise political suspicions about *Stern*'s editors.

But this discussion concerns material from recent history of extreme delicacy. *Stern* has therefore, despite its opinion, taken into account Professor Broszat's demand, and will allow an immediate inspection of the material by experts from West Germany, Switzerland and the United States.

Until these tests, carried out on the broadest basis by highly responsible bodies, have been completed and yielded a clear result, the chief editors, publisher and printer of *Stern* believe that any further discussion will serve no purpose.

Heidemann and Schmidt promptly withdrew from a discussion programme on Austrian television which they were scheduled to take part in that night.

As a first step in this new process of verification, the Bundesarchiv was informed that more diaries would be made available for a full textual and chemical analysis. Only one condition was attached: if the diaries proved to be forgeries, *Stern* was to be informed well in advance of any public announcement – at least the magazine would be able to run the story of its own folly as an exclusive.

On Wednesday 4 May accompanied by a company manager and a lawyer, Leo Pesch arrived in Zurich and removed fifteen volumes of the Hitler diaries from the bank vault. The group split up. The manager went direct to Koblenz to hand over four books to the Bundesarchiv for a check on the contents. Pesch and the lawyer drove to the Swiss forensic laboratories in St Gallen and gave the scientists eleven diaries for microscopic examination.

On the same day, from Hamburg, Gerd Heidemann set off on a two-day trip to Bavaria. He planned to visit a former employee of the Berghof now living in an old people's home near Berchtesgaden – she would swear, he was sure, to having seen Hitler write a diary. He told Walde that he would also stop off at an old printing works in Miesbach, south of Munich. The factory had at one time been run by the SS and he was certain he could obtain enough samples of pre-war paper to prove that whitener had been in use in the 1930s. And then there was Hitler's chauffeur's girlfriend – she would swear that Erich Kempka had told her before he died that Hitler used to write notes in the back of his Mercedes.

They must all trust him, said Heidemann. Everything would be fine.

In America, Peter Koch, supported by Wolf Hess, had embarked on what *Newsweek* described as a 'media blitz', with invitations to appear on *Good Morning America*, *The CBS Morning News*, *The Today Show* and *Nightline*. He gave a long interview to the *Washington Post* whose reporters were impressed by the confidence of this 'balding, trim man, sunburned from an outing at Jones beach over the weekend'. He was in combative mood. 'I expected the uproar,' he told another group of journalists, 'and expected that many incompetent people would denounce the diaries as fakes. This is because every other publishing house will envy our story and every historian will envy us.'

One man following Koch's publicity tour with interest was Kenneth Rendell, a forty-year-old handwriting expert based in Boston. Rendell had been retained by *Newsweek* when the magazine was bidding for the diaries at the beginning of April. 'Anticipating my imminent departure for Zurich,' Rendell recalled, 'I organized about a hundred samples of authentic Hitler writing, researched scientific tests that might date the material and prepared myself for a sizeable challenge.' Then, to his disappointment, the deal with *Newsweek* had fallen through, and he had been forced to watch the affair unfold from America. Koch's visit, bearing diaries from 1932 and 1945, gave him an opportunity to have a look at the material at first hand.

Rendell caught up with Koch at the Manhattan studios of CBS at breakfast time on Wednesday, as Koch was preparing for his appearance on the *Morning News*. Koch knew of Rendell's reputation and

ROBERT HARRIS

had no objections to letting him look at the diaries. Repeatedly interrupted by technicians, Rendell began his examination on the studio floor. 'Even at first glance,' he wrote later, 'everything looked wrong.' The paper was of poor quality, the ink looked modern, none of the writing was blotted ('a sloppiness I didn't expect from Hitler'), and the signatures seemed to him to be 'terrible renditions'. His immediate reaction was that both diaries were forged – the 1945 volume especially was a 'fiasco'.

At the end of the broadcast, Koch invited the American expert to continue his analysis in *Stern*'s New York office that afternoon. Rendell arrived with an assistant, an 80-power microscope and a dossier of genuine Hitler writing. The microscope showed 'no examples of tracing or other glaring technical errors', so Rendell tried a different technique. At his request, the *Stern* staff photocopied the twenty-two pages of the 1932 diary. 'We began,' he recalled, 'the tedious process of snipping out all of the capital letters and pasting them on sheets of paper. In all we assembled separate collections of twenty-one letters, and an additional assortment of numbers. We compared the diary characters with authentic characters we had pasted up earlier...'

At 9 p.m., Rendell broke off his examination for the night. 'It doesn't look good,' he warned Koch.

Across the Atlantic, in Koblenz, the President of the Bundesarchiv, Hans Booms, had been given four of the diaries by the *Stern* lawyer. He took them home with him to read. He was shocked by the content, but not in the way he had expected: it was indescribably *dull*. At midnight he turned to his wife. 'I don't care whether they are real or forged,' he told her. 'They are so boring, so totally meaningless, it hardly makes any difference.'

29

The next morning, 5 May, *Stern* appeared carrying the second instalment of its serialization of the diaries. The magazine, which had reverted to its normal habit of publishing on Thursday, devoted its cover and thirty-four inside pages to the story of Rudolf Hess's flight to Scotland. Hitler was quoted as describing the Duke of Windsor in an entry for 1937 as 'a glowing National Socialist'; Winston Churchill was dismissed in 1939 as 'the greatest poisoner in London'. The issue was also notable for a ranting editorial by Peter Koch, written before he left for America, entitled 'the Falsifiers', smearing *Stern*'s critics as part of an international conspiracy founded upon envy. Irving and Maser were historians without reputations to lose; so too, now, was Eberhard Jaeckel for daring to criticize the magazine's scoop. As for Trevor-Roper, Koch hinted that he had changed his mind partly because of his wartime connection with British intelligence. They were all contemptible. *Stern* welcomed the abuse of such people. 'More enemies,' wrote Koch, 'more honour.'

It was a masterpiece of mistiming, for at that moment, disaster was racing towards *Stern* from at least five different directions: from Koblenz, where Booms had handed over the diaries to a team of scholars to check for errors; from the forensic laboratories in Berlin which had taken samples of material from three of the diaries; from the police laboratories in Wiesbaden, whose scientists had now been handed those three volumes and were running their own tests; from the forensic institute in St Gallen; and from New York, where, at 10 a.m., Kenneth Rendell had resumed his handwriting investigation.

Within three hours, Rendell was in a position to prove what he had suspected the moment he saw the diaries. The capital letters E, H and K in the 1932 volume had striking dissimilarities to the same letters in authentic examples of Hitler's writing. 'Koch was stunned when he saw my evidence laid out on a conference table,' recalled Rendell. 'This type of systematic analysis was unimpeachable.' He wanted to know how the American could have concluded they were fakes so quickly, when three other handwriting experts had been convinced the diaries were genuine. 'He had the impression,' said Rendell, 'that all of the comparison documents provided by his magazine had come from the German Federal Archives. But I showed him that a careful reading of the authentication reports indicated that most examples were from the dossier of *Stern* and its reporter Gerd Heidemann.'

Rendell – who was reportedly paid a retainer of $8000 by *Newsweek* – wanted to tell Maynard Parker of his findings at once. Koch pleaded with him to keep quiet for the time being; *Stern* would fly him to Europe and give him the opportunity to study the entire archive if he would deal with them exclusively. Rendell agreed.

At 1.30 p.m. New York time (7.30 p.m. in Hamburg), Koch telephoned Schulte-Hillen.

The managing director of Gruner and Jahr had taken to his bed with a fever. 'Rendell thinks the diaries are forged,' said Koch when he eventually tracked him down. Groggily, Schulte-Hillen agreed with his suggestion that they should invite Rendell to Hamburg to inspect the diaries. But he refused to panic: he would wait, he told Koch, for the Bundesarchiv's verdict which *Stern* had been told would be given to them the next day. Besides, Rendell had spent only a few hours with the material; Frei-Sulzer, Hilton and Huebner had been allowed weeks and they had all been certain it was genuine.

Schulte-Hillen was still feeling confident when Manfred Fischer paid him a visit at home later that evening. Fischer had left Bertelsmann the previous November: despite Reinhard Mohn's excitement at the purchase of the Hitler diaries, the relationship between the two men had not worked smoothly. Nevertheless, Fischer had continued to maintain an interest in the project he had started in 1981. But over the past week, his pride had turned to dismay. The Hitler diaries could turn out to be the 'biggest deception of the century', he warned his successor. 'I fear we have allowed ourselves to be led by the nose.'

Schulte-Hillen shook his head. He was sure Fischer was being pessimistic. Anyway, they would both know for certain tomorrow.

The events which would eventually turn Friday 6 May 1983 into 'Black Friday' as far as the participants in the diaries affair were concerned began at 11 a.m. when the two *Stern* lawyers, Ruppert and Hagen, turned up at the Bundesarchiv to see Hans Booms.

Booms now had full reports from the scientists at Wiesbaden and Berlin. Reduced to its basic components, *Stern*'s great scoop had proved to be a shoddy forgery. The paper was a poor quality mixture of coniferous wood, grass and foliage, laced with a chemical paper whitener which had not existed before 1955. The binding of the books also contained whitener. The red threads attached to the seals on the covers contained viscose and polyester. The labels stuck on the front and supposedly signed by Bormann and Hess had all been typed on the same machine. The typewriter came from the correct period – it was an Adler Klein II, manufactured between 1925 and 1934 – but although an interval of seven years supposedly separated the labels attached to the 1934 diary and the Hess special volume of 1941, there was no evidence of wear in the typeface: the labels had been written in quick succession. The four different varieties of ink used in the books were of a type commonly found in West German artists' shops; they did not match any of the inks known to have been widely used during the war. And by measuring the evaporation of chloride from the ink, the scientists established that the Hess volume had been written within the last two years, whilst the writing in the 1943 diary was less than twelve months old.

Booms told all this to Hagen and Ruppert. They were, he recalled, 'deeply shocked' and 'shattered': 'I can still hear their arguments: "Heidemann is certain. He absolutely swears on it. As far as he's concerned, it's quite impossible that we could be dealing with a forgery. . ."'

But there could be no doubt. In addition to the forensic evidence, the Bundesarchiv had discovered a number of textual errors: for example, a law passed on 19 January 1933 was entered in the diary under 19 January

1934. It did not take the archivists long to discover the forger's main source: the two-volume edition of *Hitler's Speeches and Proclamations*, compiled by Max Domarus. 'It became apparent to us,' said Booms later, 'that if there was nothing in Domarus for a particular day, then Hitler didn't write anything in his diary that night either. When Domarus did include something, then Hitler wrote it down. And when an occasional mistake crept into Domarus, Hitler repeated the same error.' One such mistake was an entry by 'Hitler' recording that he had received a telegram from General Ritter von Epp congratulating him on the fiftieth anniversary of his joining the army; in reality, the telegram was *from* Hitler *to* von Epp. Kujau had copied the error word-for-word into the diary.

Throughout the half-hour conversation, Booms was repeatedly interrupted by telephone calls from Berlin, Wiesbaden and Bonn. Suddenly, Hagen realized what was happening: the two forensic laboratories, both official organizations, were reporting direct to the Federal Government. Booms confirmed that this was the case. But what about the guarantee of confidentiality? That no longer applied, answered Booms. The affair was now 'a ministerial matter'. There would be a government news conference to announce that the diaries were fakes at noon.

The two *Stern* lawyers scrambled to a telephone to alert Hamburg to what was about to happen. They reached Jan Hensmann. Hardly anyone seemed to be around. Hensmann rang Schulte-Hillen who left his sick bed immediately to come in. Hensmann tried to find Nannen.

Nannen was at Hamburg airport, preparing to fly to Rome for a ceremony to open *Stern*'s new Italian office. A stewardess told him he was wanted urgently on the telephone.

'It's all a forgery,' wailed Hensmann.

Nannen asked how he could be certain. The Bundesarchiv, said Hensmann. They were going to announce it in less than thirty minutes.

The sixty-nine-year-old publisher dropped the telephone, sprinted through the terminal, abandoned his luggage and his car, and jumped into a taxi. At the office, he dictated a statement acknowledging the Bundesarchiv's findings and promising a full investigation. The message was rushed to a telex machine but it arrived just five minutes too late to beat the official announcement.

*

The news that the diaries were forgeries had been whispered to the West German Minister of the Interior, Friedrich Zimmermann, during a debate in the Federal parliament. Broad smiles appeared as the news spread along the Government bench. Zimmermann told the Chancellor, Helmut Kohl. 'Now that is something,' laughed Kohl. *Stern* was an old enemy of the Christian Democrats: the discomfiture of Nannen and the rest of 'the Hamburg set', as Kohl dismissively called them, was a pleasant prospect to brighten the Government's day. Zimmermann hurried out of the Chamber to brief the press.

Zimmermann's determination to announce the news immediately was not motivated solely by party considerations. The legacy of Adolf Hitler was too important to be bandied about as *Stern* had done. Any West German government would have been sensitive about the diaries; the fact that the scandal had blown up on the fiftieth anniversary of Hitler's accession to power, at a time of intense interest in the Nazis, made the matter especially delicate. There was no question of the Interior Ministry permitting the Bundesarchiv to suppress the news that the diaries were forged while *Stern* tried to wriggle off the hook. The whole business was out of hand. It could no longer be left to a collection of scoop-happy journalists.

'On the basis of an analysis of the contents and after a forensic examination, the Federal Archive is convinced that the documents do not come from Hitler's hand but were produced after the war,' Zimmermann told reporters. 'I regret most deeply that this analysis was not undertaken by *Stern* before publication.' A press conference giving more details would be held shortly by the Bundesarchiv.

A few minutes later, the German Press Agency put out a rush statement: 'HITLER DIARIES ARE POST-WAR'. It was two weeks, literally to the hour, since the same agency had issued the announcement of *Stern*'s scoop.

In the *Sunday Times* offices in London there had been, according to the paper's own account, 'an air of considerable elation' all morning. *Stern* had finally agreed to lend the newspaper two volumes of the diaries to enable it to carry out its own forensic tests. A *Stern* courier had flown in from Hamburg and handed them personally to Rupert

Murdoch. Someone suggested to Murdoch that they should have the books photocopied. Murdoch would not allow it. He had given his word, he said, that they would be used only for scientific evaluation.

The atmosphere of self-congratulation was punctured abruptly at noon. Peter Hess, the publishing director of Gruner and Jahr, rang through from Germany with the news that the diaries were forgeries. 'It's staggering, shattering,' he said, stammering out his apologies. 'We still just can't believe it.'

Murdoch told his journalists to photocopy the diaries.

Arthur Brittenden issued a statement to Associated Press: 'The *Sunday Times* accepts the report of the German archivists that the volumes they have examined contain materials that demonstrate the diaries are not authentic. In view of this, the *Sunday Times* will not go ahead with publication.' News International announced it would be seeking an immediate repayment of the $200,000 it had paid as a first instalment for the diaries.

In Hamburg a debate was underway as to what *Stern* should do next. Astonishingly, Henri Nannen thought the magazine should cut out all the references drawn from the Hitler diaries and continue with its series about Rudolf Hess: it was still an interesting piece of journalism in his opinion. The others were horrified. The magazine would be torn apart by its critics if it tried to carry on as if nothing had happened. Nannen was forced to back down.

At the Itzehoe printing works, thirty miles north-east of Hamburg, the third issue of *Stern* to be built around the Hitler diaries was already being printed. By the time the arguments on the editorial floor had ended and the order had been given to stop the presses, 160,000 copies of the inside pages and 260,000 covers had already been printed. An additional 70,000 magazines were actually finished and in lorries on their way to the distributors; they were recalled only after frantic telephone calls. Every trace of the issue was pulped, losing *Stern* a quarter of a million marks in the process. The cover picture of Rudolf Hess was replaced by a photograph of a new-born baby.

At 2.30 p.m. Felix Schmidt addressed a hastily convened editorial conference. Everyone had to set to work to remake the next issue, he told them. He refused to answer detailed questions. Confused and angry, the *Stern* departmental chiefs drifted away. At 5 p.m. the entire staff held a meeting and elected a committee to negotiate a new code of conduct with the management.

In Cambridge, Hugh Trevor-Roper's telephone was once again ringing incessantly. 'I just don't want to say anything about it,' he told one reporter. 'I think I should only comment to Times Newspapers.'

In America, Leslie Hinton, the associate editor of Rupert Murdoch's *Boston Globe*, confirmed that the paper had been on the point of running extracts from the Hitler diaries. 'We have suspended our plans to publish,' he said in a statement to UPI, 'in view of what the German archivists said today.'

David Irving was in Düsseldorf on another speaking tour for the DVU when he heard the news from his secretary in London. It was a disastrous turn of events. He hastily dictated a statement for the press accepting the Bundesarchiv's ruling but drawing attention to the fact that he was the first person to declare the diaries fakes. ('Yes,' said a reporter from *The Times* when this was read out to him, 'and the last person to declare them authentic.') NBC sent a television crew to interview him after his speech to an audience of right-wing extremists in the nearby town of Neuss. 'They questioned whom I was speaking to,' Irving recorded in his diary, 'but I ducked the issue. As I was sitting down for the interview the whole audience streamed past behind the cameraman, several of the nuttier of them wearing the uniform and badges of the *Vikinger Jugend* [a fanatical sect of young neo-Nazis]. Fortunately NBC did not observe *them*.'

For Konrad Kujau, the newsflash announcing that the diaries were forgeries was the signal to pack up and leave Stuttgart as quickly as possible. Things had already started becoming uncomfortable for him. Stefan Aust, the editor of *Panorama*, West German television's leading current affairs programme, had managed to reconstruct the trail back from David Irving through August Priesack to Fritz Stiefel. Working from a clue dropped by Priesack that the supplier of the diaries was apparently a dealer in militaria named Fischer, Aust had begun trailing round every antiques shop in Stuttgart until someone remembered a Herr Fischer who had kept a shop in Aspergstrasse. Neighbours there told Aust that Fischer had moved to Schreiberstrasse. Aust had arrived on Thursday to find the shop deserted. He had driven straight round to see Fritz Stiefel to confront him with this information, and whilst there had actually spoken to Kujau on the telephone. 'Tell me where you are,' insisted Aust, 'and I'll come over.' Kujau had managed to stall him. But now that the diaries had been exposed, it was obviously going to be only a matter of time before a dozen other journalists followed Aust's path to Stuttgart.

According to Maria Modritsch, her lover turned up on her door-step at 7 p.m. on Friday, accompanied by Edith Lieblang. 'There was a conversation between us,' recalled Maria. 'Conny told Edith that I was cleaning for him.' Kujau insisted that all three of them leave Stuttgart immediately. Both women knew too much for him to be able to leave them behind. 'Conny wanted to go to the Black Forest,' said Maria, 'but then he took up my suggestion that we go to Austria.'

Shortly afterwards, the forger, his common-law wife and his mis-tress all clambered into a car, and this bizarre *ménage à trois* headed off to the Austrian border.

Gerd Heidemann had been incommunicado all day, driving around the countryside between Berchtesgaden and Munich trying to find evidence to shore up his crumbling scoop. The *Stern* executives were itching to get their hands on him. So too was Gina, who was having to field telephone calls from their apartment in the Elbchaussee. She refused to believe what the Bundesarchiv was saying. 'I am not sur-prised,' she told Gitta Sereny. 'We expected something like this.' Was she saying the diaries were genuine? 'Yes.' Those who said the diaries were fakes, she insisted to a reporter from the *New York Times*, were trying to 'suppress the truth'. 'It's terrible, but no matter what hap-pens, we will always believe in the diaries. . . It would have been a joy to tell the world about the Führer. We have received letters and tele-grams above all from young people who are overjoyed finally to learn the truth.' Between conversations with journalists, Gina managed to reach the couple's friend, Heinrich Hoffmann, the son of Hitler's photographer, who was also in Bavaria, undergoing treatment in a private clinic. Did he know where her husband was? Hoffmann said he did not. It was an emergency, said Gina, Gerd must ring her immediately. 'Shortly afterwards,' recalled Hoffmann, 'Heidemann rang.'

> He told me he was in the neighbourhood, but had no time to drop by. He asked how I was. I told him that his wife had rung and that he was being looked for. He said: 'Yes, that's the reason I'm in a rush – to get the last plane from Munich to Hamburg. . .' I then rang Frau Heidemann and said: 'You can relax. Gerd's all right and he's on his way back home.'

According to Heidemann's own account, he had heard the news of Zimmermann's announcement towards the end of the day on the car radio. He was 'completely shattered'. At 8 p.m. he rang the *Stern* office, and was briskly informed that they had been trying to find him all day and that a private plane was waiting on the tarmac at Munich to bring him straight to Hamburg.

The plane touched down shortly after 11 p.m. A *Stern* representative was waiting for Heidemann at the airport with a car to take him to the office. Gina was also there. At first she had been told by *Stern* to keep away, but she was determined to meet her husband. *Stern* had relented, but its official had instructions to make sure the couple did not try to rehearse a story together. 'All Gerd could say to me in the car,' recalled Gina, 'was: "I know they are genuine. I know." He looked shaken to the core.'

Heidemann faced a grim reception committee in the managing director's office: Henri Nannen, Felix Schmidt, Rolf Gillhausen and Gerd Schulte-Hillen had been waiting for him all evening. 'We are going to uncover the full story of this forgery and lay it before our readers,' Nannen had promised in an interview on West German television that night. 'We have reason to be ashamed.' No one was in any mood to listen to excuses. 'What do you have to say?' demanded Schulte-Hillen.

Heidemann said he was sure that most of the diaries were genuine. He needed more time. He wanted to meet a contact in East Berlin.

Schmidt interrupted him. 'Stop playing around. I'm sick of this performance. Let's get down to the real issues.'

Very well, said Heidemann. He opened his briefcase and placed a cassette recorder on the table. He switched it on and played his interrogators a recording of a fifteen-minute telephone conversation he had had from Munich with Medard Klapper. Klapper promised the reporter that Martin Bormann was now willing to fly over from South America to authenticate the diaries – he was an old man, he no longer feared prosecution, he would come and help Heidemann out of his predicament. Heidemann switched off the tape. The four *Stern* officials looked at one another. After a while, Schulte-Hillen spoke. 'How is Bormann proposing to get here?' he inquired.

'In a Lear jet,' said Heidemann.

There were angry and frustrated shouts from around the table. Felix Schmidt pointed out that a Lear jet did not have the range to cross the Atlantic: it would fall into the sea in mid-flight.

The atmosphere became progressively more unpleasant as Heidemann still refused to name his source. 'Lives are in danger,' he insisted. 'Nonsense,' said Schmidt. '*We're* the ones in danger.' Heidemann replied that his supplier had returned to East Germany to try to obtain the original score of Wagner's *Die Meistersinger*, one of Adolf Hitler's most treasured possessions which had also been on the Boernersdorf plane.

It was after midnight. Schulte-Hillen was unwell and Henri Nannen was beginning to fall asleep. The four senior *Stern* men decided to get some rest and Heidemann was taken downstairs to Felix Schmidt's office to face a fresh set of examiners: Thomas Walde, Wolfe Thieme and another *Stern* journalist, Michael Seufert. This session lasted until dawn.

Meanwhile, in another office, Gina Heidemann was also being subjected to some detailed questioning. Heidemann had once described driving her car over to East Germany to carry out one of the dramatic exchanges of money for diaries on the Berlin autobahn; had she been with him? Gina said she had, an answer which did not help Heidemann's credibility as at that moment he was denying that his wife had ever accompanied him. At 2.45 a.m., Gina telephoned Gitta Sereny at the Four Seasons Hotel. Sereny had flown over to cover the story of the forgery for the *Sunday Times*. 'They've got Gerd upstairs,' whispered Gina. 'They are putting him through the mangle.' By the time she emerged from the *Stern* building shortly after 3 a.m. she was in a pitiful state. She went to Sereny's hotel. 'Her hair,' wrote the reporter, 'usually neat and attractive, was tangled, and she looked as if she was in an advanced state of shock. She was trembling and crying.' Did she now believe the diaries were fakes? 'I don't know what to think,' she replied. 'Gerd always believed and swore they were genuine.' Who was the supplier? 'That's what they want to know. That's what they are asking him up there.'

As light began to break over Hamburg, Heidemann's defiance at last started to wilt. He was forced to accept that journalists from rival organizations would soon be swarming over Stuttgart. 'We simply cannot cling to the principle of protecting our informants any longer,' said Walde. At 5 a.m., Heidemann handed over 'Herr Fischer's' home telephone number. 'He used to live in Ditzingen,' said Heidemann, but he'd moved a year ago. 'I said to him: "Give me your new address", but he refused to give it to me so we always spoke on the telephone.' This was the break *Stern* needed. At 5 a.m., Seufert called the head of the magazine's Frankfurt office and told him to try to trace the owner of the number.

Was it possible, someone asked, that 'Herr Fischer' had forged everything?

'He can't have forged it,' replied Heidemann. 'He's far too primitive.'

30

Stern was given a predictable savaging in the West German press the following day. One paper denounced the magazine for its 'megalomania' in claiming it would rewrite the history of the Nazi era, 'as if this history had not already been written by the sixty million victims of the Second World War'. Another called the scoop 'a stinking bubble from the brown swamp'. An editorial in *Die Welt* summed up what seemed to be the mood of the entire country:

> Two days before the thirty-eighth anniversary of the Nazi defeat on 8 May 1945, one thing is certain: the history books on Hitler and the Third Reich will not be rewritten. Hitler's diaries, which *Stern* presented to the world at enormous cost in money and wordage, are a forgery... Mr Zimmermann is to be thanked for the fact that this upsurge of sensationalism, involving a massive attempt to falsify history, has been stopped in its tracks. Fortunately, the matter has been clarified before irreparable damage was done to the consciousness of the German people and the world.

It was clear that some heads from within *Stern* would have to be offered up to appease public opinion; the only question was – whose heads should they be?

Early on Saturday morning, Schulte-Hillen telephoned Reinhard Mohn and submitted his resignation. Mohn refused it. 'You do not carry the main responsibility,' he told him. Throughout the morning, members of the boards of Gruner and Jahr and Bertelsmann telephoned Schulte-Hillen to pledge their support. By lunchtime there was a clear consensus that the editors rather than management should face the consequences of the disaster. Koch arrived back from New York to find Nannen, Schulte-Hillen, Gillhausen and Schmidt locked in conference in Nannen's office, passing the poisoned chalice from one to another. Schulte-Hillen had the backing of Mohn, therefore he was excused. Nannen was already in semi-retirement. Gillhausen was responsible only for the design of the magazine... Koch quickly realized that it was he and Schmidt who were expected to drink. At 2 p.m., a lawyer was called in to represent them, as the meeting turned from a general discussion into a specific negotiation over severance pay.

It seems grossly unfair that Koch and Schmidt – who had never trusted Heidemann and who might, indeed, have dismissed him in 1981 – were made to carry the responsibility for the collapse of what had always been the management's scoop. Certainly, the two editors felt this to be the case, and their threats to take the issue to an industrial tribunal brought each of them enormous financial compensation: 3.5 million marks (more than $1 million) each, pre-tax, according to the *Stern Report*, conditional on a pledge of secrecy that they would not reveal the story of how the diaries affair had been handled within the company.

In London, the two diary volumes handed over to the *Sunday Times* had quickly been confirmed as forgeries. Dr Julius Grant, the forensic scientist who had established that the Mussolini diaries were forgeries, took only five hours to locate traces of post-war whitener in the paper. Norman Stone, one of Hitler's most recent biographers and one of the few scholars in Britain who could read the outdated German script, rapidly concluded that the diaries were fakes. There were inconsistencies and misspellings; above all, the diaries were full of trivia and absurd repetitions. On 30 January 1933, the day upon which Hitler assumed power, the diarist had recorded:

> We must at once proceed to build up as fast as possible the power we
> have won. I must at once proceed to the dissolution of the Reichstag,
> and so I can build up my power. We will not give up our power, let
> there come what may.

'This reads almost like a "Charlie Chaplin" Hitler,' wrote Stone. The *Sunday Times* itself admitted that nothing 'had prepared us for such an anticlimax'.

In Frank Giles's absence, it fell to his deputy, Brian MacArthur, somehow to frame an explanation for the behaviour of the newspaper, whose front page headlines had changed in two weeks from 'World Exclusive: The secrets of Hitler's war' to 'The Hitler Diaries: the hunt for the forger'. The statement which eventually appeared probably earned the paper more derision than anything else it had done in the past two weeks. 'Serious journalism,' it began, 'is a high-risk enterprise.' It went on:

> By our own lights we did not act irresponsibly. When major but hazardous stories seem to be appearing, a newspaper can either dismiss them without inquiry or pursue investigations to see if they are true. No one would dispute that the emergence of authentic diaries written by Adolf Hitler would be an event of public interest and historic importance.
>
> Our mistake was to rely on other people's evidence. . .

The statement ended:

> In a sense we are relieved that the matter has been so conclusively settled. A not-proven verdict would have raised difficult problems about publication.

This remarkable piece of self-justification masquerading as apology was subsequently attacked by a number of writers. The Hitler diaries affair was not an example of 'serious journalism', but of cheque-book journalism, pure and simple. And, as has become clear since, a 'not-proven verdict' would probably have led the *Sunday Times* to continue serialization: Murdoch's 55–45 formula required the balance of probability to tilt decisively *against* authenticity. To add to the paper's embarrassment, its colour supplement had already been distributed containing a twelve-page pictorial guide to Hitler's career: it was too late to recall it.

'What has happened to the *Sunday Times*?' asked an article in the *New York Times*, commenting on this front page statement. 'Rupert

Murdoch has, for one thing, with his talent for turning what he touches into dross.' Murdoch himself has been quoted as making three comments on the affair:

'Nothing ventured, nothing gained.'
'After all, we are in the entertainment business.'
'Circulation went up and it stayed up. We didn't lose money or anything like that.'

The last statement is certainly true. *Stern* returned to News International all the money it paid for the diaries, and the *Sunday Times* retained 20,000 of the 60,000 new readers it acquired when it began publishing the scoop.

When he had first heard that the diaries were forgeries, Gerd Heidemann had managed to cope with the news relatively calmly. The finality of the verdict had not sunk in. He still clung to the hope that the Bundesarchiv might be wrong. But by Sunday he was suffering from a bad case of delayed shock. His confidence had been shattered by his rough treatment overnight in the *Stern* building. And that, he realized, was only the beginning. Now that his three-year-old dream of bringing Hitler's testament to the world was in ruins, it would simply be a matter of time before questions began to be asked about what had happened to the money.

He later testified that his depression was such that he had considered shooting himself: he did, after all, have Hitler's so-called 'suicide weapon' and five bullets with which to do it. For part of the weekend he lay, in a state of collapse, in the lower of the family's two apartments, refusing to move. Barbara Dickmann telephoned from Rome to find out what was happening and was shocked by Heidemann's emotional state: 'He was crying, emphasizing again and again that it would become clear that most of the diaries were genuine, that I had to trust him, that he hadn't landed me in it.'

On Sunday morning, having not heard a word from Heidemann for more than twenty-four hours, Thomas Walde, Leo Pesch and Michael Seufert set out to try to find him. 'We were worried that he might be suicidal,' recalled Walde. They tried telephoning him, but there was no answer. They drove over to *Carin II*; the yacht was deserted. At about midday, they turned up outside the Heidemanns' Elbchaussee home. 'We rang the bell,' said Pesch later. 'His elder daughter appeared at the window. After much toing and froing, the door was finally opened and we were let into the flat by Frau Heidemann.' The three men told her they needed to speak to her husband. Gina said that he was staying with friends somewhere in Hamburg; she would fetch him. The *Stern* reporters were left alone while she went downstairs, apparently to try to persuade her husband to come out of his hiding place in the apartment below. Ten minutes later, the doorbell rang.

'I looked through the spyhole,' related Pesch, 'and I saw Heidemann, in his shirt sleeves, lying crumpled up on the floor by the steps. He was groaning, "Open up, open up." His wife was next to him and was trying to get him to his feet. I opened the door and Heidemann – who didn't seem able to stand – staggered to a chair and dropped into it. He was crying and choking. It was about ten minutes before he could speak.'

Heidemann presented a wretched spectacle, but his colleagues' visit was not principally motivated by concern for his health. *Stern* had been working flat out since dawn on Saturday to piece together the story of the hoax. Using information and the telephone number supplied by Heidemann, the magazine's reporters had located 'Fischer's' home and shop and found them shuttered and deserted; neighbours said that Conny and Edith had gone away. *Stern* had soon established that 'Fischer's' real name was Kujau and that his highly placed East German relatives – the museum keeper and the general – were, respectively, a municipal caretaker and a railway porter. Walde, Pesch and Seufert were under instructions to obtain more information and once Heidemann had regained his composure, they began asking him the same old questions all over again.

Seufert produced a photograph of Kujau which the magazine had already obtained from his family in East Germany. Was this 'Fischer'? Heidemann replied immediately that it was. Seufert told him that the man's real name was Kujau. According to Pesch: 'Heidemann assured us – and I believed him – that this was the first time he'd heard the name Kujau.' The questioning went on until seven o'clock in the evening and resumed again at midday on Monday.

In the interim, Heidemann received a telephone call from Kujau. The forger told him he was calling from a telephone box in Czechoslovakia where he was still trying to locate the score of *Die Meistersinger*. Heidemann taped the call. He was desperate. He told Kujau that the diaries were fakes. 'Who could have forged so much?' he demanded.

'Oh my God,' wailed Kujau, 'oh my God.'

Heidemann told him that they would both probably end up in prison.

'Shit,' exclaimed Kujau. 'You mean we've already been connected?'

'*Stern*'s going to file charges against me for sure,' said Heidemann. 'The papers are saying that I did it.'

'That's impossible.'

'Come on,' pleaded Heidemann. 'Where did you get the books from?'

'They're from East Germany, man.'

Heidemann confronted him with *Stern*'s revelation that he had lied about his relatives in East Germany.

Kujau admitted it, but said that it hadn't been his idea: 'they' had made him do it.

Heidemann later replayed this conversation with Kujau to Leo Pesch during his interrogation on Monday. 'It wasn't at all clear who "they" were supposed to be,' Pesch recalled, 'and Heidemann didn't press him ... During the telephone conversation, Heidemann kept referring to the Wagner opera score. He still seemed to believe that Kujau had delivered him some genuine material.'

Reporters and photographers had been lurking around the Heidemanns' home for several days. By Tuesday Heidemann had recovered sufficiently to invite them in for an impromptu press conference. Dozens of journalists jammed into his study, pinning Heidemann against a bookcase full of works on the Third Reich. Accompanied by his lawyer, he was described as looking 'drained' and 'subdued'. He was asked why he was still refusing publicly to identify the diaries' supplier. 'Because this man was probably also deceived,' replied Heidemann. 'He is trying on his own to clear up where they came from and if they are forgeries. While he is investigating the affair for me and while I still have some faith in him, I cannot betray his name to the public.' He would not comment on rumours that the man's name was Fischer.

That same day, *Stern* announced that Heidemann had been 'summarily fired' and Henri Nannen disclosed that the company would be pressing charges with the Hamburg State Prosecutor for fraud. Nannen said that, in his opinion, Heidemann had always believed in the diaries, but had been blinded by 'dollar signs in his eyes' and had stolen at least some of the magazine's money. 'Heidemann has not just been deceived,' he told reporters, 'he too is a deceiver.' Nannen also revealed that *Stern* had paid more than 9 million marks for the diaries.

A few hours later, the West German television programme *Panorama*, presented by Stefan Aust, scooped *Stern* by two days and named Heidemann's source as Konrad Fischer, alias Konrad Kujau.

Needless to say, Kujau had not been in Czechoslovakia hunting for the score of *Die Meistersinger* when he rang Heidemann on Monday. He was in the Austrian industrial town of Dornbirn, close to the Bavarian border, holed up in the home of Maria Modritsch's parents. Conditions were cramped and the atmosphere was understandably tense. 'Conny and Edith slept together,' said Maria, 'and I slept in the living room.'

Kujau's plan had been to stay away from Stuttgart until things cooled off. But it quickly became apparent that this was not going to happen – indeed, things were hotting up. Kujau was sitting watching the Modritschs' television when his picture was flashed on the screen as the man who had allegedly supplied Heidemann with the Hitler diaries. When it was also announced that *Stern* had paid out 9 million marks for the material, Kujau shot out of his chair. *Nine million marks?* He had received only a quarter of that sum. The deceiver had been deceived. The forger was full of moral outrage at Heidemann's dishonesty. 'He was bitterly upset,' recalled Edith. Kujau was certain that the reporter, believing him to be behind the Iron Curtain looking for the Wagner opera, had deliberately betrayed him: once his name was known, he would then never have been able to get back over the border; he would have conveniently disappeared into the clutches of the secret police, leaving Heidemann to enjoy the millions of marks which should rightfully have been Kujau's – such, at least, was the forger's conviction.

Kujau telephoned his lawyer in Stuttgart and learned that the Hamburg State Prosecutor was looking for him and proposed to raid his home and shop. It was clear that it was all over. On Friday 13 May Dietrich Klein of the Hamburg Prosecutor's office, accompanied by a group of police, broke into Kujau's premises and, watched by a crowd of reporters, began removing evidence: ten cartons and two plastic sacks full of books about Hitler, correspondence, newspaper cuttings, a signed copy of *Mein Kampf* and artists' materials. There were also Nazi uniforms, military decorations, swastikas and photographs. Screwed to the wall above the entrance to Kujau's collection was a coat of arms with the motto 'Fearless and True'.

Klein was in Kujau's house, sifting through his property, when the telephone rang. 'This is Klein speaking,' said the prosecutor. 'This is Kujau speaking,' came the reply. Kujau told the official that he understood he wanted to speak to him. He was willing to come forward voluntarily. He told Klein he would meet him at a border post on the Austrian frontier early the following morning.

At 8 a.m. on Saturday, Kujau said goodbye to Edith and Maria and made his way to the German border where Klein was waiting with a warrant for his arrest.

Kujau had agreed to give himself up. He had not agreed to tell the truth. During the long journey north to Hamburg he asked the prosecutor what would happen to him. According to Kujau, Klein told him that if he was not the man who wrote the diaries, he would be free in ten days; if he was: 'It could take a long time.'

'I decided,' said Kujau afterwards, 'to tell him Grimms' fairy stories.'

Kujau's tale – which he stuck to throughout the next week – was that he was simply a middleman: the idea that he was the forger of the diaries he dismissed as 'absurd'. He claimed to have met a man known only as 'Mirdorf' in East Germany in 1978 who had offered to supply him with Hitler material. In this way, Kujau said he had obtained a diary and given it to Fritz Stiefel. Later, when Heidemann had heard about the story, he had pressured him to provide more diaries. Kujau told the prosecutor that as a result he had renewed his contact with Mirdorf who had promised to obtain them. The books had then emerged from East Germany over the next two years through another man called Lauser. Above all, Kujau denied emphatically the allegation that he had been given 9 million marks for the books. He had passed on no more than 2.5 million, of which he had taken 300,000 in commission.

Kujau's story sounded wildly improbable, and Klein had no difficulty in demolishing large sections of it almost at once. For example, when Maria Modritsch was interrogated, two days after her lover's arrest, she identified the shadowy 'Mr Lauser' not as a Swiss businessman but as 'a man who used to come to the Sissy Bar to fix the juke box'. And if Kujau had not been aware that the diaries were forged, demanded Klein, why did he have in his house more than six hundred carefully marked books and newspaper articles detailing Adolf Hitler's daily movements? And why had the police also found several empty notebooks identical to the so-called diaries?

The questions were unanswerable. But what eventually proved most effective in breaking Kujau's resistance was the image the police could conjure up of Heidemann. Whilst he languished in prison, the reporter was still enjoying his freedom in Hamburg, telling everyone he had handed over all the money to Kujau. The idea of it was intolerable. On Thursday 26 May, his thirteenth day in custody, Kujau confessed in writing to having forged more than sixty volumes of Hitler's diaries. To prove his guilt, he wrote out part of his confession in the same gothic script he had used in the diaries. As a final, malicious embellishment, he added that Heidemann had known about the forgery all along.

It had been clear to Heidemann for some time that he had become the subject of a criminal investigation. Within hours of Kujau's arrest, on Saturday 14 May the Hamburg police had raided the family's home on the Elbchaussee along with his archive in Milchstrasse; *Carin II* had also been searched and impounded. Heidemann's collection of Nazi memorabilia and many of his private papers were seized. Four days later, the police carried out a second raid. It turned up 'nothing new' according to the prosecutor's office, but it made it obvious to Heidemann that his days of freedom were drawing to a close.

He read of Kujau's arrest in the newspapers and reacted to the growing rumours that 'Conny' was the forger with incredulity. 'I don't believe it at all,' he told Reuters: Kujau would have had to have been a 'wonder boy' to have forged so much. 'If these diaries are not genuine,' Heidemann confided to his friend Randolph Braumann, 'then there must – somewhere – be some genuine ones. Kujau cannot have made it all up alone – all those complicated historical situations. Maybe Kujau copied them up from genuine diaries which still exist somewhere.'

Heidemann told Braumann that he was feeling 'completely *kaputt*, flat out' and Gina warned him that her husband was 'terribly depressed'. The company Mercedes had been taken away; their credit cards had been cancelled; they were social lepers. Braumann felt very sorry for them. On Monday 23 May he rang and invited the couple round for a drink that evening. Gina doubted whether Heidemann would leave the flat. 'He's depressed again,' she said.

The Heidemanns eventually turned up at 10.30 p.m., and stayed drinking with Braumann and his wife until three o'clock the next morning. Heidemann was listless and full of self-pity. The other three tried to make him pull himself together, but he simply sat slumped in his chair, shaking his head. 'Everything seems to have collapsed at the same time,' he complained. 'Everything has crumbled. If only a scientist would appear and prove that the diaries, or at least some of them, were genuine.'

Braumann said that what was so astonishing was that the diaries were such primitive forgeries. Heidemann said that it was easy to say that now: 'But I never doubted. It all seemed to fit together so well. One thing followed another: first the Hitler pictures, then the things that he'd painted in his youth, then the writing from his time in Vienna, then his application to the school of art and his rejection by the professors – everything genuine, everything proven; then the positive results on the diaries. No one ever dreamed it could all have been forged.'

Braumann asked about the two police raids.

'They've taken everything away,' said Heidemann. 'Documents, photographs, all the paperwork – everything, without a receipt.'

'He was really apathetic,' recalled Braumann, 'like a man who had seen all his hopes and dreams destroyed. He didn't drink very much.

His thoughts seemed to be stuck in a groove going round and round on the subject of where the diaries came from, whether they were genuine or whether they were false.'

'I don't want to be remembered,' said Heidemann, 'as the man responsible for the greatest flop in newspaper history.'

Braumann promised to do all he could to help Heidemann, but time had run out. Three days later, Kujau implicated him in the forgery and at 10 p.m. on the night of Thursday 26 May, the reporter was arrested at his home and taken into custody.

Epilogue

A variety of theories have been advanced to explain the origin of the Hitler diaries. Radio Moscow alleged that the whole affair was a CIA plot 'intended to exonerate and glorify the Third Reich'. The CIA, claimed the Russians, had provided the information contained in the diaries and trained the forger. Its aim was 'to divert the attention of the West German public from the vital problems of the country prior to the deployment of new US missiles' and to discredit the normally left-wing *Stern*. In this version of events, Kujau was an American stooge:

> Half a century ago the Nazis set fire to the Reichstag building and accused the insignificant provocateur Marinus van der Lubbe of arson. Van der Lubbe was supposed to provide proof against the communists, and he did. Now, another van der Lubbe has been found, a small-time dealer, possessed by the mad idea of going down in history, psychologically as unstable as van der Lubbe. Even now the West German bourgeois press predicts that this new van der Lubbe will testify against East Germany. This is not just the normal style of the CIA: one clearly also detects the hand of the [West German] intelligence service and the Munich provocateurs from the circle around Franz Josef Strauss.

(The fact that the writer Fritz Tobias had established more than twenty years previously that the Nazis did not set fire to the Reichstag, and that the blaze *was* the work of van der Lubbe, is apparently still not officially accepted by the Soviet Union.) The Hitler diaries, wrote *Izvestia*, 'parted the curtains a little to reveal the morals of the Western "free press" and the political morality of bourgeois society'.

Henri Nannen, on the other hand, told the *New York Times* that in his view the affair could have resulted from 'an interest in East Germany to spread disinformation and destabilize the Federal Republic'. According to *Stern*'s rival, *Quick*, East German intelligence concocted the diaries and transported them to the West 'to provide a spur for neo-Nazis and to resurrect the Nazi past as a means of damaging the reputation of the Federal Republic'. The West German authorities took the allegations seriously enough to ask the central police forensic laboratory to examine the diaries to see if their paper and ink could have originated in the East. The anti-communist hysteria surrounding the fraud was sufficiently widespread to be cited as a reason by the East Germans for cancelling the planned visit to Bonn of their leader, Erich Hoenecker.

Another conspiracy theory was put forward by the *Sunday Times* in December 1983 after a lengthy investigation into the hoax. According to this account, the Hitler diaries were organized as a fund-raising operation by the SS 'mutual aid society' HIAG, which pays out funds to old SS men who lost their pensions at the end of the war. Despite the paucity of evidence put forward to support its thesis, the paper stated flatly that 'most or all of the money' paid out by *Stern* 'went to HIAG'. The idea was dismissed in West Germany and since appears to have been quietly dropped by the *Sunday Times* itself: not one word has appeared in the paper about the subject since 1983.

Most of these theories about the diaries reveal more about their authors than they do about the fraud. Because the figure of Adolf Hitler overshadows the forgery, people have tended to read into it whatever they want to see. To a communist the affair is a capitalist plot; to a capitalist, a communist conspiracy; to a writer on the Third Reich, fresh evidence of the continuing hold of the Nazis on West German society. This is not surprising. Hitler has always had the capacity to reflect whatever phobia afflicts the person who stares at him – as the columnist George F. Will wrote at the height of the diaries controversy, Hitler 'is a dark mirror held up to mankind'. Equally, it flattered the victims of the fraud to believe that they were not gulled by their own paranoia and greed for sensation, but were actually the targets of a massive 'disinformation' operation or giant criminal conspiracy, trapped by something too complex, powerful and cunning to resist. How else could a successful and worldly publication like *Stern* have fallen for such obvious fakes? How else could they have paid out so much money? How else could the story have been bought by someone as shrewd as Rupert Murdoch and launched, unchecked, in such a distinguished publication as the *Sunday Times*? Anyone who took the magnitude of the fiasco as their starting point was bound to look for an appropriately sophisticated plot as the only possible explanation. When Konrad Kujau crawled out from beneath the wreckage of *Stern*'s million-dollar syndication deals, people refused to believe that such an odd individual could be responsible.

There are many unanswered questions relating to Kujau, of which the most important are how and why did he learn to forge Nazi documents with such skill; his craftsmanship certainly suggests that at some stage he may have learned his trade by working for someone else. But, although it is possible that Kujau may have had an accomplice to help him write the diaries, it would appear, on present evidence, that there was no extensive conspiracy to rob *Stern*. The fraud swelled to the proportions it did only because of the incompetence displayed within Gruner and Jahr. How could anyone possibly have guessed in advance that the magazine would have behaved so foolishly? The editors, presented with a *fait accompli*, relied upon the management; the management relied upon Heidemann and Walde; Heidemann and Walde relied upon Kujau; and between them all, they managed to bungle the process of authentication. A competent forensic scientist would have established in less than a day that the diaries were forgeries: any conspirators would have been aware of that. Only the uncovenanted stupidity of *Stern*, along with a series of flukes, prevented the fraud from being exposed long before publication. The Hitler diaries affair is a monument to the cock-up theory of history. If HIAG or some similar group had really been so desperate for 9 million marks as to contemplate crime, they would have been far better served to have staged an old-fashioned bank raid.

But money need not have been the only motive behind the appearance of the diaries. It has also been suggested that they were concocted in an attempt to rehabilitate Hitler. Gitta Sereny, responsible for

ROBERT HARRIS

the *Sunday Times* investigation, has claimed that the diaries' content
is 'totally beyond' Kujau's abilities, that a 'coherent psycho-political
line' emerges, presenting Hitler as 'a reasonable and lonely man'. The
suggestion is that Kujau was told what to write by someone else: the
candidate put forward by the *Sunday Times* was Medard Klapper,
'the central organizer of the conspiracy'. Again, this now seems highly
improbable. In the first place, it greatly exaggerates the sophistication
of the diaries. They read like the handiwork of a fairly uneducated
man, obsessively interested in Hitler, who has cobbled together whatever he can lay his hands on from the published sources – they read, in
other words, like the handiwork of Konrad Kujau. Secondly, the idea
that Medard Klapper of all people might be the political brain behind
the whitewashing of Hitler seems somewhat unlikely. Is the man who
promised to introduce Heidemann to Martin Bormann once he had
undergone a '*Sippung*' any more credible as an author of the diaries
than Kujau? HIAG would have had to be desperate.

But above all, it is the crudity of the forgery which belies the
idea that it might be the product of a Nazi conspiracy. If this was
a serious attempt to present an untarnished Hitler, one would at
least have expected the conspirators to have taken some elementary
precautions. They would not have used paper containing chemical
whitener; they would have avoided such Kujau touches as plastic
initials and red cord made of polyester and viscose; they would not
have relied so completely on the work of Max Domarus as to have
copied out his errors.

What *is* sobering is to speculate on what might have happened if
these precautions *had* been taken. After all, *Stern* and News International stopped publication only because of the conclusiveness of
the forensic tests carried out in the first week of May. If those tests
had found nothing substantially wrong, the diaries would have been
printed and would now stand as an historical source. No doubt they
would have been dismissed by most serious scholars, but nevertheless
they would have been bought and read by millions. Thomas Walde
and Leo Pesch would have produced their book on Rudolf Hess and
become rich men; Gerd Heidemann would have retired with his Nazi
memorabilia to southern Spain; and Konrad Kujau, ex-forger of

luncheon vouchers, having thrown students of the Third Reich into turmoil, would no doubt have continued flooding the market with faked Hitler memorabilia.

Instead of which, on Tuesday 21 August 1984, after more than a year in custody, Heidemann and Kujau were led out of their cells and into a courtroom incandescent with television lights and photographers' flash bulbs to stand trial for fraud. Heidemann was accused of having stolen at least 1.7 million of the 9.3 million marks handed over by *Stern* to pay for the diaries. Kujau was charged with having received at least 1.5 million marks. Edith Lieblang, although not being held in prison, was also required to attend court with her lawyer, accused of helping to spend Kujau's illegal earnings.

The two men had both been transformed by the events of the past sixteen months. Heidemann looked worn out and seedy. He had grown a beard in captivity which only gave further emphasis to the unhealthy prison pallor of his skin. His first act on arriving in the courtroom was to head for the corner. When anyone spoke to him, he would look away. It was common knowledge that he had suffered some kind of nervous collapse in jail.

Kujau, in contrast, had developed into something of a star. He had sold his life story to *Bild Zeitung* for 100,000 marks. He gave regular television interviews from his prison cell. He slapped backs, exchanged jokes with his warders, kissed female reporters, and happily signed autographs 'Adolf Hitler'. And he lied: expertly, exuberantly and constantly. Every reporter who interviewed him came away with a forged diary entry as a souvenir and a different version of his career. He drove Heidemann mad with frustration. While the reporter sat alone in his cell, poring over a meticulous card-index of the events of the past three years, trying to work out what had happened, he could hear Kujau regaling a reporter with some new account of his adventures; occasionally, like a tormented beast, Heidemann would let out a howl of rage. He would not speak to Kujau; he would not look at him. It was a far cry from the days when Gerd and Gina and Conny and Edith would meet and toast with champagne their good fortune at having met one another.

On its opening day, the Hitler diaries trial drew an audience of 100 reporters, 150 photographers and television crewmen and around sixty members of the public. It was front page news for the first couple of days; thereafter interest dwindled until eventually the audience numbered only a half dozen regular court reporters and a handful of curious day trippers. The proceedings became so monotonous that in the middle of September one of the magistrates had to be replaced because of a chronic inability to stay awake.

Heidemann denied stealing any of *Stern*'s money. However, from his private papers and known bank accounts, the prosecution had no difficulty in establishing that he had spent almost 2 million marks more than he had earned since 1981, even allowing for the 1.5 million marks paid to him as 'compensation' for obtaining the diaries. The prosecutor also told the court that, although he would only be attempting to prove the smaller figure, he believed Heidemann could have stolen as much as 4.6 million marks. Heidemann's defence was that the money had been paid to him by four anonymous investors as payment for a stake in one of the reporter's Nazi treasure hunts. As Heidemann refused to name these gentlemen, his story lacked credibility. His defence lawyers managed to persuade the court to accept as evidence a series of tape recordings made by Heidemann of his telephone conversations with Kujau. These had been edited together by the reporter and effectively proved his contention that he had not known the diaries were forged. Unfortunately, whenever the discussions turned to the matter of payments, the tapes abruptly ended, strengthening the prosecution's case that Heidemann had not handed over all of the money.

Kujau's defence was handled by a lawyer of feline skill and left-wing opinions named Kurt Groenewold. At first sight Groenewold was an unlikely choice to defend a Nazi-obsessed forger: he was one of West Germany's leading radical lawyers, a friend of the Baader–Meinhof group, a solicitor who numbered among his clients the CIA 'whistleblower' Philip Agee. But it turned out to be an inspired partnership. Groenewold's defence of Kujau was based on the argument that he was a small-time con man who had been lured into forging the Hitler diaries only by the enormous sums offered by the capitalists from Bertelsmann. Whilst Groenewold dragged *Stern* into the centre of the proceedings, exposing the negligence which had allowed the fraud to reach the proportions it did, Kujau was able to play the role of a likeable rogue whose cheerfully amateurish work had been exploited by the salesmen from Hamburg.

On Monday 8 July 1985 the media returned in force to Hamburg to record the verdict. After presiding over ninety-four sessions of testimony from thirty-seven different witnesses, the judge found all the defendants guilty. Heidemann was sentenced to four years and eight months in prison. Kujau received four years and six months. Edith Lieblang was given a suspended sentence of one year. The judge said he could detect no evidence of a wider conspiracy. Stern, he announced, had acted with such recklessness that it was virtually an accomplice in the hoax.

More than two years had passed since the diaries were declared forgeries. More than 5 million marks of Stern's money remained – and, at the time of writing, remains – unaccounted for.

The Hitler diaries affair had a traumatic effect upon Stern. Its offices were occupied by journalists protesting at the management's appointment of two new conservative editors. There were hundreds of abusive letters and phone calls. The overwhelmingly left-wing staff found themselves being greeted on the telephone by shouts of 'Heil Hitler!' Politicians treated them as a laughing stock; prominent West Germans pulled out of interviews; young East German pacifists refused to cooperate with a planned Stern feature article on the grounds that the magazine was 'a Hitler sheet'. Circulation slumped. Before the scandal, the magazine reckoned to sell around 1.7 million copies. This figure climbed to a record 2.1 million in the week in which the diaries' discovery was announced. After the revelation that they were forgeries, circulation fell back to less than 1.5 million. Apart from the loss of advertising and sales revenue, the cost to the magazine was estimated by the Stern Report as 19 million marks: 9.34 million for the diaries; 1.5 million for Heidemann; 7 million (before tax) as compensation to the two sacked editors; and miscellaneous costs, including agents' fees, publicity and the expense of destroying thousands of copies containing the second instalment of the Hess serialization.

Gradually, most of the main participants in the story left the magazine. Dr Jan Hensmann departed at the end of 1983 to become a visiting professor at the University of Munster. Wilfried Sorge resigned in the spring of 1984 to run a small publishing company. Thomas Walde left Hamburg to work in another outpost of the Bertelsmann empire. Leo Pesch went to Munich to work for *Vogue*. Manfred Fischer, who initiated the purchase of the diaries, is currently the chief executive of the Dornier aircraft corporation. Felix Schmidt is now editing the main West German television guide. Peter Koch, at the time of writing, has not re-entered full-time employment. Gerd Schulte-Hillen, however, *is* still the managing director of Gruner and Jahr: he must be a very good manager indeed.

In Britain, Frank Giles returned from his holiday to find himself the target of a vicious whispering campaign. In June 1983, 'after discussions with Mr Rupert Murdoch', it was announced that he was to retire prematurely as editor and assume the honorific title of editor emeritus. According to a story which did the rounds at the time, Giles asked what the title meant. 'It's Latin, Frank,' Murdoch is said to have replied. 'The "e" means you're out, and the "meritus" means you deserve it.'

Newsweek, which ran the Hitler diaries on its front cover for three successive weeks, was widely criticized for its behaviour. 'The impression created with the aid of provocative newspaper and television advertising,' said Robert J. McCloskey, the ombudsman of the *Washington Post*, 'was that the entire story was authentic.' The morality of selling Hitler 'bothered us', confessed Mrs Katherine Graham. William Broyles appeared to disagree: 'We feel very, very good about how we handled this,' he told the *New York Times*. Seven months later, he resigned as *Newsweek*'s editor. Maynard Parker, who had been expected to succeed him, was passed over. Insiders blamed the Hitler diaries. 'That episode killed Parker,' said one. 'There were expressions of high-echelon support, but it was poor judgement and everyone knew it.'

In the aftermath of the Hitler diaries affair, David Irving's American publishers tripled the print run of his edition of the Führer's medical diaries. Excerpts were published in Murdoch's *New York Post* and in the *National Enquirer*. But all publicity is not necessarily good publicity: not long afterwards Irving was arrested by the Austrian police in

Vienna on suspicion of neo-Nazi activity and deported from the country; he is still banned from entry.

In 1985, Hugh Trevor-Roper published a collection of his work entitled *Renaissance Essays*. It was hailed by most critics as 'brilliant'. The Hitler diaries, tactfully, were not mentioned.

Fritz Stiefel, Kujau's best customer until Heidemann appeared, announced that he would not be suing the forger for damages. 'I have one of the biggest collections of fakes in the world,' he said, 'and that, too, is worth something.'

Adolf Hitler as Painter and Draughtsman by Billy F. Price and August Priesack was banned in West Germany, but appeared in the United States at the end of 1984 as *Adolf Hitler: The Unknown Artist*. A large section of it was the work of Konrad Kujau, but it would have cost a fortune to rip out the fakes and reprint the book. The Kujaus therefore were left sprinkled amongst the Hitlers, and nobody, apparently, cared: 'Even the suspect pictures,' claimed a limp note of explanation in the book's introduction, 'generally reflect Hitler's known style.' The remark echoes that made by *Newsweek* about the Hitler diaries: 'Genuine or not, it almost doesn't matter in the end'.

Perhaps it doesn't. Certainly, the trade in Nazi relics has not been depressed by the revelations of wholesale forgery thrown up in the aftermath of the diaries affair. Shortly before Christmas 1983, Christie's of New York auctioned seven pages of notes made by Hitler in 1930 for which the purchasers, Neville Rare Books, paid $22,000. In London, Phillips, Son & Neale, fine art auctioneers since 1796, held a sale entitled 'Third Reich Memorabilia' which netted over £100,000. Four small Hitler paintings, at least one of which had the look of a genuine Kujau about it, raised £11,500. Also up for sale were such curiosities as Reichsführer SS Heinrich Himmler's vanity case, removed from his body after his suicide and described in the catalogue as 'a small leather vanity wallet with fitted compartments containing comb, metal mirror, penknife by Chiral with gilt niello-work to sides, the wallet embossed in gold "RF-SS"'. Meanwhile, at the other end of the scale, operating from his garage in Maryland, Mr Charles Snyder continued to sell locks of Eva Braun's hair, allegedly scraped from her comb by an American officer who looted her apartment in Munich.

Here, rather than in any grand conspiracy, lies the origin of the Hitler diaries affair. Why would anyone pay $3500 for a few strands of human hair of dubious authenticity? Because, presumably, *he* might have touched them, as he might have touched the odd scrap of paper, or painting, or piece of uniform – talismans which have been handed down and sold and hoarded, to be brought out and touched occasionally, as if the essence of the man somehow lived on in them. The Hitler diaries, shabby forgeries, composed for the most part of worthless banalities, were no different. 'It was a very special thing to hold such a thing in your hand,' said Manfred Fischer, trying to explain the fascination which he and his colleagues felt when the first volume arrived. 'To think that this diary was written by *him* – and now I have it in my grasp. . .' After millions of dollars, two years, and a great deal more stroking and sniffing in offices and bank vaults, the diaries appeared, and have now taken their place as one of the most extraordinary frauds in history – a phenomenon which Chaucer's Pardoner, six centuries ago, with his pillow cases and pig's bones, would have recognized at once.

Index

Huebner (handwriting expert) 157,
159, 296
Hughes, Howard 10, 159–60, 260
Hutchinson's 32, 33

Independent Newspapers (New
Zealand) 217
Independent Radio News 255
Institute of Contemporary History,
Munich 120, 139, 177,
240, 291
International Creative Management
(ICM) 188, 193, 252
Iquisabel, Dr 141
Irving, Clifford 159–60
Irving, David xv, 17, 187–8, 191,
195, 283, 287, 291, 295, 301,
324–5; *Hitler's War* 4, 151–2,
191, 284; search for Hitler's
letters 19–20; see Churchill-
Mussolini correspondence
59–61, 64; meets Priesack
150–4; discoveries existence
of diaries 172–81; decides
Priesack documents are
forgeries 179–82, 187–8, 191;
financial problems 254–5, 281;
denounces diaries as forgeries
254–6, 259, 263; *Stern* press
conference 267, 268,
269–70; press interviews 273,
279; changes mind 283–4, 288;
forgery proved 301–2; Hitler's
medical diaries 324
Israeli secret service 141, 217,
226, 235
Izvestia 24, 317

Jabusch, Helmut 183
Jacobs, Eric 238

Jaeckel, Eberhard 91–5, 97, 104–7,
119–20, 192, 214, 224, 254, 268,
279, 280, 295
Jahn, Peter 190
Jakobovits, Immanuel, Chief Rabbi
of Great Britain 276
James, Brian 268
Jodl, General 5, 25
John Paul II, Pope 121
Josephson, Marvin 188

Karnau, Hermann 25
Die Katacombe 53, 67, 73
'Keepers of the Flame' 50, 90
Keitel, Field Marshal 25, 85
Kempka, Erich 25, 50, 293
Kern, Xavier 120
Kersten, Dr Felix 29
Kirkpatrick, Jeanne 10, 277
Kissinger, Henry 170, 188
Klapper, Medard 139–41, 173,
183–6, 304, 320
Kleenau (auctioneers) 90
Klein, Dietrich 313–14
Kleist document 144, 155, 156,
157, 158, 196, 203–4
Knightley, Phillip 173–4, 238–41,
250, 251–2, 259, 260–2
Koch, Peter 8, 121, 137, 161,
205, 274, 288; relations with
Heidemann 65–6, 68, 74,
184; diaries concealed from
74, 75, 76; diaries shown to
121–3; suspicions of Heidemann
168–9, 184; decision to speed
up publication 194–7; publicity
campaign 205, 208; learns
of Heidemann's payments
207–8; Trevor-Roper asked to
authenticate diaries 8, 212–13;

HAVE YOU READ THEM ALL?

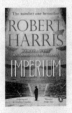
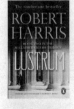
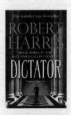

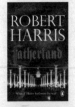
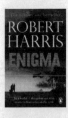

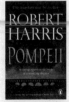
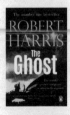
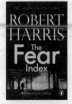

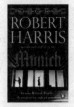

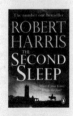
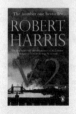
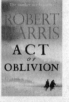